Current Issues in International Diplomacy and Foreign Policy

VOLUME ONE

edited by Colin Jennings and Nicholas Hopkinson

Current Issues in International Diplomacy and Foreign Policy

VOLUME ONE

edited by Colin Jennings and Nicholas Hopkinson

London: The Stationery Office

ISBN 0 11 702647 6

British Library Cataloguing in Publication Data.
A CIP catalogue record for this book is available from the British Library.

Wilton Park conferences bring together people in positions of influence from many countries and from diverse professional backgrounds to explore more effective ways of tackling key international issues. This volume contains substantive reports on the conferences. All papers reflect the views of the authors and their personal interpretation of conference proceedings. As such they do not represent any institutional policy of Wilton Park.

For the annual calendar and programmes of Wilton Park conferences please contact:

The Administration Office, Wilton Park, Wiston House, Steyning,
West Sussex BN44 3DZ, United Kingdom

Telephone: 44 (0 in UK) 1903 815020, Telefax: 44 (0 in UK) 1903 815244
e-mail: admin@wiltonpark.org.uk
or consult Wilton Park's website at http://www.wiltonpark.org.uk

Frontispiece illustration of Wiston House by Susanne Hopkinson

 .1 3 JUL 1999

Published by The Stationery Office and available from:

The Publications Centre
(mail, telephone and fax orders only)
PO Box 276, London SW8 5DT
General enquiries 0171 873 0011
Telephone orders 0171 873 9090
Fax orders 0171 873 8200

The Stationery Office Bookshops
123 Kingsway, London WC2B 6PQ
0171 242 6393 Fax 0171 242 6394
68-69 Bull Street, Birmingham B4 6AD
0121 236 9696 Fax 0121 236 9699
33 Wine Street, Bristol BS1 2BQ
0117 9264306 Fax 0117 9294515
9-21 Princess Street, Manchester M60 8AS
0161 834 7201 Fax 0161 833 0634
16 Arthur Street, Belfast BT1 4GD
01232 238451 Fax 01232 235401
The Stationery Office Oriel Bookshop
18-19 High Street, Cardiff CF1 2BZ
01222 395548 Fax 01222 384347
71 Lothian Road, Edinburgh EH3 9AZ
0131 228 4181 Fax 0131 622 7017

The Stationery Office's Accredited Agents
(see Yellow Pages)

and through good booksellers

Printed in the United Kingdom for The Stationery Office
by Albert Gait Ltd, Grimsby
J68438 C6 5/99 9385 9581

The Editors

Nicholas Hopkinson is Senior Associate Director at Wilton Park in West Sussex

Colin Jennings is Chief Executive and Director of Wilton Park in West Sussex

The Authors

Christopher Clapham is Professor of Politics and International Relations, Lancaster University

Virginia Crowe is an Associate Director at Wilton Park in West Sussex

Sam Daws is a consultant on UN Affairs based at New College, Oxford University

Robin Hart is an Associate Director at Wilton Park in West Sussex

Alan K. Henrikson is Director of The Fletcher Roundtable on a New World Order and teaches at the Fletcher School of Law and Diplomacy, Tufts University, Massachusetts

Richard Lambert was Secretary to the UK Delegations to Interparliamentary Assemblies, House of Commons, London and is currently Director (Planning & Residential) at the British Property Federation

Chris Langdon is an Associate Director at Wilton Park in West Sussex

Richard Latter is Deputy Director at Wilton Park in West Sussex

Contents

Foreword

The need for government policy makers to find better ways of managing major international and domestic challenges is more necessary than ever in today's interdependent world.

Wilton Park conferences are a highly effective way for politicians and government officials to explore the options with analysts from outside government. Initiated in 1946 by Winston Churchill to help re-establish peace and democracy in Europe, Wilton Park has developed a unique status as an academically independent and non-profit making Executive Agency of the United Kingdom's Foreign and Commonwealth Office. Its conferences focus on the key issues confronting government policy makers, drawing on Wilton Park's unique advantage of access to the latest government thinking and academic independence. Discussions are unattributable to encourage frank exchanges.

The quality of debate is high, with participants coming from a wide range of nationalities and professional disciplines. Many are in a position to make a direct impact on future policy (on average over 60% are politicians or officials working on the issues concerned). The residential nature of the conferences provides excellent opportunities to explore differing perspectives in depth and make new professional contacts.

This is the first in a series of volumes which will seek to disseminate the conclusions reached at the conferences to a wider audience. Over 40 conferences are organised each year, with short reports produced on each one and in-depth papers on some. This volume includes both. Each piece reflects the personal interpretation of the authors of conference discussions and issues arising. They do not represent any institutional policy of Wilton Park.

Wilton Park's academic independence is guaranteed by an Academic Council of distinguished Britons and by an International Advisory Council of OECD Ambassadors and High Commissioners in London. The conferences focus on the key political, security and economic issues confronting different parts of the world, especially areas of potential conflict. Global issues are examined, such as protection of the environment, promoting economic and social development, and ways of combating international crime, as well as prominent domestic policies such as welfare reform and the information revolution. In addition, conferences explore the latest policy challenges concerning:

- European integration and security, US foreign and security policy, and transatlantic relations;

- internal problems and foreign policies of the Russian Federation, Central and Eastern Europe, and prospects for enlargement of the EU and NATO;

- Asia's economic and security relations with Europe and the US;

- regional developments and problems in South Asia, the Middle East and North Africa, sub-Saharan Africa and Latin America.

The continuing need for a forum such as Wilton Park is underlined by the increasing financial support for the conferences from other organisations around the world. Recently these have included:

> The Anglo-German Foundation, Asian Strategy and Leadership Institute, British Aerospace, British Council, Cable and Wireless, Cathay Pacific, Chemical & Biological Arms Control Institute, Commonwealth Parliamentary Association, Daiwa Foundation, Department for International Development, Department of Trade and Industry, Dwight D. Eisenhower Institute, European Commission, European Parliament, European Policy Forum, Ford Foundation, Foreign & Commonwealth Office, Friedrich Ebert Foundation, George C. Marshall Foundation, HM Treasury, Hong Kong Government, Institute for European–Latin American Relations, Intergovernmental Oceanographic Commission of UNESCO, Japan Foundation, Netherlands Atlantic Commission, Turner Foundation, International Institute for Strategic Studies, Lawrence Livermore Laboratories, Manpower Demonstration Research Corporation, Ministry of Defence, NATO, North Atlantic Assembly, Nuffield Foundation, Rockefeller Foundation, Science Applications International Corporation, Sir Heinz Koeppler Trust, US Arms Control and Disarmament Agency, US Institute for Peace, US Mission to NATO, University of California Los Angeles.

Their support helps to bring influential people to the conferences, and is greatly appreciated.

I should like to thank all those who have contributed to this initial volume, in particular my co-editor, Nicholas Hopkinson, who has inspired the series, and our secretaries, especially Dienn Ginn, and Barbara Johnson, Judi Maledy, Jacquie King and Susan Linfield, who helped produce the reports.

I hope that you will enjoy this volume as a contribution to the understanding of major international policy issues and problems confronting the global community. The best way of exploring these issues further is to come to one of our forthcoming conferences.

Colin Jennings
Chief Executive and Director, Wilton Park

August 1998

Introduction

Wilton Park is one of those rare places where leading opinion formers come to from around the world. Perhaps even more uniquely, the senior parliamentarians, diplomats, business people, academics and journalists meet in an informal and relaxed setting where they can speak freely. The discussions at Wilton Park are confidential and unattributable, allowing direct and frank exchanges of view. This enhances the content and quality of the debate. Whilst contributions and interventions are not attributable to any one individual, the content of their discussions can be disseminated. The result is this unique policy-relevant series which provides a 'snapshot' of key current issues in international diplomacy and foreign policy.

The first volume in the *Current Issues in International Diplomacy and Foreign Policy* series draws upon conferences convened at Wilton Park during 1997. The short reports provide summaries and action points from conferences convened during the latter half of 1997. The second volume in the series, due to be published soon after the first volume, will largely feature reports on conferences in the first half of 1998.

In each calendar year, discussions at Wilton Park cover most major issues in international relations. Each individual volume alone may not provide a *tour d'horizon* because the content of each volume very much depends upon what has been discussed during a particular period of the year. However, as two volumes will be produced in the series each year, it is hoped that a timely global 'snapshot' will become apparent.

After the end of the Cold War some argued that discussion of international relations would be less vital. The opposite has been the case. Without a bi-polar framework to conceptualise the world, international relations is certainly more complex. Since 1990, issues such as controlling migration, curbing international crime and drugs trafficking, economic crises (such as Asia's), and the environment have risen up the international agenda. The end of the bi-polar world order has unleashed regional tensions that were previously suppressed. As a result, humanitarian interventions and the need to protect human rights have, unfortunately, become all the more necessary. At the same time that globalisation is making the world's economy more integrated, a number of larger states are fragmenting into smaller ones. It is ironic that the post-Cold War world is in some places a much more violent one, while in many other parts of the world, people are enjoying unprecedented peace and prosperity. The North Atlantic Treaty Organisation (NATO) and the European Union (EU) through their expansions eastwards will extend a zone of stability throughout Europe to parts of the former Communist bloc. Although some have argued that NATO has become redundant, NATO has adapted and it remains a linchpin of the international security order.

Underlying this evolving international panorama is a fundamental change in the nature of diplomacy, the 'oxygen' of international relations. One can think of no better way to start the series than with the Fletcher School's Professor Alan K. Henrikson's retrospective essay on the 'Diplomacy: Profession in Peril?' conference.

Nicholas Hopkinson
Senior Associate Director, Wilton Park

August 1998

Abbreviations and Acronyms

ABM	Anti-Ballistic Missile
ACP	African Caribbean and Pacific (countries)
ACRS	Arms Control and Regional Security
ADFL	Alliance of Democratic Forces for the Liberation
AEC	African Economic Community
AMF	Asia Monetary Fund
ANC	African National Congress
APC	Atlantic Partnership Council
APEC	Asia–Pacific Economic Cooperation
ARF	ASEAN Regional Forum
ASEAN	Association of South East Asian Nations
ASEM	Asia–Europe Summit Meeting
BW	biological weapons
BWC	Biological Weapons Convention
CAP	Common Agricultural Policy
CBM	confidence-building measures
CBSS	Council of Baltic Sea States
CBW	chemical and biological weapons
CEEC	Central and Eastern European Countries
CEFTA	Central Europe Free Trade Area
CFSP	Common Foreign and Security Policy
CIA	Central Intelligence Agency
CIS	Commonwealth of Independent States
CJTF	Combined Joint Task Force
CSCAP	Council for Security Cooperation in the Asia Pacific
CTBT	Comprehensive Test Ban Treaty
CW	chemical weapons
CWC	Chemical Weapons Convention
DAC	Development Assistance Committee
DOSFAN	Department of State Foreign Affairs Network
DRC	Democratic Republic of the Congo
EAPC	Euro-Atlantic Partnership Council
EBRD	European Bank for Reconstruction and Development
ECB	European Central Bank
ECHO	European Commission Humanitarian Office
ECJ	European Court of Justice
ECOMOG	ECOWAS Monitoring Group
ECOWAS	Economic Community of West African States
EDU	European Drugs Unit
EIB	European Investment Bank
EMU	Economic and Monetary Union
EP	European Parliament
EPA	Environmental Protection Agency
EPLF	Eritrean People's Liberation Front
EPRDF	Ethiopian People's Revolutionary Democratic Front
ESDI	European Security and Defence Identity
EU	European Union
Europol	European Police Office
FBI	Federal Bureau of Investigation
FCO	Foreign and Commonwealth Office
FDI	foreign direct investment

FIG	financial-industrial group
FRY	Former Republic of Yugoslavia
FSU	Former Soviet Union
FYROM	Former Yugoslav Republic of Macedonia
G7	Group of Seven
G8	Group of Eight
GATT	General Agreement on Tariffs and Trade
GCC	Gulf Cooperation Council
GDP	gross domestic product
GMO	Gratis Military Officer
GNP	gross national product
GSP	Generalised System of Preferences
HIC	high intensity conflict
IAEA	International Atomic Energy Agency
ICJ	International Court of Justice
ICRC	International Committee of the Red Cross
IFI	international financial institution
IFOR	(Peace) Implementation Force in Bosnia Herzegovina
IGC	Inter-Governmental Conference
ILO	International Labour Organisation
ILSA	Iran Libya Sanctions Action
IMF	International Monetary Fund
Interpol	International Criminal Police Commission
IPTF	International Police Task Force
IT	information technology
JHA	Justice and Home Affairs
KEDO	Korean Peninsula Energy Development Organisation
KHF	Know-How Fund
KLA	Kosovo Liberation Army
LDK	Democratic League of Kosovo
LIC	low intensity conflict
MAI	Multilateral Agreement on Investment
MBFR	Mutual and Balanced Force Reductions
MEDA	European Union's main framework for financial and technical cooperation with Mediterranean Partners
MFA	Ministry of Foreign Affairs
MFN	Most Favoured Nation
MLAT	Mutual Legal Assistance Treaty
MMPR	Mixed Member Proportional Representation
MTCR	Missile Technology Control Regime
NAFTA	North Atlantic Free Trade Association
NAM	Non-Aligned Movement
NATO	North Atlantic Treaty Organisation
NCIS	National Criminal Intelligence Service
NGO	non-governmental organisation
NIS	Newly Independent States
NNWS	non-nuclear weapons states
NPT	(Nuclear) Non-Proliferation Treaty
NRA	National Resistance Army
NRM	National Resistance Movement
NWS	nuclear weapons states
NZ	New Zealand
OAS	Organisation of American States
OAU	Organisation of African Unity

ODA	overseas development aid
OECD	Organisation for Economic Cooperation and Development
OEEC	Organisation for European Economic Cooperation
OPEC	Organisation of Petroleum Exporting Countries
OSCE	Organisation for Security and Cooperation in Europe
P5	Five Permanent Members of UN Security Council
PfP	Partnership for Peace
PGM	Precision Guided Munitions
PHARE	European Union Programme of Aid for Central and Eastern Europe
PIC	Peace Implementation Council
PLA	People's Liberation Army
PRC	People's Republic of China
PSO	Peace Support Operations
RMA	revolution in military affairs
RPF	Rwanda Patriotic Front
RS	Republika Srpska
RUF	Revolutionary United Front
SAARC	South Asian Association for Regional Cooperation
SADC	Southern Africa Development Community
SAFTA	South Asian Free Trade Association
SALT	Strategic Arms Limitation Talks
SCMM	Standing Committee on Military Matters
SDS	Serb Democratic Party
SFOR	(multinational) Stabilisation Force in Bosnia Herzegovina
SHAPE	Supreme Headquarters Allied Powers, Europe
SLOC	Sea Lanes of Communication
SLORC	State Law and Order Restoration Council
SNS	Serb National Alliance
SPLA	Sudanese People's Liberation Army
SRS	Serbian Radical Party
START	Strategic Arms Reduction Talks
TACIS	(European Union) Technical Assistance to Commonwealth of Independent States
TMD	theatre missile defence
TRIM	trade related investment measures
TRIP	trade related intellectual property
UAE	United Arab Emirates
UCLAF	Protection of the (European) Community's Financial Interests Fight Against Fraud
UK	United Kingdom
UN	United Nations
UNAMIR	UN Assistance Mission for Rwanda
UNCED	UN Conference on Environment and Development
UNDCP	UN Drug Control Programme
UNDP	UN Development Programme
UNHCR	UN High Commission for Refugees
UNIDR	UN Institute for Disarmament Research
UNPROFOR	UN Protection Force
UNSCOM	UN Special Commission
US	United States
USIA	US Information Agency
USSR	Union of Soviet Socialist Republics

VERTIC	Verification Technology Information Centre
WEU	Western European Union
WMD	weapons of mass destruction
WTO	World Trade Organisation

Diplomacy for the 21st Century: 'Re-crafting the Old Guild'

Diplomacy for the 21st Century: 'Re-crafting the Old Guild'

A retrospective essay based on Wilton Park Conference 503: 21–25 July 1997 on 'Diplomacy: Profession in Peril?'

Alan K. Henrikson

1 Diplomacy Today

Diplomats have been called many things throughout history – some complimentary, others less so. One description at the Wilton Park conference, 'Diplomacy: Profession in Peril?', was of diplomats as a 'priestly class', which had a certain if self-assuring appeal. I myself have suggested that diplomats constitute a *guild*, and it is that notion I want to explore in this essay. According to *Webster's*, a guild is 'an association of men belonging to the same class, engaged in kindred pursuits, or having common interests or aims'. The dictionary goes on to describe it as 'a medieval association of members of a craft or trade established to promote the welfare of that craft and its members'. That diplomats as a group display this cohesiveness, even across national lines, is noteworthy. However, it is not merely this quality of the diplomatic profession that I would wish to emphasize. Instead, the issue I would like to pose is that of the *relationship* between diplomacy's 'associative' character, or the effect it has of incorporating or bonding those who participate in it, and its 'craftsmanship', its guild-related knowledge and skills. In the parlance of contemporary political science, this technical element of craft is the diplomatic profession's capacity or competence as an international 'epistemic' community.

This relationship seemed to me to be the central theme – and problem – of the 'Diplomacy' conference: is there a significant connection between what diplomats *are*, as a somewhat exclusive body or elite community, and what they are authorized and professionally able to *do*, as a service? Is the one, the *corps diplomatique*, necessary to the actual function of diplomats? Or, perhaps, could all or most of the work being done by them now be done by others with different training and backgrounds? Conversely, does the work of diplomacy, the very nature of it, call for the existence of something like a diplomatic corps, not simply those on the *Diplomatic List* in a particular location, but the totality of all those posted at every national centre and international headquarters and involved in special negotiating tasks and field work? If the present multinational community of diplomats stationed around the globe didn't exist, would it, or something very much like it, have to be invented?

This notion of 'universality', it should be noted, is today being severely challenged by fiscal constraints and, behind these, criticism from elected representatives and a hostile public mood in some countries. As a former US Secretary of State, Warren Christopher, reported with alarm in an address at Harvard University shortly before his retirement in January 1997, 'Budget cuts have forced us to close over two dozen consulates and several embassies. If the hemorrhaging continues, we will have no option but to close more facilities' ('Investing in American Leadership', Department of State *Dispatch* [January 1997]). The assumption that governments are able and willing to support full participation in a 'universal diplomatic system', unfortunately, may no longer continue to hold, even for the largest and richest states.[1]

The very idea of a diplomatic service also has been put in question. As a fellow student of the profession, Raymond Cohen, has pointed out: 'Classic diplomacy, as it evolved over centuries in the European states system, came to reflect the values and assumptions of an *exclusive diplomatic elite*' ('Culture and Anarchy in the New Global Diplomacy', University of Leicester Diplomatic Studies Programme *Newsletter* [April 1996]). Today it is impossible to speak of diplomats as an 'elite' group in this same sense. The rearguard battle to preserve the diplomatic profession's former social exclusivity, as the participants in the Wilton Park conference learned from the accounts given by Peter Torry and Anthony Quainton, has largely been lost – much for the better, as we live in an age of openness and equality. In the case of the United States, the extraordinary diversity of the Foreign Service today is entirely logical, and appropriate to the makeup of American society.

Certainly, the 'West', including America, still enjoys certain advantages: the pre-eminence of the United States as a superpower, the centrality of Western cities as diplomatic venues, and the dominance of the English language. Yet Cohen notes that 'the balance has gradually shifted towards other civilisations and economies'. Henry Kissinger observes that the 'multi-state' international order that is emerging, or re-emerging, following the 'rigid patterns' of the Cold War will have to be constructed 'by statesmen who represent vastly different cultures'. However, the 'only available model' for them is the traditional one built by Western societies which, he acknowledges in his book *Diplomacy* (1994), 'many of the participants may reject'. As he rather indelicately puts it, these leaders include not only many inexperienced persons but also those who rose 'by means of qualities that are not necessarily those needed to govern, and are even less suited to building an international order'.

Against this background, the prime function of the diplomatic profession, both the community and their practice, has to be to hold the multi-state system together. Its guild-like nature serves that end. Diplomacy, even the academic study of it, engenders camaraderie: it draws new people inward and socializes them, inter-generationally as well as internationally. The composition of the present Wilton Park conference is an illustration of the point. This is mainly what I mean by stressing diplomacy's *associative* character. Some of this invaluable transnational bonding effect would be lost, one cannot help but speculate, if most national governments were now to move to, for example, a 'unified civil service' as the source of their representatives abroad. Some of the variations of 'privatization' and even of in-and-out 'flexibility' for diplomats that were discussed at the conference also could damage the sense, indeed the ethic, of professional solidarity or cohesion.

In my view, the diplomatic profession not only contributes to international society but also epitomizes that society. Diplomacy may even be international society's finest expression – a group of men and, increasingly, women who defend to others not only their respective 'national interests' but also an 'international' idea. This is not necessarily always a higher or transcendent ideal. However, their outlook does at least represent a vision of interconnected and shared – of internationally blended – interests. The basic subject of diplomacy is not nationalism or supra-nationalism, but internationalism. That is what its professionals 'profess'.

Nowhere is this ethos more evident, in all its perfections and imperfections, than at the United Nations. New York is 'the most powerful diplomatic center in the world', wrote *New York Times* UN correspondent Barbara Crossette in December 1996, and it is growing more so as nations use their base at the United Nations to conduct business with one another 'within the enabling orbit of the organization'. The UN is a kind of 'ecosystem', the Malaysian President of the General Assembly Razali Ismail told her. 'Most countries, including a lot of small countries, send their very best people to the United Nations', observed Thomas R. Pickering, a former US Permanent Representative at the United Nations and currently the US Under Secretary of State for Political Affairs. 'As a result, they bring special skills – and sometimes special capacities to make problems. Here it wasn't always the size of the country that counted, but in some cases the size of the ambassador and the size of the fight. ... The bulk of the countries in the United Nations have individuals representing them with nearly full powers with respect to votes'.

Getting to know them personally can pay off, therefore, when important issues are decided; moreover, not a few ambassadors return home to become foreign ministers. Contrasting bilateral diplomacy with the multilateral activity centred on UN Headquarters, Pickering noted: 'Your life in a capital is very much tied up in relations you have and your country has with the host country. The life of New York is tied up, particularly for medium or small-size countries, with a whole series of ambassadors of common ilk on issues that are dealt with in a kind of international legislature'.

In any systematic consideration of the international order as it is now and may develop into the 21st century, the body of professional-international practitioners of diplomacy must be taken deliberately and fully into account. It is, in fact, one of the constitutive 'orders' of the international system, and it has been at least since the Congress of Vienna. And, I believe, it should and will remain so. The Vienna Convention on Diplomatic Relations of 1961, about which Richard Langhorne and others have authoritatively written, partially codifies the diplomatic tradition in law. The Charter of the United Nations itself, in Article 105, establishes the general principle that diplomatic representatives of UN member countries, like officials of the UN organization itself, shall 'enjoy such privileges and immunities as are necessary for the independent exercise of their functions'.

At Wilton Park I somewhat surprisingly found myself, a distant North American (a US citizen conscious also of the Canadian experience) identifying more with what came to be referred to during the conference as the European 'Continental' view – favouring the idea of lifetime career service and the tradition of *la puissance publique* – than with the 'Anglo-Saxon' view – tending toward privatism, pragmatism, part-time-ism, etc., in the training and staffing of diplomatic positions. As the participants were candidly informed by Ambassador Quainton, a young person cannot be assured lifetime career employment in the US State Department today, and the same is probably true in some other Anglo-Western foreign ministries. A person entering at an early age 'will be guaranteed a 25-year career', he indicated, which may or may not be considered a full career; indeed some may regard it as only a semi-permanent job, like other forms of employment, and not in any deeper sense a calling, or vocation. Granting that some entrants to the American and other diplomatic services today might not even *want* a 'career' per se, one can none the less see that the difference between the Continental and Anglo-Saxon conceptions is fundamental, and appreciate its significance for the profession.

There is another, related difference that is developing. With so many technical specialists coming into foreign ministries, often laterally, there is a risk of loss of what Ambassador Luis Navega called the profession's 'humanist' perspective and Ambassador Paul Leifer called the 'pluri-disciplinary' preparation that its members should and commonly do have (precisely neither 'generalist' nor 'specialist' – a conventional analytic distinction which he faults). Professional diplomats should, themselves, have varied capabilities, so that they never have to defer entirely to others. As Sir David Hannay, a former Permanent Representative of the United Kingdom to the United Nations, said to Barbara Crossette, with reference especially to diplomatic work at the UN: 'You have to have a reasonable spread of specializations. You now certainly have to have military advice. And on the development side, you have to have people who know something about the environment, who know something about population control, who know something about wider development policies'. The head of mission himself needs to 'know something about' at least some of these subjects, if not most of them. By the end of his career, he usually does. I think of what Professor Yves Collart said of diplomats, 'Like wine, they increase considerably in value with age'. The value they have accumulated, I would again insist, is not only theirs, or their country's, alone. It is a valuable asset of the larger international community.

Besides the associative pull of diplomacy upon its own members and, through them, upon the governments and societies that diplomats represent, I would emphasize, as *Webster's* does, the 'kindred pursuits' and 'common interests or aims' that diplomacy tends to promote – in other words, the shared policy goals, not just the common professional identity and feeling. A guild activity is a cooperative public service, of benefit both within and beyond its sphere of work.

At the most basic level, what the diplomatic corps has done, and still does today, is to pursue and share information. 'An Ambassador', wrote François de Callières in his classic *De la manière de négocier avec les Souverains* (1716), 'may very probably find that his colleagues of the diplomatic corps in the capital where he resides may be of value to him. Since the whole diplomatic body labours to the same end, namely to discover what is happening, there arises a certain freemasonry of diplomacy, by which one colleague informs another of coming events which a lucky chance has enabled him to discern'. At the very highest level of aspiration, as Harold Nicolson said, following de Callières, in his 1953 Chichele Lectures (*The Evolution of Diplomacy* [1962]), the members of the 'professional freemasonry' of diplomacy 'all believed, whatever their governments might believe, that the purpose of diplomacy was the preservation of peace'. The so-called 'old' diplomacy failed to guarantee that outcome in July 1914, of course. Woodrow Wilson and other proponents of a 'new' diplomacy following the First World War sought to make up for its failure by reforming diplomacy's methods, in particular by making the diplomatic process more open, or available to the public, and also more institution-based. Hence his linkage of diplomacy to international organizations; hence his innovative proposal for a League of Nations.

The sense among diplomats, whatever their particular backgrounds or instructions, of being fundamentally engaged in a common pursuit of international peace surely endures today. If anything, the experience of the 20th century means that the mutual commitment of diplomats to seek peace or, in the words of the Preamble of the UN Charter, 'to save succeeding generations from the scourge of war', is stronger than ever before. This commitment of the diplomatic community extends far beyond the United Nations.

The kindred pursuits and common interests or aims of the diplomatic guild might be thought of, in more theoretical terms, as international 'collective' or 'public' goods; Mancur Olson and other political scientists have set out the logic of this notion in relation to wider group action. Among the goods or goals that I would, myself, specifically mention as broader common values or objectives of the diplomatic community today are these: the preservation of political stability and the integrity of electoral processes; the promotion of international law and adherence to pledged agreements; and, beyond political forms and legal necessities, the defence of time-tested norms of civility, including care and moderation in the use of language – precision in international discourse, as well as mere politeness.

That is why, with the guild-like character of the profession in mind, I would here emphasize the *craftsmanship* of diplomacy. De Callières's mutually-informing 'freemasons', in addition to knowing secret passwords and travelling safely anywhere, were first of all *masons* – artisans of a kind, having prior training, practical and useful skills, and often a measure of artistry. The techniques of a diplomat – including adroitness, insight, and flair in negotiation – are commonly admired attributes in the profession. Of course, these must be grounded in education and in experience. Academic courses and training programmes such as are available at the Diplomatische Akademie in Vienna and other institutions, including the US State Department's Foreign Service Institute or the Fletcher School of Law and Diplomacy where I teach, contribute substantially to the formation of a diplomat, as a basis for further learning in the field. Not least among a diplomat's foundations of knowledge ought to be a sure sense of his or her own country's history and that of the world at large. As Henry Kissinger, sceptical about futuristic blueprints and purely theoretical approaches, is said to have said, 'History is the only policy science'. None the less, one must today ask whether we wisely take pride in saying, as those of us who work in diplomatic academies or schools of international relations are fond of doing, that we are 'Sons and Daughters of Maria Theresa'. The diplomatic-educational tradition needs, and periodically receives, an updating (Ralph Feltham, *International Forum on Diplomatic Training* [1997], updated second edition of A.H.M. Kirk-Greene, *'Sons and Daughters of Maria Theresa'* [1993], Diplomatische Akademie Wien *Occasional Paper* [1997]).

The Preview statement of the Wilton Park 'Diplomacy: Profession in Peril?' conference posed the following question, among others: 'Is there a new professionalism and an adaptation of the traditional skills, or are still more radical changes called for?' Perhaps because I approach the subject as a historian, I incline – provisionally – more toward the 'adaptation' response than the 'radical change' answer. I am here inescapably drawn to use Harold Nicolson's phrase, the title of his Chichele Lectures in which he traced the diplomatic craft from ancient times to our own, more global period. Will his *evolution* of diplomacy be sufficient, or is *revolution* called for?

2 Diplomacy Tomorrow

There are, in the annals of diplomacy and even in recent times, remarkable examples of adaptation to changing circumstances that should give us confidence about the profession's ability to survive – and more – in the future. One of the 'Diplomacy' conference's speakers, Sir Crispin Tickell, began his study of a new problem not then on the international agenda – global climate change – when he spent a year in the Fellows Program at the Center for International Affairs at Harvard and also took a course in meteorology at MIT. His book, *Climatic Change and World Affairs* (1977), was a result of his investigation and anticipation. He subsequently went on to become one of the world's leading environmental diplomatists.

When one contemplates this story, one realizes what a difference individual learning and effort can make in expanding the horizon of an entire profession. Diplomacy, conceived of as an 'epistemic' community, is a guild unusually capable of knowledge, including technical expertise, when the logic of the world situation requires some mastery of new subjects. The physical 'science' of the environment, Sir Crispin suggested to his fellow conferees, is 'not as difficult as it looks' – much 'less complicated' than arms-control topics like SALT or MBFR, for example. 'Any sensible person with a good education' – who is willing to listen and to read carefully – 'can understand'. His is not an argument for specialization, however. In the field of environmental policy, 'generalists in the shape of diplomats' are more necessary than ever, he asserted. They should keep control, with experts (including lawyers) being kept 'in their proper place'. A major reason to 'keep generalist control' over environmental-policy negotiations is to be able to ensure, as the experienced diplomat is best equipped and placed to do, that you 'don't make obligations you can't meet'.

Subjects such as arms control and environmental policy obviously can be taken aboard intellectually without 'radical' restructuring of the diplomatic guild itself. The 'adaptation' of diplomatic thinking to new conditions and the forces that produce them can be a difficult process, however. In some cases, a diplomatic negotiator may have to pay 'a personal cost' in terms of risk to his future careeer, as Sir Crispin put it, in order to espouse positions at the international level that are not favoured at the national level, often simply because they are not well or widely understood. An example would be the experience of Richard Benedick, US representative at the negotiations which in 1987 produced the Montreal Protocol on Substances that Deplete the Ozone Layer. At one point during the Montreal negotiations, as Benedick recalls in his *Ozone Diplomacy: New Directions for Safeguarding the Planet* (1991), one powerful congressional committee chairman, Representative John Dingell (Democrat, Michigan), being from an electoral district heavily dependent on the manufacture of emissions-producing automobiles, declared that he was 'deeply concerned ... [that] our chief negotiator,

Ambassador Richard Benedick, and his EPA staff support ... are negotiating on a seat-of-the-pants basis'. This was far from being the case, but Dingell's charge and others like it from those with interests at stake, exerted a damaging influence.

In order 'to change the culture' of even a single ministry within a government, regarding the need for scientifically-based international regulation in a new field like the environment, you often 'need someone at the top to give a lead', Ambassador Tickell said. Diplomats are generally willing to learn, but naturally welcome recognition of their efforts to acquire new expertise. To make an entire institution environmentally literate, not merely to elevate a few experts, is managerially more difficult. Sir Crispin suggested how the US State Department leadership might, for example, use its relationship with Vice President Al Gore, a man personally committed to the cause of the environment. If there is someone at the top 'arranging rewards', he advised, institutional adaptation can occur very quickly. The word could be put out that: 'If you want to have lunch with the Vice President [and thereby increase the chances of your ideas finding echo at the highest level], you have to have worked on the environment. The foreign service will get the message'. Such an incentive structure could help not only to overcome inertia, fear, or indifference but also to allow officers with an independent interest in a new field to develop their individual competence in it faster.

Whether by intellectual persuasion or bureaucratic manipulation, the American and other diplomatic services have to understand the need to embrace new subjects, including sciences, and to master new techniques, including technologies. Considerable *re-crafting* of the old guild as the 21st century approaches thus may be necessary. Otherwise, it is possible that diplomats with their relatively traditional education, institutional structures, and professional codes and routines might not 'match up' to the future. In the mirror of the 21st century, which historians such as Paul Kennedy as well as futurists such as Alvin and Heidi Toffler, Paul and Anne Ehrlich, and even House of Representatives Speaker Newt Gingrich have tried to foresee, the past achievements and attitudes of diplomacy, particularly those associated with the Cold War era, might appear not to be strengths, but *déformations professionelles*. If there does turn out to be a serious mismatch between diplomats' skills and world demands, then 'radical changes', as the conference Preview warns, might indeed be in order.

Much depends, it must be apparent, on the accuracy of our picture of the future, on our intellectual prevision. Diplomacy will not need to be changed if the world itself does not change. I myself do not take an apocalyptic view regarding this. I do not foresee, as Robert D. Kaplan does on the basis of his travels around the social margins of Africa and Asia, a 'Coming Anarchy' (*The Atlantic Monthly* [February 1994]). His *The Ends of the Earth: From Togo to Turkmenistan, From Iran to Cambodia – A Journey to the Frontiers of Anarchy* (1997) none the less repays close attention. Nor do the fears of other pessimistically inclined observers seem to me quite plausible. The historical certainty of a speculative future such as that which Zbigniew Brzezinski describes in *Out of Control: Global Turmoil on the Eve of the Twenty-first Century* (1993), Daniel Patrick Moynihan describes (with Milton) in *Pandaemonium: Ethnicity in International Politics* (1993), and Samuel Huntington describes in *The Clash of Civilizations and the Remaking of World Order* (1996) is difficult intellectually to accept, given the virtual impossibility of predicting how mankind and its leaders are going to respond to the future confusing times of which these writers warn. About Huntington's ideas in particular – especially the less-noticed latter half of the title of his new book, i.e. *the Remaking of World Order* – I shall say more later.

I should make it clear that, although I myself have served as director of a futuristic research-and-discussion initiative, named optimistically The Fletcher Roundtable on a New World Order, I do not anticipate the polar opposite of world anarchy: that is, anything like globalized 'good governance' – a sort of universal version of the structures and behaviour which the World Bank and the International Monetary Fund are now insisting on as a condition of giving assistance to countries. Nor, certainly, can anything like 'world government' be expected. There does not, in truth, appear to be widespread public support for boldly progressive measures for international cooperation or management, of any kind. The notion of a 'new world order', I say with sadness as an American, whose very currency carries the motto *NOVUS ORDO SECLORUM*, is today viewed in some circles in the United States, mainly but not only on the anti-statist radical right, as a spectre to be feared almost much as the more palpable threat of increased global disorder.

Both of these extreme visions – that of planetary disarray and planetary dictation – would, obviously, further threaten the profession of diplomacy, even beyond the 'peril' suggested in the Wilton Park conference title. Diplomacy is inherently international, a middle-of-the-road idea. It takes place in, and is allowed and indeed made necessary by, a loosely organized and non-hierarchical world political system in which most participating states are – at least nominally – free, sovereign, and equal. The world contains elements of both disorder and order: between states, generally, there is less regularity than there is within them. As Henry Kissinger reminds us in *Diplomacy*, the diplomatic profession grew up within a 'multi-state' system – the evolving Westphalian international order which was described by Dr Brian Hocking in the first session of the conference. Despite the changes that have occurred, Kissinger argues, 'the rise and fall of previous world orders based on many states ... is the only experience on which one can draw in trying to understand the challenges facing contemporary statesmen'. From a Kissinger perspective, the post-Cold War pattern emerging today is most akin to the European structure of the 18th and 19th centuries. In this structure a number – a plurality – of powerful, constantly-interacting, and roughly equivalent states hold the larger system together in equilibrium. The 'new order' he envisages will contain 'at least six major powers – the United States, Europe, China, Japan, Russia, and probably India – as well as a multiplicity of medium-sized and smaller countries'. A main difference between 1815 and the present is that, as Kissinger emphasizes, international relations are becoming 'truly global'. The significance of this expansion of the system, which a number of major states (not one or two superpowers) will dominate, remains to be seen.

Arguably, it is in such a *multipolar* 'multi-state' system that diplomacy truly thrives and becomes creative. This thought lay behind the challenging argument made by Ambassador Boris Biancheri Chiappori in his opening presentation at the conference when, perhaps reflecting his personal experience and the perspective of his own country (Italy), he observed that in the post-1945 *bipolar* international structure 'many of the most important issues had already been answered, from the very beginning'.

For the United States at least, it might be objected, the Cold War period is usually viewed positively. Even some former revisionists now look back upon those four or so decades as 'the long peace'. I myself grew up during that time, and teach my students about the statesmanly 'revolution' that occurred in American foreign policy following 1945 – the Truman Doctrine, Marshall Plan, North Atlantic Treaty, and so on. The events and decisions of the 1940s and ensuing decades confirmed a positive shift in the attitude of the United States from 'isolationism' to 'internationalism', and caused it to contribute – even to lead the way – toward the building of some of our most important institutions, such as NATO, on which we still rely heavily.

There is an academically fashionable theory that formal international institutions, not just conditions of political stability, are generated by the powerful and purposeful conduct of a 'hegemon', as the United States arguably was during its 'leader of the free world' days. Against this generally admiring view of past events and efforts, the reply can be made that *some* of the international organizations of the Cold War era were rhetoric-riven and even non-functional. As the conference's initial speaker quite fairly and rightly pointed out, the United Nations Security Council was during much of the Cold War period 'a non-operating body'. Upon reflection, I am now inclined to concur with Ambassador Biancheri Chiappori in his basic proposition that multipolarity – on balance – allows greater opportunity for the activity of diplomats, for the life of the profession, than does bipolarity. At the very least, diplomats therein have more freedom of manoeuvre, more scope for exercising whatever initiative and imagination they may have. Whether 'multipolarity' summons and focuses their energy as well as 'bipolarity' has done, however, remains a question.

Ambassador Biancheri Chiappori further provocatively suggested that the current widespread trend of 'deregulation' of national economies may 'at some stage' lead to 'substituting international for national regulation'. Deregulation is 'not really deregulation at all', he postulated. *Other* kinds of agreements may have to be negotiated, on an international scale, when, for example, workers' rights cease being well protected on the national level. Thus policies that were, in the past, at best 'multi-unilateral' may become truly 'multilateral'. Moreover, there could be an increased need for negotiating rules for 'watching' – monitoring – the implementation of the new international agreements that will have to be made.

If Ambassador Biancheri Chiappori is right in his expectation, there certainly will be much more business for diplomats to do in the 21st century. It is hard to know what the political circumstances and philosophical climate will be in the future, however. Europe and America – not to mention Africa and Asia – may continue to differ in their political-philosophical orientations and perspectives. That there actually will be a demand for such super-regulation on an international scale is, I think, not at all certain, whatever the underlying common objective need for such wider controls may be. There are two very different sets of values and principles that have governed policy-making debates in recent decades: *laissez-faire* and *dirigisme*. For the present, the former – the belief in the 'magic of the marketplace', as President Ronald Reagan called it – seems to be much the stronger, and also the more generally accepted worldwide. One can at least say that, on the most basic philosophical-historical level, the international system of the 21st century will be, in comparison with the rigidified Cold War structure, relatively unconstrained from the perspective of diplomats – neither debilitatingly anarchic nor dispiritingly absolutist.

3 Some Specific Developments

Can anything more *specific* be said about the outline of the future, before considering how the diplomatic profession may be required to function in the 21st century? I see at least five major developments that could have a defining and also a guiding influence. These current developments may continue as longer trends. I shall briefly discuss these, under the following headings: the conceptual *economization* of foreign policy; the *de-ideologization* of international relations; the *decentralization* of political authority and social initiative; the *diffusion* of technology and information; and the *degradation* of the physical environment.

The first development is a shift in preoccupation from military to economic concerns – leading to what has been called the *economization* of foreign policy. This seems to apply even within governments (where security must remain the foremost responsibility), and to be a continuing trend. Although associated today with *les événements* of 1989–1991 (which did greatly reduce even if they did not entirely remove the threat of nuclear war or other major conflict among great powers), the prevailing view that economic issues should be the primary concern of political leaders began to be formed much earlier. It is important, in historical forecasting, to recognize the antecedents of current developments; only on that basis can events be connected and deeper trends projected. The tendency toward economics-first decision-making began a long time ago, back in the early 1970s. It was during the last part of the Nixon administration, apparently the very heyday of military-first 'geopolitics', when the 1973 Middle East war and Arab oil embargo forced most governments, the rich industrial countries and also oil-dependent developing ones, to recognize that their nations' financial stability and socioeconomic welfare depended on the world's natural resources (not only its petroleum reserves) and access thereto.

At the Wilton Park conference it was Professor John Stempel who mentioned the word 'geoeconomics', alluding to the work of Edward Luttwak ('From Geopolitics and Geo-Economics: Logic of Conflict, Grammar of Commerce', *The National Interest* [Summer 1990]) and others on that subject. From 1973 on, the economics and business sections of newspapers, which carried sensational stories about 'the energy crisis' and related balance-of-payments, national-debt, and petrodollar-recycling problems, began to seem somehow fundamentally more important and even more interesting than the 'high political' stories on the front pages about arms control and East–West détente. With the cessation of the US–USSR nuclear arms race during the late 1980s, the most challenging matters for governments to confront have been economic, commercial, and business-policy matters, including governmental trade promotion, on which there were excellent presentations by Jean-Michel Roy and David Morris at the conference.

This inversion of priorities on the agendas of most governments, with low-political matters becoming high-politics, has begun to affect the work of diplomacy in general. During the Secretaryship of Warren Christopher in the United States, for example, the international interests of the American business community often were put at the very top of the list of subjects taken up by the Secretary himself in meetings with foreign leaders, even heads of government. An article, 'Focus on Diplomacy: The State Department at Work', in the Department of State *Dispatch* (2 September 1996) formulates the change of priorities in this way: 'We have achieved extraordinary success by putting the bottom lines of American business on the front lines of American diplomacy'. The State Department's emphasis on support for business was no doubt reinforced by the unabashed 'commercial diplomacy' of the Secretary of Commerce during the first Clinton administration, the late Ron Brown. Although the background and personal interests of the current Secretary of State, Madeleine Albright, are different, this increased American emphasis on worldwide business expansion probably will continue. Pressures from outside the US government, as well as from within it, will demand an assertive, even aggressive, economic diplomacy, perhaps conducted more forcefully even than will be the diplomacy of international peace and security.

The second development, not unrelated to the first, is the massive deflation of Cold War ideology that has occurred. In a single, almost unpronounceable word, I refer to it as *de-ideologization*. Though the energies of the East–West struggle have not completely expired, there has been a significant reduction of interest in secular ideology – notably Marxism–Leninism but also its less rigorous 'Free World' counterparts, such as Reaganism and Thatcherism (especially in their anti-communist aspects).

This process too can be traced further back, even probably in empirical ways, simply by plotting the decline in the number of books published worldwide on Marxism, for instance. The 'end of ideology' mentioned in passing by Sir Crispin Tickell happened – arguably – not in 1989, in a sudden cessation, but over a lengthy period beginning some thirty years before. It may be remembered that Daniel Bell's famous book *The End of Ideology* (1961) has the subtitle, *On the Exhaustion of Political Ideas in the Fifties*. Bell was then referring principally to 'the old nineteenth-century ideologies and intellectual debates' of the Western world. By the late 1950s these arguments had become 'exhausted', in his view. He did recognize that 'the rising states of Asia and Africa are fashioning new ideologies with a different appeal for their own people'; these were the ideologies of 'industrialization, modernization, Pan-Arabism, color, and nationalism'. Bell none the less insisted upon the 'distinctive difference' between the two kinds of ideologies, the older Western and the newer non-Western. Some of his distinction, though it may seem pejorative and would be as likely to arouse controversy with Asians and Africans today as it did then, remains valid. 'The ideologies of the nineteenth century were universalistic, humanistic, and fashioned by intellectuals', he wrote in *The End of Ideology*. 'The mass ideologies of Asia and Africa are parochial, instrumental, and created by political leaders. The driving forces of the old ideologies were social equality and, in the largest sense, freedom. The impulsions of the new ideologies are economic development and national power'.

Even in the West during the 1950s and in the decades thereafter, public ideological expressions, including those by the American government, became to some degree masks for material and political interests. In the Eisenhower–Dulles era, in the United States and also in many places abroad, a gap emerged between official rhetoric and 'alienated' personal thought in the private domain. The American official outlook of the immediately subsequent Kennedy period was much more pragmatic, less consciously philosophical, and less given to verbosity than the Manichean world-view of John Foster Dulles had been – even if the New Frontiersmen were aggressive in their own political way.

By 1989, Francis Fukuyama, in his essay on 'The End of History' in *The National Interest* (Summer 1989), on the playing-out of the Hegelian dialectic of radically opposed spiritual forces, could gain attention by announcing virtually the end of political thinking. 'What we may be witnessing', Fukuyama wrote, 'is not just the end of the Cold War, or the passing of a particular period of postwar history, but the end of history as such: that is, the end point of mankind's ideological evolution and the universalization of Western liberal democracy as the final form of human government'. President George Bush in his inaugural message (20 January 1989) stated, similarly: 'For the first time in this century – for the first time in perhaps all history – man does not have to invent a system by which to live. We don't have to talk late into the night about which form of government is better'.[2]

The story of the de-ideologization of international relations may in fact not be completed. The re-emergence around the world of religious self-identification, in particular, complicates the narrative of ideological decline. None the less, I believe it may be registered that there are no major ideological battles, as usually understood, raging today, at least within Western societies. Current discussions about the promise, and the limits, of 'free market' and 'democratic' solutions to assorted problems in various situations around the world do not rise to past levels of grand ideological debate. The problem of social and cultural differences which the West has with the East is another matter, to which I shall later return, after an initial comment here.

A good rule of thumb, or analytic test, to determine the existence of genuine ideological warfare in international relations may be derived from a definition offered by a US Foreign Service 'China' expert and former US Ambassador to Saudi Arabia, Chas Freeman, in his *The Diplomat's Dictionary* (1997). The rule would be this: that 'ideology in foreign policy' exists as the truly dominant consideration if a foreign policy is aimed at *exporting the system of government it justifies*, and thus 'explicitly' challenges the legitimacy of the states which it addresses and at least 'implicitly' invites their overthrow. If, by contrast, a foreign policy is 'based on tolerance of diverse systems of government and realistic accommodation of antagonists, morally flawed as they may be', the foreign policy may be judged not-ideological.

The criterion may be illustrated by applying it to current US government relations with the People's Republic of China. Former President Jimmy Carter, whose own administration 'normalized' relations with the Chinese communist state in 1979, has recently argued: 'Mutual criticisms are proper and necessary, but should not be offered in an arrogant or self-righteous way, and each of us should acknowledge improvements made by the other' ('It's Wrong to Demonize China', *The New York Times*, 10 August 1997). He cited, in particular, improvements in China in the areas of religious freedom and the conduct of local elections. He acknowledged, however, continuing difficulty over the issue of Tibet. Carter's timely counsel may have been prompted by a recent adverse report of the Advisory Committee on Religious Freedom Abroad, which Secretary Christopher had set up (under congressional pressure) in 1996.

Secretary Albright, also no doubt responding to congressional and interest-group pressure, has appointed a State Department officer (not at the level of ambassador) to focus on the subject of the religious freedom of Tibetans and China's respect for the Tibetans' ethnicity – though not on the underlying issue of Tibet's independence. Thus the United States government plainly accepts the reality that Tibet is part of China. By these standards, in my own assessment, political and economic calculation has now largely overtaken doctrine – 'ideology' – in foreign policy. Being practical and successful – that is, internationally competitive – is more important than remaining highly principled – super-committed to the Wilsonian ideal of 'self-determination', for instance.

What will be the practical effects for diplomacy of this playing-out of ideology, except perhaps for such second-order if still important matters as disputes over religious freedom and ethnic autonomy within countries such as China? For one thing, political leaders and their diplomatic representatives will today meet with almost anybody – except notably, for US leaders, with Fidel Castro. Without the overarching ideological framework of communist 'East' versus capitalist 'West', few diplomatic encounters today are high symbolic occurrences – such as Secretary Dulles's refusal to shake hands with Chou En-lai at the Geneva Conference in 1954 or President Nixon's demonstrative handshake with Chou on the tarmac in Beijing in 1972. Today, most political figures – even those formerly (and sometimes for valid reason) labelled by their adversaries 'terrorists' – are allowed into the international game.

Some commentators have deeply regretted this trend. 'Diplomatic integrity and credibility have been compromised in recent years largely as a result of a popular, but mistaken, belief that all parties have legitimate needs and concerns and that if only those needs were understood and addressed, then a successful outcome could be negotiated', lamented former Secretary of State George Shultz in April 1997 in remarks reported by the United States Institute of Peace (*PeaceWatch* [June 1997]). 'This belief has led some negotiators to negotiate away principles and thus to reward violence with a seat at the negotiating table'. Such inclusiveness is perhaps practical, but, in Shultz's view, unethical.

I myself am not suggesting that an international context devoid of ideology or transcendent concern with ethics deprives diplomacy of any kind of larger 'significance'. But I do note that the reduction in philosophical content has taken a lot of the moral drama out of it, making the process more workaday – more 'normal', in both positive and, as Secretary Shultz observes, negative ways. Diplomacy, today, is simply less salient. This is in part because it is more common. It is likely to remain so in the 21st century.

A third historical development that may have an impact on diplomats and their work is a *decentralization* of authority. This has occurred within most countries, and within international society generally, and brings with it a wider participation. Much of the initiative for international action, if not necessarily the formal responsibility for it, today is being exercised by various 'subnational units'. These include cities and states or provinces as well as influential non-public bodies such as corporations, labour unions, religious groups, and academic institutions – and numerous and varied ad hoc coalitions or other combinations thereof. Diplomacy in the past has been, almost by definition, an official capital city-to-capital city relationship, taking place in and between 'centres' – Washington, London, Paris, and other national seats of government. Now the 'periphery' is involved, actively and sometimes even aggressively.

This widening of the locus of initiative in the making of foreign policy has been accepted by most diplomats, not to put too fine a point on it, with bad grace. Their attitude is at best ambivalent – well expressed, for instance, in the way they tend to employ the term, 'the grassroots', as if viewed from the treetops. Indeed, foreign policy makers and diplomatic *fonctionnaires* often have valid reason to complain of what seems, from their official vantage, lower-level interference with the proper functioning of diplomacy, indeed of government in general. Jean-Marie Guéhenno, in *The End of the Nation-State* (1995), writes: 'For the French, there can be no expression of sovereignty without the formation of a body politic'. The same, he believes, is true for the English and the Germans. 'Once there is no longer a natural place for solidarity and for the general good, the well-ordered hierarchy of a society organized in a pyramid of interlocking powers disappears. There are no great decisions from which proceed lesser ones, or laws from which decrees proceed'. Nowhere has this breakdown become more evident than in the United States, Guéhenno remarks. 'Because it was once in the vanguard of the institutional organization of power, one can see how its institutional logic is exhausted, bringing down with it in its demise politics itself!'

A recent example of locally initiated action that presents difficulties to central-government diplomats is the law passed on 25 June 1996 by the legislative Great and General Court of Massachusetts – The Act Regulating State Contracts with Companies Doing Business with or in Burma (Myanmar). This measure restricts the Commonwealth of Massachusetts in its dealings with any company, US-owned or other, that trades with or invests in Burma while under the SLORC military dictatorship. The law is not, it should be noted, a total ban; it precludes official purchasing from companies having an economic relationship with Burma unless their products or services are 10 percent cheaper than those offered by competitors. Rather than openly contest this Massachusetts legislation, some leading US corporations, including Hewlett-Packard and Pepsi-Cola, have simply bowed out of the Burmese market.

Europe has not been so accommodating. Sir Leon Brittan, the Trade Commissioner, and others in the European Union have vehemently protested against what a European Commission report calls 'a worrying new trend of US sub-federal policy-making aimed at regulating the behaviour of economic agents beyond US territorial jurisdiction'. The European Commission has filed a complaint with the World Trade Organization about the Massachusetts law. It sees that other states in the US federal system including Connecticut, California, and Texas and also even cities, notably New York, are considering procurement measures similar to the one approved by Massachusetts. Officials in Brussels, in presenting the Commission's report, stated that they are trying to 'nip in the bud' such practices (Neil Buckley, 'US: Increase in Extra-territorial trade laws angers EU', *Financial Times* [30 July 1997]).

The opposition to state government action in the 'sovereign' realm of foreign policy is of course shared by the US State Department, which fears that actions analogous to the ones taken against Burma might be taken against other Asian countries. Indonesia is one likely target, because of the issue of human rights offences in East Timor. Indonesia is an incomparably larger and richer market than is Burma – for Boeing (or Airbus) aircraft, for example. The current US Ambassador to Indonesia (formerly to China, the implicit 'background' question in this debate), Stapleton Roy, argued at a meeting in June 1997 at the Fletcher School of Law and Diplomacy ('ASEAN and the United States in the Fourth Decade: A Roundtable Discussion on Growth, Trade, Security, and Human Rights in Southeast Asia') that much depends upon the way state government measures are written. He sought, with his advice, to shape state policy. If state legislatures pass *resolutions* expressing 'concern' about human rights conditions in East Timor, their doing so 'strengthens' his hand as a diplomat, he explained. If, however, they (as the Massachusetts legislature had done) enact *laws* on the subject, in some manner or measure penalizing businesses' sales or investment in Indonesia, that would 'tie' his hands in dealing with the Indonesian government. He expressed some frustration over the fact that, as it seemed to him, American popular attitudes and local policies regarding East Timor and relations with the Indonesian government were being determined less by reports regarding the actual situation on the ground in East Timor, which the US Embassy in Jakarta well knows and can even affect, than by an entirely different communications cycle – namely, that revolving around the awarding by a parliamentary committee in Oslo, Norway, of the Nobel Prize for Peace to a Timorese Catholic bishop and human rights lawyer. Not only is this cycle decentralized, from the point of view of the State Department or US Embassy in Jakarta. It is also eccentric.

The participation in this forum of Ambassador Roy and six other US heads of mission to Southeast Asian countries was part of the New England phase of a State Department tour, a tour facilitated by the business-supported US ASEAN Council, in coordination with local governments, firms and academic institutions. Such round-the-country diplomatic sweeps are likely to become much more frequent and necessary in the coming years. Professional diplomats, in the United States and elsewhere, may have to enter directly into local political discussions in order to maintain their effectiveness on the international level. 'All politics are local', as the late Speaker of the US House of Representatives Thomas P. O'Neill, Democrat of Cambridge, Massachusetts, liked to say.

This brings me to a fourth development likely to affect the conduct of diplomacy in the 21st century: the *diffusion* of technology and information. Diffusion of information may bring, in the process, diffusion of knowledge, although users will know that 'hits' on the Internet, a measure of computer inquiries, often means 'misses' in terms of understanding transferred. As was made very evident during the Wilton Park conference, the spread of information technology (IT) throughout industry and other structures, all around the world, is putting very heavy pressure on the diplomatic profession. Even diplomats in technically advanced countries, not merely in those countries that are slower to adapt to new technologies, are struggling to 'keep up', not just in terms of mastery but also in terms of style – to maintain the diplomatic guild's self-respect as well as image in the eyes of others. 'The Department of State is the lead U.S. foreign affairs agency', as an aforementioned article in the Department's official *Dispatch* insists, perhaps as much as a reminder to itself as to others ('Focus on Diplomacy: The State Department at Work'). In no area is the primacy of the State Department, and of other countries' ministries of foreign affairs, more 'in peril' than in the sphere of international, even interstate, communication.

A word of caution is necessary here: the IT diffusion process, even though worldwide, is incomplete and imperfect; it is inconsistent over time and space. Differences in countries' levels of economic and institutional development mean that mankind's 'passage to virtuality' will be highly uneven. Thus the relevance of IT skills for the conduct of diplomacy among some societies, especially the less-developed ones, should not be exaggerated. John Gage, director of the science office at Sun Microsystems has reminded us: 'Fifty percent of today's human beings will never make a phone call'. None the less, the information revolution is spreading fast and far. The April 1997 conference sponsored by the US Institute of Peace in Washington on 'Virtual Diplomacy' at which Gage spoke explored the possibility, alarming for traditional diplomats, of a radical reduction in the amount of face-to-face or 'contact' diplomacy, driven by technology and costs.

The notion of the 'virtual teams' and even 'virtual embassies' was discussed by Joan Link of the British Foreign and Commonwealth Office and others at the Wilton Park conference. It is now possible to interconnect, for 'real-time' consultation and even joint decision-making, not only the diplomat on the scene and officials in a ministry but also those having pertinent expertise or experience (perhaps acquired from previous service in a trouble-spot country) even if they may currently be working in other regions of the world. Thus, for example, a crisis in Africa could be monitored by everyone in the British diplomatic service who might have useful knowledge of a particular problem. Especially for crisis management, the advantage of harnessing such 'virtual teams' is obvious. Virtual diplomacy also helps to offset disadvantages of the rotational system for diplomatic personnel used by most foreign ministries, and it can even compensate somewhat for actual staff reductions.

The concept of a 'virtual embassy' can easily be debunked. 'If it's virtual, it's not an embassy; and if it's an embassy, it's not virtual', as one conference participant, Jovan Kurbalija, rightly commented, drawing attention to the inescapable territorial element in any established and functioning diplomatic system. 'The priceless asset of the diplomat is that he is *there*', said the former American ambassador and State Department official Livingston Merchant ('Diplomats, role of', Freeman, *The Diplomat's Dictionary*). The *terra firma* of traditional diplomacy, however, is plainly being eroded away.

Communication, if not necessarily also conflict resolution, can be facilitated by the current revolution in information technology. Diplomatic representation itself can be accelerated and in other ways expedited. Gordon Smith, Deputy Minister in the Canadian Department of Foreign Affairs and International Trade, reflected at the US Institute of Peace 'Virtual Diplomacy' conference: 'There was a time when establishing a new embassy or diplomatic post took weeks, even months. Now, it takes a plane ticket, a lap top and a dial tone. And maybe a diplomatic passport. We can hit the ground running: this has huge implications for the mobility of our operations and what I call "just in time and place" operational effectiveness'. An example is the Canadian government's rapid opening of a new embassy in Zagreb, Croatia, at the height of the Bosnian crisis. 'It was operational within a few hours', Smith said. Thus perhaps some of the ground lost to technology and budget-cutting can be regained, by dint of those very same factors.

Real-time communication between post and ministry can have the effect of improving professional discipline. It was mentioned by Joan Link that, in the old days, a diplomat overseas could use the excuse that his message, 'unfortunately', didn't arrive in time to have an effect on a Foreign Office decision – from which he may have wanted to dissociate himself. That trick is 'harder' now, she emphasized, when you are 'face to face across a screen' in real time if not also in real space. There is an insistent hierarchy in the new instant electronic communication, in the technological medium itself, which commands attention. This somewhat cuts across older organizational hierarchies, compelling persons within them to conform and, also perhaps, challenging them better to perform.

Diplomats in the field today, although surely assisted by being not only on the spot but also in instant contact, can be personally unsettled by the ubiquity and intrusiveness of IT communication. A student currently at the Fletcher School, a young diplomat from an Eastern European country who previously had been posted by his government in Beijing, recalled during a discussion in my political geography seminar that he once had received an instruction from his ministry to check out a story that had been on CNN at home about something that, reportedly, had happened in China. He was in a quandary. He didn't know exactly what his function in this situation was, i.e. what he as a political reporter was basically expected to do. Was he, he asked himself, supposed to be merely 'confirming' CNN or actively 'competing with' CNN, or what? It was, he said, 'very stressful' – a feeling intensified by the 'extremely short' deadline that the instantaneous character of the CNN report and his ministry's response to it imposed upon him.

By contrast, Harold Nicolson, writing about diplomacy as it had evolved prior to the early 1950s, felt no such professional unease in the face of the bustling public media and communications industry of his time. 'These functions in the modern world are fulfilled by newspaper reporters, who are usually younger and more adventurous men', he simply noted. 'All the ambassador need do is to comment, in the quiet of his own study, upon the news they send'. Such tranquillity, and perhaps also the Nicolsonian wisdom that ambassadorial detachment and time for reflection can bestow, will under the new working conditions imposed by telecommunications and IT be increasingly difficult to achieve, even for the most superior and studious of diplomats.

The fifth development that will more and more affect the activity of the professional diplomat is what I have described as processes of *degradation* of the physical environment through which many peoples of the world, especially in poorer countries, are now living. Awareness of these worsening environmental conditions is part of a much wider consciousness of the finiteness of the Earth, and the irreplaceability of many of its resources. There is a growing sense of the primacy even among foreign policy makers generally not trained in science, of what geographers call Man–Milieu, as contrasted with Man–Man, relationships. Politics, in this Nature-oriented view, is physics, much as it was for certain of the *philosophes* of the Enlightenment. Natural law, or knowledge of the realities of the physical environment, should be, from this perspective, the basis for positive law, or the policies of government and agreements between countries.

It should not be surprising that, in the past, some diplomats, given their ability to travel widely, and to explore and observe in the course of their duties, have been among the pioneers of the science of Man's interaction with Nature – in effect, ecology. Among Americans, the noteworthy figure in this regard is George Perkins Marsh, US Minister to Turkey and for an extended period to the Kingdom of Italy. Marsh, on his own, undertook to study, in an unprecedentedly comprehensive and detailed way, 'the changes produced by human action in the physical conditions of the globe we inhabit', as he wrote in his classic *Man and Nature* (1864). His principal focus was the disastrous impact of deforestation – the effect of the 'felling of the woods', as he called it, upon the drainage of the soil, upon the configuration of the soil surface, and 'probably' even upon local climate. The genesis of *Man and Nature*, as Marsh himself explains, was his 'early life almost literally in the woods' of his native Vermont. According to a modern editor of his work, the geographer David Lowenthal, 'Marsh's Mediterranean travels corroborated these experiences and gave them historical depth'. Marsh's sweep was nearly Braudelian. Extensive and lengthy overseas service, for a naturistically inclined diplomat today as well, can be a stimulus to thought about the physical world and damage being inflicted upon it by society.

Even as 'virtual reality' appears to be replacing geographical truth in some respects, the imperativeness of the material needs of the world's population and the implacability of the natural forces acting upon our societies are, if anything, increased in impact. In some cases, problems caused by Nature can be amplified by Man's own seemingly-insignificant activities, as Marsh was one of the first to show. From the variations of global warming to the vagaries of El Niño, the dynamic processes of Nature seem to be pressing themselves upon us more powerfully than ever. The present political crisis in North Korea, for instance, was arguably not merely *exacerbated*, but fundamentally *caused*, by the two years of floods and two months of drought that have occurred there.

The very existence of some states, notably island countries, is being threatened by these potent factors. The violence and destruction caused by Man-motivated disruptions such as trans-border aggressions and internal civil wars can be triggered or otherwise strongly conditioned by natural disturbances, i.e. vast geological and meteorological occurrences, outside historic norms on which social, economic, and political equilibria may rest. I am here thinking not merely of the destruction caused by earthquakes, volcanoes and hurricanes, which occasion immediate international relief efforts, but also of less dramatic phenomena such as the trans-regional and even worldwide spread of disease – malaria, AIDS, the Ebola virus, etc.

Frequently connected with larger physical and social processes, including tropical forest harvesting and soil overutilization as well as rapid population increase and rural migration to cities, these natural biological threats require preventive and curative measures, on an international scale, which are much more extensive, longer term, and complicated than we have envisaged so far. These issues may be even more urgent than those arising from the danger of war. During the Wilton Park conference, Barry Fulton noted quietly that the Atlanta Centers for Disease Control have 'relations with most countries on issues that are as important as any we have discussed here today'. The point should resonate. Robert Kaplan's *The Ends of the Earth*, already mentioned, is actually frightening on the subject of these untraditional and under-appreciated dangers to our health and welfare, reaching even relatively cared-for Europe and America. 'Viruses luxuriating in Africa may constitute a basic risk to humanity', Kaplan convincingly writes. Deeply alarming, too, was the warning of Sir Crispin Tickell, when he described the increasing destruction, through Man's industrial progress, of the beneficial function of Earth's own 'natural services'. The value of these, even in accounting terms, is, he noted, many times greater than the total value of the world's current economic output. 'We are just about the first generation to be able to see what is going on around us', he stated. And this too will be 'the world of diplomacy'.

4 Old Craft: New Skills

Now I come to what most interests me, the *craftsmanship* question: that of how diplomats can respond to these and other developments which may imperil their relatively traditional trade – and perhaps even the 'multi-state' system in which they will be plying it, likely to become still more pluralistic and hard-to-manage in the 21st century. Earlier in the text of this essay, as well as in its subtitle, I have suggested the need for what I term the *re-crafting* of diplomacy, the old guild. By this, I mean something more fundamental than training in how to use the Internet – or the teaching of technological survival skills to diplomats, especially the 'dinosaurs', as the old-timers in the profession were affectionately called during the Wilton Park conference. Knowing how to explore the World Wide Web, to send e-mail, and to master a bureaucracy's intranet system are important; but they are merely questions of technique – a matter of the way diplomats work, and of the means they use, not of what they basically do. I have in mind, rather, a rethinking of the very nature of the diplomatic craft, conceived in the broader sense of what Harold Nicolson called 'method' (*The Evolution of Diplomacy*, originally published as *The Evolution of Diplomatic Method* [1954]). For Nicolson, diplomatic 'method' meant 'not only the actual machinery for negotiation, but also the general theory, in accordance with which the machinery was used'.

What are likely to be the most important and professionally distinctive crafts for diplomats in the 21st century? I shall discuss five of these, noting how in each case current skills and techniques can be reimagined for new uses. There may well be more than this number. I shall deliberately use unconventional terms, all of them playing on the 'guild' or medieval 'craft' metaphor with which I introduced this subject – whimsically perhaps, but I hope for a serious purpose. My aim is in the most vivid way possible to define, or redefine, the varied and essential roles which will help diplomats to prosper professionally and, beyond that self-protective aim, to prevail internationally in the 21st century.

It is obvious from what I have said so far that I consider – at least tentatively – that diplomacy will be more useful than ever. I am inclined further to the view that it is not possible to have diplomacy without diplomats – that is, 'a real career corps', as George F. Kennan expressed the ideal in a recent article ('Diplomacy Without Diplomats?' *Foreign Affairs* [September/October 1997]). The combined membership of the diplomatic profession, as I postulated at the beginning of this essay, is one of the very constitutive 'orders' in our organization of the world: more exactly, it is the one international community that serves that common higher purpose as well as the mutual adjustment of separate national interests. Professional diplomats are arguably the most reliable element, though not politically the very strongest pillar, of the multi-state system that has existed and is likely to govern international relations during the coming century. Professor Kennan, with whom I have recently corresponded regarding this subject, has however underlined the difference that my approach construes the term 'diplomatic corps' expansively; and perhaps I differ also in condoning and even commending a progressive and substantial re-adaptation of the methods of diplomacy.

The first modernized diplomatic craft I shall call that of the *weavers*. The term was suggested to me by the work in a very different field – art history – being done by a scholar, trained as a sociologist and in literature, who served during a recent period as the French Cultural Counsellor in New York, Dr Annie Cohen-Solal. Perhaps best known as the biographer of Sartre, she is currently doing a historical-sociological study of the 'incessant exchange' (a Sartrean phrase) that has occurred back-and-forth across the Atlantic Ocean in the imagery of modern visual art – impressionism, abstract expressionism, surrealism, and so on. After the Second World War, the United States came to dominate the international art world in almost an imperial fashion. In explaining this rise to artistic predominance, Cohen-Solal focuses on the creatively *intermediary* roles of certain individuals, and the institutions with which they were affiliated. These persons – art dealers (e.g. Leo Castelli) and museum curators in different cities (especially New York) as well as many of the painters themselves – were involved in a Europe-to-America-to-Europe-to-America intercultural activity that resembles to her nothing so much as weaving (*tissage*). It is important to note that the result of such an exchanging process is not just a higher-functioning reciprocity, an intensified trade between culturally and artistically unchanged continents. The exchanging system is itself creative. Its product can be a specific new fabric of culture – a pattern of American and European seeing, 'pan-Atlantic' in some ways, that didn't exist before.

This is, I believe, essentially what cultural diplomats can and, increasingly, should do. The essential difference between diplomats and artists (or other direct participants) themselves is that the diplomats have – or should have – a detachment that enables them better to see the entirety of what is woven, that is, the whole international pattern. They observe, and sometimes can even help to shape, a vast and distinctive tapestry. Annie Cohen-Solal certainly did a lot of creative interweaving herself when she represented France in New York (William H. Honan, 'A Shaker and Mover of Things French', *The New York Times*, 7 September 1992). 'My job is to be a go-between', she then said. 'It is very subtle. It is to detect interest and then open the door and make sure that the door doesn't close. It comes to this: I provide American institutions with French potentialities'.

Something very similar is possible for commercial diplomats. Instead of attempting to weave an 'art world' (musical community, educational community, etc.), they try to make a 'commercial world'. They can help to structure and, in a sense, even to 'civilize' the forces of economization that are powering the international system today. Their work was described, and implicitly demonstrated, at the Wilton Park conference by Jean-Michel Roy, David Morris and, from a business perspective, Howard Chase. Commercial diplomacy now involves what Morris, on behalf of Australia Inc., called 'branding', i.e. national image-patenting in support of Australia's varied business enterprises. This latter activity is a broader, more generic function than just 'networking', or interconnecting potentially interested individual business partners. We are 'really marketing the country', he said.

The resemblance of this kind of higher strategic, as well as lower-level tactical, commercial thinking to what cultural policy makers (like French Culture Minister Jack Lang) and their representatives (like Annie Cohen-Solal) do is very close, despite the differences in subject matter. Art, after all, is a commodity too. And commodities like audio-visuals, as was learned during the last phase of the GATT Uruguay Round, can have large cultural import. The objective of both cultural diplomacy and commercial diplomacy, I would myself emphasize, is ordinarily not merely a particular national interest – a French interest or an Australian interest – but a larger international interest, however nationally approached.

Sometimes the effort of the commercial attaché is, it was acknowledged by the speakers, akin to 'pushing water uphill'. Diplomats must learn to know the market, the playing field of international business being in constant upheaval, and rarely flat or level. I am here reminded of François de Callières's earlier, 18th-century gravitational analogy, 'Diplomacy a Bowling Green'. Callières then wrote: 'Thus in the approach to difficult negotiations the true dexterity of diplomacy, like a good bowler using the run of the green, consists in finding the existing bias of the matter'.

Diplomatic weaving could be particularly important in the 21st century, not only in the cultural and commercial fields but also in the socioeconomic area, such as in providing technical and other help to foster the development of countries. Development diplomacy, which typically involves the coordination of public and private efforts to support projects and deliver assistance, is an ever more important sub-craft. In the political sphere, too, there are ample opportunities for creative interweaving. One thinks of a mediator like Dennis Ross, who repeatedly has been sent by US administrations to try to resolve, or at least to manage, the Israeli–Palestinian conflict. One of his forerunners in this work was Henry Kissinger, whose earlier 'shuttle diplomacy' between Middle Eastern capitals was actually named after a device used in weaving.

Diplomatic mediation is usually a complex, long-term, and demanding process. It requires patience, sensitivity, and understanding – but also detachment and a broader view. Even though a mediator may be the representative of an individual country with a strong interest in a situation, the role he or she performs imposes a certain 'neutrality' –

that is, at least a (seeming) attitude of impartiality toward the persons or parties involved, and even an (apparent) indifference to the substance of many of the issues at stake. The goal is a higher and larger one, that of peace between the rivals and those who may back them from afar.

If there does turn out to be, as Samuel Huntington foresees, an increased incidence of 'clashes', or 'fault line wars' as he also calls them, between the West and non-West, in the Middle East or Asia or Africa or elsewhere, the ability of professional diplomats of all kinds to formulate and to maintain the cohesive effect of 'commonalities' (another Huntington term) could be – at the frontiers between civilizations – decisive. How can such commonalities be woven, and a broken world order thereby, perhaps, 'remade'?

'At least at a basic "thin" morality level', Huntington acknowledges, 'some commonalities exist between Asia and the West'. He recognizes, as others have observed and have described in greater substantive detail, that the world's major religions – Western Christianity, Orthodoxy, Hinduism, Buddhism, Islam, Confucianism, Taoism, and Judaism – 'share key values in common'. He then posits, intriguingly and consistently with the last part of the title of *The Clash of Civilizations and the Remaking of World Order*: 'If humans are ever to develop a universal civilization, it will emerge gradually through the exploration and expansion of these commonalities'.

This – the exploration and expansion of commonalities – is essentially what I call diplomatic weaving on a more philosophical plane. The need for it is the premise of the third of three rules which Huntington advises statesmen, their advisers and agents to follow. The first of these is the *abstention rule*: that countries should, generally, refrain from intervention in the conflicts in other civilizations. The second is the *joint mediation rule*: that 'core states', like the United States and Russia, should negotiate with each other to contain or stop fault line wars between states, or groups of states, representing their respective civilizations. The continuing effort of the Contact Group for Bosnia to prevent further conflict among the Orthodox, Catholic, and Muslim communities there is illustrative. This is essentially a great power-led style of diplomacy. The last of Huntington's three rules, and the most pertinent here, is the *commonalities rule*: that 'peoples in all civilizations should search for and attempt to expand the values, institutions, and practices they have in common with peoples of other civilizations'. Who among the world's 'peoples' are better placed to carry out Huntington's 'commonalities' injunction than the family of diplomats, particularly the professionals among them who are working in the cultural, commercial, and developmental fields as well as the political field? In the conflict-fraught historical context Huntington envisages, all would be labouring as international weavers.

Huntington's *The Clash of Civilizations and the Remaking of World Order* is not itself an attempt to describe in detail the process of reknitting the torn textures of international order or of interlacing new designs of shared normative understanding. The 'commonalities rule' is only briefly stated, and it appears at the end of his book. In an earlier passage, however, he cites a case which clearly indicates, though more by negative than positive example, what professional diplomats could do to articulate international norms, old and new. The example is the United Nations World Conference on Human Rights held in Vienna in June 1993. Of this Huntington writes, mainly to criticize but also to urge that future inter-civilizational polarization be prevented:

> The Western nations were ill prepared for Vienna, were outnumbered at the conference, and during its proceedings made more concessions than their opponents. As a result, apart from a strong endorsement of women's rights, the declaration approved by the conference was a minimal one. It was, one human rights supporter observed, 'a flawed and contradictory' document, and represented a victory for the Asian–Islamic coalition and a defeat for the West. The Vienna declaration contained no explicit endorsement of the rights to freedom of speech, the press, assembly, and religion, and was thus in many respects weaker than the Universal Declaration of Human Rights the U.N. had adopted in 1948.

There is a lesson in his critique for multilateral diplomacy in particular. There should have been a creative way for a multinational group of diplomats, despite the agitation of assorted human rights lobbyists and pressures back home, to have expressed a higher level of common understanding, on the basis of their technical knowledge of precedent, their habitual cosmopolitan outlook, and also a cross-national feeling of professional solidarity.

The human rights altercations that have taken place, more recently, in the context of meetings between the ASEAN group of countries and Western powers, mainly the United States, provide another example. These concern the relative importance of individual political and civil rights, on the one hand, and economic, social and cultural rights, on the other. The debate illustrates the increased need, which it ought to be possible to meet in the post-Cold War world, for re-weaving the fabric of international comity. It may not be, in the short or even in the long run, the most effective method for Secretary of State Albright and Under Secretary of State for Economic Affairs Stuart Eizenstat to 'answer' the philosophical provocations of Malaysia's Dr Mahathir on these matters. Good humour also is necessary and, happily, that has been demonstrated too, as at the ASEAN–US dialogue in Kuala Lumpur in July 1997 when Secretary Albright, dressed as Evita (thus winning her the sobriquet 'Madonna'), sang, 'Don't cry for me Aseanies,/The truth is I always loved you'.

Creating joint cultural values, where there have been differences, is, of course, an immensely ambitious undertaking. It is a suitable challenge, however, for a diplomacy of the 21st century. Particularly difficult to form in the decades ahead will be a mutually acceptable value-based relationship between Euro-America and the People's Republic of China. Alluding to the Huntington thesis, Secretary Albright has made a start. 'What we see in Asia today', she said in a lecture at the US Naval Academy in April 1997, 'is not a clash of civilization[s], but a test of civilization' ('American Principle and Purpose in East Asia', Department of State *Dispatch* [March/April 1997]). There is, as she pointed out, a 'dialogue' under way between the American and Chinese governments. There is much commentary about this in the foreign-policy journals, she noted. 'What those journals sometimes ignore ... is that, in addition to what is occurring at the official level, ties between the American and Chinese people are deepening at every level'. She went on to posit that it is 'our peoples, even more than our governments, that are bringing the old era of mutual isolation and miscommunication to a decisive and irreversible end'.

The 'ties', governmental and extra-governmental, to which Secretary Albright refers may not bind; indeed, they might not even be perceived or thought of as such, i.e. as a 'texture'. However functional for those involved in them, mere networks or liaisons do not necessarily have the consistency of pattern, overall design, or even thickness of weave which makes a figured and rich tapestry – a relationship – which will be recognized as such by the different societies, or civilizations, from which they originate. Nevertheless, with some management by culturally aware diplomats, with direction and oversight and resource support from policy makers, the threads of transpacific contact can be woven into a texture of community, perhaps in time comparable to that existing between America and Europe across the Atlantic.

This brings me to a second diplomatic craft which I should like to describe. The *framers*, I shall call them. By 'framers', I refer of course to the great diplomatic institution, or 'house', builders of the postwar period, especially those who constructed the United Nations organization. More specifically, and perhaps analytically, I refer to the international effort – which distinguishes our own time – to construct functional 'regimes': sometimes outside the context of formal organizations, and sometimes even without big, high-level multilateral conferences to establish them. These international arrangements – consisting, in the political scientist Stephen Krasner's by now standard definition, of principles, norms, rules and procedures – have been built, for example, to enforce the nonproliferation of nuclear, chemical and biological weapons. Such systems, a kind of international 'regulation', also sometimes incorporate the work of non-governmental organizations (NGOs), as 'monitors' or even as 'implementers' of a particular regime's mandates. A case in point is the Verification Technology Information Centre (VERTIC) in London, a specialized NGO whose work Patricia Lewis described at the Wilton Park conference.

Protection of the environment is another vast substantive area in which functional regimes are beginning to be formed. The early stages included the 1972 UN Conference on the Human Environment in Stockholm and its sequel, the 1992 UN Conference on Environment and Development in Rio de Janeiro. The latest phase of rule-making in the environmental field is the controversial process of putting into precise treaty form, at the conference for that purpose in Kyoto in December 1997, the 1992 framework Climate Change Convention. The Kyoto meeting, intended to set quantitative carbon-emissions targets for governments and industry, will be, as Sir Crispin Tickell frankly put it, 'the moment of truth'.

The 1992 Conference in Rio was the first of a cycle of 'global conferences'. It was followed by the World Conference on Human Rights in Vienna (1993), the International Conference on Population and Development in Cairo (1994), the World Summit for Social Development in Copenhagen (1995), the Fourth World Conference on Women in Beijing (1995), and Habitat II in Istanbul (1996). These may in time prove to be the cornerstones for other regimes in the future. Most international regime-making involves some participation by national legislators, as the regimes are law-like and usually entail some sacrifice or, more euphemistically, pooling of national sovereignties. Even if done through non-obligatory intergovernmental coordination, some sharing of national control responsibilities usually results. A high degree of trust, therefore, must be formed across national lines – between domestic law-makers and international rule-givers. The diplomatic aspect of this process is crucial. It is a combination of traditional diplomatic persuasion and modern parliamentary vote-getting – 'negotiating world order' I have called it elsewhere, having in mind the notion of 'parliamentary diplomacy' that Dean Rusk and the jurist Philip Jessup long ago spotted as a novel development.

As new organizations or regimes usually result from juristic diplomacy, rather than legislative initiative, careful attention must be paid by diplomatic framers not only to the methods of negotiation but also to the mechanisms for ultimate ratification. A 'two-level game' must be played, as Robert Putnam has described it. One part of the game is played in an international negotiating forum and the other is played in the arena of national politics. The logic of the two processes is complicated, and failure to manage both parts of the game in synchrony can produce deadlock. Lest we have other failures like the US Senate's defeat of the League of Nations Covenant or the prolonged refusal of the US government (even, at times, the Executive branch itself) to accept the United Nations Law of the Sea Convention, American diplomats especially must learn to master also the domestic-level process – 'the *politics* of diplomacy', as former Secretary of State James A. Baker characterizes this new operational milieu, one that he himself helped to create as well as prospered in. Diplomats need to think like legislators, as representatives with constituents, and not just as negotiators, as agents of principals.

And they should play it straight, speaking and acting consistently, with complete intellectual and moral integrity, in both forums. Such consistency is essential to a diplomat's credibility and good name. This is classically recognized as an asset of any trusted and successful negotiator. Honesty counts. Ambassador Navega recalled at the conference the words of a former French Ambassador at Washington. 'A good diplomat', Hervé Alphand used to say, 'is the person who can tell the truth to anyone in the government to which he is accredited without offending him, but also to anyone in his own government at the risk of offending him'. The truth itself has to remain a constant, at home and abroad.

The 're-crafting' process to which I refer should give diplomats skills and experience in dealing with legislators. At the training level this might involve more internships and higher level positions with US Congressmen and parliamentarians elsewhere. In some instances, especially in the United States, such familiarization can occur naturally, as former Congressmen are not uncommonly appointed ambassadors. One of my own former students, a mid-career Foreign Service officer who had been serving in Japan, recently worked as a State Department Fellow in the office of Representative Lee Hamilton, the ranking Democrat on the House International Relations Committee. More 'strategic' still, a diplomat can get himself or herself elected to Congress, to Parliament, or to the National Assembly. Bridges to the law-making world of whatever devising would help. Wisdom would be transported the other way, from diplomacy to the solonocracy, as well. In Washington, the chasm in diplomatic–legislative understanding has been particularly wide in recent years – most notoriously, in the State Department's awkward dealings with the Senate Foreign Relations Committee under the chairmanship of Jesse Helms, Republican of North Carolina. (Helms's predecessor, Senator Claiborne Pell, a Rhode Island Democrat, had been a Foreign Service Officer early in his career, and brought an understanding of diplomatic ways to that position.) The basic lesson remains: the framing of international norms, be it through international organizations, functional regimes, or ad hoc treaties, requires closer collaboration between diplomacy and politics.

The third craft I don't know exactly what to call, in trade-craft terms. Perhaps wordsmiths among readers will have ideas. The *printers*, perhaps. This term has the advantage of emphasizing the theme of adapting old guilds to new technology and providing access to a larger readership, or mass audience, which the development of the printing profession (out of die-cutting, goldsmithing, and silversmithing) allowed in an earlier era. The word does not, however, encompass oral expression or stress the public function of the new re-craft.[3]

What I have mainly in mind is what we have come to call 'public diplomacy', the function of press and information officers. Essentially, the idea of public diplomacy is that of exercising influence in support of a country's foreign policy initiatives or positions through the international use of public media of communications, from press to radio and television, and through the provision of (publicly available) supportive information to individuals and organizations within the target country that may be able to effect change in their government's policy. The distinguishing characteristic of public diplomacy, in its various manifestations, is its relative 'openness'.

The term itself – still considered by some traditionalists to be oxymoronic – is of quite recent origin. It was chosen in the early 1960s by Ambassador Edmund A. Gullion, then Dean of the Fletcher School of Law and Diplomacy, for the name of the new 'Edward R. Murrow Center of Public Diplomacy' at the School. Ed Murrow himself, a very stylish and innovative broadcast journalist with CBS radio and television, and later a Director of the United States Information Agency (USIA), was to have directed the Murrow Center at Fletcher, but died in 1965 of lung cancer before he could take up the position. Each year at the Fletcher School's commencement exercises, 'The Edward R. Murrow Award for Excellence in Public Diplomacy' is awarded to an individual member of the US Information Agency, where it is considered the highest such professional honour an American international affairs information officer can earn.[4]

During the 1980s the activity of 'public diplomacy', under that name, was given a new formal status and a greater role in the United States government's international informational effort. Today, even as the future of the USIA itself is in doubt, proponents of the public diplomatic function assert its centrality to the future success of American foreign policy. Other governments, too, have taken up the term. It was explained at the Wilton Park conference that public diplomacy has now become a core function of the United Kingdom's Foreign and Commonwealth Office. Another participant – the press officer in the Austrian Embassy in London, Michael Rendi – now uses the term, 'First Secretary (Public Diplomacy)', to describe his work. The concept has become 'Continentalized'.

In the context of the present discussion, it is not so much general-purpose press and information work I would highlight as it is the increasingly serious challenge of publicizing the work and importance of international institutions, including diplomacy itself. I refer more specifically to the necessary function of making international organizations or regimes that are newly formed as well as old ones we wish to strengthen more 'transparent' – 'putting the windows' (including Microsoft Windows) into their frames, so to speak. (I recall another former student, who happens to be an extraordinary linguist and professional interpreter, named Fenstermacher.) The basic purpose is to shed light – as well as to receive light. The larger, political purpose is that, in so doing, the activities of international institutions, being more open to view, can be made more comprehensible and confidence-inspiring –

hence more acceptable, more 'legitimate'. A lack of public acceptance of the decisions and resolutions of international bodies is becoming an almost 'structural' political problem today, not only in the United States but also even within some member countries of the European Union, and in other parts of the world.

At the conference there was discussion of multilateral communiqués. One veteran of multilateral diplomacy as conducted within international organizations, Ambassador Roger Beetham, noted the distinct advantage that a diplomat has in being able to draft in more than one language, English obviously being the most advantageous one to possess today. He did say that communiqués, despite their name, are 'not necessarily the best means of communication'. The communiqués of the Group of Seven (now Eight) Summits, for example, are much 'too long', he noted. A subsequent check reveals that the final communiqué of the 1996 G-7 Summit, held in Lyon, had 55 enumerated paragraphs and ran to seven densely packed pages in the Department of State *Dispatch*. The communiqué of the Denver Summit of the Eight the following year was not printed in the *Dispatch*. It could be viewed, however, through the Department of State Foreign Affairs Network (DOSFAN) at http://www.state.gov. Such World Wide Web sites are increasingly becoming the only place to find the full, documentary 'official word'.

The inherent publicity of summit diplomacy imposes a particularly heavy burden of exposition upon diplomats. This responsibility can also be looked upon as an opportunity. Early in the Wilton Park conference the comment was made by another senior and experienced diplomat, Boris Biancheri Chiappori: 'We all know in the profession that summit meetings *increase* the role of diplomats'. Their summit-enhanced role is twofold – handling the 'preparation' of the summit beforehand and then, during and after it, 'explaining what is happening [or has happened], making it all sensible'. However, another speaker with summit experience, Ambassador Koichiro Matsuura, who served as the sherpa for the Japanese government in putting on a G-7 meeting in Tokyo, opined later in the conference that 'summit diplomacy has not necessarily increased the role of diplomats'. When asked to explain his comment – on the face of it a direct contradiction of his colleague's – he made the point that, when political leaders at summit meetings negotiate agreements, diplomats themselves do not have to do so. Otherwise, diplomats themselves would have the challenge of defining the problems to be dealt with and working out the solutions to them. He did agree that diplomats have a major responsibility at summit meetings in being the ones to explicate what is happening.

In the past, Ambassador Matsuura further noted, it was usually considered sufficient to make only 'the final product' public. He referred to Harold Nicolson, who wrote in *Diplomacy* (1939) that, whereas 'policy' should be open and known, the actual processes of 'negotiation' need not be. Now it is necessary, Matsuura stated, for diplomats to explain 'the major part' of a negotiation while it is going on. And this must be done orally. As for communiqués, he said that '80 to 90 percent of what is in a summit communiqué is prepared by the diplomats in advance', but 'the remaining 10 to 20 percent' might consist of 'very controversial issues', and be 'very, very crucial' to the outcome. Thus a 'volume' approach to estimating the role of diplomats can be misleading. He gave as an example the GATT's Uruguay Round, which would 'not have been concluded successfully' had it not been for the summit, involving political leaders and their decisions, at the end.

There should not be, everyone agreed, 'secret agreements'. The existence of these among certain European powers during the First World War had been the principal reason for President Woodrow Wilson's prescribing, as Point One of his Fourteen Points: 'Open covenants of peace, openly arrived at, after which there shall be no private international understandings of any kind but diplomacy shall proceed always frankly and in the public view'. Today, we are approximating fulfilment of the Wilsonian open-diplomacy programme, with diplomats having to be 'media diplomats', as Ambassador Matsuura called them, as well as substantive negotiators. Contemporary diplomats need to be adept at phrasing – providing *le mot juste* or the 'sound bite' – and also expressive in visage and manner – offering an image that is strong and vivid, but not too 'hot', in Marshall McLuhan's sense. Radio and television, despite the increasing use of the Internet for many purposes, must be the media of choice for public diplomats working at the highest levels.

Another Wilton Park speaker, Fraser Cameron, in his discussion of the diplomacy and current policies of the European Commission, said of the presentation of the Commission's 'Agenda 2000' Communication on 16 July 1997, that it was 'handled pretty well'. Included in the announcement were the Commission's formal Opinions regarding the readiness of a number of Central and Eastern European countries – the Czech Republic, Estonia, Hungary, Poland, and Slovenia – for eventual EU membership. It also contained important proposals regarding the future financing of the Community and reform of the Common Agricultural Policy and the Structural Funds. As was pointed out in discussion, however, the impact of the 'Agenda 2000' announcement was lessened by the high noise level caused by other stories, notably the murder of the clothing designer, Gianni Versace, the very day before. This illustrates a point made earlier during the conference: it is very 'hard to predict' how the media will react to an official announcement. You can't 'rely on' them to get the word out the way you want it to go out. And, moreover, you 'can't be sure a message will get through to those whom you wish to reach'. At least, it may be said, the 'Agenda 2000' documentation was fully available on the Internet – via the European Commission's EUROPA server (www.europa.eu.int) – for those interested in and willing to seek out such information. Printing, in its technologically most novel form, thus remains essential. But the *general* public, where political support for institutions resides, is hard to reach or impress.

In considering this subject, participants in the Wilton Park conference's special discussion group on the European Commission's new External Service stressed the role of personality in public diplomacy. The importance of assuring that not only the European Commission's spokesmen but also the Commissioners themselves are conscious of, and skilled at, media presentation – on television especially – was emphasized very pointedly. *Self* presentation as well as policy presentation is necessary. The value of professional training in the art of media appearances was suggested. One particular Commissioner was described as needing a 'makeover'. A re-crafting of a drastic kind.

For the fourth new professional craft I have a name. With due respect to the Watergate culprits, I shall call them the *plumbers*. These are the members of the extended diplomatic corps who quietly help the international community rid itself of unwanted security-related problems. Usually operating behind the scenes and even underground, they are the ones more and more engaged in a conflict that the junior Senator from Massachusetts and an expert on the subject, John Kerry, calls in a recent book, *The New War: The Web of Crime That Threatens America's Security* (1997). The 'enemy' is the challenge posed to the safety, welfare and health of the population of the United States and also other countries, even those with societies that are less open, by the spread of organized criminal activity and also politically motivated terrorism.

A much more internationally coordinated effort will have to be made to arrest this threat, given the scale and complexity of it. Many of the crime rings, having vast funds at their disposal from illegal weapons and narcotics transactions and disposed to stop at nothing with so much at stake, are operating in a sophisticated way across frontiers much like multinational corporations. Some small countries, such as certain islands of the Caribbean, are being menaced by arms smugglers, drug traffickers and money launderers to such an extent that their very sovereignty is at stake. The size of the illegal drug business alone is now about $400 billion, according to a recent report of the United Nations International Drug Control Programme. This is 'larger' than the international trade in iron and steel, and also motor vehicles, and about the same size as the total world trade in textiles. Worse yet, *The Economist* (28 June 1997) argues, 'no affordable sum' spent on trying to stop the drug traffic seems to have any effect on supply, suggesting that a diversion of funds for a demand-reduction strategy should be considered.

As long as national and international policies to oppose drugs- and related arms-traffic crime continue, a certain amount of *sub rosa* diplomacy will be required, just as in dealing with terrorist movements.

The difficulty the Japanese government had in knowing how to respond to the seizure by terrorists of a Japanese ambassadorial residence in Lima, Peru, is instructive. For that government, and its diplomatic service, that episode plainly was nothing short of traumatic. Unable because of its own military history and post-World War II pacific tradition to take forcible rescue measures itself, Japan had to seek wider international help and, in the end, to defer to a Peruvian decision to intervene (successfully as it turned out).

Appropriately, among the Japanese government's particular initiatives at the Denver G-8 Summit in June was a proposal to increase coordination against attacks such as it had experienced. Under the heading, 'Counterterrorism', a publication of the Japanese Embassy in Washington, *Japan Now* (July 1997), reported after the Denver meeting: 'Based on the lessons of the seizure of the Ambassador's Residence in Lima, Japan called for cooperation to cope with hostage taking and greater information exchanges'. Efforts against 'transnational crime' also were recommended. Who should organize and carry out such efforts? What, in particular, should be the role of diplomats? I recall from the discussion at the Wilton Park conference that Ambassador Navega, for very understandable traditional professional reasons, didn't particularly like the term, 'intelligence diplomacy'. But this may be what is entailed.

The cooperative work to meet the challenge of crime and terrorism cannot and should not be left entirely to the intelligence services, the FBI and CIA and their counterparts elsewhere, including the developing Europol. Policing across national boundaries properly is an international question. To some degree, of course, the law-enforcement aspects of border control and national safety can and will be handled by domestic affairs ministries, particularly interior and justice departments. But ministries of foreign affairs must become and stay involved. They are by far the best coordinators of most kinds of transnational as well as traditional diplomatic work. There is, however, as Anthony Quainton frankly acknowledged at the conference, a problem of 'cross-cultural communication' within our governments. 'Policemen' are 'different' from us, diplomats think. This attitude makes the needed coordination difficult.

The problem of coordination, as Ambassador Quainton said, is 'the central challenge' before foreign ministries today. It is an area in which diplomats 'must use their skills'. Coordination entails, as he and other participants emphasized, coordination within governments as well as between them. Summit meetings, such as the one in Denver, usually have the effect of augmenting the role of the diplomatic professional internally, as Ambassador Matsuura pointed out from experience. By 'working closely with the Prime Minister', the diplomat in charge of summit preparations (sherpa) gains 'coordinating power' within an administration, for his ministry as well as for himself individually. Where summits are not involved, and during the intervals between other high-level international meetings requiring coordination, foreign ministries may find it difficult to stay on top.

In the field of crime prevention, to cite the American experience, the United States government in 1994 established, according to James F. Collins (Senior Coordinator, Office of the Ambassador-at-Large for the New Independent States (NIS), subsequently appointed US Ambassador to Russia in part because of this work), a 'policy steering group' composed of the diplomatic, intelligence, and law enforcement communities in Washington. Its purpose was to address especially the problem of the spread of crime in Russia and the other newly independent countries. In a noteworthy transnational coordination move, unthinkable during the Cold War, FBI Director Louis Freeh led an interagency delegation to Moscow and Kiev to discuss common anti-crime efforts. The US government, with State Department involvement, has helped to establish training programmes for representatives from NIS and also Central European countries, and to set up an International Law Enforcement Academy in Budapest.

The political and legal basis for this unprecedented transatlantic and trans-Eurasian cooperation is being laid by the negotiation of international law enforcement agreements. With the Russians, in the interest of proceeding with speed, an executive agreement, rather than a treaty, has been concluded. A treaty remains the longer-term objective with Russia, as also with Belarus and Ukraine. Of course, the completion of formal and comprehensive mutual legal assistance treaties (MLATs) requires the formal advice and consent of the US Senate. Here diplomatic plumbing and framing, very different worlds, are being brought together. 'We will … continue to consult with the Senate as we begin this treaty process', said James Collins (*Dispatch*, 3 April 1995). This whole subject matter, though radically different from the traditional and no doubt preferred activities of most conventionally trained diplomats, must increasingly be their work, at least for some of them.

I am not entirely sure what to label the fifth and last group of diplomatic craftsmen needed for the 21st century. The basic function of the group, however, is clear. It is those high-level, special appointees who are sent out to confront the world's remaining and perhaps future dictators, face to face, and to obtain the desired behaviour from them. Basically, their function is to be deterrers – the *warners*, they might be called. Curiosity, in considering this word, led me to consult *The Oxford English Dictionary* where it is explained that 'warner' can be a variation, or contracted form, of 'warrener', which is defined as: 'An officer employed to watch over the game in a park or preserve'. Thus, to apply the notion to the present subject of diplomacy, a 'warner' is more than a deterrer; he is also a watcher-over or guardian of a territory of some kind – such as a resource-rich Kuwait or a fragile Bosnia-Herzegovina. The term implies constant vigilance, even if not a continuous presence.

When confronting a potential aggressor such as Saddam Hussein, when on the verge of sending his army against a neighbour or committing some other reckless act, the diplomatic warner should be able to say directly, with conviction and effect: 'Don't even *think* about it'. In the post-Cold War era, when nuclear weapons are not so usable, such minatory diplomacy will probably be more commonly needed. It certainly will be cheaper, in terms of the costs of preparation and the possible consequences of execution.

The inescapable role-model of the warner-diplomat in our own time is Richard Holbrooke. When I mentioned this concept and Holbrooke's name to a retired US Ambassador (also a diplomatic historian), Monteagle Stearns, he said: 'Don't forget Averell Harriman, Clark Clifford, and Cyrus Vance'. As a special emissary, Richard Holbrooke a number of times has been sent to deal with the 'bad guys' of the former Yugoslavia, to impress upon them the need to start cooperating – in particular, to fulfil the commitments of the 1995 Dayton Accords which he negotiated with, or imposed upon, them. 'The timing is dictated by the fact that we've reached another crunch, that we're behind schedule on Dayton', said an administration official in explaining one particular Holbrooke mission (Elaine Sciolino, 'White House Sending Holbrooke to Balkans to Push Leaders on Peace', *The New York Times*, 30 July, 1997). During an earlier trip to the region, aimed at ending the Serbian siege of Sarajevo, Holbrooke, then Assistant Secretary of State for European Affairs, faced down President Slobodan Milosevic, Radovan Karadjic, and General Mladic. According to his own account ('The Road to Sarajevo', *The New Yorker* [21 and 28 October 1996]):

> I stood up and faced Milosevic, deliberately turning my back on Mladic and Karadjic. 'Mr. President,' I said, 'this behavior is clearly not consistent with our agreement. If your "friends" – I said the word with all the sarcasm I could muster – 'do not wish to have a serious discussion, we will leave now'. Milosevic paused, perhaps to gauge whether I was bluffing. Then he spoke sharply to his associates. As the Serbs began to argue, I motioned for my colleagues to withdraw to the other end of the patio, and we waited there, listening to the sounds of acrimonious debate. It was over in less than ten minutes.

Might not a resident ambassador, one wonders, have done as well? One inevitably thinks of the unfortunate, and perhaps unfairly judged, April Glaspie, who as US Ambassador in Baghdad in 1990 failed to dissuade Hussein from carrying out his malign plans against Kuwait. Her failure probably was, in part, a function of her being the resident ambassador in Baghdad, where she had to deal with the Iraqi government over a wide range of issues and over a long period of time. It is hard, working in such a situation, consistently to be stern-faced, on every issue. One would thereby risk becoming, and even being formally declared, *persona non grata*. The Iraqi and Bosnian predicaments and other situations like them, such as that of Cambodia to which former Congressman Stephen Solarz was dispatched in the summer of 1997, are ones which may warrant the use of special envoys. This practice is becoming more common, as Anthony Quainton pointed out in the Wilton Park conference discussion. Ease of travel is only one reason for the increased practice.

I am not here casting for persons to fill the role of international 'hit man'.[5] Genuine diplomacy is involved, not only in the representative–leader confrontation itself but also in the coordination that is necessary behind the scenes to prepare for it. To deal with the Yugoslav imbroglio requires a careful concerting of policy, not only within the US government but also within the European Council, the NATO Council, the Contact Group, the UN Security Council, the Donors Conference, and other pertinent formal and informal bodies. Particularly when 'sticks' or 'carrots' are to be brandished or proffered, close multilateral management of policy – regarding both substance and tactics – is necessary. The making of threats, like the issuing of promises, entails serious risks and costs, and must be politically authorized.

Increasingly this is being done internationally, if not collectively, through international organizations. An illustration is a letter dated 7 August 1997 from the Permanent Representative of Luxembourg, on behalf of the European Union, to the United Nations. In this communication addressed to the UN Secretary-General (S/1997/626, 11 August 1997), the European Union states its wish 'to convey a message to the authorities of the Federal Republic of Yugoslavia and to the entire population of the country'. It proceeds to 'to draw attention to' earlier EU actions recognizing the Federal Republic of Yugoslavia and, later, granting it trade preferences, at which time the European Union 'made its position clear' that it hoped 'that the [Felipe] Gonzalez report would be fully and quickly implemented'. Then, it ominously noted: 'The Yugoslav authorities have failed to take into consideration the package of recommendations made in that report'. At the end, the EU letter recorded that Bulgaria, Cyprus, Estonia, Hungary, Latvia, Lithuania, Poland, Romania, Slovenia, and the Czech Republic 'align themselves with this statement'.

Such admonitory diplomacy, despite the appearances conveyed by those who may be the ones who present it, is never entirely a solo effort.[6] Former Representative Solarz in Cambodia, though personally successful for a time in July 1997 in 'cooling down' the usurping co-Prime Minister Hun Sen, wisely emphasized to Hun Sen the necessity of allowing ASEAN to play a role in contributing to peace and stability in Cambodia. Despite the individual success of Ambassador Solarz in being the one to get Hun Sen to focus on 'details', he and other American representatives dealing with the Cambodian situation well recognized, in an American official's words, that the current ASEAN initiative was the 'best and perhaps last chance' to resolve the crisis and that the United States could not be successful if it acted unilaterally (Steven Erlanger, 'U.S. Envoy Sees Role in Cambodia for Asian Foreign Ministers', *The New York Times*,

27 July 1997). The Solarz mission coincided with the ASEAN meeting that Secretary Albright was attending in Kuala Lumpur, and Solarz reported to her, and presumably to others, there.

One American figure who has met with, and impressed, perhaps more 'international pariahs' (as he calls them) than anyone on the current world scene is the US Permanent Representative to the United Nations, Bill Richardson, Jr. His experience was partly enabled by the fact that, until he joined the Clinton administration as a diplomat, he was acting unofficially, though a member of the US Congress. 'There was a little bit of deniability on both sides', he has explained. Congress 'has oversight of the executive branch'. The President and Department of State 'have primary responsibility over the management and conduct of foreign affairs'. However, 'I think you can combine both to mutually assist both sides' (interview in *Fletcher: The Newsletter of the Fletcher School of Law and Diplomacy* [Spring 1996]).

Though until recently best known as a politician, as Democratic Representative from the Third District of the State of New Mexico, Richardson has a graduate education in diplomacy. He was also prepared for his international missions, as he has recounted, by his background as a Mexican-American, and by his cross-cultural experiences as a Congressman in meeting with the various Indian leaders in his home district. This experience at home, he believes, has increased the sensitivity he has needed in dealing with leaders of a different kind abroad. 'I have met with many with whom we've had conflicts: Cedras, Saddam Hussein, Castro, North Korea, and many others', he has said. 'You have to show a certain amount of personal respect'.

This is a subject that deserves much more study: the art and science of personal confrontation – hostile interaction, face to face – in international diplomacy. In the post-Cold War era, when many of the military and also ideological barriers to such direct contact have been removed, it is no longer necessary to 'communicate' with an adversary only by sending military 'signals' – moving warships, scrambling aircraft, revealing that your forces might go on DefCon 3, and so on. You can actually *talk* to strangers (Monteagle Stearns, *Talking to Strangers: Improving American Diplomacy at Home and Abroad* [1996]). Not only is this infinitely less expensive and cumbersome than manoeuvring forces for sheer military displays, it is now, in present conditions which are likely to continue into the 21st century, much more likely to be more effective. It is much more focused.

In scholarly terms, the wonderful work of Thomas Schelling – his classic *The Strategy of Conflict* (1963) and *Arms and Influence* (1966), which introduced the term 'compellence' and rationalized 'deterrence' – needs to be updated – for *a new age of diplomacy*. In such an age, the psychology and indeed the very physiology of interpersonal confrontation will need to be well understood. Perhaps, if only for its suggestiveness, the work of ethologists, or animal behaviourists, such as Konrad Lorenz (*On Aggression* [1966]) should be consulted, along with that of anthropologists and *human* psychologists. (Consider, for example, the comparative work of Desmond Morris, *The Naked Ape: A Zoologist's Study of the Human Animal* [1967], and Lionel Tiger and Robin Fox, *The Imperial Animal* [1971].) A verb such as 'browbeat' indicates the close relationship between animal physical aggression and psychological intimidation. I recall once hearing on television an American ambassador to a Middle Eastern country say that whenever Henry Kissinger, then his boss, was acting in domineering fashion toward him, he 'just leaned in a little closer'. Toughness can be *taught*, and probably ought to be a regular part of diplomatic training (cf. military training). One of Professor Schelling's successors at Harvard, Stephen P. Rosen, once said in a talk ('The Military, Society, and Academia', 9 September 1996), when discussing the difficulty of exerting an influence over distant and powerful adversaries: 'You've got to get in their face'. This is both very simple and very profound.

Face-to-face diplomacy becomes particularly complicated when the confrontation is between widely different cultures. Rosen was speaking at a time of difficulty in finding ways by which the United States government could exercise suasion over the leadership of China. The significance of facial and other gestures in interpersonal relations can, of course, vary with culture, sometimes in unexpected ways. Bill Richardson, for instance, when he first met with Saddam Hussein made the mistake, probably in a effort to appear (and to feel) relaxed, of crossing his legs, inadvertently showing the Iraqi leader the bottom of his shoe. Saddam got up and left. He returned only after Richardson's offence was explained to the visiting Americans, and peace was restored so that business could be conducted. Better diplomatic training – at the Fletcher School and other schools of international relations and diplomatic academies – should take account of these variations, as well as emphasizing the constants, of direct human personal interaction and of the many influences that can enhance it.

Much more than personal politeness and cultural sensitivity are needed, of course, for a diplomat or any statesman or official to accomplish large ends. To gain the release of a couple of imprisoned Americans from Baghdad is not the same thing, in order of magnitude, as preventing – as perhaps could have been done – the Iraqi leader's order to launch the invasion that started the Gulf War in the first place. A timely warning might not have worked, however. Diplomacy, even of the minatory kind, is a limited instrument, whether bluntly or subtly exercised.

5 A Final Remark

As a kind of coda to everything I have said about diplomacy and its development, I cite a further, realistic point made by Ambassador Richardson which shall be my own ultimate one. 'Fifty per cent of the success of your meeting', he said of his many celebrated encounters, 'is actually having the meeting. That is *the power* of the United States. That is a card that we use and should use more. We are held, if I may, in the world, as the remaining superpower. Whether they like us or not, we have to be dealt with' (*Fletcher* interview). Diplomacy, in any age or system – bipolar, multipolar, or, perhaps for a brief historical moment after the Gulf War, unipolar – cannot be divorced from power any more than, as has been suggested in this essay, from an emissary's political status, legal position, or personal identity. Let me contrast, if I may, this point about American power – which, it should be emphasized, can and should be an *international* asset as well as a national resource – with an observation about the more questionable power of international organizations. The cases of confrontation in which Bill Richardson was involved when he was a Congressman were bilateral ones. What happens to the efficacy of diplomacy when confrontations are multilateral, or become multilateralized? When I heard Richard Holbrooke, in a speech at Harvard about Bosnia (Manshel Lecture, 4 December 1996), almost proudly say that he had kept the United Nations out of the Dayton negotiations, I asked him why. His answer was as revealing as it was abrupt and frank. 'The UN isn't a country', he said. No United Nations official, including the Secretary-General, could state, as can the representative of the United States of America (or of the United Kingdom, France, Russia, or any other great-power member of the Bosnia Contact Group): 'The United States will do this'.

The United Nations, as an international organization made up of sovereign and equal members, cannot itself make threats or promises – wield sticks or carrots. And it – in the person of its Secretary-General, Kofi Annan – is not likely to be authorized to do so in the future by its 185 members or, probably, even by the 15-member Security Council whose decisions, according to Article 25 of the UN Charter, all members of the organization are supposed to be willing to carry out. The diplomacy of the United Nations, of the last trade-craft type I have described, is thus severely constrained. Issuing warnings may not even be appropriate for an international organization, whose imprimatur may, none the less, be essential to the success of any forcible diplomatic admonition. There is food for thought, I believe, in this observation for the European Union as well, as it attempts to develop an effective Common Foreign and Security Policy (CFSP).

Diplomacy depends not only on power but also on character. A diplomat of ambassadorial rank, 'plenipotentiary and extraordinary', partakes of the authority and also the persona of the sovereign (however this may be constituted in particular countries). In a loosely federated structure and one of widely separated powers, such as the governmental system of the United States, there may not in fact be the concentration of authority at times needed to provide sufficient backing for a consistent diplomacy. An international organization such as the United Nations and even an international body with supranational potential such as the European Union will surely have even greater trouble than, sometimes, does the United States in negotiating with purpose and impact.

How much greater, in these circumstances, is the importance of the *corps diplomatique* itself – broadly defined. As an 'epistemic' association of professionals or cadre of knowledge, diplomats can and should function – as proposed at the outset of this essay – as a kind of constitutive 'order' of the international system. They do have a measure of autonomy. Their international standing is protected, in somewhat guild-like fashion, by the 1961 Vienna Convention on Diplomatic Relations which, it was noted at various points during the Wilton Park conference, may need some updating and revising. In particular, the Vienna Convention's requirement (Article 41, paragraph 2) that all official business between states be channelled through foreign ministries, or alternative or additional ministries that are agreed upon, may need to be liberalized. However, the more heterogeneous a diplomatic service, as George Kennan has observed, the less certainty there can be that its members will be cognizant of the 'nature' and 'motivations' of their own government, let alone 'the wider spectrum' of interests and policies into which their activities must be fitted (Kennan, 'Diplomacy Without Diplomats?'). None the less, diplomats, of whatever background and training, can and do form a collegium, whose functions are internationally more important today.

The diplomatic *community* – what diplomats *are* – is, I insist, integral to and inseparable from the *service* they perform – what diplomats *do*. This 'service', as the foregoing enumeration of the different and evolving crafts of diplomacy has illustrated, is more diversified than ever. It is in need of further adaptation if not, most likely, truly radical change. The profession's somewhat privileged status is surely justified by its larger international purpose – the 'kindred pursuits' or 'common interests or aims' – to which the 'freemasons' of *le monde diplomatique* are, jointly, dedicated. Some 'Western' values of the European multi-state system which produced the diplomatic guild in its newly adapting forms – weavers, framers, printers, plumbers, and warners – may not be culturally neutral. But the skilful maintenance of international order, as a precondition of other more particular, distinctive human accomplishments, surely is. It is a common benefit. In the coming 21st century, when different 'civilizations' may be actively testing their merits and strengths, the global textures woven by diplomacy can be an assurance as well as an expression of peace.

Notes

1. One conference participant, Ambassador Charles Murto of Finland, interestingly noted that his foreign ministry received 'no new resources' when his country joined the European Union, but that EU membership had brought 'a global dimension' to Finnish foreign policy. Finland's growing interests outside Europe were evidenced, for instance, by the visit the President of the Republic made to certain Southeast Asian countries immediately after Finland became an EU member. Thus, to a degree, regional organizations directly or indirectly may contribute to 'universal' diplomacy.

2. One Wilton Park conference participant, Professor Collart, a fellow diplomatic historian, commented that diplomatic historians in recent years have been subjected to 'alarms', threatening their very *raison d'être*. Fukuyama told us that 'history is at an end'; the announcement of the present conference advised that 'diplomacy is in peril'. A double whammy. He was relieved to be assured, by the tenor of the conferees' discussion, that diplomacy 'is to stay'.

3. Participants at the Wilton Park conference suggested the terms 'herald' and 'town crier'. A couple of audience members suggested that an appropriate craft term for those diplomats, operating within organizational 'frames', who do this information-giving work would be 'glaziers'.

4. A participant in the Wilton Park conference, Barry Fulton, is himself a winner of the Murrow Award. He currently directs the 'Diplomacy in the Information Age' project at the Center for Strategic and International Studies in Washington, DC.

5. This term, which I used at the conference, triggered the most delightful suggestion, from John Hemery, of an appropriate craft-related word recalling a gangster type in Chicago in the 1920s: 'mechanic'. When mentioning this later to a student, I was told that there is also a Hollywood film, *The Mechanic* (1972), with Charles Bronson in the lead role!

6. After my presentation, a conference participant suggested the word 'knight' to designate this fifth type. It fits in some respects, including: direct appointment by and service to a 'king' such as the US President, commitment to fulfilment of a particular mission (or 'quest'), readiness to engage in verbal or other 'swordplay' if required, and, as emphasized in this paper, fraternal regard for and reliance upon one's co-equals, the less-intrepid but supportive 'knights' of the diplomatic roundtable – the whole profession.

SECTION

Papers

SECTION

Contents

1

International Co-operation Against Drugs and Crime: Are Societies Losing the War?

Report based on Wilton Park Conference 489: 27–31 January 1997 on 'International Co-operation Against Drugs and Crime: Are Societies Losing the War?'

Richard Lambert

1 Introduction

The global drugs trade is thought to be the second most lucrative on Earth: its estimated value is in the region of £300–500 billion. This means it is more valuable than the oil trade, and second only to arms. It is estimated that 99 per cent of the proceeds of this trade go to criminals. However, it has become clear that drug sales and trafficking are only one element in the activities of organised transnational criminal gangs. These organisations increasingly mimic the behaviour of multinational business, using innovative methods to diversify their activities and seek out new markets in pursuit of ever-greater profits. It may appear axiomatic that international co-operation is vital in combating this menace; however, this has proved difficult to realise in practice.

2 The Drugs Problem

Even if drugs are now simply one of a number of commodities in which transnational criminals deal, many countries, particularly in the developed world, continue to regard them as a discrete and pernicious problem because of the threat they pose to society, not simply because of the potential to harm the health and well-being of individuals, but also because of the damage to its fabric by the corruption of business, justice, politics and administration.

To appreciate the amount of money involved in the international drugs trade, it is necessary to be aware of the various stages through which heroin and cocaine pass from raw material to consumption, and to remember that the intermediary at each point will double his outlay. Thus, if a Peruvian farmer sells coca paste at 40 cents/gram, by the time it is sold by the street vendors in the US or Europe – having passed through the cracatero, who sold it on to a cocaine baron, who flew it to Colombia to refine it, then passed it through various importers and exporters through the distribution routes of Mexico and the Caribbean, or Nigeria, Spain or Rotterdam – it will sell for $1,000/gram. Heroin passes through a similar process, grown either in the Golden Triangle (Myanmar, Thailand and Laos), and passed through China or via Bangkok to Hong Kong and the wider distribution network, or in the Golden Crescent (Afghanistan, Pakistan and Iran), and moved into Europe either through the Balkan route to the south or the former Soviet states and Rotterdam to the north.

The fact that drugs are usually (though not exclusively) consumed in countries other than those in which the precursor materials are produced, the end product refined, or through which they pass in order to reach their markets, gives the problem an international element. This is further complicated by the corruption of authority which drug traffickers use to smooth their way. For example, the most common route for transporting coca paste from Peru to be refined in Colombia is to fly it out in light aircraft. A drug baron will pay in the region of US$15,000 to clear and mark out an airstrip in the jungle where the plane can land and collect it. Half of all such airstrips are provided by the terrorist organisation Sendero Luminosa, which raises an estimated $75 million a year in this way. The remainder are provided by army officers. A Lieutenant-Colonel in the Peruvian army is paid $200 per month, so there is consequently no shortage of volunteers willing to accept the equivalent of six years' salary. In the same way, it is always possible to find those who will turn a blind eye to, or even assist the hit squads, kidnapping or extortion. In countries such as Peru and Colombia, where the drug cartels became so strong as to permeate through every level of society and government, the state was widely regarded as colluding with the criminals.

During the 1980s, the consumer countries sought to compel the supplier states to act against the growers and traffickers. The US was the most prominent proponent of this combative strategy, which reached its zenith in the overthrow of General Manuel Noriega in Panama, and his subsequent deportation and trial. The American actions at the time raised questions of whether a country had the right to impose its will on another, and there were frequent accusations that the richer nations of the developed world were using their industrial and military muscle to bully their weaker neighbours over a situation which the authorities in those countries had little capacity to control, while refusing to acknowledge the contribution of their own domestic demand and the flaws in the simplistic strategy of sanctions and interdictions to constrict supply.

Substitution was doomed to failure, because for all that the Peruvian farmer received a tiny fraction of the final street price, the precursor crop was still more profitable than any alternative. An attempt to use subsidies to promote salad vegetables as a substitute crop faltered when American growers protested at their tax dollars being used to undercut their own market. Efforts to destroy the crops in the field by spraying chemicals from the air led to their being cultivated in more remote areas, or out of sight in the shade of trees. The only success was in alienating the population. Drug consignments were deliberately moved through areas which were difficult to police either because they were so remote or so populous that they became impossible to track. The main cocaine producing areas of South America border the Amazon region; from there the drug would be moved in manageable quantities through the many islands of the Caribbean. The growing regions of the Golden Triangle and Crescent were similarly isolated; the transit routes would either cross mountains and deserts to the West, or travel East, passing through numerous hands on the canals of Bangkok and in Hong Kong harbour. Nevertheless, for legitimate business, the threat of decertification by the United States was, and remains, a sword of Damocles over their heads. Decertification has been criticised as mechanistic and inflexible by many, but others have acknowledged that the governments of Latin America presented a special case, and that the threat had produced a remarkable response in terms of legislation and eradication schemes in those countries. Whether the process was appropriate for other parts of the world was still open to question.

More recently, the consumer countries have accepted that demand reduction must play a role, and have sought to increase the resources available for drug prevention and education strategies. The most recent UK policy statement, the *Tackling Drugs Together* White Paper, published in 1995, showed that in 1993, the British government spent £500 million on tackling drug problems, of which £15 million was directed towards external assistance. Similar approaches were adopted in the US, across Europe, and by the European Union, including the establishment of a high-level working group following the Dublin Summit in December 1996, and by the G7/G8. This has combined with a greater willingness on the part of the supplier states to accept that the problem was as much theirs as the consumers'. While it was undeniable that demand was the root of the problem, it was recognised as unreasonable to suggest that levels of abuse were not affected by availability. Several countries were persuaded by their own harsh experience. Nigeria, a popular transit point for cocaine travelling to Europe, succeeded in the early 1990s in reducing the level of re-exportation of drugs, reportedly by 75 per cent. The effect was to flood the domestic market, reducing prices and increasing the levels of addiction. In the same way, Brazil has recorded increased levels of consumption in its larger cities as it has sought to restrict airborne trafficking, the latest measure being the introduction of an electronic air traffic control system in 1996. Other states have found the fabric of their societies seriously threatened: the impotence of the Colombian state and judiciary to control or even impede the activities of the drug cartels undermined all intercourse with other countries; in St Kitts, the involvement of the Prime Minister in drug-related activities threatened the stability of the democracy.

3 Foreign Policy or Criminal Policy?

This begs the question of the extent to which criminal policies now influence foreign policy. The removal of a central uniting issue, whether the fear of an opposing politico-military power bloc in the Euro-Atlantic region, or opposition to apartheid in Africa, has complicated the policy outlook. Contacts are now more varied and less predictable. Because each state may need to deal with every other, the contacts are paradoxically both more localised and more global. This has increased the extent to which foreign policy is an extension of domestic policy in an international context. But the steps taken by individual countries to transnational crime will depend on their outlook. For some, crime is an added complication to their international relations: the UK, for example, needs to consider the effect of the behaviour of expatriate British criminals on its dealings with Spain or the US, the difficulties posed by extradition arrangements around the world or how the fact that northern Cyprus is becoming a centre for drugs and attracting money from Russian gangs might affect relations with Turkey. But for other countries, for whom crime seems to colour the view of the rest of the world towards them, it will be a major consideration in the formulation of policy: Nigeria is putting great effort towards demonstrating that it views drug trafficking and advance fee fraud as seriously as anyone, not least in order to avert the possibility of sanctions. It is also worth noting that, whereas in the developed world, foreign policy is a bureaucratic mechanism, in the less developed world, it can be far more dependent on the personality of individuals, and consequently much more capricious.

In the end, the ability of one country to influence another, whether by threats or persuasion, ultimately depends on their interdependence and the degree of leverage which can be exerted as a result. The American Helms–Burton Act, directed against Cuba, has proved less effective than its authors might have hoped because Cuba is not dependent on the USA, and the European nations are unwilling to be intimidated by these actions. Decertification is a major issue for the Nigerian government, even if the income from oil resources will cushion the impact on the ordinary citizen. Thus Nigerian policy is clearly influenced by the opprobrium attracted to it by the actions of criminal nationals abroad. The relationship between the United States and Israel illustrates that it is possible for small states to have leverage over larger as a result of their domestic situation.

There is an absolute need for co-ordination of international efforts against drugs, whether in terms of bilateral relations, or through multilateral agencies such as the EU, the Council of Europe and the UN. Programmes are targeted at priority areas: sources, routes and individual problematic countries or regions (e.g. Morocco, West Africa). Assistance for alternative development is still regarded as an expensive option, which is more appropriate for the US or EU to use, but which can be highly effective in focusing assistance in areas such as Pakistan or

Afghanistan. If this strategy is adopted, the donors will demand that stringent conditions are attached to the aid, effective enforcement of those conditions, and an understanding on the part of the recipient that a project which is manifestly failing will be terminated. The UNDCP is seen as a project which is improving: although UN operations are notoriously patchy, its strengths and professionalism are recognised, as are its advantages in overcoming difficulties in bilateral relations. The EU, on the other hand, is active, but thought to undermine its own effectiveness through the multiplicity of fora through which it operates in this field. As an organisation, it has not fully appreciated the foreign policy aspects of 'drugs diplomacy', rarely including drugs conditionality in international agreements, the Andean GSP being a rare exception. The UK is devoting some £30 million over three years from its Overseas Assistance budget towards drug programmes, but also emphasises that other assistance, such as police and paramilitary training to build up local lines of defence, can make an important contribution.

4 The Development of International Criminal Law

Extraterritorial actions taken against drug traffickers are justified by reference to international law. However, while it is easy to define international crime, defining international criminal law poses greater problems. The United Nations was established to prevent a recurrence of war. The organisation was given 'hard' powers to deal with conflicts, and 'softer' powers to deal with other issues. Although there is no specific mention of crime in its founding Charter, it has used the references to social issues and human rights as the basis for its involvement in the field through the General Assembly and Economic and Social Committee since 1946. The principal vehicles were the quinquennial conferences on treatment of offenders, and, from the 1970s, the Committee on Crime Prevention and Control. The debates tended to focus on criminology and penology, with little input from law enforcement agencies, and evolved a number of treaties and conventions, intended to influence the creation of national laws. This softer approach has resulted in tension when states grow impatient for action, and wish to use harder methods of enforcement against crime.

International criminal law can thus be seen as an alternative route towards maintaining order and control. It is none the less a convergence of two strands of jurisprudence, criminal municipal law and international law. There is no comprehensive, universally accepted definition of terms or criteria. A growing body of treaties and approaches have emerged, either through agreements or longstanding behaviour. The treaties which are agreed can be fairly regarded as expressions of shared values between states, but inevitably, because of differences of sovereignty, traditions of jurisprudence and the like, they must also be the lowest common denominator, in that they encapsulate only those values upon which the participating states could positively agree. Even when there is agreement on common values, it can still prove difficult actually to implement them, as has been demonstrated by the disagreements over the arrest of indicted war criminals in the former Yugoslavia. This leads to frustration, and in extreme cases, to extraterritorial action.

The UN has taken a broad view when formulating its agenda on crime. As far back as the 5th Conference on the Treatment of Offenders, it was seeking to define crime within two main categories: corporate crime (crime in business) and organised crime (crime as business). It also recognised the ability of certain crimes to corrupt law enforcement and political structures in order to place themselves beyond the reach of the law. By the 7th Conference in 1985, the talk was of national boundaries being permeated and the need for international action. This led to calls for an intergovernmental review, and ultimately to the 1994 UN Conference on Transnational Organised Crime in Naples, when the UN set itself up as a clearing house for the needs and resources to fight international crime. However, a divergence between the approaches of the UN and the individual member states also emerged during this Conference. The UN took the view that it should look at the threat crime posed to the security and stability of states, and should seek to address the three broad categories of corporate crime, organised crime, and corruption. When the states were invited to express their concerns, they offered a list of specific crimes, including terrorism; drug trafficking; money laundering; trafficking in people, such as smuggling illegal immigrants; firearms; juvenile crime; crimes against women and children; environmental crime; and car crime. The institutional pressure argued for a general instrument which would cover all crimes; the reaction of the states suggested that it might be easier to build up a corpus of agreement by dealing one by one with the areas in which there was agreement. This dichotomy has continued ever since: the UN sees its role as setting out the agenda and initiating discussion, even if that causes as many problems as it solves. For example, the 1988 Vienna Convention acknowledged that controlled deliveries of drugs, where the authorities knowingly permitted a consignment into the country in order to track it to its destination and identify the figures in the supply chain, was a legitimate tool, even though it was illegal in some states.

The ultimate solution lies in greater co-operation between states. The 1994 Conference adopted the Naples Declaration, which produced the Global Action Plan against Transnational Organised Crime. This had three basic aims: to strengthen national capabilities; to foster co-operation against transnational crime; and to strengthen and co-ordinate action against crime. But the principles were watered down in the detail. The Plan was couched in terms of roles for the states; the UN would be brought in 'when necessary' or 'on request', to assist rather than lead. This was the logical approach, in that the states were responsible for enforcing the law, and the UN did not have the resources to undertake a programme of such magnitude. None the less, it meant that the building block approach was the only way forward.

5 Transnational Criminals

The object of organised crime is to make profits and acquire power. In this sense, they resemble any business, and, like business, a criminal organisation must engage in certain activities and follow established procedures in order to achieve their aims. Today, trading in drugs is the major criminal activity, simply because it generates such vast amounts of money; consequently, almost every organised grouping is involved to some degree. Those involved will do whatever is necessary in pursuit of the trade, bribing public officials and corrupting banks and businesses, resorting to violence when this does not work. The effect of this combination of inducement and intimidation on one who is unused to it should never be underestimated. But it serves to undermine the confidence of the public in legitimate business, and in the ability of the authorities to maintain public security. Organised crime is not new. It was seen to develop in the United States within the Sicilian immigrant communities in the 1880s, and was boosted during the Prohibition era, which presented the gangs with a specific activity to focus on and the opportunity to coalesce. From there, it was a short step to recognising the potential for putting their illicit proceeds into legitimate business.

The linking of gangs was not unknown at that time, but has become much more prevalent in recent years, opening up new vistas and opportunities for the criminals, up to and including the disruption of politics and the economy. The list of concerns put forward by states is one illustration of the breadth of activity in which organised crime engages. In keeping with their tendency to mimic business, criminal gangs have proved themselves swift to adapt to changing situations and to maximise the opportunities presented by new markets. Turkish gangs, which previously smuggled antiquities from the transcaucasian republics of the Soviet Union, are known more recently to have been trafficking in nuclear materials. Nigeria is deeply concerned at the impact of advance fee fraud, where criminals play on the ignorance and preconceptions of the gullible and the greedy, sending faxes offering huge rewards for facilitating a criminal act by people purporting to be high-ranking officials or businessmen, only to disappear with the money advanced or to clean out the account set up for the transaction. It is widely believed that the distinction between white collar crime and organised criminals has broken down, and that they are now responsible for most large-scale fraud.

The rise of transnational criminality can be ascribed to the existence of the opportunities, the incentives, the pressures and the resources of modern society. Globalisation has been of immeasurable benefit, rendering borders as little more than 'a fantasy of foreign ministries'. The ease of transport enables travel and migration, as well as providing the conduit for international trade. Migrants form ethnic enclaves within host countries. The connection and loyalty to the home country will persist, however little intention they may have to return. Migrants are more often the victims of crime than its organisers, but the diaspora will provide support, recruits and cover for their criminal links, particularly if they are marginalised and alienated from the majority in the host country.

The promotion of international free trade has encouraged the development of legitimate business which can be used as a cover for illicit activities. The minimalist regulation of the international banking system has always offered potential for the criminal or tax evader to move their funds. Even the best regulated have proved to be all too susceptible to fraudsters, while the secretive nature of the offshore sector rendered it particularly attractive. The growth of a global financial system has enabled money to be moved electronically across the world with sufficient frequency to conceal its source and its final destination. When matched with a global computerised information system, it creates new vulnerabilities by decoupling security from territory, and rendering the systems susceptible to anyone with a computer, a modem and the relevant expertise. For example, there are estimated to be 250,000 incursions into the US Department of Defence computer system every year. One in five are detected; not all those detected are reported. Although the sophistication of the information system is indeed a source of power, it is a greater asset to criminals because of the expanded opportunities it offers. Furthermore, accumulating more and more information is irrelevant without the analysis to appreciate its value.

All these trends are focused and magnified in the rise of the global city, which acts as a transport hub, concentrates financial power and attracts huge populations, facilitating anonymity and criminal contact. Mega-cities are already proving difficult to control, and the problems will become more acute in the next century. Forty million people are expected to join the job market each year; without drastic action, the vast majority of them will seemingly have the stark choice between poverty and crime. Analysts argue that this implies an imminent crisis of legitimacy and authority in criminal home and host states, as the effects of crime corrode society. Most should be regarded as weak, unable to achieve anything significant in the face of organised crime. In these states, criminal gangs have an essentially predatory relationship to the rest of society. Other states may decide not to act because to do so is not in the national interest; in such societies, crime has evolved a parasitic relationship to society, using legitimate activities as a base and a cover. Eventually, society is corrupted, as government benefits from criminal acts, and may finally become collusive when there is a seamless web between crime and government. A regulatory vacuum emerges, where the states lack the capacity to enforce the law. Inevitably, where the public authorities are unable to provide, private enterprise will seek to provide the goods or services which cannot be obtained elsewhere; the private interests are likely to be criminal. Pure malice is unlikely to be as profitable as filling a gap in the market: it has even been argued that in societies with underdeveloped systems of litigation, crime takes advantage of the market opportunity to provide contract enforcement. The conclusion drawn from this line of reasoning is that if organised crime is ultimately an attempt to undermine and transcend the legitimate sovereignty of the state, it should be treated as a national security problem rather than a law and order issue, with measures to combat it being given the same priority as were security arrangements during the Cold War.

Attempts to draw out generalised global trends in transnational crime risk portraying the phenomenon as a homogeneous international monolith. The truth is far more complex. Groups may be based on particular or mixed criteria, ranging from ethnicity and region to former or current occupations. Some are organised into structured groupings, others into more fluid, dynamic networks. Formal hierarchies are unknown outside the Sicilian families; African and Pakistani groups make use of the tradition of the extended family; Asian crime tends to be based more on transactions than on organisations. It is more effective to think of transnational criminals as sovereign-free actors, linked through networks of affiliation. This makes their relationships infinitely more flexible than those between states, who require themselves to use approved channels and formalised agreements, as the criminal networks will have a great capacity for adapting and reconstituting themselves. The network is strongest when there is a bond: hence the links with expatriate communities, whose effectiveness as a base has been demonstrated by Sicilian, Chinese and Russian gangs. Indeed, it has been alleged that the main reason for the failure of Russian gangs to establish themselves in Sweden was the absence of such an expatriate community.

Transitional states are most vulnerable to transnational crime. As the countries of Central and Eastern Europe and the former Soviet Union relaxed state controls, reduced the power of the police and encouraged international trade, criminal gangs were able to gain a stronger hold on post-Communist society. Crime and the black market had flourished under the Communist regime, reaching its height during the Brezhnev era in the 1960s and 70s, when it became a parallel economic instrument, corrupting and enriching the Communist party nomenklatura. When they were deprived of their formal privileges and influence with the fall of the Party, the apparatchiks were able to use their knowledge of the economic system and structure to expand their control of the black market as it in turn grew to compensate for the shortages caused by the ending of the command economy. As this operation developed, so it became more organised. In these circumstances, privatisation of state assets was a gift, of which they took full advantage, and it is now estimated that as much as 80 per cent of all privatised share capital in Russia is owned by organised criminal gangs. New organisations also emerged, and foreign groups began to use Russia either as a base or an extended zone of operations. Greater contact with foreign business provided the opportunity to expand abroad and forge links with other criminal groupings. The states around the Baltic Sea, notably Latvia and Finland, have been a particularly important transit route. Ecological crimes are also increasing.

'Russian' crime has become shorthand for the activities of the diverse criminal groupings operating from within the former Soviet states. They are seen as having a different mentality to Latin American, Western European or North American gangs, being more practical, ambitious and direct in their search for profit. The various ethnic groups within the Soviet Union had long been diverse and specialised in their criminal activities: the Azeris were involved in opiates smuggling; Russians stole and sold state property; Georgians used a sophisticated transit system to smuggle soft fruits, and were thought to have moved into private air transports; the Ukrainians were involved in many activities; and the Chechens were employed by all for their capacity for violence. The growth of criminalisation was not foreseen as a consequence of the collapse of communism. The corruption and political and social instability has disrupted the development of a democratic social order, to the point where criminals threaten to supplant the legitimate political structure. There is a genuine fear that the successor to Boris Yeltsin as President might be a front for criminals.

6 Strategies to Combat Transnational Crime

The growing sophistication of transnational criminals has led them to evolve a wider range of risk management strategies intended to prevent, absorb and control the risks to themselves and their activities. They will look to maintain, and where possible, increase the safe havens available to them, and consolidate links with other groups. Networks are becoming ever more important in achieving the global reach that their business requires, so the gangs will seek strategic alliances in order to secure access to their markets, spread or minimise the risk to their own organisation, utilise complementary expertise and guarantee a predictable relationship with their supplier. Infiltration of the banking system and legitimate business will continue: recent evidence suggests that the construction and hazardous waste industries have become targets. A growth in extortion is expected to be matched by its diversification to encompass nuclear, chemical and cyber-threats. The combination of mega-cities and the lack of development opportunities will increase the ethnic diversity of transnational criminals (the number of identifiable African groups is already rising) and provide greater scope to develop specialists.

Societies will need to match this sophistication with their own risk absorption strategies. Rather than targeting a specific point or activity, a comprehensive holistic approach is essential, involving new combinations of expertise and new models of analysis to identify the triggers of criminal activity, allied to comprehensive methods of prevention, control and absorption. The criminals are not bound by rules, formalities and procedures, and so are more ready and able to think strategically and act quickly to deal with a changed situation. It has been argued that if society intends to attack transnational crime with any degree of seriousness, it should focus its efforts on the accumulated profits, organisational integrity and leadership, instead of attacking the products, personnel and profit-taking which characterises the footsoldiers at the lower end of the organisation, who are easily replaced. This will mean accepting that this entails a greater tolerance of lower level criminal activity as a quid pro quo for greater long-term successes.

Once the US law enforcement agencies recognised the existence and extent of the problem of organised crime in America in the 1950s, and the resultant penetration of business, politics and the unions, they were forced to acknowledge that pursuing individual crimes was insufficient. Over the next 20 years, Congress was persuaded to pass the legislation which enabled the police to investigate the activities of a number of individuals as a group, to pursue them as a group and to confiscate illegally obtained assets. This encompassed various statutes dealing with racketeering, electronic interception, the pursuit of assets and money laundering. The 1989 Money Laundering Act was seen as a watershed, in that it treated all those involved in the process as criminals, and enabled the agencies to confiscate their assets, thereby ending their business, licit and illicit. Whichever agency was responsible for the asset forfeiture was also permitted to use the confiscated funds to continue its work. Although this has been criticised as a distorting mechanism, leading to over-concentration of efforts in the areas that promised to raise most money rather than those which might prove most effective, there is no denying that it has proved an incentive. The US Embassy in London recently presented a cheque for $1.2 million to Jersey as its share of the proceeds of one particular operation. In contrast, all confiscations made by the UK agencies go to the Treasury.

The new legislation was coupled with a fresh approach by the FBI, using regional intelligence centres to target groups. Law enforcement is a highly decentralised activity in the US, encompassing some 25–30,000 different agencies, many of them locally based, with resources too limited to devote to the lengthy, manpower-intensive investigations which were required. The FBI implemented a national strategy, based on regional centres, where the main targets were identified, then investigated using complex long-term techniques, and whatever means the law would allow to find a way into the insulated criminal cells, such as undercover agents and electronic surveillance. The groups targeted included second- and third-generation Italian Cosa Nostra, which were widely infiltrated, although it proved difficult to root out the corrupt networks they had established; Italian-based organisations linked to them; South American drug traders, initially from Colombia, more recently from Mexico, whose border with Texas is impossible to police; and various Asian groups, from China, Japan and Vietnam. Attention is now turning to groups from Russia and Central and Eastern Europe, with the FBI establishing a Police Academy in Budapest to train local agents, and groups working in specific regions, such as motorcycle gangs, Jamaicans and West Africans.

Although the American experience cannot translate exactly to other countries, intelligence-based policing has become the main focus in combating transnational organised crime, providing information on which to base risk analysis and preventive strategies. The Americans' greater use of covert operations is the main reason for their greater knowledge of criminal activities. The investigations continue to be long-term projects, fraught with difficulty: infiltration is dangerous; turning an operative carries this risk, with the added uncertainty that a confessed criminal may not make a credible witness; and however carefully access is controlled, however rigorous staff vetting and however small the circle of knowledge, the prospect of counter-intelligence persists. Furthermore information gathered during the course of an investigation has to be distinguished from the evidence necessary to convict in a court of law. It may require another highly labour-intensive investigation of similar length to go through the accounts in order to obtain the evidence to secure the conviction.

7 Money Laundering

Action against money laundering is perhaps the most high-profile example of intelligence-led policing. Criminals will seek to conceal their illicit profits by mixing them with the proceeds of legitimate business. At the local level, this can be done through fast-moving, cash-intensive businesses, such as fast-food outlets or gambling; larger sums will be transferred internationally. The police have found one of the most effective intelligence techniques to be establishing a front business which criminals will then seek to use as a cover. International electronic banking has given an additional dimension to money laundering. The commercial secrecy of banking confidentiality and offshore legislation have always placed obstacles in the way of investigation; the speed and complexity of laundering by computer has intensified them. One laundering action is reputed to have taken 45 seconds to complete and 18 months to investigate.

It is almost impossible to say how much money is actually laundered. It has been estimated that the total could be the equivalent of between 2 and 6 per cent of US GNP. Levels of crime are normally assessed through victim reports, but in this case the victim's loss does not necessarily equal the criminal's gain. The criminal's propensity to spend or save, and the volume and location of savings, is hard to assess. At the lower end of the organisation, there may be a multiplier effect caused by the redistribution of money into the local economy through personal consumption; few people involved in the drugs trade are motivated by long-term financial gains in preference to immediate self-gratification. At the top, it will be physically impossible to spend all the profits. The greater the inequality of distribution, the more there will be to save. This gives rise to the question of how it is saved, and where. Money may be laundered several times through different countries, inevitably being mixed with legitimate profits, and as it moves, counted more than once.

It usually comes to rest in countries with a reputation for banking integrity and competence. In the UK, the banking system is so trusted that depositing money in an account guarantees that, to all intents and purposes, it is laundered. It is interesting to note that money laundering was virtually unknown in Brazil until the economy stabilised and inflation was brought under control in the early 1990s. Trust is fundamental to these activities, to the point where it will constrain other forms of behaviour; indeed, the requirement for trust often presents the greatest obstacle to the success of preventive policies. There is also a cultural problem. There is almost certainly more money laundering as a result of fraud or tax evasion than from drugs. Yet the City of London is reluctant to accept that its members indulge in such criminal behaviour. When instances of wrong-doing are found, it prefers to deal with the miscreants through its own regulatory mechanisms which are inevitably more lenient than the criminal judicial process. There is also an understandable human reluctance on the part of senior figures to suspect those who make money for their organisations, particularly when management bonuses are calculated on the basis of organisational performance.

There has been disagreement between the banks, which are required to report suspicious transactions, and the National Criminal Intelligence Service (NCIS) over the level of detection of money laundering in the UK. The banks have claimed that 1 in 200 reports led to a charge or conviction; NCIS, which claims a 1 in 5 success rate, viewed this as a criticism; the banks were unfazed by the response, since they had never believed NCIS's figures anyway. Despite the NCIS reaction, a strike rate of 1 in 200 on the basis of information received would usually be regarded as good, although capable of improvement. Nor should it obscure the fact that the relationship between the banks and the police is generally positive and co-operative. The system of reporting is thought to work well, revealing much which would otherwise have remained unknown, and the audit trail is greatly assisted by the banks' practice of retaining information. The role of NCIS is essentially that of a clearing house: it receives reports and distributes them to local police forces, who must then allocate their resources. It may be that NCIS distribution is too slow, or that local forces are finding the same problem in deploying resources as was experienced in the US. Every local Financial Investigations Unit has to tackle three main areas of work: preparing reports on those charged for the forthcoming court proceedings, which must take priority; then following up money laundering disclosures; proactive work, of necessity, comes furthest down the list.

What is certain is that the money trail will eventually lead to the criminals. The FBI's experience is that there is never more than one man between the criminal and his money, and the British police have found that while traffickers are prepared to admit to drugs offences, they will fight confiscation and asset forfeiture proceedings tooth and nail. Confiscation can be a long and complicated process. If the money has gone overseas, international co-operation will be required to retrieve it. There have been many developments in international co-operation in the aftermath of the Brinks-Mat bullion robbery in 1984, but the chain remains only as strong as its weakest link. Nevertheless, it is strategically important, if not always cost-effective, as it can make the difference between hurting the criminal organisation and simply reducing consumption. The Royal Ulster Constabulary has in the past used financial strategies to disrupt paramilitary organisations in Northern Ireland. The asset trail has traditionally been an under-estimated tool, however useful it has proved. Approximately a quarter of all the funds recovered are retrieved as a result of court orders allowing the police to inspect accounts. Recent UK legislation has made obtaining a production order easier, which is expected to lead to an improvement in their yield. Figures for asset forfeiture are far less spectacular than the £500 million a year which has been reported, the actual figure being closer to £30 million. To put this into some kind of context, Citibank deals with US$100 trillion every day. The police will tend to focus on getting the case to court and securing the conviction rather than targeting the maximum seizable assets. Nevertheless, the size of the figure is less important than what it represents. Money laundering is, after all, a secondary crime, and one should never lose sight of the fact that it is the primary criminal act which generates the profits. Society ought to take a tough line on the confiscation of the proceeds because it involves so many other crimes. The crucial questions are what is being laundered, why it is being laundered and how. It also vital for there to be the political will to back up the rhetoric of any strategy.

8 International Co-operation

The United Nations, the Council of Europe and the European Union are all acknowledged to have undertaken valuable work in this field over and above the multiplicity of bilateral relations. President Clinton used his speech on the 50th anniversary of the UN to stress its role in the fight against crime. The EU Summit in Dublin in December 1996 established a high-level working group on organised crime. Yet professional, political and cultural differences cause disagreements over the merits of formal structures over informal contacts, structures imposed from the top downwards by political decision or built up from the grassroots by the practitioners. There is consensus that certain approaches work, such as the construction of databases and the formation of networks of liaison officers, that excessive political or theoretical interference can be damaging, and that unnecessary duplication and overlapping should be avoided, not least to ensure the efficient use of resources. Despite clearly complementary briefs and defining conventions, Europol and Interpol appeared to be evolving a classic institutional rivalry. Such rivalries are the cause of institutional introspection, obscuring the fact that it is the substance of the co-operation which matters, not its form. If the legitimate institutions are unable to work to prevent and control crime, commerce will eventually turn to the private sector to provide.

The European Union has adopted three avenues of response to the drugs problem: through economic regulation and harmonisation, political co-operation and social policies. The completion of the single market, which allows free movement of people and capital has facilitated the activities of illicit business as much as legitimate trade. The EU has sought to introduce measures to counteract criminal activities, such as measures against the importation of precursor chemicals and a harmonisation of money-laundering legislation. The European Action Plan to Combat Drugs planned to assess the effectiveness of these and other measures during 1995 and 1996. Politically, the EU has used its powers under the Third Pillar of the Maastricht Treaty and the Common Foreign and Security Policy (CFSP) to compensate for the effects of the single market. Police forces have been given a greater role as customs found themselves overwhelmed by the volume of licit trade. The EU has sought to define a clearer delineation between police and customs and to facilitate more effective liaison between them, not least because there is an uncertainty as to what actually makes customs effective, because of the absence of tools to measure their performance. The Southern European forces are inclined to take a more vigorous proactive approach than their Northern counterparts; paradoxically, the Northern forces are more likely to have full police powers. A European Parliament Committee of Inquiry investigating customs methods within the EU was unsure which model was the more effective.

The concept of a formal European Police Agency grew from the informal Trevi system, where police authorities exchanged information to combat anti-terrorism, and the desire of a number of European leaders, most notably Helmut Kohl, to set up a European police force modelled on the FBI. The latter hope was doomed to failure. There was no mechanism for the political or judicial accountability of such a body, and no agreed method of international taxation to fund it. There have been several attempts to overcome these blocks, with varying success. UCLAF has had some success in the limited and clearly defined field of fraud against the Community budget, reflecting the experience of national anti-fraud task forces. The Schengen system's attempt to solve the question of judicial and police supervision through IT foundered when the software proved incapable of coping with the true level of entries necessary to compile an effective database. The approach was further undermined by the continued insistence of the French government that computer-based communications could not be regarded as evidence and that there was a requirement for more rigorous judicial supervision. The second Schengen agreement was a more pragmatic arrangement, which accepted the existence of different systems in different countries, and looks to see what will develop from the limited interaction which exists at present. The UK has refused to join the Schengen area, on the grounds that it is not prepared to give up its border controls, but most other EU countries believe that it will eventually be forced to accede. The Schengen accords are being incorporated in the revised Treaty being prepared by the Inter-Governmental Conference. Customs authorities, on the other hand, having accepted that their roles differ from state to state, have approached international co-operation from a practical point of view and appear to have been more successful as a result.

Interpol is a long-established body, whose status is recognised by the UN General Assembly, although it is not attached to any formal intergovernmental mechanism. Its role is to investigate all reported international crime which has already been committed, rendering it primarily a reactive organisation. It aims to promote international police co-operation for the benefit of the practitioners, operates through National Crime Bureaux in the member countries, and is geared to receiving requests for assistance. Regional co-operation is firmly established within Interpol, and regional liaison bureaux have been working to strengthen this element in recent years. The UK National Crime Bureau handles 20,000 new cases every year, with each officer holding up to 400 live files. Interpol has been described as 'a vital all-world mailing system': the communications network provides the means for law enforcement agencies throughout the world to exchange information and access the Interpol database. Although Interpol's database is secondary in nature, it is well placed to provide the analysis which is regarded as one of its most valuable services. The drawback is that, unlike criminals, the database deals in single crimes. There is a concern that if this anomaly is not addressed soon, the intelligence system will impose a constriction on the operational aspects.

The Europol Convention was only agreed by the EU member states in 1996, and will not come into force until ratified by all 15. So far only the UK has done this. Consequently, much of the discussion of the nature and activity of the agency is theoretical, based on its pre-ratification state, and the ambitions which some member states have for it. Europol is intended to be a more proactive body, focusing on a pre-defined list of serious crimes, in which organised criminals are thought to be involved, and which occur between two or more EU member states. Europol's prime function will be intelligence gathering, whereas intelligence is a by-product of Interpol's work. Trying to match Interpol's practical work would serve to detract from Europol's potential to fulfil its intelligence role. There is a distinction between the kind of information each organisation can hold on its database: Interpol retains information on those who have or are suspected of committing crime and who may become involved in crime again in the future; Europol will have information on those who have committed, or are suspected by member states as being likely to commit, crimes on the Europol list. Europol's powers are much broader than those defined in the European Convention on Data Protection, as it can hold information without concrete grounds for the suspicion. This enables profiling of criminals and their activities, the exchange of information and techniques and the co-ordination of multinational police operations. The communications system consists of a central and linked databases, programmed with analytical software in order to establish linkages which could not be achieved manually. At present, Europol is entirely dependent on national structures and ad hoc alliances, which leads to a tendency to seek to make the final arrest in the severest jurisdiction. It is anticipated that multilateral frameworks for transnational investigations will be established within the next five years. Co-operation with countries outside the EU is being established as part of the programme of tying wider concerns into the reciprocal agreements which are initially sought on trade and economic grounds, such as the pre-accession Association Agreements with other European countries, the Euro-Mediterranean Partnership, the EU/US Transatlantic Agenda and the Andean Pact 95. This economic underpinning gives Europol's agenda considerable leverage.

The establishment of Europol in itself may pose a threat to Interpol's funding. Interpol's budget for 1997 totalled FF150 million. Four of the six largest contributors are EU member states. Europol's budget for the same year is FF51 million. Interpol is thus trying to cover the world on three times as much as the EU gives Europol to cover Europe. It is arguable that the major European contributors will not wish to continue paying Interpol to duplicate Europol's work, and that it will be forced to adapt to a complementary role. Moreover, the successful growth of Europol depends upon it colonising Interpol's resources. However, Interpol's advocates respond that such Eurocentric dominance is unlikely to be accepted so willingly by the other 129 non-European countries, not least those in Africa and Latin America, which have recently signed Interpol conventions. The Europol Convention specifically mentioned that it should not prejudice existing forms of co-operation. There is a strong case for double-hatting the Interpol and Europol agencies, as the UK had done, but non-EU member countries have said that they have found Europol less willing to share information. Europol's strength lies ultimately in its political support, something for which Interpol has always struggled. There is probably a need for both organisations, and for Europol to acquire an operational capability. The most important factor is the quality of the co-operation rather than the structure.

A feeling remains that politicians should have made an effort to inform themselves as to the existing mechanisms for co-operation before imposing new ones. Many practitioners fear the negative effects of uncoordinated initiatives. Practical experience of operational co-operation has suggested several factors which can contribute towards effective co-operation. Firstly, the police forces must be sufficiently well-established to hold and retain public confidence. Legislation should be harmonised, by which is meant the achievement of interoperability between national jurisdictions, rather than the imposition of a standard. This could require lengthy negotiations and implementation periods, but the Council of Europe provides an example of having achieved remarkable results in recent years. Regional co-operation is logical, between groups of countries, such as the Nordic nations of Denmark, Finland, Iceland, Norway and Sweden, who share a common approach and legal framework. Small administrative tiers are also helpful in preventing excessive bureaucracy. Intelligence sharing at a central level, often through a system of liaison officers, has proved extremely valuable. The liaison officers established under the Task Force set up by the Council of Baltic Sea States were all appointed as the personal representatives of their Prime Ministers, and thus possessed sufficient personal and political credibility and influence to protect the liaison relationship from excessive political or theoretical interference. The strengthening of practical liaison has been reflected in the development of greater political co-ordination. The Council of the Baltic Sea States has established a ministerial working group on crime, with a sufficiently loose remit to allow it to take a broad enough view to cover the full range of potential problems. Their experience shows the value of a multi-agency approach, with the emphasis placed on personal and informal contacts between practitioners to create a framework on which to base concrete action rather than politically-driven solutions imposed from above.

9 Are Societies Losing the War?

The more apocalyptic analysts might argue that societies have already lost the war against transnational crime because the authorities have been too slow to adapt to the trends of the late 20th century. Crime, and perhaps more importantly, the fear of crime, could lead to a reversing of globalisation, as populations seek to defend themselves against the threat by becoming more insular and recreating barriers and borders. A more widely held view may be that, although there remains much to do, on all levels, practical and strategic, there are reasons for being cautiously optimistic about the outcome. There is a need to re-evaluate the balance of efforts in controlling the demand for and supply of drugs. Greater political co-operation and co-ordination, in both practical and policy terms is vital. Certainly, rivalry and uncertainty between Europol and Interpol serves no one's interests. Nor would anyone be helped if each state followed its own individual path. None the less, international co-operation is not, and can never be a panacea. The difficulties in concluding international agreements have demonstrated time and again that some states that are vital to the success of the project do not share the values the convention sought to express. Societies may have lost ground and, with the multiplication of the opportunities for crime, should be conscious of the possibility of losing more. But the human and other costs are far too high to allow societies to abandon the fight.

2

Europe's Development Aid

Report based on Wilton Park Conference 490: 3–7 February 1997 on
'Europe's Development Aid'

Robin Hart

1 Introduction

Europe's assistance to developing countries is at a turning point. The European Community development aid budget has expanded significantly in recent years, at a time when the aid budgets of member states have been reduced. Key questions are being asked about the balance to be struck between European Union (EU) member states' bilateral spending on development aid and aid channelled through the European Commission. And of the increasing proportion channelled through the Commission, where can value be added if the Commission is not to be the sixteenth European donor? There are also tensions between the EU's Lomé commitments to former colonial territories in Africa, the Caribbean and the Pacific (ACP) countries, and Europe's concern for non-ACP developing countries.

Development assistance remains an important element of the EU's relations with many countries, but it forms only part of a complex menu of trade links, political dialogue, security considerations and cultural exchange which make up Europe's foreign policy. It is widely recognised that Europe's development policies need to be a core consideration within Europe's wider Common Foreign and Security Policy.

All member states of the European Union want to see global poverty reduced. It is estimated that 1.4 billion people (and increasing) live in absolute poverty. Each year 13–18 million people, mostly children, die from hunger and poverty-related causes. Only about 10% of these deaths are caused by emergencies. Europe generally sees benefit in helping developing countries develop – whether for purely altruistic reasons or for self interest, or a combination. Decisions made in Brussels are already affecting hundreds of millions of people.

The end of the Cold War has had a profound effect on development policy. For nearly a century foreign aid helped to advance the Western recipe of market-based democracy, often based on neo-colonial lines. The Western, or some would say 'Northern', affluent society is now trying to come to terms with the new, rapidly globalising, multi-polar world. The more altruistic approach of recent years, often the result of terrible human disasters flashed into Western living rooms, has given a boost to humanitarian aid, often at the expense of longer-term development aid. There has also been a decentralisation of aid, with more assistance channelled through non-governmental organisations (NGOs) rather than directly disbursed from government to government. A re-examination of development principles across the Western/Northern donors has taken place with increasing support for poverty alleviation, the recognition of the role of women in development and the need to consider environmental issues to allow sustainable development. At the same time a more business-like approach has been applied to aid, with attempts to measure progress and value.

In the context of this changing approach to development aid the key question facing Europe now, with scarce aid funds, is how to make an effective and worthwhile impact through the variety of bilateral, European and multilateral mechanisms already in place. How should priorities be set for EU aid to balance the desire to support the poorest countries, many of which are former colonies of Europe's member states, against the recent trend to support Europe's near neighbours to the East and the immediate South? How should Europe respond to Organisation for Economic Cooperation and Development (OECD) targets to halve the proportion of people living in extreme poverty by 2015? Where can European collective aid add the most value to that contributed by bilateral aid? How can or should bilateral aid be better coordinated by Europeans? What are the best delivery mechanisms to ensure that European Commission aid is effectively distributed? How should Europe's trade policies be set to benefit developing countries? What assistance should be given to support foreign direct investment and to help develop the indigenous private sectors? Europe's aid agenda is to find effective answers to these questions.

2 Europe's Development Aid: Setting a New Agenda

The Maastricht Treaty and its Implications for European Aid

The Maastricht Treaty of 1992 stipulates that EU assistance should foster the sustainable economic and social development of developing countries, and particularly the most disadvantaged among them; reduce poverty in developing countries; assist the smooth and gradual integration of partner countries into the world economy; and support the observance of democracy, human rights, fundamental freedoms and the rule of law. It also states that the EU's development policy shall be *complementary* to the policies of the member states (Article 130u), while Article 130x requires the EU and its member states to *coordinate* policy in this area. The EU is also bound to take account of its development objectives in any of its policies likely to affect developing countries (article 130v). Hence the requirement for policy *coherence*.

Bilateral aid flows from EU member states to developing countries are effectively declining, not least because of internal budgetary pressures required for Economic and Monetary Union and in some cases because of recession. Each member state sets its own priorities for their bilateral aid based on its own objectives, knowing it is answerable to its taxpaying electorate. Northern European donors have tended to follow a more NGO-focused policy, the French a neo-colonial one, the Italians a more commercially-driven approach and the UK a good governance policy.

Now about 20% of member states' development aid is channelled through the European Community, compared with only 7% in 1970. The Commission itself is ranked as the fifth biggest donor agency in the OECD and the second largest multilateral donor after the World Bank (OECD Development Assistance Committee (DAC) figures). As the OECD Development Assistance Committee report on the European Community published in 1996 says, 'the Community is a large and unique multilateral donor in its own right'.

Setting Priorities for European Union Aid

More than one third of EU aid is channelled via the Lomé Convention to 70 ACP countries and is separately financed outside the general EU budget. Lomé is a complex package of aid and trade arrangements between the EU and ACP countries. The current Lomé Convention is due to expire in 2000.

Lomé is now, however, no longer the centrepiece of EU aid because of the increasing trend for development assistance to come direct from the EC budget, which is now almost two thirds of total EU aid. Over recent years the priorities for the EU's disbursements have changed with the volume of Community aid to Europe's neighbours increasing. Significant EU aid flows are now channelled to Europe's southern neighbours around the Mediterranean (with a 100% increase to MEDA programmes) and to Central and Eastern Europe, countries in transition and essentially middle-income countries, rather than to the traditional developing country recipients of EU collective aid. This raises questions about the priorities for EU aid, given that programmes such as MEDA are seen more as a political policy towards Europe's southern neighbours than as a development policy.

The proportion of European aid directed towards the poorest countries, as recommended by the G7 and the OECD Development Assistance Committee, is dropping. Poverty reduction is a key EU policy, as enshrined in the Maastricht Treaty. Despite the rhetoric behind European policies the poorest countries and the poorest people are not necessarily benefiting and, it is argued, aid is not being used to tackle poverty eradication effectively. In member states' bilateral programmes as much as 70% of aid is aimed at the poorest (in the case of the UK); far less of the increasing Commission aid is thus targeted. Foreign governments and aid donors do not hold a magic key to unlock the door to poverty reduction, but they can accelerate natural processes to ensure that the fruits of economic growth are widely shared and that the basic needs of the poor are better satisfied.

There is a general desire for debate about the priorities and balance of Europe's aid. However debate is difficult given the member states' varying interests – and their preference for their own flags to fly rather than one saying 'built by the EU and its member states'. The IGC, with its discussion about Europe's Common Foreign and Security Policy (CFSP) and the Lomé Green Paper, has provided opportunity for this debate which should not be missed. The member states remain in the driving seat both of their own bilateral programmes and of Europe's collective assistance through the Council of Ministers. Given the requisite political will, Europe's agenda for the future can be set.

3 Economic Development and Trade

The Role of European Foreign Investment and Support for the Private Sector

It is now realised that there has been little correlation between aid given to developing countries and economic growth in those countries. Yet economic growth is essential if a country is to reduce its level of poverty. Where significant economic growth has been achieved by developing countries this has been largely by private capital flows supporting the private sector. This is a feature of the 1990s. During the first half of the 1990s global private capital flows to developing countries increased fivefold. In 1996 capital flows, mostly financed by the private sector, approached 200 billion ECU, around eight times the volume of EU aid. The European private sector is a major source of these flows. The most dramatic impact is seen in some SE Asian 'tiger economies' where private capital flows are playing an increased role in development.

Development assistance can be used to help governments in developing countries create the conditions for private capital flow. There is a new global era of investment liberalisation and many developing countries are putting new investment laws in place. The EU strategy paper on the private sector concentrates on capacity and confidence building to allow the private sector to be the engine of growth.

In parallel to creating the appropriate economic environment for developing countries to attract foreign direct investment, Europe needs to support the indigenous private sector, building up small businesses. Donors, it is argued, could be doing more to provide *direct* support for the private sector. This assistance needs to be targeted carefully, providing support which adds value. It should only be given where it is in the recipient countries' interests and where it does not create market distortion. Operating in a business-like manner is important, through loans for instance. The European Investment Bank provides such loans; half new lending in ACP countries, for example, is directed towards the private sector. There is concern however that where the European Investment Bank (EIB), and others, subsidise loans this can cause local market distortion. And private sector finance and loans need to respond to requests, some of which are risky. Europe needs to be prepared to take such risks even when looking for financial return on its development assistance.

Donors are also considering how they can enable governments in developing countries to mobilise their own private sector. In many cases the private sector has not grown and created economic growth, most notably in Africa. This has been for a variety of reasons such as the levels of protection and tax impediments, the size of the domestic debt, the large sums of African capital invested overseas rather than in their own economies and the fact that their next-door-neighbours, and potential trading partners, may be failing states. Donors can help directly in capacity building, and in finding new approaches for financing, such as venture capital leasing. But this will only be beneficial if the environmental context is right. Strengthening the local financial sector is therefore important, providing technical assistance and expertise to banks, supporting the creation of local merchant banks and stockmarkets. Technical help to privatise ailing state industries can also be of value. This approach has benefited Eastern Europe (see below).

It is recognised, however, that economic growth is not necessarily a panacea and many of the poorest countries are not likely to benefit from such private flows.

> Increased Foreign Direct Investment is no substitute for aid. It is highly selective – going mainly to China and a handful of other growth centres in Asia and Latin America – and, unlike aid, it is not possible to focus Foreign Direct Investment (FDI) on need, or on the kind of long-term investments in people which are the key to growth with equity.[1]

Economic growth also carries social consequences for those whose lives are not improved.

Working Towards Sustainable Development

Sustained economic growth is fundamental to provide countries with the means of developing themselves and reducing levels of absolute poverty. Yet if sustainable development is to be achieved, consideration of environmental issues is crucial as part of overall development policies. Environmental considerations cannot be divorced from the resource allocation, and often priorities are set by donors on a fairly short-term basis. Many European donors work in 3–5 year cycles, whereas with forestry work, for example, a longer approach would be beneficial. Some environmental projects are easier for donors – planting forests as opposed to dealing with old nuclear reactors, for instance, in the former Soviet Union and Central Europe. The biggest environmental disasters such as desertification, industrial pollution, and eradication of forestry also regularly occur in failed states, outside the aid net.

Agreements at the Rio Summit in 1992 should ensure that environmental considerations are at the heart of development policy and projects. In practice, however, there is often a time-lag between policy awareness and implementation. For sustainable development to work recipient countries need a strengthened capacity, across the public, private and civil sector, to allow continued success after project funding has ended.

Trade versus Aid

Looking at overall policies towards developing countries, trade, in aggregate, is more important than direct assistance. In 1994 total developing country export earnings were eight times greater than their aid receipts. Trade between the EU and ACP states is, however, very small in comparison with Europe's trade elsewhere, amounting in 1995 to 3.7% of the EU's imports and 3.1% of EU exports. However to the ACP countries themselves, their trade with Europe is a crucial part of their overall trade – in many cases amounting to at least 50%, much in commodities. The share of ACP countries in the EU's merchandise market has been flat or declining for more than a decade. Many would argue that the disappointing trade performance of developing countries generally can be traced to an inadequate supply response.

To encourage trade Europe grants special privileges exempting imports from developing countries from tariff and other barriers. Complex preferential trade agreements, such as those provided by the Lomé Convention, lie at the heart of the EU's development-related trade policies. Yet preferential access to European markets has not necessarily benefited developing countries; ACP countries have better access to the European market than the Asian tigers whose economies have grown dramatically by comparison. Preferences also run contrary to the rules of the World Trade Organisation (WTO) system. The value of a preferential tariff regime to a developing country is also reduced by the fact that many other countries, and groups of countries, are also getting preferential access to the European market. And the margin of preference depends in part on the level of tariffs, which are themselves being reduced with each round of multilateral trade negotiations, such as happened in the Uruguay Round.

Europe's options in trade policy towards developing countries are complex, but one offer might be to reduce to zero, on a Most Favoured Nation (MFN) basis, tariffs on products of specific export interest to developing countries, especially those lower-income developing countries. As these countries start to solve their supply-response problems, investors can develop export-oriented industries on the basis of permanent, WTO-guaranteed access to the markets of current and potential trading partners. The EU's current negotiations with South Africa, regarding exports of agricultural products from South Africa to the EU, are not seen as an encouraging indicator of the EU's willingness to grant a meaningful increase in market access to developing countries.

One of the key commodities traded by developing countries is agricultural goods. Europe's Common Agricultural Policy (CAP) severely restricts some agricultural imports, particularly those competing with Europe's own production. And subsidised European agricultural exports hit production within developing countries. A recent example is the problems facing Namibian beef producers, competing in the South African market with highly subsidised EU beef. Reform of the CAP is seen by many to be vital if developing countries' exports are to have a fair chance in the world market.

As the world moves towards freer trade the most liberal economies will gain most; the most protected and inward looking countries least. It is these latter countries which are most likely to need a safety net. To shield them from the full force of competition the WTO should be encouraged to build an international agreement to create an appropriate clause to protect these poorest countries. This will take time but should be encouraged by European members of the WTO.

More developing countries are also becoming, by choice or necessity, more actively involved in WTO activities themselves. The WTO is a member-driven organisation and now averages around 45 meetings a week. All delegations in Geneva, and particularly those with few staff and little back-up resources in capitals, are feeling the pressure. Of the 28 Least Developed Countries who are WTO members only 10 have a permanent office in Geneva (and these cover all the international bodies in Geneva). Europe, it is suggested, could play an active part here in providing support to allow developing countries to have an effective presence and voice in Geneva.

It is argued that global free trade should mean fair trade for the poorest countries as they struggle to integrate into the global economy. Europe should recognise that it will take time for local industries to become more competitive and build up their supply for export, and this should be taken into account in Europe's development planning. There is therefore a call for greater policy coherence between Europe's trade policies and her development policies.

4 Recipients of European Aid
Lomé Partners

Preferential trade agreements lie at the heart of Europe's relations with ACP countries. A consultative Green Paper, produced by the Commission, considers the future of the Lomé relationship beyond 2000. The 'goal is clear; to revitalize ACP–EU relations; open new horizons and boost chances of success. ACP–EU relations are still a key part of the Union's identity'.[2] The Green Paper is providing a vehicle for discussion about how successful the partnership has been in promoting development in terms of economic growth. As a group, ACP countries' development performance has been disappointing compared with that of other developing countries. An assessment can also be made on the wide variety of instruments or forms of aid used, when many evaluation studies suggest that some of the instruments are now outmoded.

One of the key areas of the future of Europe's assistance to developing countries is therefore under debate. What shape should the future relationship with ACP countries take? Will there be a Lomé V? Lomé's membership is being discussed by the different parties, and the question arises of who should benefit in any new structural relationship? Should it be split into regional groupings and thus differentiation occur? Should new members be added, including all nine of the Least Developed Countries not already included within Lomé?

A less formulaic and contractual style of relationship between Europe and the ACP countries is foreseen as one option, with different levels of support to the recipients and concentrated on the poorest countries, possibly as many as 40 of the current ACP grouping. A rationalisation of all the Lomé instruments would also allow greater flexibility and could form a three-part package: of humanitarian emergency aid where necessary; direct government-to-government support through programmes by sector; and through the provision of resources to build the non-governmental sector, encouraging decentralisation of aid. Moving away from the traditional government-to-government 'project' approach to assistance towards sectoral development initiatives or budget support may be an attractive option.

The Commission's Green Paper is not seeking to offer a clear vision for the future; rather it is intended to spark debate in preparation for negotiations between Europe and the ACP countries in 1998. Likely priorities for future development assistance to ACP countries include promoting economic growth and competitiveness; engaging in greater political dialogue with partner governments on issues such as human rights, democracy and the rule of law and conflict prevention; and strengthening institutional capacity-building and political dialogue with partner governments to assist ACP countries to enter the global economy.

In terms of promoting economic growth, ACP partners will be expected to organise their policies, institutions and administrations so that private entrepreneurs are involved, competitiveness is encouraged, export growth is supported, and investment is made in their countries' future. In a number of ACP countries, achieving competitiveness in trade and investment means continuing to struggle along the long road of policy and institutional reforms, including reforms in the legal and regulatory framework, and in the consultative processes between government and civil society. Another key theme for 'after-Lomé' is, therefore, support for institutional capacity-building. Governments need support to be competent and transparent to fulfil their essential tasks of maintaining law and order and ensuring the provision of social and economic services. Europe is likely to want to see continuous movement towards reform – to ensure the public service is dedicated to achieving the collective good, not to feathering its own nest. ACP partners need training to support any institutional reform and create a pool of local expertise.

As for the trade preferences built into the Lomé package, there is considerable debate about their future. The WTO waiver to Lomé trade preferences is due to expire in February 2000 and may not be renewed by WTO members. Many have argued that continuation of a waiver, possibly with differentiations and within a future Lomé umbrella, should be pursued. Under this option regional or even bilateral trade agreements with the EU would allow for the differences within the ACP group, while maintaining an overall development cooperation agreement. But any attempt to apply preferential trade policies on a differentiated basis is likely to be extremely complex – and could be argued to be a negative tool rather than a more active one, such as providing direct financial aid or technical assistance, for example.

There is concern about the impact abolition of any current trade protocols would have on the economies of the middle-income Lomé countries, who would not benefit from any new WTO clause protecting the poorest. It has been suggested that a special WTO clause could be created to assist the poorest countries in trading. Where ACP countries are not Least Developed there is an appeal that Europe should not 'kick the ladder out from under them', particularly where the countries are dependent on a single and primary commodity.

The EU–South Africa negotiations are seen as a foretaste of what may lie ahead for ACP countries. The Commission proposes a Free Trade Area around South Africa – yet this, it is argued, could have disastrous consequences for South African industries, and the economic impact on neighbouring countries would be severe. The EU–South African negotiations also highlight the serious problem for small states over their capacity to be involved in lengthy and complex negotiations with the EU.

ACP countries themselves are being encouraged to be proactive and to take the lead in the discussions, and to have 'ownership' of the policy, although there is debate about how much the EU is prepared to cede 'ownership' in practice and about the conditionalities which will be set. The ACP countries, however, need time to develop their capacity to negotiate trade agreements, and time to accelerate the process of their own economic diversification.

Themes which could be explored further in the debate include deciding the EU's overall objectives for a new relationship, how to prevent conflict within and between developing countries, the emphasis which should be placed on basic healthcare and primary education, and the role of women in the ACP development process. The conditionality of European aid to ACP countries is likely to feature significantly in the debate, with aid increasingly linked to good governance. A complaints procedure within any successor Lomé arrangement is also recommended as part of the package for ACP countries. As the debate hots up Europe is tasked with finding a way of assisting them in tackling their problems and supporting their needs into the next century.

Central and Eastern Europe

Since the end of the Cold War, European collective assistance to countries in Central and Eastern Europe has increased dramatically to assist their transition from a command economy to a market economy and to pluralist democracy. Ways are being found of increasing the gearing of each ECU spent in development in Eastern Europe, such as loans through the European Bank of Reconstruction and Development (EBRD), interest subsidies or guarantees. The EBRD's work is project-oriented with support for private sector development, including the utilities. The British Know-How Fund (KHF), working with the non-governmental sector in providing specific technical assistance and 'know-how', has concentrated its support to Central Europe on financial services such as banking, insurance, audit and privatisation, through development of small and medium sized enterprises, management training, public administration and, to a lesser extent, support for agriculture, energy, industrial restructuring and the environment. The KHF has worked with a cross-section of private sector partners, giving operational flexibility, differentiating it from the EC PHARE and TACIS programmes to Central Europe and the Commonwealth of Independent States respectively.

For Poland's development, debt rescheduling was a very important element. Assistance, particularly bilateral aid, was flexible and timely, and much was focused on support for restructuring. The exit from support and the strategies used for phasing out development assistance will be crucial and will be linked to countries' accession to the European Union. Allowing some of these countries to 'transit' quickly away from relying on European support will free more European resources for those lower down the development scale. Some countries, such as Poland, are already themselves becoming donors, for example providing assistance to Ukraine.

There are lessons here for Europe's aid to developing countries, many of whom are trying to transform themselves into democratic market economies. Technical know-how in the finance sector, for example, can play a crucial role in their development. One key element is the level of education and literacy. Countries in Central Europe with the quickest success were also those who made the most dramatic changes, accepting the mistakes they made en route. Meetings of European donors, often including state government representatives, have helped to reduce the risk of overlap, and have enabled greater coordination of programmes, for instance a bilateral donor providing technical support to an EBRD loan.

Bangladesh: A Case Study

Bangladesh is one of the largest, poorest countries. Its total population is 120 million, increasing by 1–2% per annum. It is an aid-intensive country. Bangladesh now finances 40% of its public investments from its own resources; but aid is needed to finance the remaining 60% – with European collective support providing about 15% of the international effort. Total annual international aid disbursement to Bangladesh has remained almost constant during the past 10 years at about $1.6 billion. But the purpose, type and source of aid has changed, with project aid, rather than commodity and food aid, now the principal disbursement, with increased soft loans and more than half total disbursements financed multilaterally.

European bilateral aid commitments to Bangladesh have dropped significantly since 1990 (from $282 million to $181 million) whilst those channelled through the Commission have risen simultaneously, now accounting for about 18% of total European aid to Bangladesh. Much of the international aid flow to Bangladesh is via other multilateral donor agencies, which are themselves sponsored by European member states. Bangladesh also benefits from preferential trade arrangements with Europe under a number of unilateral Generalised System of Preferences on certain agricultural and industrial goods.

Bangladesh, as one of six countries, has been selected as a trial to improve European coordination. EU member states and the Commission are working more closely together, overcoming individual preferences in order to better coordinate their policies and actions in support of poverty alleviation in Bangladesh. ECHO, the EC humanitarian office, for example, has an ambitious disaster prevention and management programme in Bangladesh. Growing donor coordination and systemisation of aid ensures that aided projects and programmes are identified, designed and financed coherently and efficiently. The business-like discipline imposed on the country by recipes from the IMF and World Bank for macro-economic stabilisation and economic growth give Bangladesh little room to manoeuvre. European donors work within this framework. In order to prevent corruption greater emphasis has been placed by European donors on supporting civil society. Most donors now channel significant portions of aid to NGOs and other civil society organisations.

'Losers' in the Aid Cycle

There is a serious and so far unanswered question about what Europe, and other donors, should to do with the losers, those who are not receiving aid, many of which are African nations where the machinery of government has broken down. Forty per cent of Africa is not receiving European support for a variety of reasons such as undemocratic governments and poor human rights records. Yet it is precisely these African countries that are some of the poorest and that have the greatest needs. Any vacuum of development assistance is often filled of necessity by crisis management and sticking plasters of humanitarian aid, rather than more sustainable long-term development. Moreover, humanitarian assistance can lead to dependency on aid. It is a concern that humanitarian aid accounts for an ever-increasing proportion of aid budgets.

5 The Role of the European Commission

A Complementary or Competing Role with Member States?

Coherence, coordination and complementarity are key words for the Commission's relations with member states in the field of development assistance. Greater policy coherence between the Commission and member states is needed at three levels. First, at a general foreign policy level in guiding development policy and coordinating the various preferred objectives. The challenge for Europe collectively over the next ten years, if wanting to move from the sixteenth donor scenario, will be to build on the foundations of Maastricht and Lomé. This needs political will as a clear demonstration that there is no 'aid-fatigue'. Second, the practical level of coherence of development instruments used; and third coherence of all EU policies touching on developing countries. The Dutch Presidency in the first half of 1997 focused on the issue of policy coherence questions.

Coordination of development policy and practice can be seen as a route to complementarity. Greater coordination between the Commission and member states is welcomed, but who coordinates whom? The Commission may have a vocation for coordination, but this is unacceptable to many member states who have their own objectives and interests, and are responding to their own voters' and taxpayers' demands, making coordination on the ground difficult to achieve in practice. There are also differences of approach to implementation. Some member states may be absent in a particular country; some donors, most notably the Commission, operate a very centralised approach. Member states may be in the driving seat for Commission aid through the Council of Development Ministers and through the appraisal of projects, yet greater coordination between the Commission and member states' aid is not being achieved, except in some trial countries.

The developing community would profit from the strengths of individual actors being brought together, for instance through a division of labour by country or NGO and by programme sector or project. If this is unachievable there is still a need for greater coordination to avoid duplication on the ground between the Commission, bilateral ODAs and NGOs. This also raises the question of European coordination with other bilateral and multilateral donors, such as the UN and World Bank. There is often less donor coordination in the area of social support than in economic aid.

Adding Value

To avoid the criticism that the Commission is the sixteenth donor, the question is asked what can the EU do best collectively and what is the added value? Collective EU aid is of value because of its scale.

Coordination works best in such areas as emergency humanitarian aid through ECHO and food aid in emergencies where there is a single objective and overhead costs can be reduced. Coordinated programmes such as Lomé, or other structural adjustment programmes or assistance which benefit from coordination, provide added value. One approach is for the Commission, at the behest of member states, to be a wholesaler rather than retailer of aid, supporting development with general and coordinated policies but without needing to be 'in the villages' and involved in projects on the ground.

The Need for Institutional Reform

As the amount of European aid disbursed via the Commission increases, the need for *institutional reform* becomes stronger. Larger budgets place increased management burdens on the Commission to produce effective results on behalf of member states. It is the member states, however, who are themselves often reluctant to allow the Commission the tools to do the job effectively, seeing a key problem already of bureaucracy and over-complicated procedures. Many of the problems identified in the 1996 OECD DAC report on European Community aid still need addressing. The Commission is short staffed for instance, a point it readily acknowledges and which only the member states can address. Staff vary in expertise (being weaker in critical areas such as gender, population and environment) and some lack specialist technical skills; local Commission delegations could employ more local staff at reduced cost.

> If the Commission is to continue to make progress in improving its development co-operation effectiveness and to capitalise on the staff investments it is making in training and evaluation, it will require an adequate base of long-term, trained staff, and, in particular, high quality specialist staff in critical fields. The Commission needs to assure that it is not deficient in some of the key fields for working on poverty alleviation – participatory development, gender, population, health, education, environment, and the social sciences.[3]

In terms of policy, strategies for individual recipient countries need developing to coordinate and integrate the various EU development instruments. And the duration of the budgetary process, from project preparation to financing and implementation, could be speeded up. There is also not enough cross-over between directorates within the Commission to prevent policy incoherence.

Structurally the Community programme is more complicated than many donor structures, making it more challenging to ensure effective coordination, coherence and complementarity. Member states have a collective responsibility to sort this out. One proposed option is for a separate agency within the Commission to bring professional and technical functions together. Questions of accountability would still arise as would the need for transparency. In creating any new agency, lessons should be remembered from the creation of ECHO.

An evaluation study of European aid to Ethiopia (1995) highlighted a number of key issues about how EU aid could be improved, through simplifying the range of aid instruments (to Lomé and non Lomé recipients), strengthening strategic planning which is weak at country level, improving the quality of the management of projects, staffing local delegations effectively (including employing local staff at a much reduced cost – 1 fewer Commission delegate could fund 40 Ethiopians of professor level) and improving and simplifying the aid administration (creating procedural manuals, allowing delegated authority to delegates, and annual reporting). Such changes need political support and political will – the European Parliament may increase the budget lines (and set up yet more lines) but member states through the Development Council need to coordinate their policies and strategies, and provide the Commission with the tools to do the job effectively.

The Value of Evaluation

There is an increasing desire for European donors to see results and a cost–benefit analysis of Community aid to satisfy their taxpayers and legitimise EC aid. Commission evaluation has improved greatly over recent years, particularly in DGVIII, and more is being done in training Commission delegates and ACP partners but any results, which should all be made publicly available, need to be fed back into the decision-making process. There is, however, a question over the effectiveness of the evaluation process. It is viewed sometimes more as a tool for finance ministries than for aid agencies. It can only be subjective, and there are few cases where an evaluation can sufficiently capture the range of development aid used and effectively assess its long term impact and whether it is value for money. There is a call to move away from a focus on how speedily an investment can be made (often needed to disburse large funds quickly within set financial periods) to focusing on the quality of investment.

A longer-term assessment is preferable to show that aid really works. Continuous monitoring, in individual sectors for example, might be equally effective, together with account audits by the European Court of Auditors. With the PHARE and TACIS programmes, monitoring is built into the projects at the outset.

Questions remain about the independence of the evaluation function when conducted internally by the Commission. The recommendation that one Commission evaluation unit should be set up to cover the whole programme is not welcomed by many as it might mean that it lost direct contact with the aid dispensing directorates.

6 Other Actors in Europe's Aid

European Non-Governmental Organisations

European NGOs are increasingly becoming involved in lobbying EU institutions to encourage constructive debate between the many different actors and to help shape the future aid agenda. The challenge for the European NGOs is not to mirror the policy work of the Commission. The 'Elewijt process', supported by the Commission, has clarified the distinctive elements of the diverse European NGOs working in the development field, and led to the adoption of shared values and approaches. The EU-NGO Liaison Committee has set political goals, promoting Europe as 'open to the world', to enhance the quality and quantity of EU development and humanitarian assistance and to contribute to making Europe more aware of its interdependence with the South.

A code of conduct for NGOs active on the ground, together with greater coordination between them, would be valued by recipient countries, particularly where there is a proliferation of NGOs. NGO activity in Rwanda failed in this area. NGOs become competitive with one another on the ground, heightened by media coverage of humanitarian disasters, so there needs to be more effective and proactive coordination among them.

Concern is also voiced about the loss of separate identity and agenda when NGOs receive public funding. This is increasingly the case from both bilateral and collective European donors, who provide funding either directly or for contract work.

Self-examination by European NGOs of their role as agents for change in developing societies has led to greater emphasis on their role in their own societies. For example, the Real World lobby group recently set up in the UK as a broader coalition of development NGOs, environmental and democratic renewal agencies.

Local Partners

Local partners, as the recipients, remain the key players in Europe's development. Rather belatedly there is an increased desire by the donors, supported by the OECD Development Strategy, to involve the recipient partners more, encouraging them to set up and 'own' and control their development plans. This calls for a more proactive approach from both partners. Dialogue is essential to ensure local ownership of European development assistance. Local ownership means both the officials within the recipient country and the civil society, the beneficiaries of the aid.

European donors can provide resources and support for 'capacity-building' of the recipient countries, for example in training, and to cope with the numerous donor visits, repeated requests for the same information and to understand the enormous variety of aid instruments of the different donors, many with conditionalities attached. Recipients welcome greater donor coordination to avoid what has been termed the 'beauty contest' approach of different donors vying with one another. If one donor were to lead in one sector and others to accept their development and evaluation plans, the recipient country would benefit. Uganda is turning into a laboratory where donors vie with one another and where this kind of approach would be beneficial. Decentralisation of aid in cooperation with recipient countries is also seen as a positive way forward, providing an opportunity for more recipients to be involved in the decision-making processes.

7 Conclusions

As the year 2000 approaches, it is time for the EU to set a new agenda, to define a clearer role for Commission aid in the context of Europe's overall relations with the developing world. Commission aid needs to add value to that of member states and to be complementary. A reassessment of what is best done at Community level (on or off budget) and what at a bilateral or other multilateral level, based on experience and expertise, is needed. Humanitarian assistance, food aid and large-scale integrated policies such as Lomé are opportunities for collective European action. It is also recommended that the Commission move from project aid to programme aid, to be a wholesaler rather than a retailer. The aim should be to maximise the total EU effort so that Europe can contribute effectively to global development and to contribute to the OECD target to halve those living in absolute poverty by 2015.

There is a clear need for enhanced policy coherence to achieve coherent and consistent policies across the EU, linking development issues with other EU decisions. For example, EU trade and other development-related policies must not be allowed to undermine EU development policies. There must be greater political support for development interests if such policy coherence is to be achieved.

Greater coordination is needed on the ground between the many European players in the development field (whether European Commission, bilateral agencies or NGOs) to ensure they work with one another, thus avoiding duplication and encouraging all donors to work in partnership with aid recipients. Coordination at a European level has already proved effective in Central Europe and Bangladesh, for example. European donors could coordinate even more if they were to agree a greater division of labour, based on the expertise of donors, and divide up their development aid at country, sector and project level.

Poverty reduction is at the heart of many member states' development policy, yet it is not always seen to be at the heart of all Commission policy. Scarce official flows could be more concentrated on the poorest. The targets for poverty alleviation set by the OECD are based on the achievement of significantly increased rates of per capita economic growth in developing countries. Developing countries need to assess jointly with donors the kind of assistance required from public and private sector donors to help promote such growth. And serious consideration is needed over what to do with the 'losers' in the aid cycle – particularly where political conditions are unfavourable for long-term development and poverty thus escalates.

The debate about the future of Lomé provides a crucial opportunity for forward thinking and for Europe to define a new relationship with ACP countries. Europe wants to encourage economic growth and competitiveness. In greater consultation with ACP partners, it can provide more flexible assistance. Questions of membership and differentiation are still to be addressed, together with such issues as conditionality of aid and determining the most effective aid instruments, for example sectoral and programme initiatives. ACP countries need to be more proactive in setting their own agenda to strengthen their unique relationship with Europe. They also need to be given time by Europe so that the most effective future partnership can be worked out.

European donors can do more to provide support for the indigenous private sector, which itself can be an engine for sustained economic growth. Assistance through capacity building of the banking and financial sectors, or technical help and 'know-how', has added value in Central and Eastern Europe where a little aid, carefully targeted, and often to the non-governmental sector, can have a significant impact. However, economic growth does not provide all the answers, and there are often adverse social consequences for those remaining in the poverty trap. Debt rescheduling can also play a crucial role in allowing economies to grow.

Developing countries have received less benefit from trade preferences than expected. An inadequate supply-response system could be to blame and Europe can provide direct assistance to support industrial production, as well as provide more open markets, particularly in the agricultural sector. Europe should encourage the WTO to develop policies which protect the poorest countries. Europe can also help these countries in their negotiations with the WTO.

European donors can work increasingly in partnership with all levels of civil society. EU aid should be related to programmes proposed by the recipients as part of their own efforts to tackle poverty.

At the organisational level, the European Commission could disburse aid more effectively. Country strategies need developing, staffing levels need to be increased and staff appropriately trained. Greater delegated authority should be given to the in-country Commission representation which should include more locally-engaged staff. Evaluation of EU aid needs to be incorporated at the planning stage and results fed back into the decision-making process. If a new agency is created for professional and technical functions care needs to be taken to allow full transparency and accountability. Member states have a responsibility to support Commission work through the Development Council. Greater political support for increased European cooperation would do much to ensure that Europe's development aid, whether collective or bilateral, made maximum impact in assisting developing countries to fulfil their potential.

Notes

1. Judith Randel and Tony German, *Reality of Aid,* International Council of Voluntary Agencies and Eurostep, 1996.

2. Professor Joâo de Deus Pinheiro, Green Paper on relations between the European Union and the ACP countries on the eve of the 21st century, 1996.

3. DAC/OECD report on the European Community, No. 12, 1996.

3

Nato's Future

Report based on Wilton Park Conference 491: 10–14 February 1997 on
'NATO's Role in the Twenty-First Century'

Richard Latter

1 Introduction

The North Atlantic Treaty Organisation (NATO) is about to take the first formal steps towards the Alliance's enlargement. This policy will be implemented in the face of reservations in some member states and of opposition from the Russian government and despite criticisms that enlargement will involve the *de facto* re-division of Europe. The enlargement process will intensify interest in three related issues: the ratification of enlargement by member states' legislatures, coping with possible adverse Russian reactions, and developing positive links with Central European states which are not included in the list of candidates to underpin their stability and security.

The three issues are inter-related. The ease with which ratification occurs will be affected by Russian policies and by levels of perceived stability or instability in non-NATO Central Europe. Russian reactions are likely to be conditioned in part by judgements about the prospects for ratification and to include decisions about whether to distance themselves from or meddle in possible resulting confusion in Central Europe. To Central Europeans a failure to ratify enlargement would confirm the closing of one potential vital link with the West, a closure which is already suspected in capitals not expecting to be on the July 1997 lists; their reactions are likely to be conditioned in part by Russian policies and rhetoric on the issue.

To NATO states' policy makers, who have not undertaken enlargement lightly, a positive outcome to these and related problems is envisaged. While some commentators doubt the willingness of a US Congress to approve enlargement and disparage it as a means to keep Central European states out of the European Union,[1] current levels of public support for enlargement in the United States and the strong margin of bi-partisan support for enlargement in the US Congress would seem to indicate that ratification will occur in the United States and be successfully achieved in the other fifteen NATO member countries.[2]

Considerable effort and resources are being committed through the Partnership for Peace programme (PfP) to ensure that NATO cooperation with PfP partners which are not members of NATO can be so intense that partnership will match the benefits of actual membership to a very high degree: while PfP links will not include Article five commitments to mutual defence, they will be of such a quality that they will reassure Central Europeans about the Alliance's interest in their security and offer the prospect of stability throughout the region. Furthermore the commitment of Central European states to be part of the West, or at least their commitment to have positive relations both with the West and Russia, is in any case deeply-rooted enough to survive their omission from the first group of membership candidates. In this context it will be important that the Alliance chooses wisely in its pronouncements about how far enlargement should extend in the longer term. Options include an open door policy for all states based upon self differentiation as countries meet the standards set by the Alliance for membership; enlargement based upon parallel expansion of NATO and the European Union, not requiring European Union (EU) joint members to join NATO but offering them a *de facto* right to do so; or limiting enlargement to a few countries based on strategic criteria and then ending the process.[3] The selection and presentation of one of these options should be undertaken with due reference to Central European sensitivities.

Dealing with a possible negative Russian reaction remains problematical, not least because of leadership uncertainties in Moscow. The extent of any damage to Alliance–Russian relations will depend partially upon who heads the Russian government in the Kremlin. However, Russian negative attitudes towards enlargement extend across the spectrum of Russian political life and the likelihood of an adverse Russian reaction has to be faced. Recent NATO initiatives to establish a special relationship with Russia are designed to reduce Russian reservations and to develop a positive relationship between an enlarged Alliance and the Russian Federation. The eventual outcome of this initiative remains to be seen.

These issues have dominated the attention of both policy makers and observers of the Alliance in recent years, their interest in these issues being matched only by the war and subsequent peace in former Yugoslavia and the threat that the conflict represented to NATO cohesion. The emergence of the Alliance as a peace enforcer and a peace keeper developed as an ad hoc reaction to these problems and raised issues which extend beyond enlargement; namely establishing the core missions for NATO in the twenty-first century. What could and should these be?

NATO's internal adaptation provides some pointers: the development of flexible rapid reaction forces, greater interest in and emphasis on air lift capabilities and manoeuvrability of military forces, establishing Combined Joint Task Forces, and the increasing interest in and acquaintance with member states' peacekeeping doctrines. NATO is to be more flexible, but does this mean a long-term commitment to take on responsibilities extending much beyond the defence of member states and ensuring, through persuasion and cooperation but not excluding a judicial use of force, stability at NATO's immediate periphery? Or are other missions to be considered, for example the development of a collective and cooperative security throughout Europe or conducting police actions in, for example, Africa? Consideration of these issues has to be developed further although interesting pointers are already developing:

> Would using NATO for subject-matter too far removed from its familiar concerns … risk damaging its efficiency for insufficient gain? [There are divisions] … about

whether its proven utility in tackling security issues could be extended geographically, as to problems in the Middle East or East Asia; ... [there may be] no better established forum, but focus might not be easily sustained as distance diluted interest, and regional sensitivities might not be easy to handle.[4]

These are questions which should be at the centre of the debate on the Alliance's future and it is important that member states, not least Americans and Europeans who may have different perspectives, should develop a common view. This debate and hoped for emerging consensus should include general publics as well as the decision makers of member states; talk of peace dividends, falling defence budgets, other demands on government finances and attention (for example health care and law and order), have reduced public interest in foreign policy and defence issues, which in any case have never been high on the public's agenda. Adjustments made by NATO to date have successfully answered criticisms that it was an alliance of the past, but its continued relevance will have to be demonstrated to new generations of leaders and tax payers. Success in this enterprise requires clarity of thought and message.

2 NATO Enlargement
The Case For

There is general agreement within NATO that the Alliance's overall aim is to ensure security and stability of *all* states in Europe. Enlargement is being undertaken to this end, although it is recognised that it is not a panacea and that other institutions have significant roles to play: the Western European Union (WEU), the Council of Europe, the Organisation for Security and Cooperation in Europe (OSCE). However, NATO is the key institution in that it fulfils roles which the others are unable to undertake. Thus, for example, it is a means to ensure that the United States remains engaged in Europe, and that Germany is fully integrated in regional security structures, thereby avoiding the historical European problem of dealing with a Germany which is either too strong or too weak. NATO continues to ensure positive cooperation on security matters between its members and prevents any re-nationalisation of their foreign and security policies. It has become a means through which the West seeks to help Russia to succeed as a democratic state and to integrate the Russian Federation in the international system. Not least, it is the Alliance which enables Western countries to fulfil their responsibilities for maintaining security and stability in Central Europe.

It is with this last goal particularly in mind that the enlargement process will begin in 1997 with the anticipated invitations to a small number of Central European states to join the Alliance. These countries will be 'full' members of NATO, enjoying all rights accruing from, but accepting all responsibilities of, Alliance membership. They will be expected to be suppliers as well as users of security, and while it may be possible for them to opt out of non-Article five operations, they will have to accept and be fully committed to the Alliance's collective defence arrangements. In addition, clear criteria for membership have been established for potential new members. Each candidate must have a democratic polity, effective democratic control of the military, well-regulated relations with neighbouring states, and a sufficient level of military preparedness and sophistication to undertake NATO missions. While improving military preparedness may not be an immediate priority, given the lack of an immediate threat to the Alliance and the overriding necessity to strengthen Central European economies, meeting the democratic criteria is essential. The Cold War strategic compulsion which resulted in NATO offering membership to less-than-democratic states has ceased to exist, and its new mission – the building of stability – requires that new members be fully democratic.

Thus enlargement is proposed and supported because of a desire to stabilise the European security environment as far east as possible and promote the integration of, and cooperation between, former adversaries of Eastern and Western Europe. It is not founded upon any fear of a potential adversary and, in principle, membership will be open to all states meeting the Alliance's criteria. However, this commitment is constrained by the realities of geography; namely, all members must have a genuine commitment to the defence of fellow member states in all foreseeable circumstances. It is for this reason that states of central Asia and the Russian Federation are unlikely to be offered Alliance membership; West European countries are simply not prepared to take up collective defence responsibilities in central Asia or in the Russian far east. Indeed, it is concern that NATO may be taking up roles for which it is ill suited which underpins, in part, Western reservations about enlargement.

Western Reservations

While opposition to enlargement in the West has been relatively muted, there is evidence of a growing concern among sections of the policy-making elites. Some observers argue that Eastern European states are simply not ready to join the Alliance, noting for example the fragility of their new democracies, the uncertainty of civilian command over the military in some countries, and economic vulnerabilities which could yet undermine political and economic advances made to date. Others stress that there is no immediate military threat to Western Europe or indeed to the countries of Central and Eastern Europe. They therefore take the view that there is no urgency to enlarge the Alliance and that the West can afford to opt for a 'wait-and-see' policy.

In addition, many critics are concerned about the costs of enlargement, arguing that even the relatively modest amounts envisaged by the Clinton Administration are an unnecessary burden both on existing members and those states aspiring to join NATO. A further argument focuses upon the internal reorganisation of the Alliance itself; some take the view that the Alliance should concentrate upon improving levels of cooperation between the existing 16 members before considering any enlargement.

Perhaps most important are the two central arguments about the effects of enlargement on Central and Eastern Europe. There is evident concern that Central European countries which are not included in the first group of new members will be consigned to a 'grey area' of possible future Russian influence; indeed, some argue that the trauma of exclusion will suffice to undermine many of the positive political developments which are occurring in those countries and force them into accommodations with Russia which will be to their detriment and affect negatively the long-term stability and security of the continent. The likely impact of enlargement on Russia looms largest in Western concerns. Western critics argue that including new members in the Alliance will antagonise the Russian government to such a degree that a renewed East–West confrontation may result. If this is the case, what are the prospects for avoiding this pitfall?

Russian Hostility

Russian differences with NATO member states over the Alliance's enlargement are undermining significantly the more cooperative relationship which was established after the end of the Cold War. Not that cooperation has ceased completely. The continued implementation of agreed arms control measures, cooperation between Western and Russian troops within IFOR and SFOR, and the presence of Russian military officers at the Alliance's SHAPE headquarters demonstrate the continuing positive elements of the West's relationship with Russia. However, these seem increasingly fragile and vulnerable, notwithstanding the fact that there appear to be no vital differences of national interest among the parties. This is, to a large degree, the result of increasing Russian unease about its relations with the West as the decade has progressed. The Russian decision-making elites believe the West has not been sufficiently sensitive to their country's needs, and that it is exploiting its economic and political advantages to the detriment of Russian development and interests. For some, this is a result of the failure of the European powers to come to a final post-Cold War settlement; Russia has not been included or excluded from the new European order. For Russians, the West's cooperation has been slow, uneven and not effectively institutionalised. They perceived a lack of Western willingness to develop a *genuine* partnership with Russia.

It is in this context of growing concern and mistrust that the Russian policy opposing NATO enlargement has developed. While many Russians are prepared to concede privately that the Alliance does not represent a direct threat to Russia, it is the more general spread of Western influence into Central Europe and its growing ties with Central European military establishments which generate a fundamental unease based in Russian history and current insecurities. The resulting negative Russian attitudes towards enlargement have become a severe test for Western–Russian relations. For Russian decision-makers, enlargement will lead to a marginalisation of their country in European security matters, at the very time when they are pushing for greater Russian involvement in European affairs. They argue that such involvement is not intended to be sinister or overbearing; rather, there is a desire for cooperative participation in decision-making and implementation of European security policy. Many in the West accept in principle the idea of a genuine collaboration, but they remain wary of accepting a possible Russian 'veto' on Alliance decisions and actions. The problem revolves around how to ensure a genuine dialogue and cooperative decision-making while retaining the Alliance's existing ability to take, and implement, its own decisions.

A possible answer to the problem involves establishing a charter between NATO and Russia which will underpin a new, positive, cooperative relationship. While arguments persist about whether the charter should be legally binding, a status for which the Russian government is pressing, a consensus appears to be developing about the substantive issues to be covered: establishing a mechanism for Russian–NATO decision-making in the Alliance's new areas of interest (i.e. excluding collective defence decisions), and formalising regular contacts between decision-makers and military establishments to build the habit of cooperation. While the issues to be covered in such meetings remain to be established, the Russian 'wish list' includes policy and planning, specific security problems, crisis management issues, nuclear non-proliferation including theatre missile defence (TMD), air space control, and the modernisation of former Warsaw Pact militaries. While not necessarily accepting all of these proposals, the West has sought to respond positively in order to allay Russian fears. Negotiations led by the Alliance's Secretary-General have included the idea of creating a NATO–Russia Council which is intended to be not 'yet another talking shop' but a working organisation that can make joint decisions;[5] among recent NATO 'concessions' have been statements assuring Russia that the Alliance has no intention of deploying nuclear weapons on the territories of new member states and strong indications that NATO forces would not be permanently deployed in those states in substantial numbers – although military exercises could involve temporary deployments and small numbers of liaison and staff officers are likely to be permanently stationed in the new member countries.

It remains to be seen whether these and other Western initiatives will reduce Russian resistance to enlargement. This may simply be an unachievable goal, but there is every prospect that an 'agreement to disagree' can be forged while establishing a clear accord setting out the terms of NATO–Russian relations in the future. A failure to reach an agreement could severely damage the prospects for future Western–Russian cooperation: it could result in 'a slide toward a new confrontation, to an undermining of trust between Russia and western countries'.[6]

Overcoming Russian suspicions will be a long-term task extending beyond the envisaged summits of 1997:

> Russians are little impressed with American assurances that it reflects no hostile intentions. They would see their prestige – always uppermost in the Russian mind – and their security interests as adversely affected. They would, of course, have no choice but to accept expansion as a military *fait accompli*. But they would continue to regard it as a rebuff by the West and would likely look elsewhere for guarantees of a secure and hopeful future for themselves.[7]

What substantive form Russian reaction would take remains unclear. However, the prospect of it being negative looms large in Western thinking.

But it is not the only important factor. There is a clearly stated recognition that Central European states also aspire to a 'secure and hopeful future'. For those anticipating an early entry into the Alliance, membership will offer this prospect. However, for those who are 'excluded', the future may seem uncertain and insecure. Will they also 'look elsewhere'?

What about the Rest?

The principal aim of NATO enlargement is to ensure the integration of Central Europe into the hitherto 'Western' political and security system. However, enlargement is not intended to exclude those who do not aspire to membership or those countries not invited to join in July 1997. Every effort is to be made to avoid any redivision of Europe and most analysts take the view that further enlargements of NATO cannot be discounted. This will depend to some degree upon the success of the first enlargement exercise; positive results and anticipated growing Russian awareness that enlargement has not detrimentally affected its interests would make further enlargement easier. However, some observers believe that the enlargement process will be so protracted and controversial that the Alliance will be wary of beginning a second round.

Whatever the outcome, the Partnership for Peace programme is to be developed to constitute a permanent association of states who are not members of the Alliance but which will work closely with NATO. PfP will underpin a pan-European process intended to improve military cooperation between all European states, thus its agenda will extend well beyond preparing states for future membership: a new Euro-Atlantic Partnership Council (EAPC) is to be established to include PfP states in regular direct deliberations with the Alliance.

These NATO intentions have received qualified support in Central Europe. Ukraine is an active PfP partner because it enables Ukrainian armed forces to gain exposure to Western practices and doctrine and to work alongside Western militaries, for example, in the peacekeeping field. More fundamentally, it ensures that Ukraine is not marginalised in Europe while permitting it to retain its current policy of non-alignment and neutrality. However, Ukraine is also seeking a special partnership with the West similar to that being sought by Russia. Furthermore, neutrality appears to be being de-emphasised by Ukrainian spokesmen which may point to an eventual application for Alliance membership. Two key concerns govern these policies: continued concern about future Russian behaviour; and worries about the impact on Ukrainian security interests of being excluded from the Alliance's decision-making processes. Such concerns are commonly expressed by Central European states which do not expect to be included in the first round of new members:

> For Bulgaria, the membership in NATO has no alternative. The Atlantic Partnership Council will certainly occupy its legitimate place in the European Security architecture. All countries, present and future NATO members, as well as those that are unlikely to join the Alliance early or at all should actively participate in

the implementation of this initiative. The APC, however, could not serve as a compensation for the candidates waiting to be invited for accession negotiations. The enhanced partnership and the intensified dialogue should form the framework for an individualised and accelerated preparation for membership.[8]

Similar aspirations certainly exist in the Baltic Republics and all of the former Warsaw Pact states except those of the former Soviet Union. None are comfortable with the alternatives offered through PfP and all accept that the policies of self-reliance, practised for example by Finland and Sweden during the Cold War, are inappropriate for their security needs. Indeed, these two Nordic countries share the concern that they may be sidelined while vital decisions about European security are made within the Alliance.

Meeting these concerns with an enhanced PfP will be a considerable challenge; some urge that more should be done: they note that non-NATO members in Central Europe are increasingly closely linked to the European Union by virtue of their EU membership applications. They take the view that countries in this position should be linked as closely to NATO as to the EU. For example, given the Baltic states' commitments to the Petersberg tasks formulated by the Western European Union, a mechanism should be found to formalise close Baltic linkages with NATO which will inevitably develop, whatever the countries' future membership status.

Whatever the policies adopted on these issues, Alliance difficulties are founded in its efforts to achieve a number of goals simultaneously: enlargement, close cooperation with non-members, and building positive relations with Russian and Ukraine. Success in all three areas is interdependent and essential; failure in one area will adversely affect progress in the others. If achieving these goals dominates the Alliance's short-to-medium term agenda, much else remains which is in need of NATO member states' attention. In addition to repairing the consequences of past European hostilities, the Alliance faces other challenges for which new missions must be undertaken.

3 New Missions

The Unstable Periphery

The southern periphery of Europe is widely perceived to be a region of increasing instability, where military conflicts are likely to occur. Existing crises in the region reinforce this perception: civil war in Algeria, the wars in former Yugoslavia, Albanian unrest, the Arab–Israeli problem, Greek–Turkish relations, and the Cyprus issue. In addition the region is closely associated with increasingly important 'soft' security issues including migration, energy security, and the environment, as well as the problems of the proliferation of weapons of mass destruction and terrorism. These problems are perceived to affect all of Europe and not just its southern states, and many present challenges which are not readily susceptible to effective military response. How has the Alliance responded?

While there is a ready appreciation within the Alliance of these problems, some observers argue that a number of NATO member states are wary of any refocusing of Alliance attention towards 'southern issues'. The central concern of these countries and that of aspiring Central European members remains Eastern Europe. This perception has been reinforced by recent disputes between the United States and France over the future nationality of the military commander of NATO's southern region; French insistence that this should be a European has been firmly rejected by the United States, not least because it is not prepared to place the US Mediterranean-based Sixth Fleet under foreign command. A 'southern issue' has become divisive. Such differences have diverted attention from the low key but none the less important NATO efforts to develop a dialogue with a number of North African and Middle Eastern states. Furthermore, this effort has been overshadowed by the central US role in the Middle East Peace Process, by European Union efforts to increase its involvement in the Process, and by the EU's Barcelona initiative with the Maghreb states. This is unsurprising given the slow progress of the Alliance's multilateral initiative in the region and the relative coolness of Arab states' responses; there is little Arab interest, for example, in the PfP process.

Given the nature of many of the region's problems, some take the view that the European Union should play the major role in bolstering regional security through the provision of aid, increasing trade and the promotion of economic development. However, some issues remain outside its remit; notably proliferation, possible threats to Europeans visiting or working in the region, and peacekeeping. All may be and are dealt with by NATO members at the national level but many perceive a need for an increased multilateral response on these issues which should be coordinated within the Alliance. It remains to be seen whether NATO will indeed increase its interest in the region in the decade ahead. Given the linkages which exist between North African and the Middle Eastern economic failures, political instability and security problems, the case for increased liaison between NATO and the EU on these matters appears to be strong. However, when military force constitutes a key element in any response, the Alliance remains the key institution; this is particularly the case with regards to peacekeeping.

Peacekeeping

While the NATO Alliance's core mission remains the provision of collective defence, to its members it has made an overt commitment to undertake peace support operations on a case-by-case basis. The use of NATO military forces may be undertaken to facilitate conflict prevention, deployments being made to avert a crisis or to monitor a conflict, or to undertake peacekeeping with the intention of containing or moderating an ongoing conflict at the request of and with the support of all protagonists. The Alliance is also ready to conduct humanitarian aid operations to relieve the suffering of populations and to engage in peace enforcement activities during which military means are to be used to restore peace in an area of conflict, either between or within states, without the consent of the protagonists. Lastly, NATO is prepared to become involved in peace building operations, offering post-conflict assistance in reconstruction to help to cement a peace and avoid a return to hostilities.

NATO involvement in such operations is firmly based in its experience in former Yugoslavia with IFOR and SFOR. The Alliance's success to date in preventing a resumption of hostilities and in facilitating considerable reconstruction has demonstrated the positive role it can play. This said, problems have been identified which will affect crucially future Alliance action and deployments. All now recognise and accept the difficulties involved in taking political decisions to deploy Alliance forces in a violent environment; the unwillingness of most member states to accept military casualties in most circumstances, short of a major war to defend vital national interests, has been well documented. While NATO is prepared to undertake peacekeeping it is certain to insist that its mission is clear, and that troops deployed have available to them the full range of military capabilities required to undertake the operation successfully and to minimise possible casualties. Furthermore, military commanders emphasise the need for their early involvement in the crafting of possible peace agreements to ensure that suggested arrangements on the ground are feasible; the dangers of setting unreasonable goals, for example the creation of unprotectable 'protected zones' in Eastern Bosnia, loom large in NATO thinking. The need to plan quickly and effectively to deal with changing international circumstances is a clearly-stated Alliance priority.

Although future Alliance missions will certainly differ from the Yugoslav experience, the lessons learned there dominate NATO thinking. A common doctrine is being established between Alliance members for peace support operations. A key element involves the early establishment of a unity of command within the field of operation. Difficulties experienced in Bosnia are to be avoided in the future: national caveats on the use of forces, whether geographical or functional, will be resisted; all forces are to be under one command and control system, potential conflicts of interest between national contingent commanders and Alliance force commanders are to be avoided with the force commander having the authority to overrule national commanders in a crisis; language training is to be improved to facilitate better integration of NATO and non-NATO forces; and civil–military cooperation is to be enhanced to improve the effectiveness of civilian aspects of peace building.

All recognise that peace enforcement will involve casualties in the future and that the risk of such casualties is high in this type of operation. Generating political support for operations and public acceptance that these are legitimate will therefore be crucial. While the Alliance retains the capability to undertake this type of work, the balancing of collective defence and these new responsibilities during a time of falling budgets will remain problematical. The military implications of planning for these new missions are being examined by the Alliance with a view to enhancing the effectiveness of its future operations.

Reorganising for New Tasks

NATO's missions of collective defence, crisis management and the projection of stability in Europe affect critically the conduct of the Alliance's military planning. The Alliance is already organising to undertake all three tasks, recognising that it is incorrect to take the view that organising for future collective defence needs will provide the capabilities to fulfil other roles. The Alliance is adapting both its internal structures and its external policies and activities to meet these new needs. Internally, the Alliance command structures are being reviewed, Combined Joint Task Forces (CJTFs) developed and established, and a European security and defence identity given substance.

Defence planning for collective defence is being adapted to meet regional contingencies rather than a mass attack from the East; up to twenty-five joint operations are under consideration. The ending of East–West confrontation and the lack of threats at the borders of Alliance members mean that greater time to prepare to meet a threat will be available. Some further adaptation of collective defence planning will be required as new members join the Alliance.

The Alliance's commitment to undertake peacekeeping is on a case-by-case basis and will only occur with UN or OSCE mandates for the foreseeable future. In such cases it is necessary to plan for commitments of up to five years on the understanding that objectives will be long term. These need to be clearly defined; an exit strategy will be established at the beginning of an operation with a view to identifying clearly when an operation has been successfully achieved or if it has become untenable or unattainable. The need to cooperate with non-Alliance members, for example PfP partners, in undertaking peace operations has been identified; it is recognised that these countries need to be involved in the planning of an operation at as early a stage as possible. Drawing on experiences in former Yugoslavia, liaison with PfP partners will be strengthened through the CJTF process.

As part of the Alliance's internal adaptation, command structures are being reorganised and the number of headquarters is being reduced from sixty-five to approximately twenty-five and layers of command are being cut. Key priorities include: improving the integration of geographical and functional commands; integrating the CJTFs into the overall command structure; and introducing modern technologies to reduce manpower. Establishing the location of the remaining headquarters and the nationality of their commanders has proved to be problematical. However, increased European representation in the chain of command is certain and, through the CJTF arrangements, European action without US involvement can now be undertaken under arrangements agreed with the Western European Union.

Planning and reorganisation are also affected by the external policies of enlargement and Partnership for Peace. The intake of new members requires the Alliance to plan to ensure that security guarantees given to them are genuine and viable. An intensified dialogue with potential members is already under way. Regarding PfP, many new initiatives are to be undertaken to try to reduce differences between members and non-members; an expanded direct PfP partner involvement in non-Article five defence planning is anticipated. The partnership coordination cell at SHAPE military headquarters in Mons is to be reinforced. An additional priority is to improve the interoperability of Alliance and non-Alliance members' armed forces.

This reorganisation of the Alliance's work will enhance its ability to meet the demands of a more broadly-defined range of tasks. The success of these efforts will depend upon: clarity of Alliance missions and objectives and agreement that these will not be changed as an operation progresses; the creation of an effective engagement structure with PfP partners; enhancing military effectiveness by ensuring unity of command and freedom to decide and take action when appropriate; the provision of sufficient resources; and timely political guidance. This last requirement depends to a large degree on the continued internal cohesion of the Alliance and the positive involvement of all its members in decision-making; the maintenance of shared US and European interests and views will be essential.

4 Europeans and Americans – Leadership and Partnership

The United States is the traditional leader of 'the West' following the prolonged period of Cold War. US involvement in Europe was based firmly in US national interests and its security interests in the region were pursued effectively through NATO. The political consensus in Washington continues to support this position. However, to some the nature of US leadership appears to be changing. There is concern about perceived increasing US unilateralism; a propensity to act in US national interests and in accord with US views without consulting with Allies, and, at worst, acting in the expectation that they will fall in line with US policy whatever their misgivings. Others place a different interpretation on recent American actions. They emphasise the United States' position as a first among equals which is seeking partnership with friendly states, not least with Europeans, to solve international problems. Continued US strength is evident: its large and successful economy, military prowess and associated technological superiority. The lack of pressure for further US defence cuts, its capacity to generally speak with one voice on foreign policy, and the fact that it is well trusted by Europeans all ensure a continued central role for the United States in European affairs. However, while the arguments associated with relative US economic decline may have been overstated, a US recognition persists that other states are increasingly powerful economic actors and that cooperation with them cannot but facilitate problem solving. A tension between unilateralism and international cooperation is likely to persist within US decision-making structures. However, it seems certain in the European region at least that US cooperation with Europeans on security issues is assured.

What can the Europeans bring to this collaborative process? The EU's foreign policy limitations are well known, not least those demonstrated by the failure of the EU to cope effectively with the crisis in the former Yugoslavia. Can Europe develop a capacity to build a new and more genuinely cooperative transatlantic relationship on security matters? While the desire to develop a collective European security arrangement has been a long-term European aspiration, it has never achieved reality. Can the envisaged European Security and Defence Identity (ESDI) contribute to the realisation of such aspirations or is a more prosaic outcome likely?

Given recent levels of progress at the EU inter-governmental conference, it appears to be unlikely that a meaningful ESDI will develop within the European Union itself; members find it difficult enough to agree on routine matters much less those concerning national security and defence issues. Furthermore, failures in Bosnia and the relative success of ad hoc arrangements, notably those developed with the cooperation of NATO, severely dented the aspirations of those seeking a more meaningful security and defence dimension within the European Union. More broadly, the fact that total European military expenditure is only half that of the United States points towards a widening 'capability gap'; US expenditure of 17 per cent of its defence budget on information technologies and its total expenditure of 3.5 per cent of GDP on defence dwarf the efforts of individual European countries.

Nevertheless, European military and defence efforts are changing and not simply in the sense that they are being reduced. Their peacekeeping role is increasingly to the fore; training versatile soldiers to undertake new missions and their traditional war fighting role is already under way. Most European governments appear to accept the view that future conflicts in Europe are likely to be within states and, therefore, difficult to solve using 'high tech', war fighting techniques which are the United States military's 'strong suit'. European forces, properly prepared, will be well placed to undertake peacekeeping in the region, providing the political will to intervene exists.

In most foreseeable circumstances Europeans will not act alone or indeed have to act alone. Most conflicts will inevitably draw the United States in, however unwillingly: European conflicts with Russia or with the CIS, Greek/Turkish war, wars in the Balkans. An 'exclusive' European role seems most likely in the area of humanitarian intervention although even here ad hoc arrangements involving 'willing' countries appear to be most likely. The anticipated lack of universal involvement in such efforts reflects the lack of a common European view on foreign and defence policy issues. A genuine Common Foreign and Security Policy (CFSP) remains unlikely while states have different interests in and different views of international issues.

How much does this matter? Defence is not likely to be a priority for Europeans in the decade ahead; the European Union will concentrate on enlargement and economic development as will non-members, most of which are seeking closer association with the EU. These efforts will of themselves contribute to regional security. NATO it seems, will be left to deal with traditional 'hard' security problems. It remains to be seen whether this process will satisfy the interests and aspirations of the United States or indeed of some Europeans; those with aspirations to increase European attention to defence and security issues are already actively promoting this, not least through plans to enhance the credibility of the Western European Union (WEU). Many of those promoting the WEU do so in the fear that a lack of progress in developing ESDI will erode US interest in Europe over time as the problems of East Asia loom larger within the American foreign policy-making elite.

Few doubt that Europe could undertake military action alone or that it has sufficient military capability; both IFOR and SFOR involve a significant European presence. Military deployments in Albania in mid-April 1997 also demonstrated European capabilities. Problems arise, however, on the question of political will and the difficulties of reaching a consensus between European states. There is no evident source of leadership from within Europe on defence and security matters; it is unclear whether leadership from, for example, the United Kingdom, France or Germany would be welcome, not least to smaller European states already rankled by, for example, the perceived dominance of larger states in the European Union. Furthermore, differing sensitivity to casualties may affect states' decisions about a willingness to deploy their troops. While common structures can help to facilitate common interests and views, as NATO has achieved in the past, it is unclear whether there is a need for an *exclusively* European effort in this direction.

Nevertheless, there is an apparent increasing interest in deepening European collaboration, not necessarily excluding the United States; this is reflected in, for example, the greater French and Spanish involvement in NATO, increasing levels of collaboration on defence procurement, and close bilateral and multilateral military collaboration between European states. Importantly, the United States no longer appears to be concerned about such developments, having abandoned the belief that they could lead to the US being excluded from European security deliberations. However, the institutional relationship between NATO and the EU remains problematical for some; a closer link has failed to emerge. Some states oppose such a linkage while others seem more enthusiastic about an increased EU role. However, encouragingly, while progress at the institutional level has sometimes appeared to be slothful, decision-makers have proved to be flexible when dealing with genuine problems, not least in former Yugoslavia. The problem remains however, that the taking of decisions in these circumstances may be painfully slow.

For those who envisage an increased European role on security issues in the medium term, the creation of CJTFs within NATO and their availability for European use via the WEU represents a significant step forward. They point to the slow but discernible emergence in European states of deeper, common interests. This process is reflected in the regular day-to-day contacts of European officials and politicians across a range of issues; European cooperation on the export of technologies relevant to the proliferation of weapons of mass destruction; strengthening bilateral ties on military matters, notably between France and Germany and France and the UK; and the emergence of the Eurocorps and other 'European' military formations. Some argue that there is an immediate need for these successes to be reinforced to a degree which will enable Europe to act independently if US and European interests differ significantly. For some indeed, in the near term certainly a minority, Europe has to have a separate arrangement to work alone outside NATO.

The existing consensus strongly rejects this idea on the grounds that it could compromise existing beneficial transatlantic links and undermine NATO. Many point to the lack of European enthusiasm to commit resources to enable unilateral European action in cases where the United States actively opposes a given European policy. This said, if the United States is genuinely seeking a global partner for the 21st century such a partner will need to posses both the will and capacity to act in a robust manner. In the near term, it seems certain that an evolution of European military capability will occur within the NATO framework and that 'Euroforces' will be dedicated to NATO in the first instance but also usable on a case-by-case basis if the United States declines to act in a given situation. For many the Western European Union (WEU) will provide the forum through which such operations may be conducted.

NATO and the WEU have both become increasingly involved in crisis prevention since the end of the Cold War. Both institutions are enlarging, both have outreach programmes and both are seeking to deepen levels of cooperation between existing members. Furthermore, both have extended their remit beyond collective defence to security building and a promotion of stability and mutual trust in Eastern Europe and Europe as a whole. Both are increasingly political organisations although this has always been the case to some degree. Should NATO concentrate on enforcement missions and leave crisis management and prevention, peacekeeping and related tasks to the WEU? Some note that the CJTF arrangement could permit such a division of labour to occur.

Such a prospect seems unlikely. WEU involvement with collective defence issues will continue but not result in its evolution as an alternative to NATO; nor does it seem likely to become linked more closely to the European Union. The WEU will probably retain links with both the EU and NATO and develop as an organisation which is a useful instrument for undertaking action by ad hoc groups of states willing to act in a given situation. Many doubt that it will achieve a significance much greater that in its recent historical past. For example, there is little doubt that WEU members continue to look to NATO for their collective defence and East Europeans aspiring to membership take the same view; there is agreement that WEU members must be NATO members given both organisations' collective defence commitments. It is possible that WEU could abandon its collective defence commitment and concentrate on peacekeeping, etc. – this would permit its rapid enlargement as members would not automatically look to NATO for collective defence. This idea has not been well received in WEU corridors and it runs counter to the desires of those arguing for an 'exclusive' European security and defence entity.

Some observers question the utility of and need to maintain the WEU. They note that NATO can survive and fulfil its missions alone and that the WEU is not necessary for this to occur. They note that Eastern Europe is interested in NATO membership and in acquiring a link with the United States rather than any linkage with the Western European Union. They stress that while NATO has achieved a great deal in recent years, and indeed has promoted the WEU as an effective organisation, not least through the CJTF arrangement, little of importance has actually emerged from WEU deliberations and it is achieving little of practical utility within Europe. They argue that while the institution has been useful in the past, simple inertia should not be permitted to underpin its continued existence. Given the organisation's current low resource base and the confusions which appear to exist about its role, the WEU is likely to be increasingly marginalised in the debate about Europe's future security. The emergence of a robust European Common Foreign and Security Policy could change this situation, particularly if an agreement were to be made that the WEU would carry out operations at the request of the EU. The current prospects for this are at best dubious.

Debates on these issues appear, at best, esoteric to most Europeans and North Americans. They may come to question the wisdom of supporting a plethora of international institutions to deal with security problems which seem to be less menacing than those of the recent past. Is there a danger that public opinion may be apathetic or indeed disillusioned about these issues? Could complacency about the international situation combined with annoyance about the apparent competitive aspirations of multilateral institutions adversely affect public support for national defence efforts and the NATO Alliance itself?

Public Attitudes

The NATO Alliance appears to have overcome reservations about its continued utility and existence immediately after the end of the Cold War. Polls in the United States in early 1997 indicated that 61 per cent of those interviewed supported maintaining NATO. Similar polls in the Autumn of 1996 put support for NATO at 50–70 per cent in Britain, France, Italy and Germany; confidence in NATO was registered by between 60 and almost 80 per cent of Europeans interviewed, Spain being the one exception, with approximately 40 per cent support. There is every prospect that these views will be continued given continued US commitment to involvement in Europe, the success of operations in former Yugoslavia, and the deeper integration of France and Spain within the Alliance.

The adoption of new Alliance roles appears not to have affected public support; in effect the Alliance's continued presence and its enlargement are now endorsed by Western publics, less as an Alliance against a significant threat and more as a venture in collective security management for Europe. Polls indicate considerable support for NATO enlargement: between 54 and 74 per cent in the United Kingdom between 1993 and 1996; between 54 and 73 per cent in France during the same years; between 47 and 65 per cent in Germany; between 48 and 65 per cent in Italy; and between 45 and 65 per cent in the United States. However, while support is broad based it is not deeply rooted. Many respondents accept that they are ill informed about the issues and support appears to decline when the costs of enlargement are made clear.

Similarly, support is reduced when possible risks are mentioned and the commitment to support new members is clarified.

The nature of public support may become important if an organised campaign against enlargement develops. Under the impact of such a campaign, public attitudes may yet change in a number of countries. For example, US neo-isolationist tendencies could revive if Americans take the view that European states should be able to make adequate arrangements to maintain their own security. Furthermore, in the medium term pressure may revive for further reductions in military expenditure as pressure on health care, education and other domestic priorities intensifies.

To counter such possible negative developments, the Alliance and its member states will need actively to emphasise NATO's positive role as a regional manager and promoter of cooperation; publics and legislators must be aware that fulfilling this task is in their countries' national interests. While the costs of enlargement could be phased over a lengthy period, it is probably essential that the reality of such costs and indeed the risks attendant upon NATO membership should be made clear. The case must be put that such costs and risks are acceptable given the benefits of stability and security which accrue from the Alliance and its enlargement. Furthermore it must be made clear that any decision to abandon the enlargement could have disastrous effects in Central Europe and indeed for the Alliance itself.

It is encouraging to know that most critics of enlargement accept that the process cannot now be abandoned. Many are now focusing rather on how enlargement can be carried through without undermining the Alliance's ability to carry out its key functions: 'rapid, secure and frank consultations among like-minded nations about critical international issues; effective crisis management; a credible system of deterrence, under an effective integrated military command'.[9] Suggestions include delaying the new NATO/Russia Council until ratification of enlargement is completed; efforts to ensure that Russia stops its agitation against NATO enlargement and explicitly accepts all its frontier with neighbouring states; a formal Alliance declaration reaffirming its pre-eminence as the forum to which allies owe their most fundamental obligations; and a US Senate reaffirmation of the American belief in the importance of a democratic transatlantic community.[10]

While there are concerns about ratification of any enlargement agreement, this will probably occur given existing bi-partisan support for the policy in the United States and in other member countries. However, this will require on overt effort by the governments to orchestrate effectively the ratification process and to explain clearly the benefits which will accrue to Alliance members and populations as a result. It is likely that such concerted efforts will be made.

In the longer term, maintaining support for the Alliance may remain problematical. Threats to Alliance members will hopefully remain distant and abstract. An increasingly benign Russia, decreasing levels of disorder in Eastern Europe, and looked-for improvements in the human rights arena in the region may diminish the importance of perceived risks. Furthermore if military interventions by NATO are required, how they are conducted, their cost, and casualty levels will all affect critically the support for such operations and the NATO role therein. Thus, an increasingly benign and peaceful Europe may reduce public concern with and support for NATO; not least US interest in European security issues would decline, although economic and other links are likely to remain as strong as ever. However, these are concerns for the medium-to-long term and they are unlikely to disrupt the enlargement process and the Alliance's consolidation as the principal security institution in Europe for the beginning of the 21st century.

5 Conclusions

The NATO Alliance continues to play a central role in the maintenance of stability and security in Europe. It ensures that the United States plays a positive role in Europe and that its European members maintain traditions of cooperation established in the past half century; as a consequence war between the nations of Western Europe is no longer conceivable. While the Alliance continues to provide for the collective defence of its members, it is taking on new responsibilities as the century draws towards a close: responsibility for the security and stability of Central Europe; helping Russia to succeed as a democratic state and facilitating its integration into the international political system; and the organisation and conduct of peacekeeping operations.

To achieve these tasks differentiated levels of cooperation and integration will be required. The anticipated enlargement of the Alliance will not include all European states, and levels of cooperation will be affected by the wishes and policies of both the Alliance and non-member states. Enlargement itself is intended to underpin a new stable order in Europe based on mutual cooperation. It will complete the multilateral integration of Germany into Europe and, as such, represents the conclusion of the post-World War II peace. For potential new NATO members, clear pre-conditions for membership have been identified: democratic control of the military; the development of democratic polities; stable and proper relations with neighbouring countries; and modernisation and improvement of military capabilities to undertake relevant NATO missions. The anticipated announcement in July 1997 of the first group of countries which are to be invited to join the Alliance will include states which have successfully met these requirements.

However, of equal importance are future relations between NATO and European states not included in this 'enlargement group'. Cooperation with these countries is essential to the future stability of the region. Much emphasis is placed on the Partnership for Peace process (PfP), through which military contacts and cooperation are being developed between the Alliance and partner countries. The long-term goal is to establish close relationships which mirror those existing within the Alliance itself, albeit excluding the collective defence commitments of Alliance membership. PfP provides a vehicle through which different states may achieve different objectives. For the Poles it has been a means through which the country could prepare for full Alliance membership. In contrast, Swedes and Finns continue to emphasise the importance of self-reliance in their defence arrangements although their historical neutrality has been abandoned (concerns exist in these countries that they will be sidelined from security decision-making within the Alliance and the prospect of future applications for full membership cannot be discounted). In the Ukraine PfP is regarded as a means to develop experience of and cooperation with the Alliance and to avoid the marginalisation of Ukraine in security matters. A 'special' partnership between Ukraine and NATO is sought in the medium term, although the exact nature of this partnership has yet to be fully worked out.

NATO enlargement and its new mission of projecting security in Central Europe will change the security concerns of both Europeans and North Americans. While the United States' involvement in these changes demonstrates clearly its continued commitment to engagement, in Europe, it also reflects a growing concern that the United States should secure a global partner for the 21st century. Thus, while keeping the transatlantic link strong will enable positive progress to occur in Central Europe and in US–European–Russian relations, it may also underpin the emergence of a new 'balanced relationship' between equals which will enable positive US–European action across a range of international political, economic and security issues. Such a development will require consideration of three key questions: the role of the Alliance beyond Europe and its immediate periphery; the development of proactive policies to anticipate crises rather than to manage them; and the forging of a regular and positive linkage between NATO and the European Union.

Developing positive responses on these issues will be dependent upon the effective reorganisation of NATO to fulfil a wide range of roles extending beyond its traditional concern with collective defence. These new roles will include conflict prevention, crisis management, humanitarian assistance, peacekeeping and peace enforcement. The internal reorganisation needed to undertake such tasks is already well under way. Thus, for example, Combined Joint Task Forces have been established to run operations effectively. CJTFs are being designed to facilitate cooperation with non-Alliance members in undertaking these tasks. Other priorities have included the improvement of intelligence capabilities to enable the Alliance better to anticipate any possible future crisis. Procedures have been developed to ensure the unity of command during operations and the Alliance's command structures have been reorganised to maximise efficient use of resources. Work is under way to improve training and planning of operations, drawing, not least, on the lessons learned from the IFOR operation in former Yugoslavia. These changes will enable the Alliance to undertake its new missions effectively given timely political guidance, clarity of mission and objectives, an effective engagement structure with PfP partners, and adequate resources.

Provision of such resources is dependent upon continued legislative and public support in NATO member countries. Recent polls indicate high levels of support for the Alliance and its enlargement, which is regarded as a means to develop cooperation and to reduce risk. However, support is not 'deep' and the costs and risks involved are not fully understood by the general public. An organised campaign against enlargement may change attitudes. However, current evidence indicates that support for the Alliance's new regional management role is sufficiently strong in the United States Congress and in the legislatures of other member states to ensure the ratification of applications for membership. Given this commitment, it seems likely that enlargement will proceed, notwithstanding the reservations of some Western commentators.

These derive principally from an awareness of the strongly negative reaction of the Russian political elite to the proposed enlargement. To some observers, enlargement is expected to generate such a negative Russian reaction that genuine cooperative security arrangements in Europe will become impossible and a negative redivision of the continent will occur. Advocates of enlargement regard this view as unduly pessimistic. They recognise current Russian criticisms of the Alliance; Russian fears are based upon remnants of the Cold War antagonism towards the Alliance, awareness of Central European hostilities towards Russia, feelings of national weakness, perceived lack of consultation by NATO on security issues, and feelings that the West has not helped Russia sufficiently to deal with its post-Soviet economic and political problems. However, while opposing enlargement, Russian officials continue to be willing to discuss developing a positive relationship with the Alliance, including the negotiation of a legally-binding Charter to underpin NATO–Russian relations in the decade ahead. The exact nature of this Charter relationship remains to be established; for example, Russian insistence that Russia be involved in policy decisions taken by NATO on security issues has received a cool response. Alliance members insist on their right to take their own decisions and reject the possibility of a Russian 'veto'. Whether a consultative arrangement acceptable to both can be developed remains to be seen. A key difficulty arises from an apparent unwillingness on the part of the Russian leadership to adapt its attitudes towards security issues; they continue to emphasise balance of power and geopolitical considerations, and hard-core defence issues rather than the cooperation and confidence-building tenets which underpin NATO's outreach and PfP activities.

Will possible Russian intransigence divert the Alliance from its existing policies? This seems unlikely given NATO's consensus in favour of enlargement. There is some concern, although little immediate evidence, that differences between the United States and Europeans may adversely affect the Alliance's internal cohesion. Such a possibility seems unlikely in the near term given the efforts which are under way to develop a European security identity within the Alliance framework. Indeed, prospects for the success of this enterprise have been improved by a general European acceptance that the EU is unlikely to develop an active security policy in the near term. While European defence cooperation is improving at the bilateral level, notably between France, Germany and the United Kingdom, there is no broad-based European consensus on the EU's Common Foreign and Security Policy. Furthermore, European military expenditure is only half that of the United States; and Europeans lack key military means, notably intelligence gathering and force projection capabilities, to play a truly global role. It is also difficult to envisage European states having to act without US assistance; for the foreseeable future, the United States is likely to be actively involved in solving European security problems and there are few scenarios in which US support would be withheld and an exclusively European mission undertaken.

Recent French and Spanish initiatives within NATO and the Alliance's anticipated enlargement reflect a broad-based European recognition that NATO is the key European security institution. The European Union is likely to concentrate on other issues, which may have a security dimension, for example the Barcelona process in the Maghreb countries, but it will not seek to develop independent military capabilities to match those organised within the NATO structure.

This is not to say that better liaison between the two institutions could not be achieved. For some, the Western European Union offers one possible means of facilitating such collaboration. Its taking up of new roles under the Petersberg declaration, increasing cooperation with NATO, and access to CJTFs and NATO assets point towards a positive future. However, WEU has to become yet more credible and to this end improve the quality of its military advice, its political decision-making processes and develop further cooperative links with NATO and the EU. Whether it should remain autonomous or be incorporated in the EU remains subject to debate; however at a minimum it should be able to respond positively to EU requests to take on military operations in support of EU foreign policy objectives. For this to occur the difficulties associated with the differing memberships of NATO, EU and WEU need to be resolved.

Change in Europe will dominate NATO and other European institutions' attention in the near term. However it is important that developments at Europe's periphery be monitored while these changes are occurring. Problems in the Maghreb, Middle East and eastern Mediterranean appear to be growing more acute; relations between Greece and Turkey, the Cyprus issue and the Algerian civil war are but three examples of areas of high tension which could rapidly generate crises. It is important that focusing on efforts to facilitate internal reform and greater European stability should not result in a lack of attention to these issues. While many are not susceptible to military solutions, being based in social and economic ills, it is important that interested and relevant organisations should collaborate effectively in meeting different dimensions of these problems. There is a need to avoid overemphasis upon solving the receding problems of East–West confrontation while the problems of the future, for all Europeans including Russia, may lie to the south.

Notes

1. See for example, Thomas L. Friedman, 'NATO or Tomato?' *The New York Times*, 22 January 1997.

2. For an analysis of US public and Congressional opinion see, Steven Kull, 'The American Public, Congress and NATO Enlargement, Is there Sufficient Public Support?' and Jeremy D. Rosner, 'Will Congress Back Admitting New Members?', in *NATO Review*, No. 1, January 1997, Volume 45, pp. 9–14.

3. See Ronald D. Asmus and F. Stephen Larrabee, 'NATO and the Have-Nots Reassurance after Enlargement', *Foreign Affairs*, November/December 1996, pp. 13–20.

4. 'The Evolution of the Trans-Atlantic Partnership', *Ditchley Paper* 96/13, p. 2.

5. Michael Evans, 'NATO Proposes New Security Forum to Placate Russia', *The Times*, London, 10 February 1997, p. 14.

6. President Boris Yeltsin, in 'Yeltsin Turns up Heat', *International Herald Tribune,* 17 March 1997, p. 8.

7. George F. Kennan, 'NATO Expansion would be a Fateful Blunder', *International Herald Tribune,* 6 February 1997.

8. 'Bulgaria's Accession to the North Atlantic Alliance', Position Paper of the Bulgarian Government, Press Release of the Embassy of the Republic of Bulgaria, March 1997.

9. Henry Kissinger, 'New NATO Chips at Keystone of US Policy', *Daily Telegraph*, London, 11 April 1997, p. 18.

10. See ibid.

4

Future Western Military Intervention

Report based on Wilton Park Conference 493: 3–7 March 1997 on 'Western Military Intervention in the Developing World: Why, When, How and Where?'

Richard Latter

1 Introduction

The end of the Cold War and the lessons of the wars in former Yugoslavia and the Gulf have generated a fundamental review of future military requirements by Western states. As the possibility of a major military clash in Central Europe has been consigned to history, other risks and concerns have begun to emerge for which military responses may be required: humanitarian assistance, peacekeeping and peace enforcement, and counterproliferation. Nevertheless the key military responsibility for the defence of a country's territory, people and interests remains. What should be the balance between new and old responsibilities and will this result in a fundamental change in military requirements as the new century approaches?

Some effects of changing circumstances are already clear, notably in Western military expenditure. For example, the defence budget of the United States has declined by some 40 per cent since its Cold War peak. Requested funds for financial year 1997 have decreased by $9 billion from the FY 1996 authorisation.[1] Defence cuts in Western European countries have been even deeper. Paradoxically, in the post-Cold War world many foresee a greater military role in policing the 'new world disorder': many would agree with the view that 'barring a fundamental alteration in the character of the post Cold War environment, the international community will continue to mount multi-national peace operations in which ultimate success requires dealing effectively with the public security function'.[2] Such operations were not unknown in the Cold War period but they are likely to occur more frequently and many argue that their nature is changing. For example, if military deployments continue over a period of time, military intervention forces may become increasingly involved in performing law enforcement tasks in order to ensure the success of their missions. Many armies have not been trained for this work and more attention needs to be given to combined military and civilian missions in future.[3]

These changes in the military's role are taking place during a period of rapid technological progress and change. The anticipated revolution in military affairs (RMA) generates both opportunities and problems; deciding which military systems will be required for a broader range of missions is complicated and establishing priorities may be difficult. In war the penalties for errors may be catastrophic and although errors in peacetime may be less dramatic they remain costly and disruptive.[4] Indeed, undertaking more peacekeeping and peace enforcement missions, with the attendant risk of casualties, places a higher premium on making correct procurement decisions even in peacetime. Furthermore, appropriate military education and training will be essential to ensure that new missions are effective. The skills required for peacekeeping differ, for example, from those necessary in combat. Greater emphasis will be required on the 'softer' aspects of military science – resource management, civilian control, human rights – while ensuring that the 'harder' technical war fighting skills are maintained.[5] At a more fundamental level the impact of technology may change the very nature of warfare and hence the role of military forces:

> Expect to see much more intensive use of deception, stealth and redundancy as well as much smaller and stealthier platforms in order to neutralise the impact of highly accurate PGMs [Precision Guided Munitions]. Taken in aggregate, these changes call for fundamentally different approaches to the design and development of weapons systems, which, in turn, will inevitably lead to basic changes in strategy, tactics and doctrine.[6]

These changes are occurring at a time when some perceive a lack of consensus among or within Western states, notably those who are members of the NATO Alliance, concerning the missions that they and the Alliance should fulfil in the years ahead. However much work has been undertaken within NATO to clarify its missions. NATO aims include accommodating new members into the Alliance, developing a constructive relationship with Russia, accommodating European aspirations to develop a European pillar in NATO, involving France on a regular basis, keeping the United States interested and involved in Europe, preserving habits of military cooperation, promoting peace through developing cooperative military relations with non-NATO countries, and restoring peace.[7] As a result the means through which NATO states' military establishments cooperate with each other is undergoing a fundamental reorganisation; the development of Combined Joint Task Forces (CJTFs) is an example. CJTFs will also influence their relations with non-NATO military establishments. The development of the Partnership for Peace (PfP) programmes is similarly affecting military-to-military contacts between states.

NATO's changing focus is generating many practical questions, for example: whether the best preparation and starting point for military personnel being deployed on peace operations is to train for war with normal equipment; how to arrange the provision for transit and base facilities for such operations; assessing the impact of national law upon deployment and operational terms of reference; recognising the importance of communication obstacles caused by the lack of language skills and proper equipment; meeting financial costs; and providing for proper training and exercises.[8]

It is the hope that CJTFs will give NATO's military forces 'mobility and flexibility and ... make them better suited for crisis response across a spectrum of new peacetime operations'.[9] CJTF is

> a multinational, multiservice, task-tailored force consisting of NATO and possibly non-NATO forces capable of rapid deployment to conduct limited duration peace operations beyond alliance borders, under the control of either NATO's integrated military structure or the Western European Union (WEU).[10]

Making CJTF work will be difficult, for example harmonising national doctrines on techniques such as task-force deployment; defining the linkages between commands; and harmonising airspace control and the use of technologies. Divisions of labour between various commands, the interoperability of national NATO and WEU communications and intelligence systems, the nature of training and exercises, and assessment of deployment all need to be considered.[11]

At the heart of these new missions is the need to develop a capability to respond rapidly to the unexpected: 'Rapid reaction' is therefore a key requirement for Western militaries. For this to be developed three main constraints need to be overcome: political, planning and preparation, and identifying the optimum force package. Thus, if deployment is contemplated, it is necessary to clarify what policy objective it is intended to achieve; under whose auspices it is to be conducted; what constraints are to be placed on military operations; and how it is to be paid for. Planning and preparation are needed to ensure the adequate translation of policy aims into concepts of operations and force structures. After inserting initial force elements into the theatre of operations as quickly as possible, it is necessary to ensure that follow-up forces arrive with sufficient speed and strength to avoid the potential liberators becoming hostages. Once the planning processes identify the optimum force package – which will be unique to each operation – the various component units and individuals will need to be identified and placed on notice. Adequate training and resources must be made available to ensure that these problems are overcome.[12]

Considerable efforts are already under way in Western capitals and within the NATO alliance to understand these issues and to develop appropriate responses. Much has been achieved and appropriately trained, flexible armed forces will certainly evolve in the decade ahead. Nevertheless, it can be anticipated that new threats and risks will emerge which have, thus far, been unforeseen or which do not currently hold centre stage in political and military thinking. For example, the problems associated with the proliferation of weapons of mass destruction, while acknowledged in European and North American capitals, are regarded differently on each side of the Atlantic. The United States' counterproliferation initiative reflects the high priority which the issue holds for US military and political leaders; Europeans appear to be more sanguine about the problem, their interest in and devotion of resources to the issue being relatively muted. An intensification of military-to-military contacts on this question can be anticipated.

The re-configuration of Western military structures and the anticipated changes in their future role leaves open the question of where and in what circumstances intervention should actually be undertaken. In some countries and in some circumstances, for example when offering humanitarian assistance, such intervention would be welcome; although experience in Somalia showed how rapidly such a welcome could be withdrawn. When undertaken with the consent of local parties, peacekeeping operations of the 'traditional' type appear to pose few difficulties; however, if the need to use limited force arises this will require fine judgements by military leaderships and formations on the ground. Military activity will inevitably be complicated by the demands of Western democratic societies, which many believe to be increasingly averse to military casualties, particularly if the cause for which troops have been deployed is not firmly supported by public opinion. In such circumstances the role of the media and of national legislatures becomes critical, adding the further burden of effective public relations to the increasing list of developing military 'responsibilities'.

Both the Western media and publics remain sensitive about the use of military force; the justification for an intervention is likely to remain a serious issue, not least in the United States which continues to play its traditional 'leadership' role in the West. The reaction of 'targeted' countries will be central to public perceptions; short of all-out warfare in the national interest, where mobilisation of public opinion continues to be likely, lower levels of military engagement and associated complicated military decisions are likely to take place against a background of public uncertainty. Achieving cooperation between those intervening and those receiving Western assistance will help to maintain public support.

Intervention by Western forces will always be required to pass the tests of prudence and legitimacy; for Western publics intervention must be perceived to be 'just'. Failure to meet these criteria would undermine essential public support for Western military institutions. How far is this an achievable goal?

2 Justice, Warfighting and Conflict

War and Justice

For democracies to prosecute war effectively or indeed to deploy peacekeeping forces for prolonged periods, at least the tacit and in most circumstances the overt support of their populations is essential. Public hostility can severely affect a democratic state's capacity to undertake military operations; notable examples including, for example, the Vietnam War and more recently the perceived failure of Dutch peacekeepers to protect safe havens in Bosnia. Among decision makers and publics alike there appears to be a general acceptance that war should only be undertaken if there is a genuine need, if peaceful means have been tried first and failed, if the amount of force used is proper and proportionate, and if the innocent are not targeted deliberately.[13] There is a Western consensus that intervention by Western militaries must be sanctioned by the United Nations and justified in terms of relevant UN articles. In this context, it is worth noting that the UN outlaws war but recognises the right of states to national self defence and to make collective defence arrangements. Western views on the role of their militaries are generally consistent with this position; Western military action must therefore be legal.

There is some concern that increases in Western military power, notably in the United States, and the development of high technology weapon systems may make the undertaking of military operations more acceptable, not least because Western forces will experience lower casualties. However, Western publics appear to be increasingly concerned about even low levels of casualties, particularly in circumstances where the presence of national forces is controversial or not widely supported. 'Casualty aversion' will remain a central concern for decision makers considering possible military deployments. The generally-pervading view that deterrence, crisis management and conflict avoidance are preferable to military engagement seems likely to persist.

For decision makers, justice and morality represent only two of the factors involved in making deployment decisions; politics and national interest remain important. However, experiences in former Yugoslavia have tempered any enthusiasm which existed for intervention among both Western publics and politicians. Only the strongest of threats to vital interests seem likely to prompt a military action in future where high casualties are likely; humanitarian operations and low risk/low casualty operations are likely to continue. The oft-noted truism that democracies seldom if ever go to war with each other reflects this lack of enthusiasm and a recognition that warfare is not a legitimate means to solve differences between democratic states.

Difficulties arise with non-Western states or groups which do not accept this view and are prepared to use military means in conflicts with the West or with each other. Decisions about possible Western military responses are inevitably more complicated in these circumstances. However, when taking decisions elites cannot ignore Western publics, or they can do so for only a short period of time; decision makers need to win popular support for their actions and inevitably Western media play a crucial role in this process.

The Role of the Media

Can the media so influence national populations that support for government policy is assured; can the media act as a channel through which popular opinion and emotional reactions can force governments to act? Do the views of the media itself, notably of reporters and editors, affect directly government decision taking? The very multiplicity of media outlets in Western democratic societies appears effectively to preclude blanket media support for government action, particularly if such action is unpopular, ill-judged or carried through ineffectively. In such situations criticisms will inevitably be voiced. Similarly, in most circumstances the media is unlikely to force government action, particularly where governments have already assumed a clear position, developed a policy and thought through its likely implications. Only where there is a policy vacuum can media influence be expected to be significant. Even then, while the images and emotions generated by television coverage can sway public opinion and thereby influence governments, the effect of such images appears to be diminishing or subject to increasing constraints. For example, public reaction to television coverage of the disasters in the Great Lakes region of Africa has been relatively muted.

The effects of media coverage are linked to the nature of the conflict being reported. If the West is directly threatened, media support for government policy appears likely to be assured and persistent. If circumstances are more ambiguous, media views are likely to vary and related issues will be reported in a more contentious way. If a conflict occurs *within* a state, for example in Bosnia, Albania or Zaire, vivid reporting does not appear consistently to prompt an immediate desire to act either in Western publics or among decision makers. Furthermore, following experiences in Bosnia, most Western decision makers have become more sensitive to the pressures which can be exerted by the media; they are more sceptical about information and judgements made in media reports and consciously seek to react in a balanced and reflective manner, drawing on experience and information from sources other than the popular press.

Nevertheless, over the long term the reporting of international events influences policy makers' perceptions; few are immune to images and views experienced over months or years. Media opinion may also be significant in the short term if government policies go seriously awry; media reporting of failures in Somalia certainly contributed to the US decision to withdraw from that country. The taking of this decision is illustrative: the reasons for military engagement in Somalia had become increasingly unclear, casualties were rising, no visible end to the commitment appeared to be in sight, and no vital US interests appeared to be at stake. This combination of circumstances is all too likely to be repeated in future conflicts, which will tend to involve 'low intensity' violence rather than all-out warfare. If this is the case, should a reinforcing of current Western reservations about involvement in such conflicts be anticipated?

Low Intensity Conflict

Western states undoubtedly have the means to conduct low intensity military operations: funding, military capabilities, and the necessary institutional arrangements. During the Cold War, Western powers actively intervened in low intensity conflicts as part of the global ideological competition between communism and the West; a subsequent 'residual' will has persisted in favour of intervention to protect Western interests and to support international standards and good governance. However, recent negative experiences, the existence of underlying norms against warfare, and fear of casualties have generated what some term 'self-deterrence', or at least considerable caution.

Complicated low intensity conflicts abroad have tended to be viewed by Western publics as 'wars in far-away places with little impact on Westerners' lives'; the limited reaction to events in the Great Lakes region of Africa bears this out. While the desire to 'do something' may emerge occasionally, for example regarding former Yugoslavia, the importance of an issue and the perceived urgency of the need to react differ from state to state; being affected by geographical proximity, historical ties, national traditions. For example, French involvement in sub-Saharan Africa has been widely perceived to be a legitimate part of its international responsibilities. The United Kingdom, France and the United States have traditions of military intervention which are not shared by most other West European states; indeed these traditions are increasingly being questioned even in these three countries.

If this trend continues, potentially negative consequences may be envisaged, for non-intervention may have significant costs: increasing international disorder, widespread violence and the collapse of states, domestic political penalties of governments' perceived indifference, and resentment of parties to a conflict towards an aloof and indifferent international community. However, such penalties are less easy to quantify than are the costs of military deployment: the absence in the West of a 'sense of mission' to police world trouble spots mitigates against action when potential costs are weighed. Indeed, the argument has been increasingly made that there is a strong case for 'no Western intervention' because such involvement merely prolongs conflicts and postpones their eventual resolution; many take the view that it is for the local protagonists and perhaps their immediate neighbours to police their own affairs. Others strongly reject this view, arguing that inaction will eventually give rise to the emergence of direct military threats against the West or its regional allies; early action is therefore preferable not least because anticipated costs will be relatively low. Furthermore, many believe it is of central importance to the West that democratic values be defended, failing states be supported and significant dangers be faced, for example the proliferation of weapons of mass destruction.

Thus, while the vulnerabilities of the West and its vital interests are increasingly perceived to be developing – primarily in non-military areas, for example in the financial and energy sectors – military problems have persisted into the post-Cold War era and intervention cannot be precluded in all circumstances. This is most likely to occur when vital interests are at stake or when there is consensus that there is an overriding moral imperative. However, agreeing what is 'vital' and what constitutes a 'moral imperative' is difficult; for this reason unanimous Western resolve to act in a given situation is unlikely. This will be the case even when Western citizens and assets are directly threatened. At best a coalition of the willing will emerge, at worst 'confused inaction' may result. Western states' reactions to terrorism and their views on the appropriate military role in efforts to counter terrorist activities demonstrate the difficulties of achieving an international consensus.

Countering Terrorism

International terrorism has been a persistent problem for the international community over the past three decades; and it is likely to remain so given its origins in the problems associated with population growth, development and urbanisation in the developing world: poverty, unemployment, social deprivation, and growing economic inequalities. Western states have traditionally met the terrorist threat through a combination of intelligence gathering, effective and targeted policing, international cooperation on legal matters including extradition, and political and economic pressure against states sponsoring terrorist groups. Western countries have only resorted to military force occasionally.

While this range of approaches has yielded some successes, the number of incidents falling in Europe in recent years and, for example, the difficulties of acquiring accurate intelligence about small groups, particularly if they have no links with known state sponsors, mean that terrorists' 'successes' will continue. For the military to be involved in the forging of an effective response, special training to acquire particular skills is required to liaise effectively with police forces, to accept restraints on the use of force, and to deal with antagonistic civilian populations. The military is usually called upon to deal with terrorist groups when there is an understanding that military units are the only forces available with the required training, equipment and fire power to prevail in a crisis situation, for example, to rescue hostages from heavily armed groups. Military units may also be called in to deal with the consequences of a terrorist action, for example, aiding casualties or dealing with explosive devices. Most Western elite military forces have prepared for such emergencies for many years on a routine basis and their involvement in this type of operation is generally accepted. In contrast, suggestions that military forces be used to exact 'retribution' or to undertake pre-emption are more controversial.

Few embrace with enthusiasm the use of military forces to these ends. The difficulties of retribution and pre-emption are all too evident: the likelihood of civilian casualties, the difficulty of retaining the moral high ground, the possible ineffectiveness of operations given difficulties in locating terrorist groups, and the possibility that action will provoke more vigorous terrorist responses. Caution is needed when considering the use of military force against terrorist organisations. While the location of potential targets and the effectiveness of a military response may be higher if attacks are directed against a known state sponsor of a terrorist group, the costs associated with this option remain high. International condemnation of such action has been widespread in the past and is likely to be so in the future. Without the evolution of a common international view on terrorism and the agreement of international norms against terrorist activities, the likelihood of an international consensus emerging over the use of military force is unlikely. Even where the threat of terrorism is broadened to include the possible use of weapons of mass destruction (WMD) forging a consensus remains problematic.

Countering the Proliferation of Weapons of Mass Destruction

The dangers of Western military intervention are highest where the use of nuclear, biological and chemical weapons is possible or likely. The potentially disastrous consequences for Western states and forces which are subjected to WMD attacks are exceptional. For this reason many take the view that it is an open question whether intervention will ever be undertaken against opponents with convincing WMD capabilities. It is for this reason that the Western response to WMD has been firmly rooted in efforts to prevent potential adversaries from acquiring such weapons; Western arms control and non-proliferation policies, exemplified by the various international non-proliferation treaties and export control regimes, have achieved considerable success in recent decades. However, they are far from being totally effective and proliferation has continued to occur albeit at a relatively modest pace. Accordingly, many perceive an increased need to develop effective policies designed to deter the use of WMD, principally by a small number of perceived 'rogue' states. The increasing number of states possessing WMD, particularly chemical and biological weapons, has complicated decision making in the post-Cold War world; many regimes possessing

WMD are perceived to be less predictable and more willing to take risks than were the governments of the Cold War protagonists.

The concern is that the motivation to acquire WMD and regimes' rationales for WMD use do not follow the pattern set during the period of East–West confrontation. For example, some regimes acquiring WMD do not view them as weapons of last resort to avert a possible defeat but rather value their potential early use to prevent military intervention by stronger neighbours or adversaries in the West. Possible motivations for WMD use include deflection of US and allied military threats, defeat of Western forces, preventing defeat of the possessor state, disrupting possible coalitions, revenge, and deterrence. For non-state actors, possible motivations to acquire WMD are even more complex including, for example, ideology and religion.

Understanding the motivation of proliferators is vital when considering how best to respond to their possible future activities. Anticipated early use of chemical or biological weapons by adversaries means that Western priorities must include protection of intervening forces, logistics support (for example ports and airfields) and related civilian workers, improving early detection and personal protection capabilities, and developing effective vaccines. If WMD are expected to be used only as a last resort, a Western priority will be to ensure that policies and military operations are conducted in a manner designed to ensure that an adversary has options available other than WMD use.

Deterring use of WMD remains highly problematical. The actions of an opponent with WMD cannot be predicted with 100 per cent certainty, not least because in many cases acquisition of WMD has been undertaken to deter Western military action. Can the threat of using nuclear weapons effectively deter use of chemical and biological weapons? Should such an explicit linkage be overtly made? Some take the view that a 'firebreak' should be maintained between nuclear and chemical/biological weapons, not least because any linkage would undermine Western efforts to reduce the importance of nuclear weapons in international relations. Others believe that a linkage is essential if Western pronouncements that WMD use will be responded to 'in full measure' are to seem credible. Any decision to use nuclear weapons will inevitably be difficult and perhaps time consuming; a Western decision to use nuclear weapons cannot be assured. Prudence dictates that other options should be developed as a matter of urgency.

A key aim must be to ensure that Western forces can operate and prevail in nuclear, biological and chemical environments. By demonstrating to a potential user that they will not benefit from WMD possession or use, deterrence will be enhanced. To achieve this goal the United States government has identified as priorities for its counterproliferation initiative: the improvement of passive defence measures including detection and personal protection for its military personnel; developing a credible active defence capability including theatre missile defence systems; and procuring equipment and planning for effective counter force options including the destruction of bunkers housing WMD and WMD production facilities. However these US priorities are not fully shared by many of its Western allies and more cooperation and coordination will be needed if a truly 'Western' response to the WMD threat is to evolve. This may prove to be difficult given the apparent differing priorities which are being set by European governments whose defence planning appears to be focusing upon peacekeeping and related tasks rather than prevailing against WMD-equipped adversaries in a major war.

Can a 'division of labour' be anticipated whereby the United States will take the lead in dealing with large scale military threats and the Europeans increasingly provide the forces required to undertake peacekeeping and peace enforcement activities? Are forces in Europe or indeed the United States equipped to take on these 'new' tasks which have emerged in the last decade?

3 Humanitarian Assistance, Peacekeeping and Peace Enforcement

While Western intervention to provide humanitarian assistance and to undertake peacekeeping or peace enforcement operations since 1990 has involved difficult experiences, not least for those acting under the UNPROFOR flag in Bosnia, such operations led to a refocusing of Western military thinking and priorities. New missions have required significant adjustments of military organisation and planning. In addition, undertaking these missions has resulted in increased levels of cooperation between Western states and their militaries, for example between the UK and France in Bosnia, and has also facilitated positive contacts between former Cold War adversaries in Europe. Indeed, humanitarian assistance and disaster relief have proved to be areas of significant cooperation between Western states and Russia even during the recent period of cool relations as NATO enlargement plans unfolded.

Disaster Relief

Western countries have traditionally organised their responses to natural or man made disasters unilaterally or through the United Nations. This approach remains largely in place, but both NATO and the European Union have become increasingly involved. The principles governing NATO's role in disaster assistance have been explicitly stated:

- the overriding decision on whether or not to respond to a request to assist in disaster relief is with the individual government of a nation. Normally, this will be in response to an approach from the government of a stricken country, the UN or other relevant organisation;

- NATO will not seek to create an independent humanitarian role for itself on its own account, nor will NATO insert itself as another layer in the organisation of international disaster relief;

- the alliance will not duplicate or cut across the work of other international organisations set up specifically to deal with international disaster assistance;

- civil assets remain at all times under national control.

NATO's role is threefold: to act as necessary as a medium for information sharing and cooperation among NATO member countries, PfP countries and relevant international organisations; to take on any assisting coordinating role as may be identified; and to provide disaster assistance where appropriate NATO resources are available. The Alliance's role is to act as a catalyst and to facilitate rather than to be the initiator of relief. In addition it has, through its PfP programme, undertaken training, workshops and planning activities to improve PfP partner/NATO cooperation.

Such NATO initiatives have been well received in Eastern Europe. Indeed, a sometimes troubled relationship with Russia has not undermined Russian enthusiasm for the further development of such cooperation. For the Russian military, responding to national and man made disasters has traditionally been regarded as an integrated element of national security. The Russian EMERCOM agency has coordinated this activity and has been assigned considerable resources, including its own airlift capability, to carry out its work. Russian economic difficulties have encouraged the development of cooperation with NATO and Western states. EMERCOM is seeking to maximise its coordination with relevant national and multinational agencies and non-governmental organisations (NGOs).

The positive effects of such cooperation have been evident during the IFOR and SFOR operations in former Yugoslavia, where humanitarian assistance and disaster relief efforts have been a key element in NATO/PfP partner cooperation. They have also fulfilled an important function of improving the general levels of cooperation between the militaries of Eastern and Western Europe. Indeed, this holds true across a wider range of problems and activities; the lessons of former Yugoslavia loom large in the evolution of Western peacekeeping activities.

The Lessons of Former Yugoslavia

The conflicts in former Yugoslavia are widely perceived to have been damaging to Western institutions and the cohesion of the West's primary security organisation, NATO. The Yugoslav wars demonstrated the limited ability of Europeans to handle security crises in the region and the continued need for US engagement and allied unity to meet security crises. Clarity of purpose and decisive action are essential. The US-brokered Dayton Agreement, and the NATO military action against Serb forces which predated it, enabled NATO Alliance members to act in unison and put their all too public differences behind them. However, problems remain, not least because of the avowed US intention to withdraw its troops from Bosnia in 1998. It is unclear whether European states will be prepared to keep their troops in Bosnia if the United States does not. While Europeans have the military capability to undertake such a role their willingness to do so remains uncertain.

The harsh lessons of the past five years will affect this decision. Humanitarian assistance and peacekeeping will only be undertaken with the consent of all local parties; such operations are deemed to be impossible during a period of open warfare, when the withdrawal of consent by any of the protagonists will put at risk Western forces, not least because of their widespread and thin deployment when supporting humanitarian assistance. The fact that the presence of UNPROFOR represented an obstacle to the use of force by NATO has deeply affected Western thinking. Arising from this experience is the UN view that humanitarian assistance should only be undertaken when cease-fires are in place and peace settlements are firmly under negotiation. Without UN enthusiasm or mandates the prospect of Western intervention to fulfil humanitarian goals appears to be limited.

Western states involved with the Yugoslav conflicts share the perception that clear mandates for action and agreed lines of communication are essential if the West is to become involved in similar future operations. A lead organisation for military activity has to be clearly designated with the authority to command troops on the ground. Western countries are improving training and procuring necessary equipment to undertake peacekeeping operations in the future. The need for effective international cooperation in conducting such operations has hastened the development of NATO's CJTFs, speeded French decisions to reintegrate within the Alliance, and resulted in the German decision to deploy combat troops in IFOR. These decisions have improved the prospects for future cooperation between Western European militaries and governments.

Nevertheless, all are aware that the problems of Bosnia have not been 'solved'. While there is no war because of the Western military presence, genuine peace seems a distant prospect and reconciliation between the parties and reconstruction of the region's economy have been limited at best. Few refugees have returned to their homes, war crimes remain unpunished and human rights abuses continue. The rearmament of the parties to the conflict is proceeding apace; few are unaware of the consequent problems and the possibility that fighting will begin again. This prospect reinforces Western reservations about similar Western involvements in other areas in the future; many argue that intervention has failed to deal with the fundamental causes of the Bosnian conflict and that they will not be resolved while Western forces remain in place. Others believe that such forces should remain where they are until a 'sea change in local opinion' occurs and genuine peace is a possibility. This would require a long-term commitment to keep troops in Bosnia, perhaps for a generation, and it is unclear whether Western governments will be prepared to commit their forces and resources for such a period of time.

However, it seems certain that this will not be the case unless genuine efforts to undertake reconciliation and reconstruction occur. In Bosnia, they seem at best distant prospects. Is this negative assessment broadly applicable in other circumstances or can Western involvement generate a more positive result given the adoption of suitable policies?

Ending Conflict and Promoting Reconciliation

Western countries have differing views about the involvement of the military in reconstruction and reconciliation activities. European perceptions are dominated by recent experiences in Bosnia while US attitudes also derive from the outcome of operations in Haiti and Somalia.

The United States' military priority is conducting full scale war fighting operations effectively; until recently the US armed forces have been less concerned with peacekeeping. The US military tradition of active involvement in reconstruction, which reached its apogee in Germany after the Second World War, has been largely abandoned. The majority of US military officers appear to take the view that civilian agencies are best suited to undertake economic reconstruction, education, the developing of constitutional and legal systems, and establishing effective police forces. While US military help may be given to civilians in these areas, as occurred in Panama in 1989 and more recently in Haiti, its role remains supportive.

This approach governs US operations within IFOR and SFOR. Considerable efforts have been made to facilitate the work of civilian agencies and NGOs. A number of European forces have been more proactive, their militaries having long associations with peacekeeping operations throughout the Cold War period. Rather than emphasising the need to deploy overwhelming force (a key tenet of US military operations), the European emphasis is on playing a policing role, remaining neutral, encouraging reconciliation, working with and listening to local leaders and effectively applying military expertise to maximise the positive impact of civilian authorities and NGOs.

Differences of approach are grounded firmly in the differing national traditions of national military establishments. For example, British forces, with their colonial traditions and their ongoing security function in Northern Ireland, routinely train for and experience the types of tensions which inevitably prevail immediately after a period of war and instability. Canadian and Nordic forces draw upon their global peacekeeping traditions. Countries from the developing world bring different perspectives.

Forging a unity of purpose and approach between peacekeeping forces drawn from many countries may be as difficult as the task of reconstruction and reconciliation which they are deployed to encourage. In the European context, the lack of a fully-developed NATO peacekeeping doctrine remains problematical. Nevertheless, it is possible to overemphasise the difficulties; while achieving genuine progress in Bosnia has proved to be elusive, this has not occurred because of failures by deployed military forces. Notwithstanding differences of national perspective, the effective maintenance of peace and order, an essential prerequisite for any progress, is a significant achievement. It is perhaps unreasonable to expect nations' armed forces to achieve more. Should they be charged in future with broader missions, a restructuring of military organisation and activity would be required which would extend far beyond changes that are currently under consideration in most Western national capitals.

4 The Changing Military
Establishing Priorities

Discussions about the future role of the military in reconstruction and reconciliation efforts point to the need to define clearly what types of 'interventions' are to be undertaken. Political and military leaderships need to define military core missions and to establish priorities between them. The overall capacity to react militantly to threats and risks differs appreciably from state to state; only the United States currently possesses the full range of military capabilities required to enable it to deal with most if not all eventualities. While the United States sets its own priorities, others in the West are influenced in their decisions by relevant judgements about likely US support. All face increased uncertainty about the nature of future threats and risks and this complicates planning.

A few Western countries continue to retain an independent national capacity to conduct high intensity warfare and to maintain a full range of military capabilities with substantial air, sea and ground forces. In contrast, states not seeking to act alone, which anticipate military action only in cooperation with others (usually under a UN flag) have decided not to develop some capabilities or to abandon others. Thus, states electing only to become involved in operations where there is little or no local resistance train and equip their armed forces accordingly. The respective importance attached to the conducting of high intensity warfare, to peacekeeping and peace enforcement, or to a possible combination, critically affects planning, organisation and priorities: for example, infantry training, logistic priorities, selection and funding of equipment, procurement patterns, and transport capabilities. Priorities may change over time; for example United States and French military reviews in 1996 and 1995 respectively affected their military posture significantly; the UK defence review in 1997 may have a similar effect. The relative importance of air, navy and ground forces may change as could levels of funding and procurement programmes.

High intensity conflict (HIC) is ill defined and means different things in different services in different countries. It is also blurred by the increasing need for advanced weaponry for peace support operations. HIC can 'do' low intensity conflict (LIC) tasks, but not vice versa. HIC forces can concentrate violence decisively to bring about opportunities for conflict resolution which LIC forces probably cannot. The US is concentrating on HIC and, if other Western countries do not, and do not ensure interoperability with the US, there will be *de facto* role specialisation. This could lead to a situation in which the US is 'safe' in the HIC tasks and provides escalation dominance for Europeans undertaking dangerous LIC tasks. This would deepen European dependence on the US with negative consequences for an envisaged European Security and Defence Identity.

A commitment to international cooperation affects fundamentally the establishing of priorities. For example, Western cooperation through NATO is underpinned by the understanding that collaborative efforts enable each member state to maximise its military capability and security at a cost far below that which would be required by each state acting independently. United States–European cooperation has been cemented through the Alliance and seems certain to continue, although the CJTF/ WEU arrangements being put in place offer at least the prospect of Europeans acting together independently of the US in future.[14] However, it is highly unlikely that European states will undertake 'national' military operations (with the possible exceptions of France and the United Kingdom in highly specific circumstances). Moreover, all states are subject to a continued process of budget reductions; these are likely to result in an increased emphasis on role sharing and divisions of labour between states. If this does occur, there is a need to ensure that defence cuts do not result in the abandoning of what is essential for stated or reasonably anticipated future missions.

A possible means to offset the effects of budgetary pressures is to increase cooperation with non-Western states, i.e. to develop even broader 'coalitions of the willing'. Such coalitions have already been active, for example in the Gulf, Somalia, and Cambodia where Western forces have collaborated with Arab, African and Asian forces respectively. Improving this cooperation will require more regular contacts including training in such activities as peacekeeping. This may be a future role for NATO which could develop training programmes, under UN auspices, although any institutionalising of such training could best be located in a developing country. The benefits to the West would not only be financial; extending and intensifying collaboration would help to reduce the possibility of future conflict.

Establishing priorities is also affected by the technologies available to military establishments to carry out their missions. Technology influences both the effectiveness of individual personnel and of military organisations; it also directly affects the way in which military operations are conducted.

The Effects of Technological Change

Technological improvement helps the military to achieve its goals at the operational and tactical levels; it facilitates intelligence gathering, force projection and extraction, achieving goals at less human cost to both intervention forces and adversaries. Subject to funding restrictions, the availability of suitable technology determines the degree to which doctrinal objectives can be met.

Technological innovations have expanded the reach of Western military forces, and their ability to deploy forces into theatre as quickly as possible. Air-to-air refuelling, innovations in air lift and navigation, the development of all-weather cargo delivery, and unmanned on-station air surveillance have all contributed to recent Western military improvements. Technology has enabled Western militaries to expand their knowledge about potential and actual targeted enemy states. The development and deployment of new sensor systems has contributed significantly, including longer range platforms, multidimensional sensors, the combination of sensors of different types, and the higher speed micro-processing of data collected. The better integration of information gathered is a current priority but benefits were already evident during the Gulf War. Paralleling these achievements is a recognised need to constrain the awareness of an adversary; Command and Control Warfare is being developed to disrupt an enemy's capacity to witness and comprehend Western military actions. The overall aim is to speed friendly forces' reaction times and to slow an opponent's responses to the point where enemy armed forces degrade substantially.

Technology has also expanded the engagement options of Western forces, enabling them to conduct operations while minimising damage and casualties to a level commensurate with political aims. The use of technologies to incapacitate enemy forces temporarily will further refine Western options. Similarly the development and use of precision weapons and associated guidance systems, and recent reductions in their cost per unit, have given Western militaries new options. Further improvements in warhead design and the development of possible new novel systems including laser weapons, will further enhance precision and hence minimise collateral casualties. This is an important goal, if the West wishes to speed the tasks of reconciliation and rebuilding after a conflict.

These new capabilities directly affect the prosecution of Western-led military operations. Some analysts emphasise the growing importance of air power and the fact that the possible simultaneous targeting and destruction of numerous targets in enemy forces will facilitate the rapid breakdown of an enemy's ability to wage war. In contrast the development of non-lethal options is important for peacekeeping. While not without their problems, including accidental fatalities, they may reduce the level of violence in difficult situations and facilitate the protection of Western forces with the minimum use of force. To enable the West to undertake both high intensity warfare and peacekeeping operations, the cultivation of effective air and ground forces will be required: while aviation with its powerful stand-off capabilities may come to the fore during war fighting, effective ground forces will be essential to prosecute effectively peacekeeping missions. The relative importance of these types of advances will depend upon the type of operation being undertaken.

The undertaking of both types of operation may become easier for Western forces in the near-to-medium term given the possible development of a technology gap between developed and 'developing' countries. A significant, growing conventional military superiority may accrue to the West as a result of technological innovation and its successful integration into military activities. This superiority may, of itself, prove to be problematical in that it may cause potential adversaries in the developing world to resort to WMD in their efforts either to deter Western military intervention or to wage war against the West. Even at the conventional level the impact of technology will not be one sided; technology dependence may make for vulnerabilities which potential adversaries will be able to exploit. Information warfare may prove to be particularly damaging, although increasing the levels of delegated command within Western armed forces will permit continued operations even if central command and control facilities are damaged. Dealing with this type of problem is of central concern to Western military analysts and practitioners who believe the synthesis of technological change and organisational innovation constitutes a *de facto* revolution in military affairs (RMA).

The Revolution in Military Affairs

If technology continues to 'deliver less than promised at greater cost' this does appear to be less the case than in the past. Useful technology is not always 'high tech' and, increasingly, much is coming from the civilian sector rather than being developed in military programmes. Furthermore, technology may have a varied impact in differing situations; for example, air delivered precision-guided weapons may be less important than improved individual body armour when conducting peacekeeping operations in a highly urbanised setting. Nevertheless, technology does appear to be offering opportunities to improve military capabilities substantially across the entire spectrum of intervention. Does this constitute a revolution?

Revolutionary changes in military organisation and capability have been generated by technological changes in the past: examples include the introduction of the longbow and, more recently, the development of aviation. The nature of and balance between military operational concepts, military organisation, command and control of military forces, and armaments can be altered fundamentally, although this is often not recognised immediately. Such a change may be occurring at the end of the twentieth century as new operational capabilities are being developed and deployed. The United States Department of Defence, particularly concerned that this may be the case, launched the US RMA initiative in 1984 to examine its possible consequences.

Three classes of technology are perceived to be particularly important; intelligence, surveillance, and data processing in combination could promote full awareness of what is going on in a 40,000 square mile battle area in real time. C4I technologies could enable a US or Western commander to interpret information received, establish what is occurring, plan how to counter negative developments, and instruct friendly forces how to react. US and Western forces would be able to determine exactly where force is to be applied, and how much force is needed, and enable costs to both friend and foe to be minimised.

The US view is that the RMA will occur but its timing is unsure. The full integration of anticipated changes within the US armed forces is not expected to occur within the next ten to fifteen years. The US is committed to undertaking an 'American RMA' by the year 2010, to provide the US with agile and flexible forces able to respond on short warning and to bring to bear maximum possible military force with the minimum possible casualties. Current US programmes are focused upon ammunition and weapons systems, enhancing technological awareness, C4I, and power projection.

The capacity to introduce these changes will be critically affected by levels of future defence funding. Budget cuts would result in a slower introduction of new technology and the later emergence of the anticipated revamped US forces; however, as most countries are reducing their defence spending, potential adversaries' capacity to respond to US changes will also be postponed to the more distant future. How far the United States will press ahead in the next decade remains uncertain; possibilities include rapid prosecution of the RMA and cutting existing forces to fund change; maintaining current force levels and introducing technological innovation over a longer period; or a mixture of the two approaches.

Whatever the rate and extent of change this will not go unnoticed in the rest of the world. Potential adversaries will certainly look for possible means to counter increasing US conventional power and a related enhancement of 'Western' military power. Possible options include the development of weapons of mass destruction (as discussed above) or preparing to conduct low-level conflict to minimise the effectiveness of the Western high tech superiority. Reactions will be determined not least by the attitudes of countries in the 'developing world' towards anticipated Western military intervention. These need not always be negative and indeed Western action may be welcomed by many developing states if it supports those states' national interests or the broader maintenance of international order.

5 Reactions Outside the West

The reactions of non-Western states to intervention will be governed largely by the nature of that intervention, whether it is conducted with the consent or otherwise of local parties, and the goals for which it is being pursued. Whereas humanitarian assistance and peacekeeping operations are likely to be well received, peace enforcement or open warfare will certainly be resisted by target states and the reaction of other developing countries will range from the positive to the negative. To a degree, attitudes are determined by post-colonial traditions of hostility towards continued influence of colonial powers in the developing world. The desire to resist perceived 'meddling' by the West in 'Third World' affairs remains strong. This has been reinforced over the years by negative Western reactions to such Third World hostility; concerns have been reinforced in recent years by the growing Western perception that 'new' threats to the West come from the 'South' in the post-Cold War era. Indeed many points of issue exist which generate North–South frictions: arms control and related export controls, development assistance, aid and trade, and the continued economic influence of former colonial states and the United States.

Notwithstanding these problems, the reactions of developing countries to a Western intervention are likely to be determined by states' national interests. Where interventions are perceived to be legitimate, that is, duly sanctioned by the United Nations, reactions will tend to be more positive. However, those issues which feature strongly on the West's international agenda – non-proliferation, counter-terrorism, restoring democracy – will not be viewed as legitimate reasons for military intervention by a number of developing countries. Charges of dual standards, and of variable application of standards, will inevitably be levied. For example, military efforts to forestall nuclear proliferation will be condemned as hypocritical if Western nuclear powers are involved and will prompt charges of inconsistency if such an action is not undertaken in all cases. It is unclear, however, whether the prospect of such criticism would affect Western behaviour.

Of more influence may be the improving military capabilities of developing countries. It is possible to envisage the evolution of a number of medium-level military powers whose capabilities would give the West cause for concern when military operations were under consideration. Notwithstanding the anticipated benefits of the revolution in military affairs, full-scale warfare with, for example, China or India would be a daunting prospect for Western leaders. As industrial development accelerates in a number of so-called developing countries their capacity to wage war will improve: ballistic missile and cruise missile technology is proliferating; the use of indirect responses including terrorism is an increasingly used option, WMD are potent potential deterrents; low levels of violence over a considerable period, and resulting regular casualties, prompt Western anxieties.

For the West to overcome these and other possible difficulties, many argue that a cooperative arrangement with like-minded states in the developing world is essential. As the likelihood of Western intervention appears to be declining, at least in the near term, the wholehearted support of the vast majority of states in the international system will help to encourage involvement when it is required, and to ensure that interventions undertaken are prosecuted successfully. This will require a positive political collaboration between North and South which has yet to materialise; it is an open question whether it will develop as the century draws to a close.

6 Conclusions

While the possibility of future Western military intervention in the developing world cannot be discounted, enthusiasm for such intervention is at best muted. Experiences in, for example, Somalia and Bosnia have increased Western governments' caution about undertaking humanitarian assistance operations, peacekeeping and peace enforcement. Many take the view that interventions are likely to be undertaken only where vital national interests of Western states are perceived to be at risk or where a Western military presence is welcome and the risk of unacceptable casualties is low.

In the short-to-medium term the West has the military capabilities needed to undertake effectively such interventions; although there is some concern that capabilities will erode over time if no major security threat to the West arises and few, if any, deployments of Western forces occur. Publics and politicians may well question the need for maintaining sophisticated defence establishments in such circumstances. However, the anticipated revolution in military affairs (RMA), combining the introduction of new technologies and the reorganisation of military structures and procedures to maximise their exploitation for military purposes, is expected to enhance significantly the military effectiveness of a number of Western states.

Western capacity to intervene effectively is assured if the United States is an active member of the intervening coalition. Some doubt the capacity of Europeans to act effectively without US support; for example, noting their relative weakness in intelligence gathering and airlift. Others believe the military capability to conduct an intervention probably could be assembled eventually by European states, using, for example, civilian shipping and aircraft, if the political will exists to undertake action.

An intervention to defend vital national interests is likely to be prompted by a significant military threat which will require a high intensity military response; the very nature of such threats, for example to national homelands, to close allies or to vital energy supplies, would require a forceful reaction. However, low level conflicts may also lead to Western involvement because they undermine international stability which is perceived to be desirable in the West. For this reason, and others including a moral imperative, military operations can be envisaged which do not involve open warfare. A combination of national interest, public pressure and media concern can prompt more limited interventions. While the media cannot force a government to act, its influence on decision makers cannot be discounted in a crisis for which governments are unprepared.

The Western view persists that 'prevention', using for example economic aid and diplomatic means, is preferable to 'intervention', which merely reflects past failures of anticipation and policy. While expensive, peacekeeping over long periods – Cyprus and Lebanon are notable examples – is arguably cheaper than and preferable to the possible alternative: costly and destructive military conflicts which may draw in neighbouring states and affect Western interests. The costs of possible war should not be discounted when calculations of cost effectiveness are being made.

For these reasons, maintaining a military capability to undertake peacekeeping and peace enforcement remains desirable. However, the readiness to undertake more 'traditional' missions has to be preserved. Attempting to undertake both missions is not cost free; for example training costs inevitably rise and the combat readiness of troops undertaking peacekeeping operations is reduced.

Given Western reticence about intervention and concern about costs, the development of cooperative links between regional powers in the developing world and Western states is desirable. There is some Western enthusiasm for helping regional powers to police their own regions; for example, Western states have supported peacekeeping operations undertaken by African countries in Africa. The West could play a greater role to support such regional efforts.

However, cooperation needs to take due note of persistent resentment in the 'South' regarding Western 'imperial' and 'colonial' traditions, echoes of which are to be perceived in 'Southern' views of Western policies on, for example, intervention, rogue states and arms control. Ending consequent mistrust and suspicion is no simple task. However, progress can be made at the functional level, for example, by facilitating cooperation in such areas as civil defence and disaster relief; regular contacts and cooperation in this field can build confidence as has occurred between NATO and Russia, notwithstanding their differences on other issues.

Some take the view that a rejuvenation of UN involvement with intervention issues could contribute; the UN is able to confer a legitimacy on intervention operations and provides a forum within which the countries of the North and South could overcome their residual suspicions. However, for this to occur the fairly jaundiced views of some Western states about the United Nations would have to be re-examined.

Given Western perceptions that international threats to vital Western interests are currently low, some take the view that low-level and intra-states conflicts should simply be left to run their course: Western aid and involvement is deemed merely to prolong conflicts and thereby increase levels of human suffering and disruption; ring-fencing conflicts is the preferred policy. However, it is unclear whether this option offers good prospects for long-term stability and security. Nevertheless, there will always be analysts who take this view, given Western governments' caution about intervention and their legitimate concerns about expending national blood and budgets in seeking to achieve what may be unachievable, namely regional stability and reconciliation. However, persistent conflict and instability undermine development programmes, are wasteful of aid and assistance, and disrupt international trade and business. Prudent and judicial deployment of military forces can help to minimise these costs.

The West currently stands at a crossroads. In one direction it will be inward looking and act only to defend its own vital interests in the developing world. As that world changes and, for example, China, India and the nations of South East Asia become in many respects 'developed', the utility of this policy will be increasingly questionable. In another direction lies a more proactive policy: seeking to build an evolving cooperative relationship with like-minded states (and there are many) in the developing world. The West may intervene but only with the cooperation of others.

It remains unclear whether the West will become more introverted or more engaged with the developing world; however, inward looking coalitions and states have historically been unable to protect themselves from the disruptive vagaries of the broader international system. While a possible third option, that of the West policing the world's unstable regions and preventing intra-state conflicts, is increasingly unlikely, building a cooperative relationship between the West and developing countries appears to offer at least the prospect of securing the stability and security for which past interventions have been undertaken. For this to occur, it is important that interventions are widely supported in the international community and that they are seen to be just.

Notes

The author gratefully acknowledges the comments on HIC and LIC offered by Rear Admiral Richard Cobbold CB FRAES presented in the section on 'The Changing Military'.

1. See Stuart Johnson and James Blaker, 'The FY 1997–2001 Defence Budget', *Strategic Forum,* No. 80, July 1996, Institute for National Strategic Studies, pp. 1–4.

2. Robert Oakley and Michael Dziedzic, 'Policing The New World Disorder', *Strategic Forum,* No. 84, October 1996, Institute for National Strategic Studies, p. 14.

3. Ibid.

4. See David Kirkpatrick, 'Choose Your Weapon: Combined Operational Effectiveness and Investment Appraisal (COEIA) and Its Role in UK Defence Procurement', *Whitehall Papers* No. 36, 1996, Royal United Services Institute, p. 165.

5. See John A. Cope, 'International Military Education and Training: an Assessment', *McNair Paper* 44, October 1995, Institute for National Strategic Studies, pp. 1–72.

6. Abe Singer and Scott Rowell, 'Information Warfare: an Old Operational Concept with New Implications', *Strategic Forum* No. 99, December 1996, Institute for National Strategic Studies, pp. 1–4.

7. See Stanley R. Sloan, 'NATO's Future: Beyond Collective Defence', *McNair Paper* 46, December 1995, Institute for National Strategic Studies, pp. 1–73.

8. See Paul Latawski, 'Practical Cooperation in Joint Operations, Including Peacekeeping', in *Cooperation and Partnership for Peace: a Contribution to Euro-Atlantic Security Into the 21st Century, Whitehall Paper* No. 37, 1996, RUSI, pp. 57–65.

9. Charles Barry, 'NATO's Combined Joint Task Forces in Theory and Practice', *Survival,* Vol. 38, No. 1, Spring 1996, International Institute for Strategic Studies, pp. 81–97.

10. Ibid., p. 84.

11. Ibid. (for more detailed discussion).

12. See Sir Thomas Boyd-Carpenter, 'Operational Capability into the Future: Rapid Response', *RUSI Journal,* October 1996, RUSI, pp. 26–27.

13. If weapons of mass destruction are used, a disproportionate response may be envisaged in order to deter future WMD use; although even this view is controversial and has not been subject to regular public debate.

14. Europeans will still have some dependence on the US. American capabilities not only 'enable' at the lower end but also provide escalation 'control' and 'dominance' at the high end.

5

Oil and the Middle East

Report based on Wilton Park Conference 495: 17–21 March 1997 on 'Oil and the Middle East Economies'

Richard Latter

1 Introduction

The low price of crude oil in the international markets in the late 1990s was perceived to be generating severe economic problems in a number of Middle Eastern states which were of such magnitude that the future security and stability of some countries and regimes was believed to be in jeopardy. Social and political tensions appeared to be exacerbated by evident stagnation of national economies and the cost of the Gulf War, which made it increasingly difficult to maintain expensive social and economic infrastructures such as free health care and education. The possibility of introducing new or higher taxes seemed real.[1] The increase in oil prices during the second half of 1996 ameliorated local governments' economic problems and reduced the pressure for speedy economic reform and linked political change. Indeed, in some countries in the region economic prospects appeared to be bright:

> although it is one of the world's smallest countries, the Gulf state of Qatar is very rich: it is on the threshold of an astonishing building boom for gas and other projects worth $21 billion. Activity on this scale has not been seen in the Gulf since the Golden Days of the 1970s.[2]

However, long-term problems persist which may become more acute more quickly if oil prices again fall.

What are the prospects? The oil price is affected by global economic factors including, for example, levels of economic growth in Western countries, the rate of expansion of Asian economies and their related energy demand. Prices are also affected by political factors, notably events in Iraq and Iran and the reaction of the international community to them. Their current status as 'rogue' states has limited significantly their ability to export oil and gas products; a resurgence of exports from these countries could reduce prices and affect the economic well-being of their neighbours in the Arabian Peninsula.

Of similar importance are developments in the non-oil sectors of Middle Eastern economies. The levels of economic development and growth vary considerably among the states of the region; while some are booming and receiving significant inflows of foreign direct investment, others are struggling with the problems associated with burgeoning populations, stagnant economic growth and long-term environmental degradation. A significant improvement in the region's overall economic performance will be essential if sufficient jobs are to be created for the growing population and adequate infrastructure and welfare provisions are to be put in place. Success or failure in this endeavour will affect directly the political, economic and social stability of the region; failures will inevitably generate social tensions and disaffection with the existing ruling elites.

The shocks of rapid and repeated change associated with the development of modern technologically-based economies generate many challenges to Arab societies which are fundamentally based on adherence to one religion, close family ties, the use of a single language and an overall common world view. A widening generation gap, weakening family ties and the burgeoning youthful population result in increased questioning of traditional forms of authority. Rising expectations and declining work opportunities in public sectors further complicate the situation. Whether traditional elites will be prepared to share their influence and power with a growing middle class remains to be seen. Tensions in Bahrain, Qatar and Saudi Arabia, sometimes taking a violent form, point towards a possibly turbulent future.

Faced with potential internal disruption the states of the region also continue to grapple with geopolitical realities which generate regional tensions and divert attention away from economic development and internal political reforms. The continuing friction between Israel and its Arab neighbours, uncertainties about future Iraqi behaviour and continuing tension between Iran and the Arab world impede efforts to develop regional co-operative ties, not least at the economic level. Current difficulties with the Middle East Peace Process seem to preclude any meaningful economic contacts between Israel and the Arab states, complicate relations between the Arabs and contribute to difficulties experienced by Western governments and business in their relations with the Arab world. Whether Western countries, notably the United States and the members of the European Union, can act effectively to facilitate reconciliation between the Middle East region's protagonists remains an open question; while limited success has been achieved in the past the persistence and depth of mutual antagonism and suspicion appears to be unabated. In these circumstance the short-to-medium term prospects for the region's economies appear to be modest at best.

Much will depend on the continued availability of regular and steady oil revenues upon which economic and political stability have been founded. Can this resource be relied upon in future years?

2 The Future Role of Oil in the Region

Demand for oil and related products remains strong and has been growing steadily at approximately 3 per cent per annum in recent years. Rising demand has been driven by the growth of Asian economies, principally those of China, South Korea and the South-East Asian 'Tiger Economies'. Sources of oil supply remain diverse. For example, non-OPEC production has increased steadily and met two thirds of increased demand in recent years. Furthermore, while production and demand in the former Soviet Union have both fallen, a significant surplus remains which is, in fact, larger than many anticipated. As a result OPEC production has not been required to meet most of the increasing demand and it increased by 'only' 1.2 million barrels per day (mbpd) between 1991 and 1996. It is likely that future increases in demand will also be met partially from non-OPEC sources and that no major increases of OPEC production are to be anticipated. Prospects of major production increases in other OPEC countries would be further limited by any large-scale resumption of Iraqi production.

Thus, a lack of demand-led pressure to increase OPEC production seems likely to continue. Although non-OPEC oil is more costly to produce, the difference in production costs is falling as better extraction techniques and related technologies develop. Furthermore, technological innovation is enabling previously 'exhausted' oil fields to be reopened and recovery rates for existing fields are improving year by year. Western governments remain supportive of production efforts in non-OPEC countries; continued advantageous tax arrangements and many other benefits are likely to ensure that non-OPEC production remains attractive to international oil companies.

Paralleling these developments, the behaviour of some OPEC producers is further reducing the likelihood of demand driving rapid increases in Middle Eastern production. The overall OPEC production ceiling of 24.5 million barrels per day is being exceeded by about 2 million barrels per day. Most of this 'overproduction' is occurring in Venezuela as it reopens previously closed oil fields. Venezuelan exports are largely to the US market and Venezuela has supplanted Saudi Arabia as the United States' largest oil supplier. In Europe, North Sea oil production (6.1 mbpd in 1997) is forcing out African and Nigerian oil which is now going principally to the Asian market. As a consequence of these trends Middle Eastern exports are also increasingly being sold in the Asian market, rather than in Europe or the US.

This may have serious economic and political implications for the Middle Eastern region. While China is currently a ready market for Middle Eastern oil and has every prospect of providing a growing market for the foreseeable future, political considerations within China itself could prompt decisions to control economic growth and thus limit oil imports. Economic downturns in other Asian economies would have similar adverse effects on Middle Eastern exports.

Tight demand could force up oil prices and require increased Middle East production, if companies decide to increase their, currently low, levels of oil stocks; rebuilding commercial stocks would generate a short-term increase in demand and perhaps require increased output in the Middle East. However, there is little evidence that the oil companies intend to embark upon such a policy.

In this situation many anticipate large swings in the international oil price. Resulting uncertainties about future revenues and prices cannot but complicate the planning of Middle East producers and the running of government programmes financed from production revenues. However, the impact of such uncertainty differs in different states in the region. While some are well placed to surmount associated problems, for others the economic consequences may be severe. This may yet prove to have serious implications for interstate relations in the region.

The Gulf States

Oil revenues have provided the basis for a bargain between the ruling elites of the Gulf states and their citizens. Gulf revenues enabled regimes to provide income, work and goods for local populations which have remained politically quiescent in return. This bargain worked well until the early 1990s and was based on local traditions involving the rule of local extended families which maintained close links with largely tribal populations and their leaderships and with important powerful local business communities. The importance of oil in the world economy also ensures that local regimes receive significant foreign protection from their larger and more martial neighbours.

However, the substance of this bargain is under increasing strain, not least because local populations have come to view the largesse of the ruling elites as a right to which they are entitled rather than something which requires loyalty. Moreover, uncertainties about future levels of oil revenue are occurring at a time when the significant financial reserves built up by Gulf states during the 1970s have been all but exhausted. Efforts to cushion the impact of falling oil prices in the 1980s, financial support for Iraq in its war against Iran, and financing of the Gulf War against Iraq severely depleted local reserves. The poor state of reserves increases the importance of current oil incomes and their predictability. But drawing up budgets for government expenditure is difficult in a situation in which, for example, each dollar rise or fall in the oil price represents a material difference to the Saudi exchequer.

These problems have been further complicated by some lax spending. Despite the efforts of the Saudi government to improve its finances, a deficit of 10 per cent was returned in 1996 at a time when oil revenues were unexpectedly higher than had been anticipated. The deficits of other countries in the region are little better or worse: Kuwait 15 per cent (1996–97), Oman 12 per cent (1997), Qatar 20 per cent (1996–97), United Arab Emirates 25 per cent (1996–97). While local leaders have realised the significance of the economic problems they face, little practical action has occurred. Many argue that cutbacks in government expenditure are necessary, but these have proved politically difficult to undertake and the increased oil income in the second half of 1996 diminished the urgency of the problem. None the less, the pressures of a burgeoning population and their demands for services, including health, water, energy, at cost price, or at no cost, will be difficult to meet. Cuts in defence expenditure, high by international standards, have proved to be difficult in an insecure region which has experienced two major wars since the early 1980s.

The fact that the local regimes provide large numbers of jobs within government bureaucracies, 80 per cent of the Saudi budget is expended on wages for example, further inhibits efforts to balance income and expenditure. The high outlays on wages result in relatively low levels of investment in infrastructure or enterprises which could generate additional sources of revenue. Furthermore, a lack of suitable skills in the local populations and their expectation of white collar high-income jobs have hampered efforts to enhance the productivity of local workforces.

Although some progress has occurred to reduce government expenditure and to increase revenue from non-oil sources, this is insufficient at present to make a significant difference. The combination of uncertain future income, derived largely from oil, with rising expectations requiring higher expenditure, and low reserves, causes some observers to express concern about the future stability of Gulf state regimes. Unable to finance the aspirations of their consequently restive populations, the future of existing rulers has been questioned. However, in two countries which are experiencing the severest economic problems, local rulers have been able to retain power through the use of repression and force. The heirs of Ayatollah Khomeini in Iran and the regime of Saddam Hussein in Iraq remain in control despite the impoverishment of their states.

Iran

Total Iranian energy production equals approximately 5 million barrels of oil per day of which 2 mbpd are consumed within the country. Gas production is rising as a proportion of this total while oil production is falling. The low level of domestic prices, at 6 cents per litre or 5 per cent of the European price, has generated high levels of domestic demand and waste. The continuation of current trends to the year 2010 would result in the domestic consumption of all Iranian production. However, the development of the country's gas potential would avert this situation and enable Iran to continue to export at significant levels.

The development of envisaged oil and gas projects requires huge levels of investment which cannot be generated within Iran itself. The involvement of foreign oil companies is essential. Total estimated required investment for the energy sector is between 60 and 80 billion dollars between 1997 and 2010. For example, maintaining current oil production at 3.6 million barrels per day will require investment of between 15 and 20 billion dollars. Development of new offshore and onshore fields will cost 10 to 12 billion dollars, gas injection projects 3 to 5 billion dollars, and new refineries and associated activity 2 to 3 billion dollars. Investments required in the petrochemical and gas industries are estimated at 8 billion dollars and 25–32 billion dollars, respectively. Projects on this scale are attractive to international oil companies. However, their involvement in Iran has been effectively precluded by its recent internal politics and troubled international relations. Thus, changes at the political level appear to be essential before Iran's potential as an energy producer can be developed to the full. What are the prospects for such change?

Few doubt that Iran is indeed changing; while the image of the Khomeini revolution persists, two decades have passed and revolutionary fervour has significantly diminished. The election of a perceived moderate, Muhammed Khatami, in the elections of 23 May 1997 reinforces this perception. His unexpected victory, with 69 per cent of the vote on an 88 per cent turnout, demonstrates the widespread popular dissatisfaction with Iran's ruling regime, not least among the young. However, the Iranian government is not monolithic and has a highly diffused power structure in which rival centres compete strongly. Such competition has prevented the cutting of subsidies in the energy sector in the past and it will undoubtedly limit the new president's capacity to effect changes in energy policy, in Iranian domestic political arrangements and in foreign policies.

That change is needed seems certain. The poor state of the Iranian economy, which has been damaged severely by the revolution, the war with Iraq and chronic mismanagement (not least the post-war credit boom which has resulted in a huge national debt) lies behind the popular vote for president elect Khatami. Improving the situation will depend upon an improvement in Iran's international standing; recent Iranian 'charm offensives', emphasising the country's reliability and prudence in international affairs, reflect a recognition of this fact. Such efforts will need, however, to be backed by action in a number of areas, notably, improving relations with the United States (addressing particularly US concerns about terrorism, Iran's opposition to the Middle East Peace Process, and weapons of mass destruction issues); and coming to an accommodation with the Gulf states and Saudi Arabia, notably in disputes over islands in the Gulf.

Positive developments in these, and other, areas would enable the many European companies which are interested in working with Iran to expand their operations in the country. Such involvement remains inhibited by Iran's poor image with many companies deriving from its perceived 'hostile' foreign policy, and its record of internal repression. In addition, hostile US reaction to Iranian policies has focused on isolating Iran economically and developing an economic boycott of the country; companies with assets or interests in the United States are well aware that dealing with Iran would threaten their position in North America.

Whether this situation will change in the near term remains an open question. Many take the view that ideology remains important in Iran and this will make it extremely difficult for the new president or other 'moderates' to be constructive. US policy appears unlikely to change until significant changes in Iranian policy have occurred. Given this impasse, the prospects for large-scale international investment in Iran appear to be poor. In these circumstances a significant expansion of the Iranian energy sector is unlikely and the revenues that this would generate will not be available to finance the social and economic programmes which are essential to meet the aspirations of a growing and increasingly youthful population. The potential for instability in the longer term is evident and the reaction of the regime to associated unrest is likely to dictate its evolution in the decades ahead. In Iraq, similar problems have cemented the control of the repressive Saddam Hussein regime.

Iraq

Very little Iraqi oil has been exported in recent years following the imposition of UN sanctions at the end of the Gulf War. The small amounts permitted to finance humanitarian assistance do not affect significantly the international oil markets. However, a considerable capacity for production and export has been maintained in the country and it is estimated that Iraq could export 2 to 3 million barrels per day once sanctions are lifted. The existence of a skilled work force and the anticipated inflow of Western capital and expertise would ensure this level of production. It may be anticipated that existing vigorous rules on the national ownership of oil assets may be relaxed to facilitate a rapid return to full production. It is clear that Iraqi financial resources are such that they would be unable to finance the expansion of production nationally and that foreign investment and involvement will be essential.

Such changes cannot occur until the removal of Saddam Hussein and his immediate coterie of supporters. The United States is firmly opposed to any lifting of sanctions while the current government remains in place and will certainly veto any attempts in the UN Security Council to end or reduce economic sanctions. The departure of Saddam and the arrival of a new regime would probably permit the early ending of sanctions, although some observers believe that this will occur only after the passage of some time when the nature of the new regime has become clear. Others take the view that sanctions will be removed more rapidly given anticipated pressure in the international community to facilitate reconstruction in Iraq and to exploit economic opportunities which the arrival of a new regime would prompt. Any lifting of sanctions is likely to be conditional upon Iraqi good behaviour regarding the maintenance of international inspection regimes for weapons of mass destruction and the negotiation of acceptable agreements with near neighbours regarding reparations. Assuming sanctions are lifted and oil production increases rapidly, what are the implications for the region and its oil economies?

The addition of 2 million barrels per day of oil exports in the international oil market is likely to drive prices down but it is unclear how far they would fall. This would generate problems for Saudi Arabia and the Gulf states who would have to compete with Iraq to maintain market share. For Saudi Arabia in particular this may pose problems given current Saudi efforts to increase their production capacity. The maintenance of idle capacity is costly and any slowing of world demand for oil would exacerbate problems caused by an influx of Iraqi oil. It is possible that Saudi Arabia could attempt to pre-empt Iraqi re-entry into the oil market by increasing its market share through selling oil at lower prices, an option not available to other important producers. Some observers believe that this policy is likely if Saudi Arabia significantly increases its production capacity. The success of such a Saudi policy cannot but be detrimental to Iraqi interests and would also adversely affect Iranian efforts to expand oil production in the future. Saudi success could prompt Iraqi efforts to expand production as quickly as possible and to make a linked decision to sell oil cheaply in order to generate required revenues and to undercut Saudi prices and market share. Such a policy would require the active involvement of foreign companies and capital, and a confrontation between Saudi Arabia on one hand and an Iraqi/oil company coalition on the other may be anticipated. A possible Saudi response could be to liberalise the terms upon which foreign companies participate in its oil industry which would 'divert' company attention away from Iraq. Whatever the eventual scenario, many take the view that a Saudi–Iraqi confrontation of some sort is inevitable.

The intensity of such a confrontation derives in part from both countries' heavy dependence on oil production for government revenues and indeed as a proportion of GNP. In the longer term they, as other states in the region, need to diversify their economic activities. This issue is not a new one and indeed economic diversification away from oil has been an issue among Gulf oil producers for more than twenty years. What are the prospects for action?

3 Broadening the Region's Economic Base
Privatisation and Investment

Analysts in the Middle East note that most countries are not participating fully in the ongoing transformation of the world economy, with its free flows of capital, ideas and technology. While some states have started to liberalise and open up their economies, for example Egypt, some have reduced tariffs, for example Jordan and Tunisia, and the Gulf Cooperation Council (GCC) has recently permitted foreign share ownership, privatisation is perceived to be proceeding too slowly. Gulf states are aware of the situation and their public rhetoric, at least, emphasises the need to adjust their economies. Constraints on future possibilities include existing debt, growing populations which need work, and high public sector wages bills. To overcome related problems many take the view that significant inflows of foreign direct investment (FDI) will be required.

Existing international flows of FDI are largely bypassing the Middle East; FDI in the region totals only $2 billion per annum of which most goes to Saudi Arabia and Egypt. Unwelcome government policies have much to do with this but the low levels of inter-regional trade, 8 per cent of the region's total trade, also act as a disincentive. Attracting foreign capital is also linked to providing investment opportunities for domestic saving; these are limited given the high levels of 'state' ownership in the region, not least in the oil industries. The relative fragility of the region's non-oil sectors is reflected in low levels of non-oil product exports; Finland alone exports more than the entire Middle Eastern region's total of 33 billion dollars. How can this situation be changed?

Some take the view that a fundamental shift in priorities, from politics and religion to economics, is required among the region's leadership elites. More specifically, proposals made include reducing spending on armaments; making efforts to be more competitive in the world market; introducing more democracy and the development of more open societies where information can be readily shared; and reducing and modernising local bureaucracies. The prospects for such fundamental changes are unclear. While the low levels of oil prices in 1995 prompted efforts to cut expenditure and raise charges for services, these reforms all but stopped when the oil price recovered in 1996. As a result, the deficits of most countries in the region continue to increase. Proponents of reform continue to press their case nevertheless. They know that little privatisation has occurred and that it should be expanded considerably. An overhaul of the region's financial structure is deemed to be essential and a revamping of legal and educational systems is required. The governments need to encourage long-term investment and to ensure that creditors are fully protected under the law and have access to quick decisions when problems arise.

Equally importantly, existing levels of corruption need significantly to be reduced. Furthermore, levels of 'non-productive' government spending will have to fall and a higher proportion of such spending be devoted to investment. Legal reforms should be undertaken with a view to encouraging a strong private sector. Of critical importance will be the future use of the region's human capital, much of which is wasted, not least because women are forbidden to work in many countries; changing this situation will be politically difficult and it is unlikely to occur in the short term given prevailing social attitudes.

Privatisation of local economic activity will inevitably require a transfer of ownership either from the state or from the ruling families which continue to govern. The *de facto* unity of state and family will make this process difficult; privatisation will in fact involve a transfer of power within the country and this may not always be welcomed by existing rulers. Some take the view that an effective policy of privatisation would undermine the ruling families' power bases and that this will therefore not be countenanced by rulers set on retaining their positions. The associated need to deregulate national business, finance and related areas of government activity, and to permit free flows of information and transparency in business dealings, would also require significant adjustments on the part of ruling families.

In the longer term as regional economies grow and people become more involved in economic activity, demands for a more significant involvement in the political process are likely to occur. However, the reaction of existing leaderships to these changes is not pre-ordained and there are signs that many recognise the need for adjustment, not least to ensure a continued prominent role for the ruling families in their state's national life. However, while many rulers understand that political liberalisation will be needed, it is clear that they will move slowly in order to ensure that change occurs in an orderly and non-violent fashion. As a consequence, privatisation, as a motor for political change, will itself be permitted to develop slowly. How significantly will this affect the development of the region's non-oil sectors?

The Non-Oil Sectors

Economic diversification away from oil has long been a significant goal of oil producers. However, oil and gas still account for over a third of GDP in GCC states and the GCC average for non-oil exports of local origin is 12 per cent of total exports. However, the aim of Gulf governments to strengthen the role of the private sector and to provide jobs for local people and gain access to advanced technology cannot be achieved by oil extraction. While the region's gas reserves offer the prospect of significant positive economic development, this road shares the drawbacks of oil in that is dependent on overseas markets, and has limited labour requirements. Nevertheless, increased global demand for gas may be anticipated and its undoubted benefits will positively affect local economies. What other areas offer significant prospects?

Many take the view that agriculture offers little promise as demonstrated by the Saudi government's decision to allow lower subsidies and tightened quotas to bring down local levels of wheat production. Its percentage of GDP is small, for example less than 1 per cent in Kuwait and 7 per cent in Saudi Arabia. Significant increases in production are unlikely because of high costs; furthermore, the overuse of non-renewable water resources is a significant negative factor.

Most countries' governments are seeking to increase their manufacturing sectors. Oil refining still accounts for a high proportion of manufacturing GDP, the remainder being split between export-oriented heavy industry (for example petrochemicals and aluminium) and light industries serving local markets. Heavy industry tends to be dominated by a small number of big companies while light industry is carried out by a large number of small private enterprises, often staffed by 8–10 people. Prospects for the petrochemical industries are promising. Total Arab petrochemical output is high and co-ordination of investment to meet anticipated increased demand should enable the region to keep in step with global requirements. Nevertheless, competition in the region and further afield is increasing, not least in key Asian markets where, for example, India and China are also increasingly large petrochemical producers. Analysts anticipate a strong world demand for aluminium and Gulf producers seem well placed to benefit from this.

The generally positive prospects for the large heavy industrial concerns are mirrored in other sectors. Policy initiatives have been developed, including offset arrangements, to attract investment into new industries and speed technology transfer. Offset arrangements have been applied extensively in defence contracts in the region but have also come into play in the civilian sector, for example in contracts with AT&T to provide telecommunications equipment in Saudi Arabia. Deals involving electronics, aircraft accessories and sugar refining, among others, are in place and results are generally perceived to be positive. Most of these successes are occurring in Saudi Arabia and the approach has been less successful in Kuwait and the UAE. Dubai is rapidly moving away from oil production as the mainstay of its economy; it is investing heavily in services, including tourism and trans-shipment, to this end.

Such programmes are all the more important given the uncertainties of interstate flows of funds and investment between Arab countries. Remittances from rich states to poor Arab states, either on a governmental basis or involving remittances by Arab workers to their families, have been disrupted in recent years. The 1980s' fall in the oil price reduced demand for foreign Arab labour, principally from Egypt, Yemen and Lebanon, in the Gulf states. Many expatriot workers returned home after the Gulf War and family remittances declined further. In addition, government aid has declined since the early 1980s, not least because of other demands on Gulf state exchequers. In countries which provided the bulk of expatriate labour to the Gulf, the result has been increased unemployment and falls in investment flows. These adverse effects encouraged some states to begin economic reform. Whether this reform will be able to overcome many of the inherent problems of the region remains to be seen.

For example, the Middle East remains dangerously short of water. In 1987 agriculture accounted for 87 per cent of the Middle East's water use and 25 per cent of its cultivated area was irrigated. World-wide, agriculture accounted for 69 per cent of water use and only 15 per cent of cultivated land is irrigated. Considerable investment will be needed to address even part of the problem; leaking pipes account for 40 per cent of 'water use' in Syria for example. Furthermore, a radical rethinking of water pricing will be necessary in many of the region's states which currently charge their customers for water at cost or below cost price. This inevitably encourages waste. Furthermore, extraction is poorly regulated in many countries and there is clear evidence that non-renewable sources of water are being diminished. All this is occurring at a time of increasing urbanisation and industrialisation; many take the view that without a radical rethinking of attitudes regarding water use many countries will face a grave crisis in the medium term. Unfortunately the prospects for dealing with this problem are slim given the political sensitivities of introducing higher charges for an essential commodity; many are fearful that the introduction of commercial pricing would cause widespread unrest. The linkage between economic 'imperatives' and political stability could not be clearer.

4 Economics Affect Politics

The Demand for Welfare

Providing social welfare and employment for the region's burgeoning population is a key challenge for its governments. Insufficient revenues from oil income, underdeveloped non-oil sectors and the narrowness of the tax base in oil producing countries point towards an inability to provide welfare support for the unemployed and underemployed of the region.

Traditionally, in the Gulf region, welfare support has been provided through religious groups and the family. In Saudi Arabia welfare support is underpinned by Islamic principles and tribal systems. Islamic values emphasise that individuals are responsible for the just distribution of wealth in their societies. Tribal groups and the extended family system which persists in the country provide welfare for the population, particularly for women who are discouraged from working. Meeting the rising aspirations of a young population, whose needs would have been met from oil revenues in the past, is increasingly difficult. Unfortunately, elevated expectations have been accompanied by the growth of a 'dependency' culture, where receiving state aid is without stigma and incentives to work are few.

The all-encompassing nature of state support has minimised individual responsibility, with subsidies and support being provided, for example, for food, water, free health care, provision of land, interest-free loans, and government dowries to subsidise marriages. Most of these provisions are not subject to means testing and a class of dependent people has emerged with few, if any, skills and a 'relaxed' work ethic. The labour required to service these provisions and meet local needs is provided by an extensive expatriate labour force; economic downturns and related unemployment have raised ethnic tensions between different expatriate groups as well as between the local Arab population and expatriates. Furthermore, rural poverty persists because wealth distribution has been uneven. Required cuts in health and education have affected particularly the women and children of rural populations. While private charity is filling some gaps, a fundamental economic restructuring, including the encouragement of women to work, appears to be essential.

Many note that the lack of freedom to work for women represents a significant burden on the Saudi economy. If existing plans to replace the expatriate work force with local workers are to be brought to fruition, women will have to be permitted to work. This will not, however, of itself solve the problem. Education needs to be reorganised to provide practical useful skills and to encourage a work ethic. Many take the view that greater emphasis must be placed on the individual's responsibility to provide for his/her own well-being.

However, given the conservative nature of Saudi society, the difficulties of changing attitudes towards welfare provision and 'proper' women's behaviour cannot be underestimated. This said, the inexorable rise in population and anticipated shortfalls in revenue point towards a future where means testing of welfare will be introduced and its provision, through subsidies and other means of support, will be increasingly linked to productive employment. Such changes would alter the fundamental nature of many Gulf societies; the differences between, for example, Saudi Arabia, Kuwait and the UAE with their varying degrees of social mobility demonstrate clearly the likely nature of such change. How will such social change affect the region's economic performance?

Social Change

Labour, capital and natural resources are the key factors driving economic growth and development. Political and social conditions strongly affect economic performance and Middle Eastern economic prospects are believed by many to be highly dependent upon future political and social developments. Some analysts emphasise the negative impact of past economic decisions on their countries' social fabric and take the view that this remains damaging for future economic prospects.

The high oil-related earnings available to Gulf states after 1973 offered an opportunity for integrated economic development. Two choices were available: to adopt a long-term development plan taking into account human requirements – this would have been a slow process, have involved relatively little spending and the region's peoples would have been prepared over time to operate effectively in an industrial environment and undertake associated skilled employment; or to undertake large capital investment projects to build up countries' infrastructure largely using imported labour and materials. In most cases, notably Saudi Arabia, the second approach was chosen. The large projects undertaken were built by foreign companies and labour and financed with petrodollars. The long-term results of this policy have been negative. For example, the majority of the local population remain outside the economic production system. The capital-intensive, high technology projects required relatively low levels of human investment from within the region and a lack of investment in human capital has resulted. No indigenous skilled workforce has been developed to maintain the costly infrastructure which has been built.

Furthermore, the negative consequences of past policies are not confined to the underdevelopment of local skills. Many argue that the inability of local political systems to adjust to changing economic circumstances has adversely affected the region's social development: corruption has become widespread, anticipated enhancement of women's status has been checked, inefficient and ineffective bureaucracies have burgeoned. Aggressive investments in human capital and the widespread involvement of the region's populations in economic development would have required the evolution of a firmly-rooted civil society with effective legal systems, applicable not least in the business sector. Some argue that the concentration on large capital projects, their manning by expatriate workers and the lack of local involvement has resulted in a political system which is ill-suited to change and not schooled in the disciplines required to facilitate genuine broad-based economic development.

'Solutions' to this problem require constructive action by the very governments which are being criticised. They need to restructure their economies and spending. Priorities should include redirection of government spending into productive investment, with less being spent on defence and large infrastructure projects; the development of a free capital market not subject to government control, thereby liberating local funds which are available for investment; restructuring the legal system to become more responsive to economic needs and commercial life; and retraining the local labour force to meet modern requirements.

Whether such changes will be initiated remains an open question. While organised groups in Western civil society press governments effectively for policy changes, few such groups exist in the Gulf states; without such pressure will local leaders take the road of reform? If they do not, and the signs are mixed, will political change be forced upon them if living standards fall as a consequence?

Political Change?

Many take the view that pressure for change does exist in the Gulf, but that its influence is gradual and long term. They note the increased emphasis on technical education. Efforts in, for example, Abu Dhabi to privatise energy and water sectors are positive pointers. Nevertheless, 'tradition' and the roles of the ruling families remain strong. Is there a genuine interest in the 'Western model'? Some observers take the view that Gulf leaderships are not interested in accepting Western models; while adopting Western technologies and some elements of Western lifestyles, their political instincts are rooted in the region's traditions and they take the view that the countries' problems can be met through changes within existing political systems.

Optimistic observers argue that the Gulf states' leaderships are well placed to deal with the problems of merging traditional and modern elements within their societies. They note that governments are already carrying through changes which will, with good fortune and stable oil prices, address problems that give rise to social and political tensions. In Saudi Arabia, for example, plans exist to generate the jobs needed for a growing population. An estimated 800,000 new jobs will be required over the next five years and these will be provided through a combination of retirement, economic growth and replacing expatriate workers. Government subsidies for the creation of jobs will be provided although the public sector is expected to provide most of the vacancies. In addition, in the defence sector there is a new emphasis on training local people and recruitment of more Saudis, local content clauses and joint ventures. An extra 15 million riyal has been allocated to education and its spending is being reoriented. The health care system is being reorganised to make it more effective. New money is to be provided for public works. Government budgets are to be more closely monitored by the Ministry of Finance and problem areas, including water, the national airline and power companies are to be reorganised.

It is possible that these initiatives will serve to maintain prosperity and ensure a distribution of wealth which will help to maintain social stability. Will prosperous Saudis seek political reform? Many observers doubt this. They take the view that the recent reorganisations of the Saudi Council of Ministers and the inclusion of Western-educated, experienced personnel will improve the performance of government. The Saudi Majlis is maturing, its selected representatives having growing influence on taxation issues and the running of government-subsidised utilities. However, these changes are unlikely to lead to a rapid erosion of the ruling family's power or to the granting of legislative responsibilities. The largely closed nature of the ruling family's decision-making is likely to continue, and there appears to be little widespread pressure for this situation to change. The autocratic traditions of the region, albeit sometimes in benign form, remain entrenched. That dissent exists has been demonstrated by violent events but few believe that it represents a threat to regime stability in the near term. Effective internal security agencies are focusing their activities against religious conservatives, many of whom are perceived to have ties with Iranian operatives. Other less radical potential leaders of opposition appear likely to be co-opted into the governing system. While the arrangements through which the people are able to inform and advise their leaders about problems and aspirations remain informal they persist none the less, being based on the traditions of tribal society. Provided the rulers remain sensitive to their peoples' aspirations the stability of the Gulf states' political systems seems assured in the short-to-medium term.

Can external political factors and crises threaten this situation? Would a collapse in the Middle East Peace Process exacerbate Arab states' problems to a degree which would call their future stability into question?

5 Implications for Security

Economics and the Peace Process

The nature of the linkage between the Middle East's economic development and the historic rivalry between Israelis and Arabs is unclear. Would a failure of the Peace Process adversely effect the region's economies? There is a 'received wisdom' that the Middle East is an area of vast economic potential which is being squandered because of conflict and the resulting diversion of resources and attention away from economic development. It is a fact that the GDP of the Arab world is broadly equal to that of Spain, and the Spanish economy is more diversified. Nevertheless, steady growth is predicted in the region given reasonably stable oil prices and economic reforms. Furthermore, European initiatives under the Barcelona process should make a significant impact in the Maghreb region. Nevertheless, the negative economic consequences of confrontation are recognisable: higher levels of costly arms purchases, economic boycotts of Israeli goods, uncertainties regarding foreign direct investments in states bordering Israel, and a lack of Israeli–Arab trade.

Would a successful conclusion to the Peace Process alter this situation? Many take the view that arms purchases will continue anyway given mutual inter-Arab uncertainties. Israel will continue to look to the West as its primary trading partner rather than its Arab neighbours. The Arab boycott of Israeli goods has already ceased and, many would argue, the paucity of FDI in Arab states has more to do with their internal condition than their differences with Israel. Nevertheless, the multilateral element of the Middle East Peace Process has focused in part on economic issues as a means to increase Arab–Israeli contact and co-operation. However, progress at the multilateral level is linked closely with the bilateral elements of the Peace Process. The Arabs link them explicitly; for example, Syria's President Assad will not participate in multilateral discussion before a resolution of the Golan Heights and other bilateral issues. Even those Arab states involved in the multilateral process explicitly acknowledge this linkage.

Some progress has been made in the regional economic group with a view to establishing mutually-beneficial links; underpinning these efforts is the assumption that increased trade and more closely interlinking economies diminish the possibilities for war. The Copenhagen Action Plan of 1993 identified specific projects for action including transport and education. With the support of the European Union, 'fast track' projects have been developed, involving Israel, Jordan, Palestine and Egypt, to upgrade countries' border posts and to establish a Bank for Economic Co-operation and Development. Support for the economies of the West Bank and Gaza has also been forthcoming. Three meetings of the group have been held on the Middle East and North African economies and to promote economic collaboration but the last, in 1997, was the least productive; Egyptian criticism of Israeli policies and the Peace Process appeared to undermine progress made at previous meetings.

Outside the small group of core states involved in these meetings the involvement of Arab states is minimal. The Gulf countries in particular are little engaged politically and there appears to be little prospect of their financing any new initiatives. Their commitment, or otherwise, to economic reform is little affected by the Arab–Israeli dispute. Indeed, the same may be said for Iraq and Iran where other factors weigh heavier in their respective economic policies and prospects. Indeed, governments which may already be criticised for required economic reforms seem unlikely to pursue a vision of Arab–Israeli peace which will merely serve to draw additional criticism upon them. The current high level of Israeli–Palestinian confrontation and the dubious future of the Peace Process offer little incentive for Arab governments to develop initiatives for economic co-operation.

The people most likely to suffer in this situation are those living in the West Bank and Gaza, whose economy remains vulnerable. For them, and indeed for Jordanians, a genuine peace would offer the prospects of economic development and eventual relative prosperity. Current mutual suspicions appear to make this a distant prospect and the hardening of attitudes on both sides serves merely to reinforce Palestinian resentments about perceived inequalities and Israeli domination. Given this impasse and the lack of genuine economic incentives, how can positive progress be promoted? Is there a significant role to be played by actors outside the region?

US Policies

The key external player in the Middle East region continues to be the United States. The US remains engaged in the Middle East to promote and defend its national interests; for example, while the US is increasingly less dependent upon Gulf oil it remains committed to ensuring that low cost oil resources in Saudi Arabia and the Gulf states remain available to the industrial world. Its commitment to the Middle East Peace Process remains firm and talk of abandoning the process because of current difficulties is firmly rejected.

The Peace Process is one of the four key elements driving US policy. Others include maintenance of political and economic stability in friendly states; and the containment of Iraq and Iran. US policy *vis-à-vis* Iraq is unlikely to change until there is a change of regime in Baghdad. The maintenance of economic sanctions, supporting the work of UNSCOM and allowing Iraqi oil sales to fund humanitarian assistance remain the cornerstones of US policy. US manpower and resources will continue to be committed in the region to ensure the containment of any Iraqi military threat. This policy is mirrored to a large degree with regard to Iran. Iranian support for terrorism, its opposition to the Middle East Peace Process, its efforts to acquire weapons of mass destruction and continued human rights abuses reinforce US policy. The US remains committed to economic sanctions, notwithstanding the criticisms of its European allies; the view is taken that these are effective and affect the Iranian regime's behaviour. While dialogue between the US and Iran is not precluded on the US side and no preconditions have been established, contacts will only be developed if organised on an official level by the Iranian government. Without significant changes in Iranian policy the prospects for a dialogue remain minimal.

The US government has sought to maximise international co-operation in its containment efforts, but it has been prepared to act unilaterally where allied support has not been forthcoming, notably with regard to the introduction of the Iran Libya Sanctions Action (ILSA). The US aim is to prevent investment in Iran in order to limit Iranian capabilities to cause trouble in the region or further afield. There appears to be little prospect of this policy changing as there is no constituency in the US pressing for a change in policy. European opposition to sanctions has not altered US policy and is unlikely to do so. While these differences give rise to some friction, in some areas, notably the implementation of the Wassenaar Agreement on technology transfers, US–European co-operation works well. US pressure on Russia and China to prevent nuclear related exports to Iran is likely to continue.

The US military presence in the Middle East remains a significant source of influence. It is generally welcome in the Gulf and the US has sought to be responsive to Arab states' sensitivities regarding bases and the stationing of troops. While not without difficulties, the US presence is encouraged by local regimes; the need for US protection against powerful potential adversaries, and the provision of military equipment and training reinforce close US ties with the Gulf states.

Notwithstanding the generally positive picture, there is evidence of a ground swell of opinion within local elites stressing the need for greater US consultation on issues of mutual interest. Concerns that US policy makers may adopt an increasingly unilateralist approach have become evident. US policy makers are aware of this trend and are emphasising the need for senior-level discussion with both local states and European allies to maximise a commonality of approach to the region's problems. For example, the efforts of the European Union envoy to the Middle East Peace Process have been welcome in Washington as supportive of American efforts. Given the continued difficult security problems in the region, such co-ordinated policy and action would undoubtedly be welcome.

6 Conclusions

The health of the international oil industry has a direct impact on the economies of many Middle Eastern states. Their future economic, political and social development will depend upon income earned from their oil industries. In the near term, prospects look promising given anticipated growing world demand for energy and continued restrictions on Iraqi oil production. However, it is uncertain whether anticipated increased demand for oil products will be met from Middle Eastern sources. The future price of Middle East oil is also uncertain given the competition of potential alternative suppliers.

In early 1997 it was believed that increases in Middle Eastern production would be sold primarily in the Asian market. Demand in Asia may be suppressed for political reasons in some states in the region, notably China, which would adversely affect Middle Eastern sales. Given the variables involved and uncertainties about future trends it is likely that oil prices will be volatile for the foreseeable future. This will inevitably complicate economic planning and decision-making of Middle Eastern governments which are dependent on oil sales for most of their revenue.

Such difficulties appeared to threaten the economic well-being and political stability of a number of Gulf state oil producers in 1996. Cuts in government spending and services and increasing taxation offer a potential way forward, but little practical action in this direction has occurred as yet. While the short-term rise in oil prices experienced in the second half of 1996 enabled action to be deferred, rising expectations of growing populations mean that oil income is unlikely to be sufficient to meet popular aspirations or to maintain healthy Gulf economies.

This is particularly the case in Iran with its large population and a stagnating economy which suffers from the adverse effects of the country's political and economic isolation. Rising internal demand for energy, driven by artificially low domestic pricing and subsidies and by high levels of waste, is reducing the amount of oil available for export. Between 60 and 80 billion dollars will be needed over the next 13 years to maintain current levels of oil production, to develop the petrochemical industry, and to exploit and export production from the country's extensive gas reserves. Sufficient foreign direct investment and involvement of multinational energy companies is unlikely in the current political situation. Whatever the results of the May 1997 election, power will remain diffused among competing groups within the Iranian ruling elite and little change can be expected in Iranian foreign policy in the near term. As a consequence the Iranian energy industry will remain starved of investment and its potential underdeveloped.

This negative picture is repeated, albeit with greater intensity, in Iraq. Should UN sanctions be removed, the country has potential rapidly to increase production and it possesses the last major unexploited source of easily recoverable oil in the world. Such a change in Iraq's fortunes is dependent upon the removal of Saddam Hussein and his regime from power. If and how soon this will occur remains an open question. The resulting increases in Iraqi oil production and exports would reduce the oil price, which could have adverse consequences for other Middle Eastern suppliers. Competition between Iraq and Saudi Arabia could be particularly intense in such circumstances.

Given these uncertainties, economic diversification away from oil remains attractive to Middle East producers not least as a means to strengthen the role of the private sector, to provide jobs for growing populations, and to gain access to advanced technology. The principal focus will be on manufacturing industry: export-orientated heavy industry, petrochemicals and aluminium for example, and light industry serving local markets and generally constituted by small private enterprises. How far these sectors can be developed in the face of international and indeed expected intra-Gulf competition remains an open question. Gulf state applications for World Trade Organisation (WTO) membership appear to confirm their understanding of the need for liberalisation as a stimulus to investment and trade. However, economic progress continues to be adversely affected by high levels of defence spending. The 1992 defence budgets of Arab countries totalled $416 billion and these excluded expenditure on conscription, security-related expenditures and arms imports. It is unclear whether this is sustainable in the long term.

The positive effects within the region of the 1996 increase in oil prices remain important: demand for Arab workers in the Gulf has increased as have related worker remittances to their home countries. An upswing in international trade and improvement in the European economy has increased demand for Maghreb exports. Good rainfall in North Africa led to a sharp rise in agricultural production in Morocco, Tunisia and Egypt, which enabled GDP to increase at healthy rates. The short-term prospects for Arab non-oil producers have improved. Whether this combination of circumstances will be repeated in future years is uncertain.

To improve future prospects the Arab economies need to be integrated fully into the rapidly changing world economy. The liberalisation of local economies and their opening up to foreign investment is essential. The huge flows of capital in the global economic system are largely by-passing the Middle East. For the region to become attractive to investors, and thereby underpin economic development and diversification, it is important that the governments of the region focus more on economics than politics and religion; decrease spending on arms; open their economies to competition in the world market; encourage democratic decision-making; reduce burdensome bureaucracies; encourage privatisation of national assets; modernise their financial infrastructures; and revamp their legal and education systems.

Implementing these and other changes is no mean task. However, oil income alone can no longer support the health care, education, housing and other needs of the region's population. A culture of welfare dependence has developed in the Gulf states which, if fractured, could result in widespread social disruption. Finding other sources of income to finance welfare offers a partial solution; in addition, a change of popular attitudes is essential whereby incomes are linked directly to economically-productive activity and welfare provision is focused primarily on those in genuine need. While change will inevitably be gradual and must take due account of religious sensitivities, it is essential that suitable, educated and motivated workforces are available to carry through the required economic changes which will be necessary to maintain and increase the Gulf region's prosperity.

Such economic development will not take place in a vacuum. Political and social factors will critically affect progress. For sound economies to be developed it will be necessary to establish long-term development plans which take into account the provision of adequate human resources to support economic development. People need to be prepared for and able to work in a newly-constructed industrial environment. While investment in physical infrastructure and capital projects is important it needs to be linked closely with the available human capital in the region. Local regimes appear to be recognising the importance of these factors and adjustments in government policy are occurring, albeit slowly. There is concern that rapid change could undermine internal stability and threaten both the envisaged economic reforms and the position of existing regimes.

While political change is likely to be firmly rooted in the region's political traditions, with family and tribal influences remaining strong, there are signs that the Gulf's ruling elites have concluded that more broadly-based and public decision-making is required. While key decision taking remains firmly located inside the ruling family circles, more frequent and wider access to the holders of power and heightened sensitivity to the needs of, for example, business elites seem likely.

Many take the view that this gradualist approach offers the best prospect for orderly and progressive change. However, the possibility remains that dramatic political events may overwhelm the region. A collapse of the Middle East Peace Process and linked violence cannot but damage the prospects for economic and political change. Government spending will be diverted into defence expenditure, potential investors in the region will be discouraged, and low levels of intra-regional trade will continue. The limited progress made to date in developing economic links between Israel and its Arab neighbours will inevitably be threatened. However, the logic underpinning the desire for economic reform in the Arab countries will not be undermined and it is likely that economic reform will continue, particularly in states far removed from Israel, whatever the short-term effects of progress or failures in the Peace Process. This said, the achieving of a peace cannot but contribute positively towards the progress of economic development in the region.

It is for this reason, among others, that United States and European powers have sought to facilitate reconciliation in the region. The United States' role remains central to the region's future. Its commitment to the Peace Process appears to be firm as is its support for oil producers and US allies in the Gulf. The policy of containing its perceived adversaries, Iraq and Iran, remains in place; notwithstanding the criticism that this has generated in the Iranian case, notably from European states which have refused to impose the economic sanctions against Iran called for by the United States. Within the Gulf region, there appears to be a recognition that US leadership remains important and a positive benefit, but there is also concern that the US should do more to consider the views of its friends in the region who have positive contributions to make to the evolution of US policy. There is evidence that this is occurring, notably with regard to Iran where the current Administration appears to be at least considering a re-evaluation of its current 'containment' policy.

However, while the US role remains central to the evolution of security questions in the Middle East, its economic future remains dependent upon the actions and attitudes of the peoples and governments of the region itself. While oil wealth has brought good fortune and comfort to many, the maintenance and improvement of the region's growing population will require a movement away from oil 'dependency' to broadly-based economies which are firmly integrated in the global economic system. This is all the more the case in Arab countries which do not have significant oil reserves. While healthy oil prices may do much to facilitate the success of such a transition in oil-producing states, sound political leadership, economic flexibility and, perhaps above all, a genuine commitment of all concerned to economic restructuring will be essential.

Notes

1. See Richard Latter, 'Prospects for Peace in the Gulf', *Wilton Park Paper* 116, March 1996.

2. 'Big Boom for Qatar', *Foreign Report,* 13 March 1997, p. 67.

6

Maintaining Stability in East Asia

Report based on Wilton Park Conference 501: 17–20 June 1997 on
'Prospects for Peace and Stability in East Asia'

Richard Latter

1 Introduction

The longer-term prospects for peace and stability in East Asia depend principally on the answer to one question: 'what role will China seek to play in the region?' In the nearer term, the looming crisis on the Korean Peninsula is likely to feature strongly in the deliberations of the region's governments, but dealing with China's future international actions and policies will be the central focus of their attention at the turn of the century.

> In the early 1990s, it became clear that China was a rising power. By the mid-1990s, there was considerable evidence that China planned to use its new-found influence in an assertive way. The second half of the decade will demonstrate whether the outside world is prepared to restrain as well as engage an assertive China.[1]

China's rise is linked firmly to its economic growth, ranging from 9.9 to 11.1 per cent in the 1980s and 1990s, and associated increases in military expenditure. Continued Chinese growth is anticipated, albeit at slower rates, at a time when other states in the region are increasingly concerned about their future economic prospects. The reasons for such concern vary: at one extreme North Korea appears to be on the verge of economic collapse, which prompts fears of possible 'irrational' military action by its leadership; in contrast the Japanese economy suffers from the ills of a mature capitalist economy. The 'Asian Tigers' are not immune:

> Once touted as Southeast Asia's fastest-growing economy, Thailand is staring at a prolonged period of hardship. Even the most bullish forecasts anticipate a slow recovery, and official estimates of GDP growth weigh in below 6 per cent this year, compared with 8.7 per cent in 1995. Pessimists predict a devaluation of the currency and a shakeout of corporate Thailand. Watching all this, investors in the region are wondering whether the Thai dynamo has now become an economic domino – one that will somehow crimp the growth of Thailand's booming Southeast Asian neighbours.[2]

The social consequences of an economic downturn may exacerbate internal tensions in many of the region's states. Religious and ethnic differences, continued poverty and a growing gap between rich and poor, generational differences and demands for wider access to political decision-making already generate tensions, sometimes violent, which adversely affect the prospects for sustainable stability.[3]

Increased internal instability cannot but adversely affect inter-state relations in a region in which the potential for an increase in international tension appears to be growing. Likely flashpoints include Korea, Taiwan, the South China Sea, and the emergence of other disputes cannot be discounted.

Much depends on China. Will it 'inevitably become more like the West – non-ideological, pragmatic, materialistic, and progressively freer in its culture and politics'?[4] Is it correct to view the country as 'militarily weak and unthreatening: while Beijing tends toward rhetorical excess, its actual behaviour has been far more cautious, aimed at the overriding goals of economic growth and regional stability'?[5] Some argue that this view is obsolete, noting increased Chinese military power and its emergence as a great power rival of the United States: 'Driven by nationalist sentiment, a yearning to redeem the humiliations of the past, and the simple urge for international power, China is seeking to replace the United States as the dominant power in Asia'.[6]

Others take a different view. While recognising that US–Chinese relations could develop in a number of directions[7] they note that the foundations for a positive relationship do exist:

Economic connection could be one pillar (of cooperation). China's reliance on US capital, technology, and investment has been the primary motive behind Beijing's efforts in overcoming frequent conflicts in bilateral relations. Meanwhile, the high expectation of the US business community of benefiting from one of the world's largest and fastest growing economies played a decisive role in President Clinton's decision to de-link the Most-Favoured Nation (MFN) trading status for China from its human rights performance. Security cooperation could be the other area where the Sino-American relationship might again find some common direction. Since both countries have stakes in and the capabilities to maintain regional stability, their respective national interests converge on this point.[8]

Whether US–Chinese relations will develop in such a benign fashion remains an open question. Given such uncertainty, countries in East Asia are adjusting their foreign, security and defence policies to seek to anticipate possible negative developments in future. For example, Japan has re-emphasised its commitment to its defence links with the United States. While some take the view that trade differences and rising anti-Americanism in Japan could undermine this link[9] even they appear to take the view that positive initiatives on the US side can overcome any difficulties. Furthermore, problems in Korea and the coolness of Chinese–Japanese relations point to strong US–Japanese links for the foreseeable future; this is all the more likely given the widely perceived continued lack of internationalism in Japan and its diplomacy of 'the three "Ss": silent, smiling, and sleeping'.[10]

While China may represent the 'most forceful catalyst for change' in Japanese diplomacy, developments in Korea could have a greater impact in the near term:

Given the glacial pace of reforms in North Korea, the possibility of North Korean collapse and the subsequent reunification of the Korean peninsula under South Korean terms is very real. Such an outcome could trigger a wholesale restructuring of security relations among major powers that have vital interests in the region.[11]

More negatively, the possibility of open conflict between the two Koreas cannot be discounted, with inevitable negative consequences for regional security and prosperity. Even a peaceful reunification of Korea will generate problems not least because unification is likely to take place 'in a security environment without institutions':[12] parallels can be drawn with German reunification and the importance of NATO, the EU and OSCE in ensuring that this occurred in a benign environment.

Regional institutions have played an important role in South-East Asian security deliberations in the past decade, although they have functioned in a relatively benign regional security environment with few inter-state frictions. The Association of South East Asian Nations (ASEAN) and the ASEAN Regional Forum (ARF) are generally regarded as 'successes', having facilitated political dialogue to influence the climate of international relations between states in such a way as to ensure conflict avoidance and the management of differences. However, future problems are already emerging: the enlargement of ASEAN to include Burma, Cambodia and Laos will make consensus and cooperation more difficult and the controversies over Burma's inclusion may prove to be damaging. The future of ARF may be adversely affected by non-ASEAN ARF members who question ASEAN's capacity to lead a forum which is concerned with the broader East Asian region.

Even in South-East Asia, current institutional arrangements, with their emphasis on consensus may not be well placed to deal with increasing inter-state tensions, notably those associated with the Spratly, Paracel and other island groups:

> In several ways the dispute looks like a model for the new kind of conflict which is likely to plague East Asia over the next few decades . . . The struggle now being waged is for control, not of people, but of resources in the fastest growing, energy-poorest region in the world.[13]

The procurement of modern weapons by states party to the dispute, notably air and sea capabilities relevant to control of large maritime areas, is an indicator that, in this context at least, faith in the ASEAN process may be declining. Inevitably its success or failure will be influenced by the policies of the major powers which are active in the region. Is their influence likely to be benign?

2 Policies of the Major Regional Powers
China

The Chinese government seeks to establish China as a comprehensive great power (i.e. both economic and military), with a major voice in the East Asian region. To achieve this, modernisation and economic development are deemed to be essential; to this end, regional stability and cordial relations with neighbours are a Chinese priority. As a result, a provocative or aggressive Chinese foreign policy is unlikely. However, Beijing's actions are more unpredictable, and may possibly involve the use of military force, if perceived vital interests, notably regarding Taiwan, are threatened.

Chinese economic growth has been impressive in the past decade and its benefits to China are such that continued economic development is the central priority of the Beijing government. Official plans explicitly aim to establish China as a 'medium' developed country in the next quarter of a century. Yet this is to be achieved without undermining domestic stability; there are to be 'no more cultural revolutions'. Political reform is to be introduced gradually in order to ensure that there is no disruption of development by political turmoil; political opposition is little tolerated as a result.

The effects of rapid economic and social change have yet to emerge; while certainly beneficial for many in the short term, growing wealth and disparities may give rise to social tensions, for example between generations, and political conflict. Furthermore, the country already faces an uncertain political future as the role of the Communist Party is to be called increasingly into question in the decade ahead. As economic growth continues, new interest groups are likely to challenge the Party's exclusive control of the country's politics. Many take the view that its legitimacy is already eroding. This need not inevitably lead to internal disorder, but a tension between those pressing for political change and those seeking to retain power is inevitable.

Internationally, the Chinese government seeks cooperation with its neighbours rather than 'isolation' or 'expansion'. China's security concept emphasises a reliable defence which is to be balanced against economic development goals; increased security through closer bilateral cooperation; and engaging in multilateral dialogue and confidence-building measures (CBMs), for example in Central Asia. Chinese spokesmen emphasise their country's benign role in the East Asian region.

This positive picture contrasts with the generally negative Chinese view of the United States and, to a lesser degree, Japan. The US continues to be depicted as a regional hegemon still playing Cold War games. Reservations about the United States' presence in the region are regularly included in Chinese government statements, and there is concern about the perceived US–Japanese 'containment' of China. These negative views were reinforced by US fleet deployments during the 1996 Taiwan crisis and, more recently, by US–Japanese agreements to strengthen their military-to-military cooperation.

Taiwan remains a sensitive issue for the Beijing government which insists that Taiwan be reintegrated within China and resists strongly notions of Taiwanese independence. Many take the view that China would use military force to prevent this occurring. The modernisation of the Chinese military is being organised with this eventuality in mind, as well as being designed to meet broader security concerns such as a possible re-emergence of Russia as a major Asian power, a revival of Japanese militarism, and the emergence of an adversarial relationship with the United States. However, any Chinese military operation against Taiwan would face formidable obstacles and Chinese success in a military confrontation is not assured. A failure of mainland Chinese forces would damage severely Chinese international standing and undermine the government's domestic authority. For these reasons, Chinese leaders may not readily take up the military option in a future crisis.

Most neighbouring countries do not foresee a Chinese military threat in the next decade and some believe that it is also unlikely to materialise in the longer term. For the countries to the south, largely members of ASEAN, the response to emerging Chinese power has been one of 'engagement', of seeking areas of potentially fruitful cooperation, both bilaterally and multilaterally. This approach has been maintained despite ASEAN reservations about the Chinese policy in the South China Sea and concern about the lack of transparency regarding Chinese military goals and planning which leads some analysts to 'think the worst'. Anxiety is increased because it remains unclear whether military priorities are being set by the government in Beijing or by elements of the People's Liberation Army (PLA). This said, there is little interest in the region in seeking to prevent China from becoming a great power.

This is believed by many to be inevitable; it is the uses to which such power may be put that cause unease. The hope of ASEAN countries is that a powerful China will be a cooperative partner in the region rather than a disruptive element. This view lies at the centre of US policy towards China.

The United States

The United States will remain militarily active in the East Asian region to support its national economic, political and security interests. The nature of the US presence will alter as circumstances change but it is likely to continue to deploy 100,000 troops in the region and to enhance its force projection capability. Significant changes are only likely to occur if there is a major regional crisis. ASEAN countries generally view a strong US presence both as a counter to Chinese power and as a positive influence on Japanese foreign and security policies. In South Korea, the US is perceived as a vital ally ensuring the country's security *vis-à-vis* its northern neighbour. The overall US goal is to facilitate the maintenance of a stable, prosperous region in which the US plays a major stabilising role in cooperation with the region's states:

- The United States seeks a more equal partnership with Japan in which Japanese military capabilities remain complementary to those of the United States; the US is encouraging Japan to adopt a more proactive security role in the region, but subject to clear limits and guidelines.

- The United States supports the peaceful reunification of Korea and is seeking to act as a broker between the two Koreas, a role which it is likely to continue in the future between a reunified Korea and Japan.

- The United States supports the development of a prosperous, tolerant and cooperative China and recognises its potential as a possible partner in Asia; the US consistently advocates a peaceful accommodation between the Beijing government and Taiwan.

Achieving these goals will be complicated by differences in the American policy-making elite over such issues as human rights in China, trade with Japan and China, and the inclusion of Burma in ASEAN. The often widely differing views expressed in the US press, by the Congress and by the Clinton Administration, project, at best, a muddled foreign policy image and, at worst, are used selectively by anti-American elements in Asia to criticise US policy. The US debates about Asian contributions to US election funds further complicate US policy-making. There is an evident need to ensure that official policy is effectively projected by US Administrations to overcome the potential negative consequences of reported internal differences.

However, clarity alone will not enable the United States to bring about the US–Japanese–Chinese harmony which it desires. Achieving this will be difficult given current Chinese suspicions about the US role in the region. The Chinese view of the US presence has vacillated from cautious acceptance to outright opposition. Current Chinese statements are openly critical of the US, and many take the view that the long-term Chinese goal is to act as the principal regional power broker, supplanting the United States: a unified Korea would result in the withdrawal of US forces, and in the longer term a US troop withdrawal from Japan would occur. While recognising the importance of good Sino-US relations, the Chinese perceive a declining US interest in genuine partnership and an emerging US view of China as a competitor within the region. The United States policy on Taiwan is a source of particular irritation. Chinese officials question the credibility of US public pronouncements urging

Taiwanese restraint in its dealings with Beijing. Noting the prompt US military reaction during the 1996 Taiwan crisis, many Chinese take the view that the United States is *de facto* encouraging Taiwanese separatism. US spokesmen report these views and continue to emphasise the need for US–Chinese cooperation. The Chinese response has been cool. During 1997, the focus of Chinese criticism has concentrated increasingly on US–Japanese relations following the unveiling of the US–Japanese defence guidelines review.

From a US perspective, the review was prompted by experiences during the Gulf War when Japanese support was largely financial, and securing cooperation with the Japanese armed forces to facilitate the prosecution of the war proved to be difficult. Alarm about Korean nuclear weapons programmes and linked missile development reinforced Japanese perceptions that there was a need to define clearly the extent of and limits on future military cooperation. A deliberate effort has been made to make the review transparent by the issuing of an interim report in the spring of 1997. The defence guidelines were intended to gauge the reaction of states in the region.

The 'new' US–Japanese arrangement has caused concern in Beijing, principally because of a perceived ambiguity about the geographical range of future Japanese military operations. The Chinese fear that US involvement in a future Taiwan crisis will inevitably involve Japan, given the envisaged collaboration. In addition, the criticism is made in Beijing that US–Japanese policies seem to be predicated on past Cold War concerns, the primacy of military factors in regional security, and the possible need to 'contain' China in the future.

US analysts reject such concerns, noting, for example, that the guidelines explicitly include a commitment to continuing Japan's traditional post-war role in the region. They also note that the Japanese armed forces are being reduced to approximately one quarter of a million, while the People's Republic of China has standing forces of two and a half million and is a nuclear power. They regard Chinese expressions of concern about rising Japanese military power as at best disingenuous. American observers take the view that the key problem in US–Chinese relations remains Taiwan rather than Japan. Thus Chinese criticisms of US development of ballistic missile defences in collaboration with Japan are not founded in concerns about Japanese policy but rather fears that subsequent deployment of such systems in Taiwan would strengthen that country's capacity to resist future Chinese influence.

US observers emphasise that the US–Japanese guidelines do not represent a treaty or war plan and that they are open to public scrutiny. The fact that they contain no geographical delineation does not imply a threat to neighbours' security; it reflects the fact that the contingency planning involved addresses risks and problems which have yet to emerge. The aim is to agree what can be done, not where it will happen.

These views are generally supported by policy-makers and analysts in Japan.

Japan

The US–Japanese alliance remains central to Japanese security policy. However, the alliance is no longer intended to contain the Soviet Union, and its function of restraining possible Japanese militarism is also largely defunct. While the emphasis of Japanese security policy is increasingly on enhancing regional security, in addition to defending the Japanese homeland, much is unchanged. Japan continues to provide bases for the US in return for American security assurances. As a consequence Japan remains dependent on US forces for its defence and is not seeking to be militarily self-sufficient. The US–Japanese Treaty of Mutual Cooperation and Security continues to cover action in response to an actual or imminent armed attack against Japan and upon the provision of appropriate Japanese logistical support for US military operations in the (broadly defined) Far East region. However, changing international circumstances led Japanese policy-makers to conclude that a further elaboration was required regarding Japanese–US cooperation in support of US operations in the region. The US criticism of Japanese 'cheque book' diplomacy during the Gulf War and Japan's lack of preparedness to undertake possible response options during the 1994 crisis with North Korea pointed to a need to clarify the US and Japan's respective roles, both in the event of an attack on Japan, and if the crisis were to occur in areas nearby.

The resulting guidelines cover collaboration in normal peacetime circumstances, if Japan is physically attacked, or if problems arise in areas surrounding Japan which may affect Japanese stability and security. The guidelines do not specify possible contingencies because both governments maintain that their alliance is not directed against any state in particular. Furthermore the guidelines review is being conducted on the understanding that there will be no change in any rights or obligations existing under current bilateral US–Japanese security arrangements and that changes will occur within the limitations of the Japanese constitution.

The interim guidelines report lists 40 items in 15 fields of cooperation to deal with the emergency situations near Japan; they cover: humanitarian activities, relief and transfer operations for refugees, search and rescue operations at sea, non-combat and evacuation operations, minesweeping in Japanese territorial waters and on the high seas, and inspection of unidentified ships to ensure the effective implementation of economic sanctions against an aggressor. Japan will provide additional land and facilities to US forces and allow the US military to use Japanese defence force facilities and civilian ports and airports for supply and other purposes. Information-sharing will be increased. Japanese provisions and materials, including petroleum oil and lubricants but excluding weapons and ammunition, will be made available to US vessels and aircraft when requested.

These measures reflect the continued high level of Japanese–US cooperation on security issues. Nevertheless differences of view regarding likely security threats exist in Japan and the United States. For example, 75 per cent of American respondents favour Japanese cooperation with US military action in the event of a conflict between Taiwan and China, while 54 per cent of Japanese oppose such cooperation. In another poll, 45 per cent of Japanese surveyed thought of China more as an ally than an adversary, while 59 per cent of American respondents said that they thought of China as a rival. Their respective perceptions of threats also differed; US respondents ranking threats as: China (34 per cent), North Korea (24 per cent), Russia (7 per cent), while Japanese ranked them as Korea (54 per cent), China (19 per cent), Russia (8 per cent). Despite these differences a significant commonality of views persists: for example, 60 and 64 per cent of Americans and Japanese, respectively, support the recognition of Taiwan as an independent nation. The problem of Korea is a priority concern to governments in both countries.

Despite these similarities and differences Japanese spokesmen emphasise repeatedly that changes in policy are not intended and will not affect the prevailing *status quo* within the region and Japan's significance within it. This contrasts somewhat with the view in some US circles that Japan's role should indeed change significantly and that it should take on a far greater responsibility for the maintenance of regional stability and security. In the near term such a change in Japanese policy appears to be extremely unlikely.

However, the onset of a regional crisis could alter this situation. The outbreak of violence on the Korean peninsula could provide the catalyst for such change.

3 Possible Regional Crises
The Korean Peninsula

Concerns that a violent crisis could occur in Korea are founded on fears of a possible internal collapse in the North Korean state, deriving from the current reported famine in the country which could prompt its leadership to attack South Korea in a desperate attempt to maintain its position. How realistic is this scenario?

The North Korean state has been remarkably stable over the past four decades, and a successful and peaceful transfer of power in 1994 pointed towards continued stability. Indeed, the political system remains much as it was, the country being run by a small non-democratic clique backed by the country's military. Despite the existence of major food shortages, the government has continued to function effectively and the population appears to remain loyal. There is evidence of a loosening of economic structures to facilitate increases in agricultural production; local leaderships appear to be active in meeting localised problems. In these circumstances the collapse of the North Korean state appears to be unlikely. Indeed, its government appears to be more open to contacts with the outside world than it has in recent decades. International organisations are now permitted to work inside the country; for example, the United Nations Development Programme (UNDP), the International Red Cross, the International Atomic Energy Agency (IAEA), and various humanitarian agencies. Furthermore, regular links are maintained with the United States government, and the onset of the four-party talks with the US, China and South Korea is encouraging. This said, the North Korean leadership appears to continue to take the view that the country is isolated and threatened; hostility towards South Korea and close US–Japanese ties appears to be unabated.

In contrast, South Korea is a successful state. It is fully integrated in the international economy, has achieved high economic growth rates and a 'developed' country standard of living. However, the South Korean government remains fearful of the North and is concerned that the United States may negotiate agreements with North Korea without South Korean consent and against South Korean interests. Recent corruption scandals have damaged national confidence, and the approach of presidential elections reinforces current political uncertainty. A likely result is a lack of innovation and a degree of incoherence in South Korean foreign policy development. While the country remains committed to reunification with the North, this is regarded as a long-term project. In the near term South Korea is seeking to increase contacts between the countries with a view to increasing mutual trust and cooperation. The prospect of combining the economic strength of the South with the human and natural resources of the North is an attractive one which reinforces interest in reunification. At a practical level, contacts between the two Koreas are being developed, not least through the implementation of the Nuclear Reactor Deal designed to prevent the emergence of North Korea as a nuclear weapons power. However, there is little expectation that such contacts will lead to a rapid rapprochement between the two countries, much less to reunification. For this to occur, it is likely that a new generation of political leaders will have to emerge in both countries.

However, there are signs that economic factors are easing the path towards future collaboration. By the 1970s, the North Korean leadership were aware that their country's economic performance fell well below that of South Korea. The rise in oil prices damaged North Korean raw material exports, and the country defaulted on loans as a result. Little foreign credit or foreign direct investment has flowed into the country subsequently because few potential donors and investors were prepared to risk a second North Korean default. In an effort to overcome these problems, an Economic Zone was created in the early 1990s to encourage trade and investment. And this has been a modest success. For example, the South Korean government now permits South Korean companies to invest in the Economic Zone. Many take the view that this type of economic cooperation will provide the underpinning for improved political contacts in the longer term.

The South Korean government continues to promote the idea of a gradual reunification, beginning with people-to-people contacts, followed by the creation of a transitional body which will work in cooperation with both governments and which will be superseded eventually by one government after elections in both countries. Considerable South Korean economic support for the North, not least during the current food crisis, is intended to advance the reunification process. However, such assistance is given upon the condition that peace is maintained on the peninsula. Is there any likelihood of war breaking out?

South Koreans continue to fear that this is a genuine possibility, pointing to North Korean domestic problems, the high state of readiness of the North Korean armed forces and their professed chemical and biological weapons fighting capability, and the bellicose statements of North Korean military spokesmen. It is unclear whether these elements constitute a genuine threat to South Korea. Fiery statements by North Korean generals are largely intended for domestic consumption. North Korea rightly fears US military capability which it would inevitably face in any conflict. There is no Chinese or Russian support for war. Furthermore, North Korean military exercises appear to be organised largely in response to South Korean and US exercises and not to be governed by independent North Korean preparations for war. However, little is taken for granted in Seoul, and South Korea meets perceived uncertainties by the dual approach of deterrence and engagement.

South Korean deterrence of North Korean aggression remains firmly rooted in the maintenance of a strong alliance with the United States.

Two thirds of the North Korean army is located within 100 kilometres of the armistice line between the two countries, and a military attack is believed to be possible with very little warning. While many take the view that South Korea and the United States would prevail in a military conflict, the damage to South Korea would be extensive, particularly in Seoul, given its location near the armistice line. South Korean armed forces continue to maintain a high degree of military readiness; reform priorities include the development of a more integrated South Korean–United States command structure and the securing of more sophisticated independent South Korean intelligence-gathering capabilities. South Korean observers note that the effectiveness of the alliance is dependent upon the maintenance of high South Korean morale and determination to resist North Korean aggression. There is some concern that the South Korean people have become increasingly sceptical about the possibility of war and that their enthusiasm, for example, for service in the military reserves, is declining. Internationally South Korea continues to seek Chinese and Russian cooperation to exert positive influence on North Korea. South Korean bilateral engagement efforts have focused on arms control and confidence-building measures, but little has been achieved given North Korean reticence. South Korea supports the development of positive links between North Korea and other countries in the region, and it is largely responsible for the funding of the Korean Peninsula Energy Development Organisation (KEDO) project involving the provision of nuclear reactors and fuel to North Korea. The possibilities that these efforts may lead to a positive outcome have been strengthened by the North Korean agreement to participate in the four-party talks.

While the precise timing of, agenda and site for these negotiations have yet to be established, the four countries have agreed that the central aim will be to replace the 1952 armistice agreement with a permanent peace agreement. Whether this will take the form of a formal treaty, and how military disputes that may occur in the meantime should be settled, have yet to be resolved. The US has proposed that North and South Korea establish new ways to reduce military tensions and avoid inadvertent war by establishing a 'hot line', military exchange visits, and notification of military manoeuvres. The US has indicated its willingness to help North Korea meet its food shortages by supplying fertilisers and pesticides to increase yields and assisting in reforestation programmes.

It is unlikely that rapid progress will be made in these talks, and few anticipate a dramatic breakthrough. However, even the prospect of eventual harmony on the Korean peninsula gives rise to concern in some quarters, because they fear a diminution of the US interest in, and presence in, East Asia as a result. Such concerns are already evident in a number of ASEAN countries, not least because of the possibility that a crisis may develop between China and the ASEAN states over the South China Sea.

The South China Sea

The possibility of conflict in the South China Sea arises from the existence of overlapping sovereignty claims, notably in the Spratly islands group, by China, Taiwan, Vietnam, Malaysia, the Philippines and Brunei. Such claims to sovereignty are made in their own right, but the anticipated existence of significant seabed resources, including oil, and exploitation of the region's marine resources reinforce the interest of states in securing effective control over parts of the sea. Nearby states without direct claims, for example Indonesia, Singapore and Thailand, are concerned about the impact of such claims on regional security and the possible outbreak of hostilities which could threaten the safety of sea lanes of communication (SLOC) and the international trade on which they thrive. US and Japanese concerns also focus on the SLOC issue and the potential adverse effects that conflicts would have upon intra-regional trade and the carriage of goods through the region. However, the importance of the issue to these countries does not match that of the claimants themselves, not least because many take the view that seaborne trade, already diminishing in its national importance, would simply be diverted to the east.

Efforts to resolve the rival claims have been undertaken largely on a bilateral basis or in the context of China–ASEAN meetings. The involvement of external powers, for example Japan and the United States, has been minimal. There is a general consensus that Chinese attitudes and policies will determine whether amicable solutions can be arrived at.

Chinese claims to sovereignty over much of the South China Sea are largely rooted in references to past history. However, the claims have more recently been framed with due reference to the Law of the Sea, although Chinese interpretations of the Law, notably the definition of the Paracel islands as an archipelago, remain controversial. Chinese claims have been forcefully presented, but these have been tempered by recent statements that there should be no use of force in resolving differences, that freedom of navigation should be maintained, and that agreements should be consistent with the Law of the Sea. The Chinese approach has been to urge other states to shelve disputes about sovereignty and to cooperate with China on the development of the sea's resources. While initially wary of other than bilateral contacts on these issues, the Chinese agreement to discuss it in the multilateral ASEAN forum is regarded by many as a positive step. Chinese spokesmen stress the need for continued negotiation on the issue and emphasise that it is but one of a number of important questions which govern Chinese–ASEAN states' relations. They note that the perceived advantage of China dealing bilaterally with smaller claimants has been abandoned and that, for example, a code of conduct established with the Philippines in 1995 included a Chinese agreement not to move unilaterally on Chinese claims.

This 'benign' view of the Chinese policy is questioned by a number of ASEAN states which, while noting the positive nature of Chinese statements, point to the Chinese occupation of the Mischief Reef and recent frictions in Shoal, as evidence of Chinese expansionism.

Criticisms of Chinese actions and policy with regard to the South China Sea are widespread in the ASEAN region. For ASEAN countries, Chinese behaviour on the issue is a litmus test of its intentions regarding its southern neighbours. There is disappointment that the Chinese authorities have not been prepared to go further in promoting confidence-building measures and technical cooperation in the region. Many regret the perceived lack of clarification on how the Chinese government anticipates joint development of resources evolving. There is a belief that the Chinese government resents the fact that other countries in the region have successfully promoted their interests during past periods of Chinese internal crisis and introspection. Fears remain that China is not genuinely committed to seeking a compromise and implementing confidence-building measures in the South China Sea. Even the Chinese statements that the Law of the Sea will be applicable in resolving the issue generate concern; many note that the Law of the Sea is not helpful in establishing states' sovereignty, but is rather intended to facilitate cooperation once sovereignty has been established. The lack of a dispute-resolution mechanism further inhibits the utility of Law of the Sea provisions.

Many urge the opening of a genuine dialogue between China and ASEAN states on these issues, possibly using informal non-governmental contacts in the first instance. There is a need to identify possible triggers of potential conflict in order to ensure that conflict does not occur accidentally. Contact at the annual ASEAN–China senior officials' meeting offers an additional possibility. Bilateral talks and meetings at the ASEAN Regional Forum offer further opportunities. However, in order that successful initiatives can be launched, it is necessary for the ASEAN countries to develop a common view of the issues and to explore in detail possible 'solutions'. Common positions have already been established on some issues: the peaceful resolution of the overlapping claims and not to take any action to prejudice any other claims; and a common ASEAN stand on the incursions in the Mischief Reef claimed by the Philippines. However, ASEAN still needs to cooperate more closely to formulate additional common positions and policies. If such efforts are successful, China may be more willing to cooperate on the South China Sea.

There are indications that the ASEAN states recognise that a joint position will be necessary in future, not least because they are unable to deal effectively with China on an individual basis. A common ASEAN policy will emerge, if at all, only after a period of deliberation, and a positive Chinese response to an ASEAN view is by no means certain. Is there a possibility that conflict will break out in the meantime? In the near term this appears to be unlikely given restrained Chinese behaviour; ASEAN policies remain largely reactive. While Chinese policy cannot be predicted with certainty, the extent of Chinese control over much of the South China Sea appears to be a medium-to-long-term goal and, as such, is unlikely to provoke a crisis in the near term. An opportunity exists for developing an effective ASEAN–Chinese dialogue which could lead to a positive resolution of existing differences. Given their shared interest in continued economic development and regional stability to this end, disputes will remain low key in the near term. However, disquiet about the issue continues to grow, and the re-equipping of ASEAN states' naval and air forces to increase maritime patrolling capabilities reflects this disquiet. In order to avoid possible future military confrontations, it is essential that a concerted effort be made to resolve existing claims. This will be beneficial not only for regional security, but will also ensure that human and financial resources remain dedicated principally towards improving the region's economic progress, which is, of itself, a key factor in the maintenance of future regional stability and security.

4 Stability and Economic Progress
Maintaining Economic Growth

Thailand's financial crisis in the summer of 1997 followed a downturn in the country's exports and waning confidence among foreign investors and creditors. The crisis forced the Thai authorities to float the baht, and this triggered speculative attacks on currencies throughout South-East Asia. Concerns that the meteoric progress of East Asian economies could be consigned to history were reinforced by these events. While continued steady economic growth is predicted by many observers, others point to changes in the international economic system and in the economies of the region which point to a more troubled future. While the economic progress of Japan, South Korea and Taiwan is well advanced, continued economic progress in South-East Asia appears to be more uncertain. This is not to argue that economic collapse or disaster is imminent, for many of the region's acknowledged strengths remain: the US role in providing stability, eager and relatively cheap work forces, proximity to markets, sustained political and social stability, relatively open economies which encourage foreign direct investment, relatively low levels of taxation, the abandoning of import substitution for export-led growth, efforts to share out earned wealth, high levels of saving, significant investments in infrastructure and skill development, and public–private cooperation.

This said, further steps will need to be taken to sustain future economic growth. For example, bottlenecks in production need to be removed and increased resources made available for skill development and education. Rapid increases in population need to be diminished. The growing environmental problems associated with rapid development will need to be addressed; not least the collapse of the burgeoning cities which provide the engines for development has to be avoided. Continued liberalisation of local economies must occur, and their products must remain competitive. Problems associated with ageing populations, rapid urbanisation and the globalisation of the international economy must be met. Furthermore, South-East Asian industrialists will need to develop increasingly sophisticated products at competitive prices as new producers of relatively unsophisticated products emerge to compete in the world economy. Some take the view that economic growth in the region will inevitably decline as the region's economies achieve maturity. They note that the world market is not large enough to absorb all of East Asian production, although this view is contentious. There are uncertainties that the American market will be as open to East Asian products as it has been in the past. Some take the view that past growth has been too heavily dependent on capital mobilisation and involved insufficiently increases in productivity per worker. Others contest this view, noting that predictable variables point to continued positive economic growth prospects. They expect the region to enjoy continued political and social stability, a high level of commitment to development in the region, the maintenance of highly capable management elites, and growing local markets for local production.

These factors indeed point towards a positive future, and the relatively benign nature of inter-state relations in South-East Asia appears to offer an international environment conducive to continued progress. In contrast, the emergence of social and political frustrations within the region's states could affect adversely continued economic progress. That frustrations exist has been demonstrated by, for example, political disturbances in Indonesia, a coup in Cambodia, the persistence of separatist movements in the Philippines, East Timor and Irian Jaya. Thus far these manifestations of frustration have been effectively contained by national governments. Their continued success in these efforts would enable economic progress to continue, albeit at slower rates. What are the prospects that social change and related difficulties can be effectively managed?

Managing Social Change

Does continued economic growth portend an increase in popular frustrations and social disruption? While failures to maintain economic growth would almost certainly generate significant social disruption, continued economic growth does not guarantee stability. Sections of society will gain from economic progress while others are disadvantaged. Both groups may become frustrated because of a lack of involvement in the countries' political processes. Government incompetence and its inability to deliver adequate services quickly enough will generate frustration. Corruption angers those struggling to advance themselves honestly. Adverse effects on minorities and the environment, for example, will generate opposition to government policy.

Frustrated groups will be motivated by a variety of circumstances. They will include: those not benefiting from economic growth; those whose livelihoods are undermined by change; those with obsolete skills; and those who are unable to compete in a burgeoning economy. Even the economically successful, for example the growing middle classes, students and intellectuals, may become increasingly critical of governments' inability to develop democratic decision-making processes. The problems associated with the particularly rapid economic development of East Asian economies may exacerbate the frustrations of these groups. Solving these problems is no simple task, and governments are unable to respond quickly or effectively to social and international trends which affect fundamentally the living standards and life styles of the region's peoples. For example, the economic and social pressures of globalisation are undermining economic and social arrangements which have heretofore been regarded as permanent. For example, notions of life-time employment are being abandoned in Japan and Korea, and governments and companies are reducing the level of protection granted to workers against redundancy. The Chinese abandonment of a centrally planned economic model in favour of a market economy system is but the most extreme manifestation of this change.

Whether such adjustments will enable governments to oversee economies which provide a reasonable standard of living and security for Asian populations remains an open question. Many take the view that this will only be achieved through the efficient employment of the region's labour resources; countries will be unable to provide a western-style welfare state to support the elderly, the young, and the unemployed. As a consequence widening income gaps between rich and poor and the continued existence of widespread poverty may be anticipated; while the 'trickle-down effect' will bring improving living standards to many, relative poverty is likely to persist and inequalities may generate dissatisfaction and unrest. Inequality and poverty are likely to be compounded by the infrastructure problems associated with the region's urbanisation, problems which are associated with the major cities of most of the developing world. However, such differences are also likely to develop between the urbanised and industrialising core of a state and the largely agricultural periphery, not least because government policies tend to favour urban development. These differences may in turn exacerbate ethnic and religious differences in culturally diverse states; these have manifested themselves in the past through frictions between Chinese minorities and indigenous peoples, religious differences between Hindus, Christians and Moslems or a combination of all three. Will such differences generate *political* frustration?

Many take the view that this need not be the inevitable result of economic and social change. Much depends on how economic growth and rising affluence are managed, not least how they affect the wealth of the population at large and the perceived income gap. Growing wealth must be used to reduce the incidence of poverty and, where possible, provide a minimum social safety net. Government policies should seek to ensure as wide as possible access to public goods and services. It will be necessary for them to underpin and promote the principle, practice and equality of opportunity, and to make available at least the prospect of social mobility. Furthermore, governments need actively to promote the evolution of a genuine civil society, and they should seek to extend participatory democracy. Of particular importance is the need to establish clearly the principles of the rule of law and of equality before the law – the integrity, honesty and competence of political leaderships and bureaucracies are not only intrinsically desirable, but will provide an example to others which will encourage the application of these principles more widely.

The issue of democratic rights and the rapidity with which democracy should be encouraged has proved to be controversial in Asia. Debates about the existence of 'Asian values', the need to rewrite the UN Charter on Human Rights, and frustrations about western criticism of local labour laws and human rights records have prompted some of the region's leaders to overtly criticise the introduction of 'western' democratic values and systems in the region. Put simply, such leaders argue that democracy is a luxury which can only be introduced after economic development has occurred; they argue that its premature introduction leads merely to political unrest and instability which, in turn, undermines economic progress. Others in the region refute this view, noting that it represents a means through which the privileged merely seek to protect their own position. Others accept that Asian institutions will inevitably evolve in unique directions, but that this need not preclude their movement towards democratic and open decision-making. While economic success is essential to the legitimacy of many regimes in the region, they will need to respond to the political demands of new generations as they emerge; there is little reason to expect their demands to exclude a desire for 'good governance', equality of opportunity, and the prospect of reasonable living standards. While many of the region's leaders point to the dangers of rapid political change, it should be recognised that resisting pressure for such change will not be cost-free. A lack of flexibility, whether through a refusal to entertain the possibility of political change at all or through the too-gradual introduction of changes, could spark the very unrest and violent reaction which leadership elites fear most. While this does not appear to be an immediate prospect in most of the region's states in the near term, it is impossible to discount it. Countries will have to face the issues associated with the transferring of political power, not only within existing ruling elites but also between these elites and those which are likely to emerge in the decades ahead, whether from the growing middle classes, organised labour, or from ethno-religious groupings. Will such transfers of power occur peacefully?

Transferring Political Power

In recent decades the countries of East Asia have generally been ruled by one party (Japan, Singapore, China, Malaysia), a family clique (Taiwan, Indonesia, the Philippines), or the military (Thailand, Indonesia, Burma). These groups were associated with national independence and nation-building; their legitimacy has generally been reinforced by positive economic development. Nevertheless, while most ran their economic systems effectively, and problems which have arisen were repressed, many changes have occurred within their societies which will affect political succession in the future. For example, more players will be involved in any succession in the future; new power groups and new generations will inevitably seek to be involved at some stage. However, political diversification in pluralistic societies is difficult in young nation states; it is for this reason that many oppose any change which would endanger existing stability. In East Asia, even those seeking change tend to emphasise the need for a gradual and peaceful transition.

This message is presented by most of the region's leaderships, which perceive themselves as embodying national progress and economic success. Attitudes are generally paternalistic, and leaders are not slow to claim credit for the stability which has encouraged foreign direct investment and economic progress. These ambitious leaders have played a central role in the modernisation process and have assumed powerful central positions within the state. Many take the view that the peoples of the region are comfortable with this situation and that there will be little overt pressure for dramatic change. Nevertheless, events in one or a number of states in the region can affect thinking elsewhere. For example, any disintegration within China would inevitably encourage secessionist movements elsewhere, not least in East Timor and the southern Philippines. It is therefore in the interests of all of region's regimes that political successions proceed smoothly; ASEAN reactions to the coup in Cambodia in the summer of 1997 demonstrated governments' sensitivities.

Few regimes in the region appear to be seeking to resist change completely. Even with the possible exceptions of Burma and North Korea, changes of regime cannot be discounted completely. Indeed, it may be that the very intransigence of the regimes could lead to the political instability which most other regimes in the region fear and are therefore seeking to avoid. Elsewhere, new actors are emerging and existing leadership cliques are changing. For example, the political involvement of the army in Thailand and in Indonesia appears to be diminishing to some degree, although they remain powerful actors in the political process. However, factional differences and generational change and associated internal divisions are diminishing their influence. The prospect of radical or revolutionary change would undoubtedly provoke a military reaction; however, the prospects for radical change in the region seem limited.

Radical change would involve the emergence of a new leadership elite with different ideologies and policies. Such a radical transition is unlikely, not least because existing leaders are managing effectively their relations with their citizens. Most are seeking to involve their peoples in the process of economic transition, and the existing system has facilitated wealth distribution to a sufficient degree to underpin incentives to keep existing political systems in place. While many accept that radical change will occur given existing global challenges, there is little interest in adopting any new ideologies. The peoples of the region do not wish to lose the prosperity with which they are becoming familiar and to which all aspire. For example, the decline in the numbers of 'absolute poor' in Indonesia from 40 per cent to 12 per cent of the population in the last 30 years represents a significant achievement; those remaining in poverty aspire to the living standards of their more prosperous neighbours. There is therefore a community of interest within the population to maintain the existing system. The generally pragmatic policies of governments and their encouragement of foreign direct investment are supportive of these aspirations, and public education programmes have ensured that there is a widespread understanding of the economic changes which are under way. This is not to say that people are uncritical of their governments. However, their criticisms do not generate demands for the overthrow of the system, but rather the replacement of a particular leadership clique or party. Most analysts take the view that popular attitudes are resistant to any political succession which would adversely affect progress, and that the region's populations are generally appreciative of strong leadership. All accept that evolution will occur, but take the view that it will be gradual.

This positive picture is reinforced by the emergence of intellectual communities, business groups, non-governmental organisations, environment and social movements which form the basis for a future evolution of civil society. The fact that these groups are encouraged by governments which have generally sought to co-opt opposition groups, has reinforced this process. Government support for a wide range of associations including labour unions, chambers of commerce, women's associations and professional groups strengthens this pattern. The existence of these organisations permits people to express their discontent and to channel their political aspirations in a positive way. However, these networks are generally conservative and work for change within the existing political systems. Their role facilitates the transition from arbitrary decision-taking by the existing leadership elites towards a more transparent and consultative process. Thus in a number of East Asian states, governments have succeeded in extending and refining the mechanisms for exercising political influence. In return, organisations and associations are expected to engage in self-discipline in order to protect the freedoms which they have been granted. To a degree, the emergence of a loyal opposition appears to be occurring in a number of states.

However, it is unclear whether this will lead to the emergence of western-style democracy. Removal of leaderships and their replacement remains subject to the undue influence of 'peer groups' in the ruling elites. Personalisation of government remains a factor in political life, and some fear the consequent erosion of bureaucratic expertise and judicial independence. An undue influence on personal networks and contacts, and the related emergence of political dynasties in some countries, may diminish the effectiveness of government in future. Others note that the emergence of a politically active middle class is dependent upon its membership achieving economic independence; they note that significant sections of the middle classes in East Asia are beholden to governments for employment and their economic well-being. Their interest in acquiring political influence may consequently be diminished. This said, most observers take the view that political trends in what is a diverse region are generally favourable and that considerable successes have already been achieved. They note that economic development inevitably leads, and has led, to political changes to meet new circumstances. Caution and gradualism dominate elite thinking, not least because of the newness of most of the region's states. However, there appears to be a general appreciation that the second and third generation of leadership elites must govern within the rule of law and not act as 'great men' and 'fathers of the nation'. Emerging leaderships will need to be more responsive to the demands of their citizens. While political institutions will inevitably evolve to suit local conditions, the influence of western culture is already evident and affecting significantly the attitudes of local elites and populations. That this has generated a hostile reaction by some does not mean that the evolution of more open and pluralistic societies can be checked in the longer term. However, the impetus for democracy in whatever form must come from within the states of the region if it is to be firmly rooted. With the exception of the remaining communist regimes in the region, few oppose the idea of popular participation in their countries' political life. At issue is the timing and nature of this involvement.

5 The Way Forward
Prerequisites for Stability

While economic growth need not necessarily result in more secure and prosperous populations or in the wealth generated being evenly distributed, the condition of most of Asia's peoples has improved. For this reason, many foresee a benign security environment in East Asia over the next 10 to 15 years; namely the absence of armed conflict between its nation states or of efforts by any of those states to exercise hegemonic power over its neighbours. For past successes to be continued and stability maintained, the region's governments will have to cope with the global diffusion of new and emerging information technologies which will have economic, social, cultural and political consequences as dramatic as those experienced in the region in the past half century. The globalisation and personalisation of electronic communications may yet undermine the authority of nation states and facilitate a devolution of power to sub-national and trans-national movements, not least those that draw on ethnic, religious or cultural loyalties. The role of the nation state in assuring the security of its citizens may be affected. Since the end of the Cold War, the security threat to states and their populations from other states appears to be declining; armed conflicts in the last decade have been overwhelmingly intra-state affairs. However, non-traditional threats to security are increasing, including, for example, drug-trafficking, organised crime, and ethnic conflicts. Intra-regional migration generates suspicion and friction as well as hope for the migrants.

Problems associated with population growth and, in some countries, the ageing of populations will pose considerable economic and social problems. Ageing populations, supported by fewer people of working age, will generate pressures on social structures and economic systems, not least because the cost of medical support is likely to rise. In countries with rapid population growth, still above 2 per cent in the Philippines and Vietnam, providing sufficient job opportunities, infrastructure and social support will represent a formidable problem. Immigration is likely to increase as people seek work, and this is already causing problems between the Philippines and Japan and Singapore, between Singapore and Thailand, and between Malaysia and Indonesia. In addition, the region faces formidable environmental problems. Although these have tended to be downgraded by existing leaderships, which regard environmental concerns as an impediment to economic development, a new generation of more sophisticated leaders increasingly recognises the likely future consequence of environmental degradation. Not least, the impact of increased demand for water and the consequent exhaustion of cheap supplies of water could seriously affect the region's levels of food production, tourist development, and the quality of life in the region's burgeoning cities.

The issue of food security is of increasing concern, not least in North Korea which experienced widespread food shortages and perhaps famine in 1997. Some fear that China's demand for grain will overwhelm the world's grain production capacity. Although some Chinese experts call for an end to China's obsession with self-sufficiency in grain and an increase in China's production of income-earning export crops, the current leadership appears to be wary of importing food stocks on a regular and significant scale. However, as the country's economic strength is consolidated, the commercial importation of food at world prices may become increasingly attractive. This path has already been followed by Japan, which is now the largest food-importing country in the world ($38 billion in imports in 1995). Rapid income growth in East Asia will be an important engine of agricultural trade expansion in the region and globally.

To finance such imports, economic growth is essential and this will require increasing amounts of energy. The demand for energy is growing rapidly in the Asia–Pacific region; at present growth rates the needs of Asia for oil will nearly double by the year 2010. However, the region's production of oil is set to decline, and imported oil will become even more essential for the region's economic prosperity. East Asia will therefore become overwhelmingly dependent on oil imports from the Middle East; this level of dependency may create a degree of uncertainty and insecurity. For this reason, Asian states are looking to other energy sources: for example, natural gas, nuclear power and renewable energies such as hydro-power and geothermal power. However, in the near term it is likely that coal will increasingly be used to generate electricity. This will have serious implications for the region's environment and the global climate.

These formidable issues will be faced by states which have relatively weak governmental institutions. A combination of severe problems could overwhelm states' capacity to respond. This said, many analysts continue to take an optimistic view about East Asia's future prospects. All recognise that little can be taken for granted and that substantial efforts will be needed in four key areas to ensure the construction and maintenance of durable regional security: the development and maintenance of political pluralism, addressing the problems associated with economic growth, the creation of a regional society, and the maintenance of a robust regional balance of power.

It is a widely accepted truism that political pluralism is necessary to sustain economic growth. While recognising that pluralism can be dangerous and difficult in its early stages, modern economies inevitably generate pluralistic societies. The impact of pluralistic forces on the political process has to be managed effectively if negative consequences in foreign policy are to be avoided. In East Asia, the impact of pluralistic politics is already evident. For example, the democratic process in Taiwan is affecting foreign policy; a president seeking votes in a democratic system has sought to generate support by projecting internationalist policies and undertaking foreign visits which led to the 1996 Taiwan crisis. Similarly, South Korean politics influences that country's policies *vis-à-vis* North Korea, and this may generate instability and indeed irrational policy. There is a growing popular perception in Japan that China is a threat; this will inevitably affect Japanese policy in the future. These types of problems cannot be ignored, and governments in the region would do well to consider how to manage them effectively.

Many in the ASEAN region take the view that economic success represents the key to the region's future stability and prosperity; if the economy is successful, then everything else will be. This comfortable truism needs to be examined, for growth inevitably brings challenges as well as benefits. Successful economies in the region and richer populations will inevitably require increased imports of food, energy and capital. This will involve a degree of competition which will need to be managed peacefully. The development of effective institutions in the region to facilitate this process will be beneficial. Such a mechanism is likely to have to concern itself with difficult questions in the years ahead: the position and role of Chinese minorities in South-East Asia, Japanese–US problems on economic and trade issues, and the growing Chinese trade surplus with the United States.

The work of such institutions would be facilitated by the creation of a sense of regional society. Efforts have already been made in this direction through ASEAN, the ASEAN Regional Forum, and the Council for Security Cooperation in the Asia Pacific (CSCAP) process. However, their successes should not lead to a false sense of confidence that all problems can be managed in the future. Contacts with Europe, through the process, have been useful in that they have necessitated East Asians to develop collective attitudes and policies when dealing with Europeans speaking through the European Union mechanism.

For these cooperative efforts to bear fruit, a stable balance of power in the region is essential. Maintaining this balance cannot be left to the United States alone. A continued US presence will require the participation of allies which are prepared to share costs and risks. That the US remains prepared to act unilaterally was demonstrated during the Taiwan crisis; however, the lack of support from Asian capitals was noted, and US interest in maintaining the regional balance will inevitably decline if support for the policy from friendly governments is muted. The United States–Japanese relationship is crucial; relations between the countries must remain positive if US engagement in the region is to be assured.

Attending to these pillars of regional society will absorb the attentions of the region's governments in the decade ahead. While most observers agree that the region will begin the next century with many advantages founded in the progress of the last three decades, these may yet prove to be more fragile than many anticipate. For example, the consensus politics which has underpinned the work of ASEAN will be more difficult to maintain as the organisation expands and deals with a wider range of issues; controversies over the entry of Burma may be but an early indicator of more difficult intra-regional political relations in the future. The future actions of the great powers in the region cannot be predicted with total certainty; the policies of an emerging China are unclear, and possible US reactions are dependent upon Chinese policy. While Russian influence in the region has declined in recent years, its involvement in the area appears likely to increase in future; recent positive contacts with Japan and arms sales to Indonesia are pointers in this direction. Japanese reluctance to develop a more forceful foreign policy in the region is predicated upon continued US support and anticipated benign Russian and Chinese policies. As a new generation of political leaders emerges in Japan in the decade ahead, existing policies may come to be questioned, particularly if international circumstances change.

Set alongside these 'traditional' powers in the region, the emergence of ASEAN as an actor of considerable significance appears likely. While the US presence remains generally welcome among ASEAN members, most are engaged in a process of military modernisation with the emphasis on force projection capability. The acquisition of such capability may point to future increased assertiveness either by ASEAN as a group or by individual ASEAN members in the pursuit of their economic, political and military interests, not least in the South China Sea region. How may ASEAN best be used to avoid the development of crises in the future?

ASEAN and ARF

The future of ASEAN will depend principally on its continued utility to its members. This will depend upon how well members handle their domestic agendas, relations with fellow members, the expansion of ASEAN, and promoting the region's interests. A key test will be posed by the current expansion of the organisation.

Few doubt that negative consequences could arise following expansion. These include increased difficulty in maintaining consensus because of the diversity of counties; the possible emergence of a two-track ASEAN; the changing political and economic image of the organisation following the inclusion of poorer states; the limited capacity of new members to participate fully; the introduction of additional bilateral problems; and the negative consequences of including Burma. However, they point to the positive effects of enlargement: the greater influence of a larger organisation; the common interests of a group of small-to-medium powers and their evolution of common views on international issues; and the strength of the existing ASEAN culture and its positive effects on new members, and the engagement of new states.

Future priorities of ASEAN will include strengthening economic and functional cooperation rather than political or security cooperation; managing its relations with Burma well; closing the gap between the old and new ASEAN members; institutionalising its work; managing territorial issues successfully; developing the organisation as a counterweight to China if and when necessary; and managing trans-border activities.

The ASEAN Regional Forum (ARF), a newer body which is still developing, is expected to have a different focus, not least because it covers a larger area and involves a broader membership. Many take the view that its future evolution is dependent upon US and Chinese attitudes; their support is deemed to be crucial to the future evolution of a positive multilateral forum for problem-solving. This said, some progress has already been made. The ARF's achievements include increasing mutual understanding; providing a venue for small powers to make an impact; providing multilateral contacts for the Chinese and Russian governments; and developing confidence-building measures. Future ARF priorities should include promoting a sub-regional security arrangement for North-East Asia, including North Korea; undertaking a fuller examination of perceived threats in the region; increasing interest in cooperative security; and institutionalising preventive diplomacy efforts.

Some observers have expressed concern about the compatibility of the ASEAN and ARF agendas. Both seek to promote cooperative security. Indeed, the ARF was established with the intention of using the same security model which had evolved in ASEAN; promoting confidence-building and conflict management, and acting as a diplomatic community on regional issues. ASEAN's success owed much to the absence of any interest in developing an alternative form of security cooperation in the region, and because its initiating role was acceptable to the major Asia–Pacific powers.

ASEAN's successes have included the integration of Indonesia within the South-East Asian community and the facilitation of engagement with China. It is unclear whether ARF-based dialogue will have a similar benign political impact on regional order. However, participating states appear to be committed to using the forum as a means to improve the regional political climate, although the ARF is far from addressing preventive diplomacy and dispute-settlement issues. In addition, the underlying North-East Asian reluctance to accept the legitimacy of an ASEAN Regional Forum with ASEAN as its 'prime driving force' will generate problems in future. ASEAN is ill-suited to deal with the security concerns of North-East Asia. A key ASEAN interest within the ARF remains the maintenance of its distinct identity and role within the forum, not least to ensure that the association is not subordinated to the major Asia–Pacific powers. These tensions are likely to remain and may affect the ARF's institutional performance. Amelioration of such tensions could therefore contribute significantly to the promotion of cooperative security initiatives in East Asia.

6 Conclusions

Many predict the maintenance of a benign security environment in East Asia for the next 10 to 15 years, arguing that few major inter-state conflicts or serious threats to states' internal security are likely to emerge. This positive future is, however, dependent upon the successful adaptation of the region's states to problems associated with economic globalisation; growing and in some cases ageing populations; environmental degradation associated with development; the maintenance of economic development and trade; and maintaining adequate access to key resources, not least food and energy.

To meet these challenges and to continue the economic and social progress made in recent decades, four central pillars need to be maintained which underpin the region's security: (a) the creation and extension of political pluralism will be essential to sustain economic growth, although the difficulties of doing so in the early stages of economic development must be recognised; (b) economic growth must continue and access to important resources be maintained; wealth generated through development must be more widely spread to ensure that the peoples of the region have a stake in its continued stability; (c) a sense of regional society needs to be developed, a process which has already begun through the ASEAN and CSCAP processes; and (d) a balance of power must be maintained within the region; this cannot be done in future by the United States alone.

The United States will remain engaged in the region because of its own national interests, political, economic and military. Current US troop levels will remain stable for the foreseeable future unless an unlooked-for crisis emerges. US aims are to promote a stable and prosperous region in which cooperation with active partners, notably Japan and a peacefully reunited Korea, will be possible. The US seeks harmonious relations with China; in the near term there will be a need to demonstrate to China that closer US–Japanese military links, exemplified through the recent defence guidelines review, are not directed against China. Internal differences may be expected within the US over its China policy, with some pressing for more engagement and others demanding a tougher stance, for example on human rights and arms exports; differences of view between the Congress and Clinton Administration will complicate relations with China. It is important that US Administration policy is clear and effectively presented to the Chinese government.

Chinese reactions to US policy and the broader security environment will be dictated by two key ambitions: to develop as a comprehensive great power (i.e. both economically and militarily); and to have a prominent voice in the region. To achieve these goals, Chinese priorities are economic modernisation and growth, which the Beijing government recognises require a stable and peaceful international environment. The Chinese government will not, therefore, seek confrontation on the international stage but it may react militarily if perceived vital interests, notably Taiwan, are threatened. Modernisation of the Chinese military will continue to meet possible contingencies. Concern that US–Japanese military cooperation is intended to contain China remains strong; many Chinese believe that the US is more interested in regional hegemony than genuine partnership. However, the Chinese reaction thus far has not been to develop an adversarial relationship with the United States. Additional Chinese concerns focus on the possible re-emergence of Russia as a regional power and in the near term the revival of Japanese 'militarism' in the region.

This seems to be an extremely remote possibility as Japanese policies do not envisage any major expansion of Japan's security role in the region or significant changes in the status quo. An adaptation of policy is occurring following the disappearance of the Soviet threat which involves a greater readiness to participate in efforts to enhance regional security rather than simply concentrating on the defence of the Japanese homeland per se. Japan is not militarily self-sufficient and continues to rely on United States forces to supplement its own efforts. Recently-announced guidelines to clarify the responsibilities of the two countries are not perceived by the Japanese as representing a major change in policy, merely elaborating in detail how the countries will cooperate during peace-time, if Japan is attacked, or if they wish to react to a regional crisis. The aim is to agree in advance who can and will undertake what actions in a given situation. These efforts derive from a Japanese recognition that 'cheque book' diplomacy, as practised during the Gulf War, needs to be supplemented if US–Japanese ties are to remain close. Furthermore, worries about North Korea, following the nuclear crisis of 1994 and associated revelations about North Korean missile capability, appear to have persuaded the Japanese authorities that more detailed planning on US–Japanese military cooperation is desirable.

North Korea remains a source of concern to neighbouring countries because of its internal difficulties, not least the recent widely reported food shortages, its role as a supplier of missile and WMD technologies, and its perceived continued military threat to South Korea. Most analysts do not expect a total collapse of North Korea to occur; a generational transfer of power has been achieved successfully and the government appears to be functioning effectively despite current crises, and the armed forces remain loyal. Furthermore, contacts with the outside world appear to be increasing. This is encouraging for states in the region, notably South Korea, which are working to ensure that North Korea achieves a 'soft landing'. South Korea remains committed to reunification but this is only to be achieved in an orderly and peaceful manner. South Koreans continue to look to the United States to counter North Korean military capabilities and to deter possible North Korean aggression, but they couple this with a policy of engagement with their North Korean neighbours. Efforts are under way to develop arms control and confidence-building measures at the bilateral level, although the North

Korean response has been meagre. The recent agreement of North Korea to participate in four-party talks, involving China and the United States, to advance cooperation between the two Koreas is encouraging. The prospects for reunification appear to be limited in the near term although a consensus 'in favour' appears to exist in the region: significant progress may only occur when the Korean War generation pass from the scene.

Korea is but one of a number of potential flash points in the region. Efforts by Taiwan to achieve full independence, for example, would undoubtedly provoke a forceful reaction from mainland China. In the South China Sea overlapping territorial claims, notably those between China and its southern neighbours, are giving cause for concern. Multilateral efforts to stabilise the situation before it gets out of control have been initiated by ASEAN: suggestions include agreeing to defer consideration of sovereignty issues while confidence-building measures are developed; jointly developing resources pending the resolution of claims; and referring claims to the International Court of Justice. China's traditional insistence that the issues be handled bilaterally has been modified through its agreement to discuss them in the ASEAN forum. Chinese claims to much of the South China Sea are based on historical precedence and, more recently, Chinese interpretations of the International Law of the Sea. South-East Asian states fear Chinese 'creeping expansion'; for them the South China Sea issue is the key test of China's intentions towards the region and Chinese arguments that it is but one of a number of important questions are coolly received. Nevertheless it is arguable that the ASEAN states need to develop a unified position to deal effectively with China. Furthermore, agreement will be difficult if China continues to see the issue as one involving sovereignty. The potential for misunderstanding or the onset of a crisis remains significant.

The resolution of this and similar problems will depend in part on the future evolution of regional multilateral institutional arrangements, notably ASEAN and the ARF. Their future development will depend upon how members handle their own domestic agendas; the nature of bilateral relations between members; ensuring an expanded ASEAN works effectively; maintaining ASEAN coherence; and facilitating and promoting the region's interests effectively. Problems include maintaining consensus in a larger organisation; the possible development of a two-track ASEAN; living with the new political and economical image resulting from the inclusion of poor and socialist regimes; the limited capacity of new members to participate effectively; the introduction of additional bilateral problems; and some of the negative consequences of including Burma. To meet these problems ASEAN priorities must include strengthening economic and functional cooperation; managing the Burma issue well; closing the gap between old and new members; effective institution building; successful management of territorial issues; more intense economic cooperation; effective management of transport issues; and developing as an effective counterweight to China where necessary. The more recently established ARF has, thus far, achieved only modest success, not least in the area of confidence-building measures. Key future priorities should be the inclusion of North Korea and the promotion of a sub-regional security arrangement in North-East Asia. Many believe that an increase in US and Chinese commitment to the ARF will be essential for its future success. It remains an open question whether the ARF, through its process of dialogue, will have a benign political impact and facilitate regional order; it has a limited remit to cover contentious issues but it is underpinned by structures of economic cooperation and achievements. Although embryonic and unable to address effectively preventive diplomacy and dispute settlement issues, interest in the ARF remains as a means of improving the climate within which regional relationships are conducted. Possible difficulties include the continued underlying North-East Asian reluctance to accept the legitimacy of ASEAN as the ARF's 'driving force'. ASEAN's central role in the ARF facilitates its continued existence as a distinct identity; this could be difficult to maintain if the major Asia–Pacific powers opt to take leading roles in the forum. Tensions within the ARF may well affect institutional performance.

The future of these institutional arrangements and the evolution of inter-state relations will be strongly affected by the region's economic performance, associated social changes, and the capacity of the region's states to transfer political power with minimum disruption. Positive progress on these areas will undoubtedly serve to diminish international tensions. While continued economic progress cannot guarantee regional stability, being but one of the four pillars upon which this is built, its importance cannot be underestimated. What are the region's economic prospects? The received wisdom is that past progress will be continued into the future notwithstanding acknowledged problems of economic bottlenecks; the need to develop further human resources; managing demographic problems; addressing environmental difficulties; maintaining external security; continued liberalisation of economies; and maintaining competitiveness. An open international trading system must remain, and key markets, notably the United States and Europe, must remain open. Further increases in capital per worker, low by international standards, could positively affect future development. Productivity by worker should also be improved and the region's products will have to 'move up' the technological ladder. Effective leadership, internal stability and entrepreneurial flexibility are essential to ensure that the current economic successes are maintained. In the longer term, environmental degradation, which some believe to be occurring on an alarming scale, will need to be addressed.

Political frustration need not be the inevitable result of economic and social change. Much will depend upon how economic growth and rising affluence are managed: how increasing wealth is deployed to narrow the income gap; how poverty is reduced and a social safety-net provided;

how as wide as possible access to public goods and services is arranged; how equality of opportunity and social mobility are promoted; and how constructing civil society and extending democracy is undertaken. Economic development must be accompanied by the effective implementation of the rule of law and be complemented by honest and competent political leadership and bureaucracy. Any prolonged economic slowdown in the region, which results in an increased inability of governments to deliver economic well-being and better living standards, would compound existing frustrations. These are rooted in a perceived lack of involvement in political processes, frustration with government incompetence and a resulting lack of available services, and anger with corruption. Potentially frustrated groups include the non-beneficiaries from economic growth; those squeezed out by economic change; those with obsolete skills; the non-competitive; the economically successful who desire democracy; and political opponents of existing establishments, particularly if these are repressed.

Thus far these problems have been manageable; continued future success will require competent, flexible and clear political leadership. Solving the problem of 'how to compensate the losers' will be particularly problematical if, as many argue, providing a western-style welfare state is impossible because of the cost. Other answers will have to be provided.

Given continued economic progress and a reasonably benign international environment, the peoples and governments of the region appear to have time to consider and resolve these problems. The existing generation of rulers, whether political parties, prominent families or the military, have built upon a legitimacy established during periods of nation building and economic development to run effective systems of government. Concerns about the transition of power from one generation of leadership to another have proved to be largely unfounded in the majority of the region's states. In recent years political leaderships have changed without resulting widespread turmoil in Japan, the Koreas, China, Taiwan, Vietnam, the Philippines and Singapore. Only in Indonesia is there widespread concern that the passing of the current leadership may result in significant turmoil. In most countries the view appears to be taken that change should be managed in a consensual and gradualistic way, not least because radical change is perceived as threatening to existing prosperity and positive economic prospects. The legitimacy of governments is firmly rooted in economic progress and the associated improvement of living standards; while people express various concerns, they appear to be generally unwilling to overthrow existing political systems. Furthermore, the fact that the region's governments, to varying degrees, have proved to be flexible in their approaches to dealing with popular discontent has generally defused tension. Methods employed have not always been benign and the use of force is not unknown, but change has generally not been forbidden per se, but rather has been postponed to a distant future. While the prospects for political change differ from country to country in a diverse region the trends seem broadly favourable.

Notes

1. *Strategic Survey* 1996/97, The International Institute for Strategic Studies, 1997, p. 161.

2. Nayan Chanda and Michael Vatikiotis, 'Let this be a lesson', *Far Eastern Economic Review,* 12 June 1997, p. 71.

3. For more detailed discussion see, Richard Latter, 'Maintaining Stability and Security in South-East Asia', *Wilton Park Paper* 121, July 1996.

4. Richard Bernstein and Ross H. Munro, 'The Coming Conflict with America', *Foreign Affairs,* Vol. 76, No. 2, March–April 1997, pp. 18–32.

5. Ibid.

6. Ibid.

7. 'there exist three scenarios for the future of bilateral relations: antagonism; a seesaw between confrontation and cooperation (which end the seesaw tilts to depends on time and common ties); and partnership'. Wu Xinbo, 'Changing Roles: China and the United States in East Asian Security', *Journal of Northeast Asian Studies,* Spring 1996, pp. 35–55.

8. Ibid.

9. See G. Cameron Hurst III, 'The US–Japanese Alliance at Risk', *Orbis,* Vol. 41, No. 1, pp. 69–76.

10. Yoichi Funabashi in Jean-Pierre Lehmann, 'Tearing Down Opaque Walls', *The World Today,* May 1997, pp. 136–139.

11. C. S. Eliot Kang, 'Korean Unification: A Pandora's Box of Northeast Asia?', *Asian Perspective,* Vol. 20, No. 2, Fall–Winter 1996, pp. 9–43.

12. Ibid., p. 34.

13. Richard Lloyd Parry, 'No Plain Sailing in the Desert Island Dispute', *Independent,* 20 May 1997, p. 12.

7

Building Political Stability in Sub-Saharan Africa

Report based on Wilton Park Conference 506: 8–12 September 1997 on
'Building Stability in Sub-Saharan Africa'

Christopher Clapham

1 Introduction

The post-independence era in sub-Saharan Africa has come to an inglorious end. The overthrow and death of former president Mobutu symbolises the failure of the assumption that political 'stability' could be achieved by the maintenance of autocratic and corrupt regimes, whose aspirations were restricted to staying in power and accumulating wealth for their rulers, at no matter what cost to their citizens. It has been accompanied by a recognition on the part of the industrial world that the days when outside military forces could prop up or reconstruct states which no longer enjoyed the support of their own peoples have likewise passed into history. Even though Africa remains deeply embedded in an increasingly globalised world, and external actors will continue – for better or worse – to have a key part to play in the affairs of the continent, the central roles will have to be played by Africans themselves.

Many of the actors who will play those roles are already on stage. The transition to democratic rule in South Africa has not only ended the saga that began with decolonisation in the later 1950s, and removed a major source of deliberate destabilisation in the southern part of the continent, but has also brought the weight of Africa's most economically developed state on to the side of regional economic integration, and the peaceful resolution of disputes through democratic means. Still more encouragingly in many respects, several of the states which in the past had been by-words for human misery, civil war and economic decay, including Ghana, Uganda and Ethiopia, have come under the control of new governments with very different agendas for economic and political reconstruction from their predecessors. The addition of the newly renamed Democratic Republic of the Congo (DRC, formerly Zaire) to this number, should it be successfully accomplished, would add a critical weight to the movement for reform. There are encouraging signs, spread through much of the continent, that Africa's long period of economic decline may have been reversed.

No one could pretend, however, that the creation of effective and accountable systems of government in sub-Saharan Africa, and a resulting sustained improvement in the quality of life for its more than half a billion people, will be anything but a long, uncertain, and extremely difficult task. The roots of poverty and instability sink deep into the continent's past, and into a natural environment which continues to impose enormous difficulties for any sustained process of development. Encouraging developments in one part of the continent constantly have to be set against disasters in another. There are very few consistent success stories, and states which at one moment appeared to show the way forward, have very often turned out only a short time later to be in need of rescue themselves. Liberia (once the fastest growing economy in the world), Ghana (the standard-bearer of radical African nationalism), Somalia (Africa's only genuine nation-state), and Nigeria (the oil-rich giant of the continent), all reveal the fallacies of hope. After some forty years of independence, none the less, some lessons have been learnt, usually the hard way. This paper is concerned to summarise them, and to suggest where the search for political stability in sub-Saharan Africa may go from there.

2 Some Basic Questions
What is Political Stability?

At its simplest, 'political stability' means that governments stay in power: governments that remain in power for a long time are stable, whereas governments that are constantly changing are not. By this definition, Africa has had a number of extremely stable governments, to set against the familiar stereotype of instability. Presidents Banda of Malawi, Houphouet-Boigny of Côte d'Ivoire, and Mobutu of Congo/Zaire, together with Emperor Haile-Selassie of Ethiopia, ruled for thirty years or more, far longer than any leader in the supposedly stable West. The True Whig Party of Liberia, until its overthrow in 1980, was the oldest continuously governing party in the history of the world. A significant number of African countries, including Botswana, Cameroon, Côte d'Ivoire, Gabon, Kenya, Malawi, Senegal, South Africa, Tanzania and Zambia, have had no unconstitutional change of government in more than three decades of independent statehood.

Though these examples caution us against too ready an assumption that Africa is a chronically unstable continent – and in Africa even more than most parts of the world, it is the bad news that makes the headlines – they also show up the weaknesses of so crude a definition. The 'stability' of imperial Ethiopia and True Whig Liberia lasted no longer than the regimes which defined it, the collapse of which left appalling conflicts in their wake; that of South Africa rested on an institutionalised system of oppression; and Mobutu not only misgoverned Congo/Zaire, but destroyed much of the economic and institutional base on which lasting stability depends. A more complex but also more rewarding conception of stability needs to emphasise not just the survival of the regime, but its ability to reflect and adapt to the values, aspirations and identities of the people whom it governs. Ultimately, a government can be stable only if it is legitimate (accepted by its people as the rightful power), and effective (capable of meeting its people's needs). No government, no matter how longlasting, whose activities turn many of its people into internal or external refugees, can by this criterion properly be regarded as stable. Stability thus calls for both accountability and good government, and stable governments in Africa have in this respect been sadly few.

Another aspect of stability calls for attention: the survival of the boundaries of the state itself. In this respect, despite (or even perhaps because of) the artificiality of the frontiers bequeathed to it by colonialism, Africa has been extraordinarily stable. The only derogations from the principle of respect for existing frontiers upheld by the Organisation of African Unity, the recognised independence of Eritrea and unrecognised secession of Somaliland, have restored colonially created territories which had been incorporated into neighbouring states. The contrast with Europe, in which all but a very few states have experienced major territorial upheavals in the twentieth century (many of them in the last decade), is startling. The capacity of African states to maintain their territories, as the legacies of the colonialism that created them die away, none the less remains to be tested.

Why Does Political Instability Matter?

In the early years of African independence, 'political instability' was reflected largely in military coups d'état. Though some of these were violent, only rarely (as in Nigeria after 1966) did they lead to serious civil conflict. Often, they involved little more than the replacement of a few elite individuals; in Benin (then Dahomey), which experienced a plethora of coups with negligible violence between 1963 and 1972, it was possible to regard them as the equivalent of Italian cabinet crises. This easygoing approach no longer holds. Especially since the mid-1970s, political instability has engulfed whole states and regions, bringing death and misery to very large numbers of Africans. Since the dead are uncountable, whereas refugees impose themselves on the attention of the international community, the clearest measure of the damage caused by political instability is provided by the numbers of refugees, to whom should be added the massive (but far more difficult to count) populations of internally displaced people. Throughout the first half of the 1990s, between five and six million Africans were classed as refugees; Africa's position as overwhelmingly the world's largest generator of refugees in relation to total population provides the clearest indictment of the quality of much of its government.

But even though bad government has been the source of many of Africa's problems, the history of recent instability proves that government is needed. 'State collapse' in Liberia and Somalia has resulted in some of the worst suffering on the continent, as rival warlords have fought over the spoils, and orphaned children with firearms in their hands have roamed unrestricted by anything but the rules of gang warfare. The troubles of both countries may be ascribed in large degree to the brutality of the regimes which preceded the breakdown of order, and call for a very different kind of government, more effective but also more responsive than that which they have experienced in the past. How such a government can be created is the critical problem.

In the era of economic globalisation, political instability has further consequences which are no less important for being less immediately striking. The absence of capital is no longer a serious barrier to development: the capital markets of the industrial world are full of eager fund managers, looking for somewhere to put their money. What makes the difference is the infrastructure, measured not just in roads and power supplies, but in the skills and discipline of the labour force; and the security provided by peace and working legal systems which are needed to assure investors that their money will be safe. All these things require stability, in the form not just of regimes which are likely to be able to stay in power and keep the peace, but also of a commitment to good governance, in place of the rapacity with which at least a number of African governments have frightened away the capital and skills that are needed to provide the economic underpinnings (and thus the human welfare) on which stable government must ultimately rest. That Africa has received a minuscule share of the foreign direct investment going to developing countries, and that this investment has been heavily concentrated in extractive industries providing high returns on capital, has been due at least in part to the poor quality of its political environment.

Why Has Africa Been So Unstable?

This is no place to attempt any comprehensive analysis of the sources of instability in Africa, but it is none the less essential to emphasise that instability derives, not just from specific and rectifiable errors, or from the failures of a few individuals, but from far more deep-seated causes. Building political stability can thus only be a slow and uncertain process, and may not in all cases even be a practicable one. Most basically, much of Africa has from the earliest times been unconducive to state-building: its rainfall either irregular, or falling in uncontrollable deluges; its soils poor; its peoples sparsely scattered, and subject to debilitating diseases. Though parts of the continent – Ethiopia, the Great Lakes, parts of West Africa, Great Zimbabwe – have supported effective states over a long historical period, in others considerable ingenuity has been needed to create structures of political authority, and these have often been hard to reconcile with modern statehood. Somalia is perhaps the extreme example. Second, the rapid and often brutal way in which African societies were incorporated into the global system – initially in many areas through the slave trade, then through colonialism – both laid the foundations for modern state systems, and also made them peculiarly difficult to manage. Not only did their frontiers cut across indigenous social formations in ways which obstructed the creation of coherent political communities, but the very institutions of government itself were alien and imposed. The money to pay for these institutions was generated from the export of primary commodities at often volatile prices.

The first generation of independent African leaders, often for very understandable reasons, sought to ward off the dangers of instability by means which ultimately exacerbated it. They clung rigidly to the boundaries inherited from colonialism, for fear of the upheavals that might be unleashed were the possibility of redrawing them to be raised. They suppressed opposition movements of all kinds, for fear not only of the threat presented to their own tenure of power, but also of the divisions within states that might result were they to be permitted. They developed highly personalised systems of rule, which certainly afforded them personal gratification, but also chimed in with pre-colonial structures of authority in societies in which commitment to the bureaucratic forms of government introduced under colonialism was slight. The demands of statehood led to the extraction from their fragile economies of resources which these could ill afford, not least in order to pay off an ever expanding number of state employees, the most dangerous of whom were armed. Though Africa had its share of corrupt, brutal and foolish rulers, many of the problems of governance in the continent arose from the circumstances in which newly independent Africans had to rule. These cannot easily be changed.

3 Ways That Did Not Work
The Failure of Dictatorship

Much of the initial reaction to instability in Africa, both from African states themselves and from the international community, thus essentially consisted in suppressing its symptoms. Multi-party democracy was suspect, because it provided a voice for subversive ideas, and its suppression in all but a very few African states aroused remarkably little adverse reaction, either at home or abroad. Overt hostility to the imposition of single-party states was largely restricted to the disappointed leaderships of opposition parties, most of whom in any case soon found a niche in the governing party when they were permitted to do so. External protests were negligible. The successful imposition of Nigerian federal government control over the secessionist republic of Biafra, after a bitter and costly war, reinforced the principle of respect for the territorial integrity of African states, which was then applied to apparently analogous situations, such as those in Ethiopia, Sudan and Zaire.

A case could indeed be made that the demands of state-building necessarily precede such Western luxuries as the development of multi-party democracy. A Mengistu or a Mobutu were on this view needed to do for Ethiopia or Zaire what Louis XIV and Robespierre had done for France, or Peter the Great and Stalin for Russia. There was little in the experience of the currently industrialised states to support the contention that stability and development were inherently related to democracy; even in the United States, where the connections were closest, constitutionally guaranteed freedoms had signally failed to apply to that substantial section of the population who were of African descent. In the post-independence era, moreover, external support for African regimes, no matter how autocratic, was exceptionally high. The principles of state sovereignty built into the Charter of the United Nations, and still more strictly into that of the Organisation of African Unity (OAU), were readily interpreted to mean that issues of domestic governance were 'internal affairs', in which outsiders could not legitimately interfere. The division of the world between blocs led by rival superpowers with opposing ideologies of political and economic management left plenty of room for African rulers to seek external help. The superpowers in turn could usually be induced to support client rulers who looked to them for support, regardless of whether these made more than token efforts to adopt the ideology associated with their patron. The former colonial powers too, especially France, helped to sustain friendly regimes in their own bailiwicks. It was a good time to be an African dictator.

The problem, however, was not that African dictatorships failed to measure up to some Western standard of democracy and justice. It was that, simply as dictatorships, they did not work. The most brutal dictatorships did not create the most effective states; instead, they created the greatest dangers of state collapse. The Somali state, always built on uncertain foundations, crumbled beneath the attempts of Siyad Barre to impose a disciplined and hierarchical structure of government. Liberia survived 130 years of corrupt and exploitative Americo-Liberian rule, but could not cope with Master-Sergeant Samuel Doe. Idi Amin and the second Obote government did much the same for Uganda. Mengistu in Ethiopia, the most serious of Africa's would-be Stalins or Kim Il Sungs, fostered the civil wars that eventually overthrew him. The level of opposition fomented by dictatorial rule proved to be more than a match for the forces of repression that the dictators, even when supported by external powers, were able to bring against it.

The Unworkability of External Reform

The failures of post-independence African statehood gave rise to external demands for reform, long before these had been accepted by any but a very small number of African states themselves. For outsiders, indeed, African states were the problem, and the solution correspondingly lay in a takeover of African governmental functions by benevolent external institutions. This attempted takeover – almost, indeed, a recolonisation – was the *leitmotiv* of outside policy towards Africa, from the early 1980s through to the early 1990s. It took a number of forms, all of which were doomed to failure because Africans could not, ultimately, be managed from outside.

First in the field, from the early 1980s onwards, were the structural adjustment programmes fostered by the International Monetary Fund and the World Bank. Since their ostensible mandate was to set the conditions required for further external loans to African states, and the terms of reference of the two institutions explicitly prohibited involvement in the domestic politics of member states, these were able to sidestep some of the issues of sovereignty posed by more overtly 'political' intervention; but they none the less involved a takeover of the domestic economic management of target states, using loan conditionalities as leverage to force states to change policies that were viewed by the funding agencies as harmful to economic development. As the Bank and Fund reviewed their policies over the subsequent decade, a number of lessons became clear: first, that economic reform could not be separated from changes in political management; second, that policies needed to be specifically tailored to the circumstances of individual states; and third, that these policies had little chance of success unless they were 'owned' by the African governments which would have to implement them. Policies that were initially designed to substitute 'the market' for the damaging interventionism of African states thus came to require an increasing level of involvement, and hence of leverage, for those states themselves.

An analogous process applied to the later attempts by outside powers, dating largely from after the end of the Cold War in 1989, to impose conditionalities in the spheres of multi-party democracy, respect for human rights, and 'good governance'. Still less than programmes for economic reform could these be imposed from outside, a lesson made all too clear by the experience of Kenya, where the Western powers used explicit economic pressure to force a reluctant president Daniel arap Moi to hold multi-party elections, but were unable to prevent him from manipulating the results, or subsequently reverting to levels of corruption and human rights abuse little different from before. Programmes designed to improve administrative effectiveness and transparency necessarily required external agencies to work closely with the governments that they were seeking to reform.

The third and most obtrusive element in the attempt to improve African governance from outside involved direct external military intervention, either on explicitly humanitarian grounds or as part of a peacekeeping operation. In the eyes of some commentators, notably including the well-known expatriate Kenyan political analyst Ali Mazrui, this might extend to some form of external trusteeship for African states which had proved incapable of satisfactorily managing their own affairs. It was even suggested that many Africans would welcome a return to something close to colonial rule. By far the most ambitious attempt to implement such an agenda, the United States-led intervention in Somalia from 1992 onwards, rapidly exposed its deficiencies, and became a turning point for external attempts to reform Africa in many different ways. While it remains open to question whether a better managed operation could have achieved success, it soon became apparent that outside powers did not possess the capacity, and were not prepared to pay the costs (especially in the lives of their own soldiers) that effective intervention would have required; human rights abuses by some of the intervening forces scarred the idea of humanitarianism itself. The ignominious withdrawal from Somalia in 1994/95 left the Western world without any coherent and implementable concept of humanitarian action, a deficiency that has yet to be rectified. Nor did the record of external peacekeeping in Angola at the time of the failed 1992 elections, or in Rwanda during the 1994 genocide, do anything to restore confidence in the willingness or ability of the international community to intervene effectively to guarantee political order and human welfare in Africa. The withdrawal of UNAMIR from Rwanda at precisely the moment when it could – with adequate support from UN headquarters and participating states – have done much to prevent the slaughter, left an abiding sense of betrayal on the one side, and of shame on the other; the subsequent French intervention, *Operation Turquoise*, further discredited the plausibility of disinterested humanitarian action.

The project of external reform has also been deeply associated with the role of foreign non-governmental organisations or NGOs, drawn overwhelmingly from the liberal capitalist societies, which especially from the time of the Ethiopian famine in 1984 have become increasingly engaged in Africa. NGOs, which have a long and for the most part honourable history stretching back to the campaign against the slave trade, express a sense of common humanity and global social responsibility which should not be disparaged. At a time when Africa's economic decline and the end of the Cold War have sharply reduced its commercial and strategic importance to Western governments, NGOs have articulated demands, arising from their own home societies, that the continent should not be neglected. In addition to the money that they have raised themselves, they have been a potent influence in preventing the further decline of aid budgets, and their field experience has often proved invaluable. Their flexibility, capacity for rapid reaction, resources and accumulated skills, together with their constituency in their home societies, have put them at the head of the external response to African problems. The world as well as Africa would be a poorer place, both morally and materially, without them.

The relationship between Western NGOs and the African states and societies in which they operate has none the less been highly problematic. NGOs have become the victims of their own success; and in particular, as the most visible representatives of external involvement in the quest for a solution to Africa's problems, they have become, willy-nilly, an expression of political power. Often, they appeared to take over quasi-governmental functions which were properly the responsibility of the state itself. Their concern in some cases for 'advocacy', the belief that they should publicly stand up for the interests of the poorest or most oppressed sections of the population, clashed with their ability to carry out their other functions. A 'contract culture' emerged, in which NGOs acted as the local agents of governments and international institutions, which channelled their aid through NGOs – not least of course because of their field expertise, operational efficiency, and concern for the welfare of local populations – but led to the agency becoming in some respects dependent on its source of funding. The dangers were even greater when NGOs depended not just on governments but on their home civil societies, and needed to remain constantly in the eye of a public on which they relied for financial support. This led to a symbiotic relationship between NGOs and the Western media, in which some NGOs at least were under constant pressure to find a new 'emergency' to keep themselves going, while the media in turn searched for ever more gruesome images. The role of the media has certainly changed since the early 1980s, when Obote could get away with murder in Uganda by keeping them out; one result of the increasing penetration of African states over the last decade is that this is now much harder to manage, and that African governments can be made more directly accountable for human rights abuses, at least to external opinion. The Rwandan genocide of 1994 showed both the positive and the negative effects of this change. On the one hand, the killings could not be concealed, and promoted a massive external reaction; on the other, they provided the pretext for fund-raising campaigns by outside NGOs, many of which had little to offer on the ground, and often only undermined the attempts of the new Rwandan government to re-establish a viable and accountable political order.

The 'new humanitarianism', most stridently advocated by Bernard Kouchner, founder of *Médécins sans Frontières*, with his claimed *droit d'ingérence* or right of intervention, puts the problems at their clearest. M Kouchner consistently figures in opinion polls as the most admired individual in France, and has been appointed to ministerial positions in French socialist governments under both Mitterrand and Jospin: a prominent humanitarian role translates directly into domestic political power. The right of the international community to intervene directly in pursuit of humanitarian goals, regardless of principles of 'sovereignty' which have often served to reinforce the power of corrupt and brutal dictators, has reflected the moral certainties of the post-Cold War West. At the same time, the Western social values which it asserted have often, even when a plausible claim could be made for their universality, been difficult to implement under the very different political, social and economic conditions of Africa. Here too the experience in Somalia, where funds provided to relieve suffering had been readily appropriated by warlords with an interest in exploiting it, badly undermined the confidence of the NGO community. The 'imperative' of helping needy people wherever they may be, regardless of political considerations, was readily exploited by groups, like the former government of Rwanda in the refugee camps of what was then Zaire, with far from humanitarian agendas; the fact that some of the NGO personnel in Goma had previously worked in Khmer Rouge camps in Thailand made all too clear the failure of much of the NGO community to learn from its mistakes. In Goma as in Somalia, aid became a source of instability, rather than a means to alleviate its consequences. Most of all, however, an aggressive approach by those NGOs which regarded African governments as a major source of the problems that they were trying to resolve, necessarily impeded the establishment of the effective and accountable indigenous political order which provides the only long-term basis for stability.

In short, the attempt by external agencies – whether international financial institutions, peacekeeping forces, or non-governmental organisations – to take over Africa, and impose the necessary measures which African states have been unwilling or unable to implement themselves, has proved little more successful than the previous attempt by African leaders (backed by external aid and acquiescence) to impose solutions through the diktat of the overmighty African state. A great deal has none the less been learnt from it, and provides the basis for reforms which promise to be more sustainable.

One critical lesson that has emerged concerns the divergence between substance and agency. On the whole, though with very considerable caveats in particular cases, the *substantive policies* proposed by external institutions appear to be the right ones. In particular, economic reform along broadly 'liberal' lines is essential. A retreat by the state from a counter-productive and often corrupt engagement in direct economic management is inevitable. Integration into the global economy provides the only means through which African economies can develop, and should be welcomed rather than treated with suspicion. Many important lessons about micro-economic development have been learnt, especially in the area of peasant agriculture, and need to be put into effect. In the political sphere, regardless of whether Western liberal multi-party systems are appropriate, centralised dictatorship has evidently failed. African governments can only survive by making themselves responsive to the needs of their own peoples, and by devolving many functions which they have exercised at central level. A respect for basic human rights, even if this is imposed by external pressure – from the media, specialised NGOs, and ultimately outside states and international institutions – is both good in itself, and essential for stable and effective government. The 'good governance' agenda, for honest and effective administration, must likewise have an integral role in the construction of political stability.

At the same time, the *agencies* through which these policies must be implemented can only be African ones; and despite a considerably enhanced role for indigenous non-governmental organisations, private African businesses, and local institutions, as well as for cooperation at the regional and continental levels, the key agency must moreover be the African state itself. Yet the African state has been a considerable part of the 'problem' in the past, not merely because of individual culpability and gratuitous 'bad government', significant though those have often been, but because of weaknesses built into the very structure of African statehood: the artificiality of their construction; the fragility of their social and ecological base; the difficulty of generating political authority, and of managing efficient governmental institutions; the financial dependence on exports of primary products for which prices have generally been both volatile and declining. Building political stability in sub-Saharan Africa is most basically a matter of resolving this contradiction between the policies that have to be implemented, and the institutions that have to implement them.

4 Points of Departure

The prospects for resolving this contradiction have been considerably enhanced by a widespread recognition within Africa that the old ways have failed, and that new approaches are needed if the dismal record of the first three decades of independence is not to be repeated. The upsurge of demands for democracy with which Africans across the continent greeted the fall of the Berlin wall, and the demise of dictators like Ceausescu in Romania, was not only or even mainly the result of 'political conditionalities' imposed by external donors. The chain of causation was the other way round: the spontaneous and often very courageous outbreak of popular opposition to dictatorial regimes alerted the outside world to democratic aspirations which it had previously ignored. It was perfectly predictable that the subsequent experience of running multi-party systems would be a mixed one, with as many failures as successes; but the central principle of the accountability of African governments to their own peoples has been successfully asserted, and even though rulers with little popular support may continue to stay in power through a mixture of force, fraud and adept manoeuvre, the days of the old unchallenged single-party state and autocratic leader have gone.

Second, the transformation in South Africa has had a massive impact, at least in the southern part of the continent. The ANC government certainly resembles in many ways the newly independent regimes in other African states, some three decades earlier; it faces even greater pressures to meet the inflated expectations of its domestic constituency, and it is having to undergo a learning process in effectively using its potentially considerable diplomatic leverage in the region, and in the continent as a whole. Its instincts none the less are firmly on the side of reform of the way in which Africa has been run, a commitment indicated by President Mandela's support for democracy and human rights elsewhere in the continent, and by the adoption of an 'African Renaissance' as the watchword of Vice-President Mbeki.

The most remarkable change, however, has been the emergence of a new group of leaders in several of Africa's previously least successful states. Sometimes described as the proponents of a 'new Africanism', these notably include regimes that have come to power in the Horn and the Great Lakes regions after bitter and often prolonged insurgent warfare. The doyen of them, in terms of period in office, is President Museveni of Uganda, whose National Resistance Army (NRA) seized Kampala in January 1986. Just over five years later, in May 1991, the Eritrean People's Liberation Front (EPLF) led by Isaias Afewerki captured Asmara, at almost the same moment that the Ethiopian Peoples' Revolutionary Democratic Front (EPRDF) under Meles Zenawi overthrew the Mengistu regime in Addis Ababa. The Rwanda Patriotic Front (RPF), most of whose senior officers including its leader Paul Kagame had served in the NRA, took over in the aftermath of the genocide in mid-1994, and in turn supported Laurent Kabila's Alliance of Democratic Forces for the

Liberation of Congo/Zaire (ADFL), which ousted Mobutu from power in Congo/Zaire in May 1997.

These leaders and movements differ significantly from one another, and indeed from regimes with comparable agendas like that of President Rawlings in Ghana; but they have enough in common to be grouped together, and embody a similar set of attitudes towards the key issues of stabilisation and reform. First among these is a fierce sense of *ownership*. Most of them emerged intellectually from the student radicalism of the 1960s, and several were at one time Marxists. Inspired by liberation wars from Algeria to Mozambique, and by the works of Mao Zedong, they sought a genuine independence through guerrilla warfare, and in most cases spent years of struggle before their eventual triumph. Many of their closest friends died along the way. These are, in short, men and movements which have power because they have fought for it, won it, and in their own eyes earned it. They have no sense of obligation to anyone beyond their own comrades, and the people who supported them in the struggle. They are not inherently anti-Western, but their generally friendly relations with major Western states (and notably the USA) derive not from a sense of dependence or even a common ideology, but from a prudent recognition on both sides of a need for allies.

They do not, accordingly, share any commitment to Western-style multi-party democracy, which they generally regard as both divisive and threatening. In countries such as Ghana and Uganda, and in some respects DRC, multi-partyism is viewed as the preserve of old-style politicians, who used it for selfish ends. While they have been induced by external pressure to hold elections which they could be reasonably sure of winning, their idea of democracy is much closer to the original Marxist ideal, and expresses a belief that their movements derive from the people, and serve their interests. Their commitment to human rights, which is likewise deeply felt, derives not from the legalism of the Western tradition but from the experience of suffering under some of Africa's most brutal regimes. The difference is perhaps most tellingly expressed by the contrast between the procedural concerns of the UN's Arusha tribunal on the Rwandan genocide, and the determination of the RPF to find and punish those whom they hold responsible.

In other respects, however, the 'new African' leaders have much in common with Western projects of reform. They share a belief in the need for transparent, honest and responsible governance, and a disgust for the corruption of earlier elites. During the war years, movements such as the NRA and EPLF were dedicated, disciplined and efficient, and took fierce measures against any of their own members who were regarded as betraying positions of power and trust. They have sought to carry a similar sense of accountability into government, along with the civic education and institution-building programmes that marked their years in the bush: the extension of the national resistance council system in Uganda provides the clearest example. For the most part, they have abandoned a belief in state socialism, which in the hands of earlier regimes had itself become an instrument of exploitation, and have been converted to the virtues of the market – though with an emphasis not on big international companies, which were often all too intimately associated with corrupt African governments, but on African smallholders and traders.

Diplomatically, the new leaders despise the old consensus on state sovereignty and non-interference in the domestic affairs of other states, expressed in the Charter of the OAU, which both Isaias and Museveni have publicly attacked. They themselves benefited enormously from covert support from neighbouring states during their own struggles, and have been quite open in their sympathies and even material support for like-minded movements in other countries: Eritrea, Ethiopia and Uganda support the SPLA in Sudan, just as Uganda supported the RPF in Rwanda, and Uganda and Rwanda in turn supported the ADFL in Congo/ Zaire. This makes them uncomfortable neighbours for old-style regimes, like Daniel arap Moi's Kenya. On the whole, they have been prepared to accept African conventions on maintaining the old colonial frontiers, but more from convenience than conviction: Meles Zenawi in Ethiopia was quite prepared to see Eritrea become independent, and has introduced a constitution which explicitly recognises the right to secede. President Museveni's statement that he does not want to change frontiers, but to make them irrelevant, puts the point neatly.

For Western states, looking for African partners in the project of continental reform, the 'new Africans' have been welcome but also uncomfortable allies. In many respects, they provide just that bridge between substance and agency that is the key to building stability. They often, indeed, make better partners than some of the new regimes that have emerged from multi-party elections: they are more disciplined, more committed, less likely to represent just another section of the old elite, or to need to take account of the shifts and manoeuvres of multi- party politics. They are in particular far better placed to push through programmes of economic reform, overriding when necessary the protests of hitherto privileged interest groups that are adversely affected by them.

In other ways, however, they make awkward bedfellows. They resent what they regard as external interference in their own internal affairs, as illustrated by the spat between Ethiopia and the United Kingdom in mid-1997 over 'human rights' conditionalities in the new British government's aid policies. The supreme self-confidence of the Eritreans in their capacity, having won their thirty-year war for independence, to deal with their problems themselves, can make cooperation difficult for even the most sympathetic allies. They have resisted pressures to introduce Western-style political systems, and they are no more likely to be willing to relinquish power voluntarily than the most entrenched old-style dictator. But the deepest differences lie – in Ethiopia, Rwanda, and most of all the new Democratic Republic of Congo – in the area of human rights, where a Western commitment to liberalism runs up against African governments' sense of their need, and their right, to clean up the rotten systems that they inherited. The killings which (though the numbers are uncertain) unquestionably accompanied the ADFL victory in DRC have brought this issue to the centre of attention.

Western NGOs have often found themselves at the sharp end of these differences. In large part, this has been because NGOs offend the African sense of ownership: they have taken it upon themselves to perform tasks which 'new African' governments not only regard as their own responsibility, but which they believe that they must be *seen* to perform if they are to re-establish legitimate relations between the state and its own people. In some cases, and notably in post-genocide Rwanda, the role of NGOs – whether working in Rwanda itself, or amongst Rwandans in refugee camps outside – has been particularly insensitive. In part, too, NGOs have simply made awkward witnesses to events which governments sought to conceal, the killings at Kibeho camp in Rwanda in April 1995 providing a particularly clear example. Paradoxically, NGOs have often found it harder to work with governments that they viewed sympathetically, than under old-style African regimes where their sense of their own mission was clearer.

The 'new African' movements provide no readymade solutions to the problem of creating political stability. Each has grown out of its own experiences, and has sought to introduce solutions tailored to its own particular situation. Many of those experiences, moreover, have been so traumatic that few would wish to duplicate them, no matter how successful the learning process that eventually emerged: that Eritrea or Uganda should provide models for a new Africa shows how profound are the depths from which projects of reform have arisen. Nor are the reforming governments in all cases necessarily here to stay. While some appear to be firmly established, others are fragile: the tide that has seen them spread from Uganda to Ethiopia and Eritrea, Rwanda and DRC, may yet continue to flow – to Sudan, perhaps Kenya, even into West Africa – but it may ebb. And while many elements in the new agenda attract wholehearted support from the West, others raise considerable misgivings. There is in particular a ruthlessness about the new leaders which runs counter to the idealism (and very possibly the naivety) of Western governments, civil societies, and especially NGOs. What the new generation of leaders have made clear, though, is that Africa's future lies overwhelmingly in its own hands. There is room for a measure of partnership with the outside world, but not for dependence on it. Outside states and multinational organisations remain much more than mere onlookers in Africa, but they are no longer the masters of the game.

5 Rebuilding Shattered States

Building political stability in Africa is not a uniform process. It has to start from very different points, and proceed in varying ways. The greatest challenge of all is presented by those states which have suffered from such levels of conflict, breakdown and destitution that the very foundations on which to rebuild have all but disappeared. Such states are far from being rare or exceptional, but cover substantial areas of the continent. Liberia and Sierra Leone in West Africa are relatively isolated; but a continuous swathe of territories which are or have been in turmoil extends from Chad, through Sudan to Eritrea and Ethiopia, Djibouti and Somalia, Uganda, Rwanda and Burundi, Congo/Zaire, and Angola, with Mozambique as a further example. Other states, such as Congo-Brazzaville and the Central African Republic, are clearly in danger, while a similar fate cannot be excluded for Africa's most populous state, Nigeria.

Whatever the attractions of early warning schemes or other forms of pre-emptive action, designed to prevent state collapse before it gets out of control, these have had little impact in the past, and are unlikely to prove any more successful in the future. There has been no problem in identifying either the states most at risk, or the counter-productive actions of incumbent regimes which have predictably led to their own downfall. The Doe government in Liberia, which ploughed its own self-destructive path despite the efforts of the United States to establish basic levels of good governance, democracy, and respect for human rights, provides the clearest example. The Abacha regime in Nigeria, the al-Beshir one in Sudan, or the government of Daniel arap Moi in Kenya are no more responsive to external guidance. Ultimately, there is no governing Africa from outside. Nor has military intervention in the midst of civil war, as in Somalia or Liberia, achieved its objectives. In many ways, despite its success on occasions in meeting immediate humanitarian needs, it has only impeded and delayed the emergence of long-term processes of conflict resolution.

At the same time, the experience of Africa's shattered states has produced some important and constructive lessons. Several of these states have started to embark on processes of reconstruction. Ownership, as always, has been the critical factor: the process of rebuilding has begun only when an organised and determined group of indigenous political actors has set about trying to create a form of government which would not replicate the failings of the old one. Exactly how such a government might operate is something that varies from state to state. There is room especially for difference over the terms on which different parties or factions can or should be incorporated into the new political order: whether through a multi-party system; or by opening up the reform movement to create some form of broad-based government; or even by a quasi-judicial process to determine which survivors from former regimes should be excluded from any further participation in political life, and which should be readmitted. Devices ranging from the South African

Truth Commission, through the human rights trials in Ethiopia and Rwanda, to the open but non-party political structure in Uganda, represent different responses to the problem.

One essential element in rebuilding must however be an inclusive political formula: a mechanism through which all sections of the community are enabled to belong to, and offered the chance to participate in, the new political order. In Africa, this most critically involves the ethnic dimension. States which exclude parts of their own populations from full membership in the political community – as Tutsis were from Habyarimana's Rwanda or Banyamulenge from Mobutu's Zaire, or as Christians are from al-Beshir's Sudan – cannot create a viable political settlement. It is moreover all but inevitable that new political forces will be drawn disproportionately from some ethnic or religious groups rather than others, and a first priority must be to ensure that those who are less well represented are not made to feel excluded. Ways of doing this may differ; the high risk strategy pursued in Ethiopia of offering each 'nationality' its own regional government, with a right of secession built into the constitution, may backfire. But some attempt to grapple with the problem is needed. As Nobel Prize winning economist Douglass North has reminded us, making economies grow is essentially a matter of getting people to work together; exactly the same is true of creating effective political institutions.

The role of the outside world in supporting political settlements calls for finely balanced judgement in particular cases. There is always the danger that too intrusive a role may weaken the critical sense of domestic ownership, and produce settlements which cannot work once the outside pressures that imposed them are withdrawn. The remarkably successful settlement in Mozambique probably represents the furthest that external involvement in conflict resolution can go, and this in turn derived from peculiar features of the Mozambican situation. In particular, both the Frelimo government and the Renamo opposition were so dependent on external support that once the diplomatic situation allowed – notably with the transition to majority rule in South Africa – it was possible to induce each side to accept a negotiated settlement. The level of consensus within the international community was likewise a critical factor. A divided international community, conversely, could create no effective mechanism for dealing with an entrenched 'spoiler' such as Jonas Savimbi in Angola, who had access to the financial and military resources needed to sustain an independent existence, once the negotiated settlement failed to achieve his objectives. The Arusha accords on Rwanda were another tragically failed attempt at outside mediation; and in Uganda in 1985/86 and Ethiopia in 1990/91, as in Congo/Zaire in 1996/97, there was really nothing for the outside world to do except await the outcome of the military confrontation.

Once a viable political settlement is in place, there is of course an important role for the outside world, in providing the government with the resources and expertise which are then badly needed to consolidate it: for the restoration of basic infrastructure, disarming and demobilising former combatants, removing landmines, resettling refugees, training civilians as well as former soldiers for peacetime occupations, and a multitude of further essential tasks. Even this apparently straightforward involvement is not, however, unproblematic. For one thing, it has to be carried out in a way which sustains the new political order, and as already noted, this can create difficulties especially for NGOs: used to doing things themselves, often accustomed to regard governments as corrupt and inefficient, guided by their own priorities, they can easily find themselves at odds with the very government that they are there to support. There are, however, more basic issues in the relationship between a fragile regime and the international community. The regime will want to consolidate its position, while donors will want to reassure themselves that they are not merely giving *carte blanche* to a new government which is no less autocratic than its predecessor. Some conditionalities must necessarily be built into the aid relationship; where they should be drawn calls for delicate judgement. It would for example be unreasonable to expect the newly installed Kabila government in DRC to submit itself instantly to multi-party elections, as demanded by opponents whose relationship to the Mobutu regime is at any rate open to question. At the same time, some commitment to democratic values and respect for basic human rights is clearly called for. These issues become especially sensitive when – as in Rwanda and Ethiopia, as well as DRC – there are evident clashes between the demands of regime consolidation and respect for rights. African regimes for their part are sometimes confused by the proliferation of 'special envoys' from different states and international organisations, all pursuing their own agendas, and careful coordination between them is needed if their involvement is to be both constructive and effective.

6 Combining Economic and Political Reform

For states with reasonably viable governments, a rather different set of priorities come into play. Critical among these is the need to combine the reforms needed to create a dynamic economy on the one hand, with the construction of effective political and governmental institutions on the other. Two basic points can be made at the start. First, a failure to reform must eventually be fatal. Whatever mistakes were made (and they were numerous) by the international financial institutions (IFIs) in seeking to impose structural adjustment programmes, these programmes derived from an accurate recognition that Africa's inefficient and usually corrupt state-managed economies were incapable of bringing about any sustained development, and that failures of economic management bore a large part of the blame (along with external factors) for the continent's dismal economic performance. Nor were its political and governmental institutions in any better shape. Second, the processes of economic and political reform (or non-reform) are necessarily very closely linked. Recognition of this relationship, which has become increasingly widely acknowledged since 1989, has been highlighted in the World Bank's 1997 *World Development Report*.

How the relationship actually operates is likely to vary widely from case to case. While it is simple to postulate a 'virtuous circle', in which legitimate government is needed to implement economic reforms, and successful reforms in turn enhance the legitimacy of the government, the connection can easily work the other way round: reform is always likely to be painful, and the more overdue it is, the more painful it is likely to be; its costs are immediate, and bear directly on specific and often powerful interests, whereas the eventual benefits are slow to appear; and newly democratic governments are unlikely to risk unpopularity, and may well need to keep themselves in power by maintaining a fragile coalition which makes decisive action difficult. Both the Ghanaian and the Kenyan governments abandoned economic reform in order to win their first multi-party elections in 1992, with lasting damage to their economies. These experiences help to explain why strong governments with a clear sense of their own mission have sometimes provided better prospects for reform than weak and elected ones, even though Africa's most authoritarian governments, and especially its military ones, have also been the most corrupt and inefficient.

The conversion of the IFIs to a recognition of the need to manage economic reforms in such a way as to enhance rather than undermine political stability derives far more from their experience in Eastern Europe, where political factors have been paramount, than to anything they have learnt in Africa, but it is none the less welcome. It opens the way to an acknowledgement that governments must be fully committed to the reform process, so that programmes must be carefully negotiated with them, in a way that is appropriate to their local political circumstances. Contrasting examples of the relationship between political management and economic reform are provided by Uganda and Madagascar. In Uganda, the Museveni government espoused structural adjustment soon after coming to power in 1986, following a short and unsuccessful experiment with the socialist policies which came most readily to a leader with his radical background. Museveni's position was then strong enough for him to be able to resist external pressures for multi-party democracy; but the 'no-party' democracy which he introduced instead produced a far from subservient parliament, in which bargaining with regional interests was needed to implement reforms such as the privatisation of state corporations.

Madagascar had a far more switchback experience: the socialist experiments of the Ratsiraka government from 1975 onwards had such a disastrous effect on debt, inflation, and even food supply that by 1983 it was forced to turn to the IMF for rescue. That programme, negotiated in almost total secrecy, received little commitment from government or society, and had equally little effect, until an extended structural adjustment facility was introduced with far greater commitment in 1989, and brought about at least the start of a turnaround. This was not enough to prevent Ratsiraka from being ousted from office after a multi-party constitution was introduced in 1992, but his successor, Albert Zafy, shied away from reform, leading eventually to the re-election of Ratsiraka, by now a committed reformer, in 1996. The Madagascan experience indicates that both political and economic reform must be part of a learning process, on the part of people as well as government, rather than a set of policies imposed on each of them from above.

What is common to both the Ugandan and the Madagascan cases is the establishment of an indigenous political process, through which reforms can be proposed, discussed, adapted and implemented. Other states need to create their own appropriate institutional settings, through which an analogous process can take place. Specific political mechanisms, such as electoral or federal systems geared to the structure of individual states, need to be developed in such a way as to enhance both consensus and accountability. In a rapidly changing continent, new forms of political power – often based on commerce, religion and professional expertise, as well as on the more familiar forces of ethnicity and regionalism – have emerged, and call for integration into political life. It is thus necessary to develop social and governmental institutions which create confidence domestically, as well as among prospective outside investors. A free press, as an instrument of transparency and accountability, is an obvious example, even if that too requires a learning process, in which opposition newspapers need to curb a tendency to indulge in entirely negative reporting, and governments their outrage at any comment that betrays a lack of respect. Independent African newspapers, especially outside South Africa, lead a hand-to-mouth existence, with poorly paid and qualified journalists, small circulations, and often stridently partisan political agendas.

The central institution in the reform process, however, is the judicial system. The rule of law, encompassing respect for property rights and the enforceability of contracts, is an essential ingredient of sustainable development; but the need to ensure personal as well as economic security extends well beyond the simple protection of investments. In part, this is a matter of establishing appropriate procedures, for example to ensure the proper appointment and training of judges, or good conduct on the part of the police force; but the issues involved are far more cultural and social than they are technical. A strong sense on the part of many African rulers of the reverence that is due to their own authority, coupled with the difficulty on the part of oppositions of combining criticism of the regime with respect for its right to rule, remain powerful obstacles to the rule of law. If lucrative contracts are awarded to the president's relatives, to the detriment of other indigenous entrepreneurs, formal constitutional provisions are unlikely to create much confidence. Standards of day-to-day policing in much of Africa remain extremely poor, and can only be improved by consistent and determined pressure from the top.

The question of *how*, if at all, it is possible to create effective institutions in a hitherto unwelcoming environment remains to be answered. External aid programmes in 'good governance' often recall the unavailing efforts at institution-building – such as the attempt to introduce British-style local government institutions – in the period leading up to independence. No such programme will succeed unless it can draw on indigenous experience. Perhaps one of the most important changes brought about by the NRM regime in Uganda has been to make ordinary soldiers as well as policemen accountable for any abuse of power, a change that derives in Uganda from bitter memories of the Amin and Obote regimes. In Ghana likewise, the memory of the 'preventive detention' of many of the country's leading citizens in the Nkrumah period helps to reinforce opposition to arbitrary government. As these examples indicate, the demand for the rule of law in Africa does not merely involve external pressure to introduce Western legal precepts for the benefit of foreign businesses, but often springs all too vividly from a recognition of the damage done by previous abuses of power.

7 The Regional Dimension

The role of 'regionalism' in Africa has changed dramatically since the days when it referred to the creation of a plethora of organisations formally dedicated to economic integration, almost all of which were entirely ineffectual. Despite a formal commitment to the maintenance of existing boundaries, the frontiers between African states have in practice softened or even crumbled, as traders, refugees, and even guerrilla insurgencies have crossed them almost at will. As a result, the region has become a critical arena within which political stability has been threatened, but within which it can also be maintained. The idea that correct relations between neighbouring African states can be maintained by insulating them from one another, through mutual acceptance of conventions on respect for existing frontiers and non-intervention in the internal affairs of other states, is no longer sustainable. Decisions that ostensibly fall within the competence of individual states have profound effects on their neighbours, in the way that the withdrawal of citizenship from the Banyamulenge community by the Mobutu government affected Rwanda. Refugee movements, invariably created by conditions within the state of origin, have led to massive cross-border population flows which, in the 1990s, have become increasingly volatile, politicised, and sometimes criminalised. They can no longer be insulated, through the implementation of UNHCR protection rules, from the politics either of the country of origin, or of the country of refuge. The 'new African' regimes especially have shown themselves willing to aid resistance movements directed against the governments of neighbouring states, in just the same way that they had themselves been aided in earlier years. Relations between neighbours have to an appreciable extent replaced connections with the superpowers and the former colonisers as the critical determinant of state security.

For African states, like states in any other part of the world, regional stability must ultimately rest on a domestic political order which is both stable in itself, and broadly shared between neighbours. It was therefore almost inevitable that upheavals within African states, and especially those brought about by guerrilla warfare, should also have profound effects on regional security. At the same time, it is now far more widely accepted than before, both that African states have a right to concern themselves with developments within the territories of their neighbours that affect their own security, and that regional security must ultimately depend on democracy, good governance and respect for human rights at the domestic level. African states have likewise increasingly recognised that regional security is their own responsibility, and that effective continental peacekeeping mechanisms need to be developed. How these mechanisms affect the issue of national 'sovereignty', the permissible limits of influence by larger and more powerful states over their smaller and weaker neighbours, and the informal groupings of African states along lines determined by ideology, language or external alliance, remain very sensitive issues.

Varying levels of progress towards the establishment of a stable regional order have been achieved in different parts of the continent. Even in southern Africa, however, where the conditions seem to be most favourable, considerable difficulties remain. While regional leadership is predestined – on grounds of size, economic development, and even military strength – to lie with South Africa, attempts by the ANC government to define its regional role have as yet been largely ineffectual. Denials on both sides notwithstanding, tensions remain between the government in Pretoria and that in Harare, which until the end of the apartheid era occupied the central role among the front line states. Awkward diplomatic arrangements have been needed to accommodate the claims of Presidents Mandela and Mugabe within the new structure of the Southern African Development Community. Attempts by President Mandela to mediate in disputes over the 1997 Zambian elections were viewed by the Chiluba government as unwarranted interference in favour of the ANC's old ally, ex-President Kaunda, while South Africa also had little to show for its attempts to mediate in the 1996/97 war in Zaire.

In West Africa, Nigeria's oft-asserted leadership role has likewise been affected by its aborted democratic transition, illustrated by the incongruity of the Abacha regime's attempts to present itself as the defender of democracy in Liberia and Sierra Leone. The overwhelming victory of Charles Taylor in the Liberian elections arouses understandable concern, both over issues of good governance and human rights, and over his willingness to curb the expansionist tendencies which once saw him claim a substantial area of Sierra Leone as part of 'Greater Liberia'. Taylor had close connections with the Sierra Leonean RUF, which exercises considerable influence over the military regime in Freetown, while the ousted elected government, then based in Guinea, sought international support for its return. The bases for regional stability in West Africa, in short, are extremely uncertain, while the critical east-central region remains in a state of open warfare, focused especially on Sudan, but affecting every state in the region.

Considerable controversy has been injected into regional relations by the role of private security forces, most prominent among them the South African-based group Executive Outcomes. Viewed on the one side as a source of stability, bringing order to troubled areas in which normal peacekeeping forces were unwilling to operate, this has conversely been regarded as a recolonising army, closely associated with the armed forces of apartheid South Africa and the covert operations of international mining companies. The very mention of 'mercenaries' in Africa continues to evoke memories of Congo in the 1960s, and the overthrow of African governments by dubious bands of foreign adventurers. Regardless of the temporary successes that they have achieved in some cases, such enterprises may undermine the development of effective long-term security structures, which must derive from the societies which they need to protect.

Executive Outcomes and its competitors do however draw attention to the links between regional security and economic development. Even though regionalism neither can nor should shelter African states from the global economy, the region remains a critical setting for economic transformation. Just as being in a region which is viewed favourably in developmental terms, such as South-East Asia, can provide enormous benefits, so African states have been badly disadvantaged by the negative image of the continent. Regional collaboration is needed, not just for infrastructure, but for the maintenance of international currency and investment regimes, and for the reduction of cumbersome frontier formalities. This cannot however be divorced from political rivalries: in southern Africa in particular, it has been closely associated with the search by South African corporations for investment opportunities north of the Limpopo, not only in mining but in consumption goods (with South African Breweries well to the fore) and the energy sector. Given its wealth, not only in minerals but in hydro-electrical potential, Congo/Zaire presents a particularly attractive target, provided that sufficient stability can be assured to justify the long-term investments that power supplies especially require. This stability can only be achieved, however, provided that governments in the region are self-confident enough not to feel the need to secure their borders against threats, real or imagined, from outside.

8 What Role for the Outside World?

The plea for Africans to be left alone to pursue their own solutions to their own problems is a vain one. The continent is inescapably part of a wider global system, not only economically and militarily (only South Africa is a major arms producer), but as part of a world society linked together by the news media and at least some sense of common humanity. Even the most self-confident of 'new African' leaders look outside the continent for essential resources. Outsiders are drawn in for a mixture of reasons: humanitarian conscience or even guilt; a need for Africa's resources, especially in minerals; power projection – lessened but not entirely removed by the end of the Cold War; and a desire to protect their own societies against evils perceived as emanating from the continent – refugees or economic immigrants, narcotics, AIDS.

This outside world is itself both varied and divided. Few major world actors have significant interests in Africa, France being the main exception. Their policies towards the continent are both low on their overall scale of priorities, and heavily influenced by pressures from their domestic societies. Western humanitarian organisations, along with a limited number of major corporations (mostly engaged in mineral extraction), may be more significant actors in Africa than the governments which nominally represent them. United States policy towards Africa is chronically uncertain, lacking leadership both in the Administration and in Congress. France, hitherto by far the most activist external power in Africa, is engaged in an irreversible process of transition, and none of the traditional pillars of its African policy any longer appear to be viable. The old networks are rapidly fading, in a way made most visible by the deaths of François Mitterrand and Jacques Foccart on the French side, and Felix Houphouet-Boigny and Mobutu Sese Seko on the African. And although France remains substantially the largest bilateral aid donor and investor in the continent (with over two-thirds of that investment now going to non-francophone Africa), both the aid budget and the franc zone are threatened by the demands of European monetary union. The European Union is making long overdue attempts to bring coherence to its own African policies, especially by directing aid towards major political priorities in conflict prevention and management, but its capacities are limited. The new British government, too, is attempting to reorder its priorities.

But Africa's external linkages extend beyond the 'traditional' connections with the major Western powers. East and South-East Asian states have been extending their economic interests, and in some areas have acquired a significant political presence. The level of Malaysian investment in southern and especially South Africa is remarkable, while Chad, as France withdraws, has been bankrolled by Taiwan. The very public struggle for pre-eminence in South Africa between Taiwan and the People's Republic of China now appears to have been won by the PRC. Western Europe and the United States, in short, are not the only players in the game. These changes, coupled with an increasing self-assertiveness among African leaders, have left Western states in the unaccustomed position of needing to respond to African initiatives, rather than imposing their own. The US government's proposals for an Inter-African Force, the centrepiece of former Secretary of State Christopher's 1996 visit to the continent, suffered badly from inadequate diplomatic preparation. Nor, despite perennial French suspicions of an Anglo-Saxon conspiracy, was US policy during the central African crisis of 1996/97 any more successful: its attempt to prevent external intervention failed, and the attempt to bring pressure on Kabila, notably through a call for early elections, lacked any credibility. For France, the central African crisis was still more traumatic: still reeling from deep disquiet about its links with the *genocidaires* in Rwanda, its botched clandestine attempts to recruit a mercenary force on Mobutu's behalf revealed it to be ineffectual as well as unprincipled. No more in France than in the United States is there any domestic political constituency for further military adventures in Africa.

Africa none the less remains on the international agenda, and while much has been heard of the 'marginalisation' of Africa, the continent is in some respects at the forefront of post-Cold War international relations, especially over humanitarian issues. Within the new world order, Africa has acquired an invidious place as the symbol of human suffering, a role which is often inappropriate and even offensive, but helps to assure a continuing level of concern. But while popular perceptions of Africa remain deeply negative, both in Europe and in the United States, governments and major corporations have recognised the signs of economic recovery, and are cautiously exploring the possibilities for further engagement. Even though the aid budgets of most European Union states are under severe pressure, especially from the demands of monetary union, there are signs of a budgetary turnaround in the United States, which may release more funds for Africa. President Clinton and Secretary of State Albright visited the continent in 1998. They and other Western leaders will have to do a great deal more listening, and appreciably less talking, than has been their wont. Difficult areas of difference or collaboration remain to be worked out, notably in the field of human rights. But after a long period during which African states have been on the receiving end of demands and initiatives imposed on them from outside, the balance is starting to shift.

9 Conclusions

Political instability in Africa derives from deep-seated causes, which cannot easily be remedied. A long timescale is needed, and progress is likely to remain both uneven and uncertain.

Lasting solutions can only be devised by Africans, and within Africa. The African dimension is primary; the external dimension, though significant, is secondary.

Political stability requires the creation of effective states, which must deliver, and be seen to deliver, basic services to their people. However, African states and societies vary considerably. No single political or economic formula can apply to them all, and solutions must be tailored to their individual circumstances.

One common element must none the less be a recognition, by significant political forces within each African state, of the need for governments which are accountable to, and serve the interests of, the peoples whom they govern. The forcible removal of regimes which do not recognise these principles is however only likely to lead to an improvement, if it is brought about by viable internal movements with a commitment to good governance.

Measures to cope with the ethnic diversity of African states, such as federal systems, must depend on specific circumstances. Though on occasion the formation of separate independent states may be the only solution, no substantial redrawing of existing boundaries is to be expected.

The introduction of Western-style multi-party systems likewise depends on circumstances. In many cases, it has greatly improved existing levels of transparency and accountability, and contributed to improved governance, but it may not always do so. Mechanisms such as electoral systems must be carefully designed, so as to ensure adequate representation without exacerbating social cleavages.

The key to rebuilding shattered states lies in the emergence of an inclusive political movement, dedicated to honest and efficient government. Immediate adherence to Western democratic norms cannot however be expected: good government has to come first.

Economic reform is essential, but must be carefully related to political conditions. Reform will not work unless governments are fully committed to its implementation.

Next after the maintenance of basic civil order, the creation of effective legal systems is the most critical requirement for stability and development. This is however far more than a technical task, and calls both for changes in social norms and for dedication and restraint on the part of governments.

The conventions on 'non-interference' in the internal affairs of other states are rapidly declining. Regional relationships are thus emerging as critical to stability. These require mechanisms to ensure close consultation between neighbours, and even to bring pressure on states which threaten regional stability.

The role of non-African states in seeking to assure stability in the continent is declining. These must be prepared to take a secondary and supportive role. The role of external non-governmental organisations is also likely to decline. These need to adapt their operating practices to working with self-confident African governments, and to ensuring that they support and do not undermine local political institutions.

8

Nuclear Weapons in the Twenty-First Century

Report based on Wilton Park Conference 515: 1–5 December 1997 on 'Building an Effective International Consensus Against Nuclear Proliferation: What More Can Be Done?'

Richard Latter

1 Introduction

As the century draws to a close, it is appropriate that the future role of nuclear weapons in the international system should be reassessed. Furthermore, there is a need to examine the possible future development of efforts to prevent the proliferation of nuclear weapons in the twenty-first century. What should be the near and long-term aspirations of those seeking to reduce the importance of nuclear weapons and what balance is to be struck between near and longer-term objectives? Should the priority be the continued reduction in the numbers of weapons held by nuclear weapons states (NWS) or should a clearer commitment to total disarmament be sought? How are those favouring disarmament to persuade those who continue to believe that nuclear weapons have a utility? What should be done about states who continue to seek to acquire these weapons?

Many take the view that there is a need to begin a serious debate on how to improve the effectiveness of non-proliferation regimes while assuring their long-term utility. Ensuring the effectiveness of the Nuclear Non-Proliferation Treaty (NPT) will require the resolution of fundamental differences between states about its long-term purpose: should it maintain a system in which a small number of states possess nuclear weapons and the rest refrain from doing so, or is the goal the eventual achievement of complete nuclear disarmament? Strong differences between states are likely to emerge on this issue as the NPT review process develops.

2 Fewer Nuclear Weapons or Total Disarmament?

Many are concerned that severely reducing the number of nuclear weapons held by states will be dangerous. Some analysts note that reductions of states' nuclear arsenals to very low numbers will be difficult to achieve in a situation in which threshold nuclear weapons states are extending the range of their delivery vehicles; mobile missile systems are increasingly deployed; antiballistic missile systems are proliferating; and there is continued evidence of a Russian nuclear war-fighting capability. Furthermore, verification of disarmament agreements is increasingly difficult at lower numbers which, in turn, would lead to greater uncertainty and perhaps higher instability. In addition, it is impossible today to establish clearly the actual numbers of nuclear weapons held by various states, particularly the numbers of tactical nuclear weapons; it will therefore be difficult to be certain that some of these weapons have not been hidden. Also future clandestine production cannot be entirely discounted. There are concerns that low yield testing of weapons systems may not be completely detectable.

Even if these problems are overcome or put to one side, there are serious concerns that the existence of low numbers of nuclear weapons may stimulate proliferation because states depending on the nuclear umbrellas of others will be less certain of their viability and therefore seek to develop their own weapons; some states may seek to match, for example, the lower holdings of the US. Furthermore, fewer weapons and launchers may increase the 'attractiveness' of pre-emption because a successful first strike against few targets may appear to be 'doable'. Low numbers will require a return to the targeting of cities rather than smaller military or nuclear targets, which many would regard as a retrograde step. Low numbers of nuclear weapons may also require rises in expenditure on conventional capabilities to 'ensure' states' future security. For the United States, going down to very low numbers would preclude the maintenance of its existing air, sea and ground triad.

These types of reservations draw criticisms as 'old thinking'. Some commentators urge greater efforts to enhance trust, through confidence-building and transparency, to a degree to which nuclear weapons will either be unnecessary or irrelevant; the example of the lack of concern in the United Kingdom and France about one another's nuclear capabilities is often given. However, achieving this state of affairs at a global level is, at best, in a distant future and the problems associated with 'low levels' need to be considered comprehensively and a clear picture developed of the conditions under which low numbers of nuclear weapons would be both acceptable and safe.

Progressing from low numbers to complete nuclear disarmament is certainly a distant prospect. Currently two opposing views exist, one emphasising the risks of keeping nuclear weapons and the other those of not keeping them. It is possible to take the view that nuclear weapons will be abolished only when they have been abandoned: nuclear disarmament will occur when and if there has been an extended period of disinvestment, disinterest, and disuse of nuclear weapons. The need is to establish not only a nuclear-free world but also a nuclear-free peace.

Discussion of the conditions necessary for a nuclear-free peace have barely begun. However, it is possible that shaping changes to the interstate system could narrow and perhaps eliminate nuclear roles. Inevitably steps in this direction will change perceptions of what 'zero' will be. For example, the movement below 2000 warheads will require a redefinition of the strategic relationship between the US and Russia; neither seems currently prepared to abandon deterrence given the uncertainties of the international system. Movement below 1000 warheads will require the 'trilateralisation' of the core strategic relationship to include China and it is unclear whether Russia and the US are ready to accept 'parity-based' relations with Beijing. Furthermore, France and the United Kingdom will also need to be included in the equation. Effective measures will have to be developed to deal with so-called 'rogue regimes' and the security concerns of 'defensive' nuclear powers – Israel, India and Pakistan – will need to be addressed.

Moving from this situation to complete nuclear disarmament is difficult to envisage. However, it is likely that deterrence-based relations between states would remain and they would depend upon forces in being for immediate threats and latent capabilities for the longer term. There would be residual potentials for wild fire proliferation and the use of other weapons of mass destruction (WMD), for example biological weapons. States would be transparent about their defence activities to a degree which is unimaginable in current circumstances. Furthermore, there would be heavy reliance on collective security or, possibly, the development of a multipolar system dominated by regional hegemonies. Reliable punishments would need to be available for possible application against states developing or using nuclear weapons.

Thus, movement towards nuclear disarmament will involve a spectrum of deterrence and reassurance problems in relations among the major powers, among regional adversaries, and among the recipients and providers of security guarantees. Many take the view that the 'reassurance' role of nuclear weapons will be of continued significance in the decades ahead. Continued possession will be reassuring to the major powers who will seek to continue the prevailing peace among them, and they will also reassure states who fear the onset of a post-Cold War era of greater anarchy and less reliable protection from the major powers.

It is possible to envisage an acceleration in the rate of reductions, possibly in response to a future crisis, accident or use. Perhaps more likely, however, is a slowing of reductions resulting, for example, from a

stalling of negotiations and related reductions as a result of a breakdown
of political will in some or all of the parties; a decay of the negotiated
nuclear order, whether START or NPT; a devolution of political initiative
from the US; or the emergence of a competitive reconstitution of nuclear
capabilities arising from changing political circumstances.

Given these future uncertainties, decision-makers in the NWS are likely
to consider it prudent to retain an 'adequate', however defined, nuclear
capability while, perhaps spasmodically, supporting and leading non-
proliferation efforts. For many, the retention of limited nuclear
capabilities is deemed to provide the essential element of stability
required to take risks in pressing forward with reductions. It should be
recognised, however, that it is unlikely that all states will accept this
view even if it is accepted by the existing NWS and most other countries.
For this majority, however, a medium-term utility for nuclear weapons
is evident. For example, possession of small nuclear arsenals ensures
that there are few benefits for potential 'rogue regimes' in covertly
producing nuclear weapons with which to threaten their neighbours.
Similarly, some argue, nuclear weapons will continue to diminish the
attraction of developing huge conventional military capabilities.

Should, however, a blueprint be established for eventual disarmament?
Probably not. Setting aside the problem of securing agreement on its
content, it may be counterproductive. A shortlist of essential elements
for such a blueprint may of itself suffice to diminish enthusiasm for the
whole project: the need for trust between most if not all nation states;
the need for complete and adequate verification; the need to end the
chemical and biological weapons threat; and the need to assure complete
defence dominance, for example through the widespread availability of
ballistic missile defences. The list, and it is far from inclusive, is so
formidable that it merely serves to discourage any effort to pursue the
desired outcome.

A key requirement in promoting nuclear weapons' reductions and
non-proliferation must be the maintenance of support for these goals in
the vast majority of countries which have elected not to acquire nuclear
weapons. To achieve this, their ambitions and anxieties must be
considered by the NWS. A recent survey of 17 non-nuclear weapons
states (NNWS) which actively support the NPT gave clear pointers into
their motivations. These did *not* include, for example, an absence of
perceived security threats or utility for nuclear weapons; the provision
of nuclear guarantees through alliances with nuclear weapons states; a
lack of technical capability to develop weapons; or pressure from existing
nuclear weapons states. Decisions not to acquire nuclear weapons tended
to be based upon elite and popular attitudes, although their relative
importance varied in different countries. A common element often
included a normative aversion to nuclear weapons associated with deep-
rooted anti-militarism. Furthermore, anti-nuclear policies are often
regarded as a means to demonstrate independence from larger more

powerful neighbours or the nuclear weapons states. Such policies may be associated with a multilateral approach to foreign policy and the desire to play the role of 'good citizen' in the international system. There is also often a related concern that the wealth of the state be used to promote the welfare of its population rather than the promotion of international foreign policy objectives.

Decisions not to acquire nuclear weapons appear, therefore, not to be grounded in security considerations alone. This may be relevant when considering how best to deal with states which are not supportive of the NPT regime. For example, normative aspects of the NPT and their consistent application need to be re-emphasised and NNWS are well placed to do this. In addition, active NNWS could attempt to facilitate the reintegration of 'rogue regimes' into the international system; help their integration into multilateral institutions, not least those which will help them to improve their economies; encourage non-governmental organisation and 'track II' contacts at informal levels; and promote open and frank debates about their (the threshold/breakout states) policies and aims. The role of the NNWS has, thus far, been undervalued in the debate between the NWS and those not subscribing to the NPT regime. The possibility of these states acting as 'bridge-builders' between the NWS and those who doubt the utility of the NPT should be explored. They may be particularly able to facilitate progress given their often considerable economic resources which could be mobilised to generate economic incentives in support of non-proliferation efforts.

Consideration of nuclear non-proliferation and possible nuclear disarmament cannot be conducted without paying due reference to the existence of other weapons of mass destruction, namely chemical and biological weapons (CBW). How far is the removal of their menace essential for progress to be made in the nuclear field?

3 The Biological Weapons Threat

The dangers presented by the proliferation of CBW appear to be increasing. For example, 25 states are now believed to have offensive chemical weapons programmes. It is generally accepted that CBW offer a wide range of applications and have genuine strategic, operational and tactical utility. Do nuclear weapons have a role in deterring CBW acquisition or use? If so, should the aim be to deter initial use, repeated use after an initial incident, all use, or merely strategic use? Some argue that nuclear weapons should also be used to deter conflicts where chemical or biological weapons could be used, or to deter intimidation backed by CBW. A case can be made in support of nuclear deterrence in all of these circumstances.

However, the effectiveness of nuclear deterrence depends upon the rationale and viewpoint adopted by decision-makers who are considering the acquisition or use of CBW. Their ideas of costs and benefits may differ from those prevailing in the Cold War, for example, being influenced by such factors as pride, anger, revenge, a perceived lack of alternatives. For deterrence to be credible, it will need to be calibrated to meet a given situation and backed by appropriate rhetoric, technical capabilities and, at need, appropriate action.

There are strong differences of opinion on whether or not nuclear weapons are appropriate to deter CBW. Arguments 'against' include claims that it violates the existing 50-year taboo against the use of nuclear weapons; it violates promises made under existing nuclear security assurances; nuclear use would be disproportionate and increase the 'cost' of CBW use beyond what is reasonable; the threat of using nuclear weapons is not credible, is disproportionate and is immoral; it may set a precedent that nuclear weapons not be used in different circumstances; use sets a bad precedent which weaker states will follow; use of nuclear weapons could provoke more CBW use because of the targeted states' perceived need to 'win' a conflict, avert defeat or seek vengeance; and that there are effective alternatives, for example, the use of 'high-tech' offensive conventional weapons and/or of effective defensive systems.

Arguments 'in favour' of possible use of nuclear weapons include claims that popular rage about a CBW attack will demand a devastating response; threats to use CBW to avert defeat may require a nuclear response; a BW campaign should be stopped to prevent further casualties; inaction would be politically damaging, for example to relations with allies; a lack of response would contribute to the idea that CBW use is acceptable; belligerent reprisal is permitted under international law; and that there are no good alternatives in some circumstances because conventional forces cannot deliver an adequate response, it is unclear how they would be targeted, and they would take too long to prepare.

Whatever the strengths of these arguments, nuclear weapons will be held by a minority of states for the foreseeable future. However, they need not be central to their defence doctrines nor need their role in deterring CBW be overtly stated. It remains probable that nuclear weapons would only be used in extreme cases, but CBW use may constitute such a case.

What are the implications of this for the future of arms control efforts? There will inevitably be a tension between deterrence and arms control; there is a need to think seriously about non-nuclear methods of deterring CBW use. It is also necessary to consider the impact using nuclear weapons may have on the winning of any future peace. This said, there is also a need to consider whether the use of BW will represent a seminal event within the international community which would require an overwhelming and decisive response.

Ideally, the search for solutions to these problems should involve the pursuit of non-nuclear options, and the existence of nuclear weapons should not be permitted to undermine efforts to develop possible alternatives, including enhanced conventional military capabilities. The current circumstance, in which nuclear weapons states do not have the capacity to respond in kind to a CBW attack and can only rely on a possible nuclear response, is undesirable, not least because it will be difficult to decide how to use nuclear weapons in such circumstances; for example, what should the targets be: populations, military installations, leaderships?

It is far from clear that allies would support the use of nuclear weapons which could leave them hostages to subsequent non-nuclear retaliation. This would particularly be the case in circumstances where chemical or biological weapons were used to a limited degree or if related casualties were low. If nuclear deterrence is to remain a cornerstone of defence policy, it is necessary to clarify what it involves in a post-Cold War world and what the expectations of both allies and enemies are. There is a need for consistency of purpose among allies and to decide whether ambiguity about possible nuclear use is desirable or not. It should be recognised that for nuclear deterrence to succeed, it inevitably involves the threat of punitive use.

To forge an international consensus on these issues will require careful deliberation in national capitals and cooperative effort by national decision-making elites. Many would argue that future success in such efforts will require consistent and expert leadership. From where should such leadership come? Readily available possible candidates include the existing NWS and, perhaps, the three threshold nuclear weapons states. What are the prospects that they will provide leadership at the beginning of a new millennium?

4 Who Should Lead?

The United States

A key element of US nuclear weapons policy involves the securing of an eventual nuclear-free peace. To this end, the US Administration supports the NPT as an essential framework within which future arms control and arms reduction efforts are to be conducted. In the nearer term, American priorities include living up to NPT commitments through continuing deep reductions in the US nuclear arsenal; moving forward on a START III agreement; and avoiding the creation of new roles for nuclear weapons. Outside the NPT process, priorities of the current Administration include negotiating a Fissile Material Cut-Off Treaty, ratification of the Comprehensive Test Ban Treaty (CTBT), implementing the Chemical Weapons Convention (CWC) in practice within the United States, and supporting efforts to secure a protocol to the Biological Weapons Convention (BWC) to enhance the Convention's compliance regime.

In the medium term, the United States is considering promoting additional initiatives which include developing new conventional weapons arms control measures; actively seeking to reduce regional tensions which underpin WMD acquisition; assisting the states of the former Soviet Union to control and oversee effectively their stocks of fissile material; and considering how excess plutonium may best be destroyed, by whom this should be undertaken and how such destruction should be supervised.

More broadly, the United States is seeking to facilitate the maintenance of a stable international economic environment in the belief that this is required to provide the financial resources necessary, for example, to fund the Korean Peninsula Energy Development Organisation (KEDO) and fissile material disposal in Russia, and finance United Nations (UN) and other arms control efforts.

This substantial programme of work is not without its critics. Many argue that the United States is doing too little to raise the profile of arms control domestically and internationally; they argue that the United States should do more to point out the benefits of arms control and to persuade audiences that costs incurred are well spent and worthwhile. The anticipated demise of the Arms Control and Development Agency in Washington is felt by many to be sending the wrong message. Furthermore, there is concern about future US ratification of the CTBT because of Congressional worries that the Treaty will undermine the future viability of the US nuclear stockpile.

These criticisms are forcefully countered by representatives of the Clinton Administration. They note that the United States remains actively engaged in all multilateral arms control fora. They assert that the United States government has not lost interest in arms control, but that it is concerned that initiatives be cost-effective, practical and contribute to US national security goals and international stability.

Additional criticisms of current US policy involve a perceived US movement towards linking nuclear weapons with the deterrence of CBW. Furthermore, US efforts to influence the international arms control agenda prompt considerable resentment; for example, American initiatives to affect Indian and Pakistani policies regarding nuclear weapons are strongly resented, particularly in India. More broadly, in the Non-Aligned Movement (NAM) there are many who remain doubtful about the sincerity of the United States' commitment to eventual total nuclear disarmament.

The degree to which such doubts damage American efforts to promote non-proliferation is debatable. It is inevitable that the pursuance of non-proliferation and arms control goals will give rise to differences between nation states; these will not always be surmountable by constructive and cooperative effort, even if this approach is desirable. For it to succeed, however, United States' and other initiatives must receive widespread support within the international community, not least from its more powerful players. Many take the view that China will have a crucial role to play in promoting the arms control agenda of the twenty-first century. Are decision-makers in Beijing prepared to undertake this role?

China

Chinese interest and involvement in arms control and non-proliferation has increased since the end of the Cold War; for example, it has opted to join the NPT and accept related obligations. The end of the Cold War is perceived in China to have brought opportunities for China to participate in arms control efforts as the United States and Russia undertake deep cuts in their nuclear arsenals. Positive opportunities are perceived to have been created by growing international interest in the non-proliferation agenda; increased awareness that the use of nuclear weapons will not produce 'winners'; the cooling of many regional 'hot spots'; and greater interest in multilateral and regional confidence- and security-building, as exemplified through, for instance, the NPT, CTBT and various nuclear weapons-free zones.

Chinese analysts emphasise the following continued problems: the large numbers of nuclear weapons remaining and their importance in 'great power' relations; the lag between changing circumstances and old nuclear strategies; the inherent inequalities of the international system; the spread of nuclear technology to produce power; and uncertainties regarding the future policies of 'threshold' states. Chinese observers suggest that these problems may best be met through the strengthening of the non-proliferation regime and by the provision of unconditional negative security assurances to all NNWS. These assurances should include not only No-First-Use but also more nuclear weapons-free zones. They emphasise that the Anti-Ballistic Missile (ABM) Treaty and the Missile Technology Control Regime (MTCR) should be observed strictly, this being of particular concern given Chinese unease about the possible deployment of US theatre missile defence systems in East Asia. They also call for implementation of the CTBT and the negotiation of a Fissile Material Agreement. There is an increasing understanding of the need to increase transparency about China's own nuclear programmes and of the concerns which Western states have in this regard. There is an apparent willingness to improve control over exports of contentious materials and dual-use technologies and a revamping of the Chinese legal system is being undertaken to this end.

The Chinese take the view that they will join the nuclear disarmament process at 'the appropriate time' which is defined in terms of when 'No-First-Use' has been embraced by all the NWS; when US and Russian stockpiles drop below 1000; when the UK and France are prepared to join in; and when China's multiple bilateral relationships permit it to do so (any use of disarmament to 'contain' China is unacceptable).

While China's policies are generally welcomed in the international arms control community, some misgivings persist. The concept of 'No-First-Use' is not accepted by, or acceptable to, many states which regard such guarantees as unreliable at best and 'ill-intentioned lies' at worst. These views have yet to affect Chinese thinking which appears to continue to take the view that 'No-First-Use' agreements constitute useful confidence-building measures. There is a residual concern about Chinese export policies, the lack of transparency about Chinese nuclear holdings, and about the continued Chinese production of fissile material. Those seeking to engage China more actively in the multilateral arms control process are pressing for further progress on these issues. Nevertheless, there is some concern that the conditions currently set by the Chinese leadership for early entry into disarmament discussions may simply be unattainable and therefore represent a means to avoid such participation for the foreseeable future.

This would be regrettable if, as many believe, the Chinese must be persuaded that they have a central role to play in forging a consensus against nuclear proliferation. As the major rising power with a historical antipathy to existing international norms and institutions, its future attitudes towards them will have far-reaching implications for the alignment of other rising powers. The future of non-proliferation will be well served by a genuine commitment of Chinese authorities to fulfil their legal and political obligations as a Permanent Member of the Security Council to protect the peace by compelling states to honour their Treaty obligations.

The Europeans

The three European nuclear powers, Russia, France and the United Kingdom, must similarly be charged to meet these responsibilities.

Russia has proved to be a cooperative partner with the US in arranging the mutual reduction of their nuclear stockpiles. Its declaratory policy has been supportive of the NPT and other arms control regimes. Difficulties have been encountered, however, with the implementation of arms control agreements: financing reductions in the numbers of weapons and their destruction has proved to be difficult in a state struggling with economic decline. At the political level, the lively politics of the Duma have complicated both the ratification of treaties and their implementation in practice. This said, Russia has put to good use assistance received from former Western adversaries, particularly the United States, to dismantle nuclear weapons systems, dispose of fissile material, and to provide employment for Russian scientists formerly employed in nuclear weapons-related industries. Russian ratification of the CWC represented a further positive step.

However, there are continuing concerns about the depth of Russian commitment to future arms control. For example, the CTBT and START II have yet to be ratified by the Russian Duma. Organised groups exist which oppose further Russian disarmament, arguing it reflects a decline in Russian influence and international status which should be arrested. Many are concerned about the lack of transparency about Russian programmes, including, for example, biological weapons-related research; the destruction of nuclear material; numbers of tactical nuclear weapons held in the Russian inventory; and details about Russian nuclear doctrine. Others point to a lack of rigour in Russian export control policy which is permitting, for example, transfers of nuclear material and expertise to Iran. There is an overriding concern that the Russian security policy elite is not committed to de-emphasising the importance of nuclear weapons in the international system, but is rather relying more heavily on Russian nuclear capabilities as a means to offset a relative decline in conventional military capacity and to maintain great power status in the international system.

Given the ambiguities about future Russian arms control policy, the uncertain direction of its future domestic political arrangements, and the impact of the cost burden on its capacity to carry through the implementation of existing commitments, it is unlikely that Russia will provide a source of leadership on arms control matters in the near-to-medium term. Many believe that France and the United Kingdom, for different reasons, will similarly be disinclined to push through new arms control initiatives.

Since the end of the Cold War the UK has moved to a true 'minimum' deterrent based solely on the Trident submarines. The rationales for its retention include the provision of general existential deterrence; the prevention of a major conventional war in Europe; maintaining a partnership and risk-sharing with the United States; maintaining the UK's international status; providing a separate centre of decision-making on nuclear issues and thereby enhancing the credibility of Western coalitions; maintaining a tangible link with the US and thereby underpinning US nuclear guarantees; utility as weapons of last resort; and maintaining current capability as a cost-efficient bridge to the next generation of nuclear weapons. Many of these rationales generate considerable scepticism, although existential deterrence and retaining a 'stepping stone' towards future nuclear capabilities seem prudent if it is expected that nuclear weapons will continue to be a significant element in international relations for decades to come.

The ongoing UK defence review has excluded the UK nuclear deterrent and nuclear strategy issues and a fundamental review of UK policy is unlikely to occur until 2003–5, when a decision will be needed on whether or not to replace the existing Trident systems. Many anticipate little innovation occurring in UK policy until the Trident debate begins. The emphasis until then will be upon prudent management of a small, minimum deterrent coupled with active support for arms control and non-proliferation initiatives. Practical efforts will focus upon the implementation of the CTBT, encouraging greater Chinese involvement in multilateral arms control fora, implementing the 93+2 initiative, supporting UNSCOM activities in Iraq, providing financial support for the KEDO project, supporting CWC implementation, and promoting the finalisation of a BWC compliance protocol. It is possible, although perhaps unlikely, that economic pressures may prompt an earlier reassessment of the UK's nuclear position as the relatively high costs of maintaining the nuclear option divert funding required to develop and maintain the conventional power projection capabilities which many believe to be essential if the UK is to be involved in the solution of the international problems of the early twenty-first century. Whether this would lead to serious consideration of abandoning nuclear weapons remains to be seen.

The recent reductions in the French nuclear arsenal point to the maintenance of a 'minimum' nuclear capability in future. Surface-to-surface components of the French nuclear force have been dismantled, the air-delivered component is being reduced and the nation's submarine force is limited to four ships. The future evolution of French nuclear thinking will be dominated by political factors: the behaviour of the US, Russia and China; the future of European integration; and relations between the NWS and the rest of the world.

From a French perspective, the future benign behaviour of Russia and China is far from assured. French observers are critical of Chinese 'posturing' in the NAM while they continue modernising their nuclear forces. They note a Russian tendency to sign arms control agreements but to fail to ratify or implement them. Note is also taken of the US tendency to maintain a 'large hedge' and reconstitution capability. A stronger Europe can develop a more balanced relationship with the US and this, in turn, will require Europeans to do more to defend and promote common interests. While the nuclear issue is not a priority in the transatlantic debate or indeed within the European integration debate, there are the beginnings of a discussion on these issues amongst defence analysts. This will need to be pursued further, for it will be difficult for Europeans to make a greater contribution to transatlantic defence without developing a clear view of the future place of nuclear weapons in European defence. This may prove to be difficult to achieve as European integration proceeds, given the strong differences of view which exist between EU member states on nuclear issues. Until these differences are resolved it is difficult to envisage Europeans playing a central role in advancing the arms control agenda.

The Threshold States

The three 'threshold' states, Israel, India and Pakistan, view arms control and non-proliferation efforts principally in terms of their regional security concerns. Their contribution to the evolution of the future arms control agenda seems likely to be limited at best.

Israel's approach to non-proliferation is based upon policies of nuclear self-restraint, support for global non-proliferation, and the promotion of regional disarmament. Israel continues to espouse a policy of 'not being the first to introduce nuclear weapons into the Middle East'. Pressure of external military threats and internal defence planners urging that nuclear weapons be factored into the nation's defence both constitute challenges, as yet unsuccessful, to the maintenance of this declaratory policy. However, there is an international consensus that Israel does in fact possess nuclear weapons. This said, the use of these weapons is understood to be extremely unlikely, being contemplated only in the direst circumstances, which remain undefined.

Nuclear disarmament is a regional rather than a global issue for Israel and linked fundamentally with perceptions of the country's security. The unfavourable conventional balance of forces in the Middle East, negative proliferation trends – notably regarding CBW – and the continued hostility of regimes to Israel's existence point to few changes in Israeli policy. The Arms Control and Regional Security (ACRS) talks between 1991 and 1995 led to greater interest in regional arms control in Israel and consideration of various options including, for example, the development of a WMD and missile-free zone in the region. The change in political circumstances since 1995, not least the stalling of the Peace Process and continued Iranian hostility, have prevented further progress.

Indeed, there is diminishing enthusiasm for arms control in Israel because of perceived negative proliferation trends such as the extension of the range of ballistic missiles in the region through the introduction of SCUD Cs; the move to BW in some Arab states; and greater interest in non-conventional warfighting in the Arab world. Israel's perception of Egyptian obstructionism in the ACRS process constituted a further discouragement. Israeli attention is turning more to passive and offensive defence options. Support for accession to the CWC has declined. Therefore, while the possibility of progress on arms control cannot be discounted entirely, for example 'track II' contacts remain fruitful, the conditions to make much progress simply do not exist given the high levels of tension in the Middle East.

A similar situation obtains on the Indian subcontinent, where India and Pakistan are engaged in a ballistic missile development race and each country possesses the capacity to produce nuclear weapons at short notice.

Indian affirmations of the country's right to possess nuclear weapons and its rejection of multilateral arms control agreements have been particularly strident. India rejects the idea of third parties mediating between India and Pakistan and will not accept a 'roll back' of the two countries' nuclear programmes. Indian experts regularly describe non-proliferation treaties as 'Western creations' which are both discriminatory and racist. They reject the view that the five nuclear powers are in some sense 'responsible' and other states are not. The argument is repeatedly made that if the P5 are to have nuclear weapons, India is entitled to also, particularly given the existence of Chinese and Pakistani nuclear capabilities. The impact of these views on Indian policy has been considerable including, for example, the rejection of the CTBT, of the NPT's indefinite extension and of the MTCR. Indian politicians are particularly critical of US efforts to encourage non-proliferation, describing them as hypocritical and hegemonic. For critics of Indian policy, these views are perceived to be based in the 'politics of grievance'. The election of a new Hindu nationalist government in India may simply lead to a reinforcement of these views in Indian policy-making and could lead to the emergence of India as a declared nuclear power.

Should this occur, Pakistan is likely to follow suit and tensions in the Indian subcontinent will rise as a result. Such a change would overwhelm the modest bilateral efforts which have been made to improve relations between the countries in recent months. Maintenance of the existing nuclear *status quo* will be required if the introduction of CBMs and the forging of more political and economic links are to bear fruit. Many take the view that a sea change in bilateral relations will be required before arms control can flourish. However, others believe that the situation in the area is too dangerous and volatile to permit inaction. They argue that efforts to alter the current situation can usefully be attempted and assisted by external actors. India's insistence that total disarmament must be on the agenda for any progress to be made is rejected.

For those arguing that there are opportunities to cap and roll back South Asian nuclear programmes, the priority is to avert full weaponisation and the deployment of nuclear weapons. To this end, the following approaches have been suggested: the continued judicial application of sanctions regarding key technologies; the development of political incentives; the maintenance of 'track II' contacts facilitated by the United States; strengthening sanctions on conventional arms (which will influence the thinking of the country's military establishments); and giving significant economic incentives (which must, however, be conditional upon their constructive use for development and the strengthening of the democratic societies which will be needed to permit a real debate about nuclear weapons to occur). The impact of these efforts will be gradual, and the compliance of India and Pakistan with international non-proliferation norms is unlikely in the immediate future.

5 (Re)Gaining Compliance

Non-compliance with the NPT regime moved towards the top of the non-proliferation agenda after the revelations about covert North Korean and Iraqi nuclear programmes. While obligations of states under the NPT are clearly set out, they remain open to interpretation. For example, the NWS are obligated not to help NNWS to obtain nuclear material which could be used in a weapons programme, but implementation of these obligations has not always been effective and it is unclear how far exports of, for example, dual-use items should be included. Denial of such items may contravene the NWS obligations under the NPT to assist NNWS in the development of nuclear industries for peaceful purposes. Interpretation of these and related provisions may be more or less benign and states can differ on whether non-compliance with NPT rules is in fact occurring. Many ask 'who is to decide if non-compliance has occurred'. The Treaty provides little guidance because it does not include explicit provisions about non-compliance and how to deal with it.

It is recognised today that different levels of compliance exist: 'administrative non-compliance' (e.g. failure to finalise safeguards agreements within the required two-year period), and non-compliance with basic NPT-related undertakings. The difficulties of dealing with the latter are increasingly understood, and there is an awareness of the need to deal with such instances on a case-by-case basis. There is also an evident need for firm action and this has been regrettably absent in the past; for example the UN has done little about non-compliance following the UN Security Council 1992 statement that proliferation constitutes a threat to the peace.

Possible options to improve on this record include increased use of the International Atomic Energy Agency (IAEA) through the application of strengthened safeguards; more effective probing of problems and the consequent alerting of the international community; greater use of the UN Security Council which must make it clear that proliferation will not be tolerated; institutionalisation of commitments to non-proliferation through strong statements by each of the Permanent Members of the Security Council and the NPT depository states; using UN Security Council dispute-resolution powers to encourage low-key discussion; using the NPT review process to report on compliance and raise questions if needed; using regional organisations, for example the OAS or ASEAN, to address regional compliance problems; and encouraging international organisations to promote education on relevant issues and to instil public support for compliance.

There is a need to generate a sense that non-compliance is unacceptable and to build a robust political consensus and the political will to act against non-compliance when it occurs. This will require not only sanctions, which can contribute to ensuring that states do not profit from non-compliance, but also addressing the legitimate security concerns of states who might opt for nuclear weapons. Furthermore, deterrence and denial will not provide complete answers; a large measure of international cooperation will be essential if the provisions of the NPT regime are to be implemented fully and effectively.

To make the regime more effective, it will be necessary to do more than discuss issues of process regarding how to put non-compliance on the international political agenda. There is an urgent need to examine the substance of (re)gaining compliance once non-compliance is determined to have occurred. The consequences of failing to gain full compliance by North Korea and Iraq have yet fully to be considered. The future compliance of states in unstable regions will inevitably be affected by the performance of the NPT regime in dealing with existing violations. Again, the issue of taking the lead to ensure compliance is relevant.

It seems unlikely that the Permanent Members of the Security Council will act to secure compliance by any state without some measure of international support. To secure this support, it will be necessary to increase transparency about the means used to determine that non-compliance has in fact occurred. However, gaining international support will also require a broad international consensus that the treaties and institutions which embody the existing world order serve the interests not only of the most powerful states but also those of a wider international community. That community will need to be persuaded that non-compliance cannot be dealt with simply by dealing with political sources of conflict; that this approach is not effective in the case of states with offensive purposes. In this small group of cases, containment and counter-proliferation will be necessary; the current unease felt in many states about US counter-proliferation policies will need to be overcome. They will need to consider military and other options, including for example paying states not to acquire nuclear weapons, and the use of bilateral as opposed to multilateral pressure. Without seeking to establish a blueprint for action, which inevitably cannot foresee all possible circumstances, there is a need to consider how best to respond to non-compliance and what practical measures are necessary, be they legal, financial or military, and whether they involve coercion or inducement. What can be done to encourage progress?

Many take the view that much can be achieved through the NPT review process and a further strengthening of the regime.

Strengthening the NPT

The 1995 NPT conference established a process whereby progress on the regime's implementation is to be evaluated at five-yearly intervals. Regular preparatory committee meetings are to be held to prepare for the Review conferences. The first such 'Prepcom' meeting in 1997 was a generally harmonious affair, although it marked continued deep differences between states regarding the future of the regime. A need remains to identify common security interests which will help to underpin positive progress. To this end, proposals have been made that a voluntary group of 'bridge-builders' be established to facilitate the negotiation of solutions to differences between states and to examine contentious issues. The group could facilitate the forging of interest-based coalitions to identify emerging problems and press for solutions. The group would work informally between and during Review meetings.

An additional suggestion involves the creation of an Executive Council to develop positions to support the UN Security Council when and if difficult decisions regarding non-compliance have to be made. The Executive Council would serve as a 'grievance mechanism' within the NPT regime which could, for example, help to convince NNWS that restrictions on states are justified in a given circumstance and not merely arbitrary. The Council would fulfil the functions of a permanent secretariat and clearing house to provide rational and reasonable oversight of non-compliance allegations.

Many argue that 'bridge-builders' will be essential as differences between states emerge during the review process. There will be different views on the need for and desirability of a treaty on security assurances which South Africa is promoting; the need to increase transparency about nuclear material holdings and transfers; and the need to respond effectively to growing pressure for total nuclear disarmament. Some take the view that failure to address these types of issues over the next decade will lead to a weakening of the NPT and that a group of disgruntled states is likely to suspend membership of the regime, although they may elect not to produce nuclear weapons.

Many believe that the solution to these problems cannot, however, be sought exclusively through the review process. Recent efforts to improve the effectiveness of IAEA safeguards demonstrate that other approaches can be fruitful.

Implementing 93+2

The IAEA has sought to strengthen its safeguards system following the discovery of clandestine nuclear weapons programmes in Iraq and North Korea. The so-called 93+2 programme was agreed in May 1997. Measures include securing:

- information about, and inspector access to, all aspects of states' nuclear fuel cycle, from uranium mines to nuclear waste and any other location where nuclear material intended for non-nuclear uses is present;

- information on, and short-notice inspector access to, all buildings on a nuclear site;

- information about, and inspection mechanisms for, fuel cycle-related research and development;

- information on the manufacture and export of sensitive nuclear-related technologies and inspection mechanisms for manufacturing and import locations;

- the collection of environmental samples beyond declared locations when deemed necessary by the IAEA;

- administrative arrangements that improve the process of designating inspectors, the issuance of multi-entry visas (necessary for unannounced inspections) and IAEA access to modern means of communications.

It is anticipated that these measures will enable the IAEA to gain as complete a picture as practicable of a state's production and holdings of nuclear source material, the activities for further processing of nuclear material (for both nuclear and non-nuclear application), and of specified elements of the infrastructure that directly support the state's current or planned nuclear fuel cycle. The intention is that increased access for inspectors be provided to help assure that undeclared nuclear activities are not concealed within declared nuclear sites or at other locations where nuclear material is present. Inspection mechanisms are to be provided for instances where there appear to be inconsistencies between information available to the Agency and the declarations made by states regarding the whole of their nuclear programmes.

These strengthened safeguard measures, especially the environmental sampling provisions, promise tangible improvement to the verifiability of the NPT. However, the flood of protocol ratifications expected may mean that the IAEA will have to divert resources from existing approaches as it begins to implement the new ones embodied in 93+2. Additional funding is required to ensure that the full range of approaches available to the IAEA can be carried through in practice. Such funding should be made available.

6 Conclusions

Ensuring the effectiveness of the NPT regime will require the resolution of fundamental differences between states about its long-term purpose. Differences between states are likely to emerge in the NPT review process and, to enhance the prospects of resolving them, it has been suggested that: (a) a voluntary group of 'bridge-builders' be established to act informally to identify emerging problems and press for consensus-based solutions; and (b) a permanent secretariat/clearing house be created, to be elected by the NPT membership, which would receive and evaluate allegations of non-compliance within the NPT framework.

Additional proposed steps to support the regime include establishing a treaty on security assurances to the NNWS; placing nuclear material transferred from military to civilian uses under IAEA safeguards; more transparency by the NWS about their nuclear fissile material holdings; and implementing the 93+2 agreement. Undertaking this programme of work will be controversial and there is an urgent need for the implications of these approaches to be thought through in detail.

Strengthening IAEA safeguards through the 93+2 protocol, that is the auditing by the IAEA of states' national accounting of nuclear material, is already under way. The overall aim is to ensure that undeclared nuclear activities are not concealed within declared nuclear sites or at other locations where nuclear material is present. Effective implementation of these arrangements requires the provision of sufficient funding over the next five years to establish the system. Furthermore, the fact that the NWS have indicated that they will not accept these arrangements in their entirety is bound to generate demands by others that they must be applied universally. Both issues could adversely affect the implementation of these new arrangements.

Overshadowing these issues are differences between states about the wisdom of continuing to reduce the numbers of nuclear weapons to very low levels and the possible eventual achievement of total nuclear disarmament. Reducing the world's nuclear arsenals to very low numbers is perceived by some to be destabilising and to increase the risk that nuclear weapons will be used.

Some take the view that such concerns should be overridden in a more cooperative post-Cold War situation. Given anticipated pressure for reductions both within NWS themselves and from the governments of the NNWS, NWS governments will have to consider the issue during a period of uncertainty about future trends in the international system. However, there is a requirement to maintain international peace and stability which overrides other considerations, and nuclear weapons may continue to be useful to the maintenance of such a peace. This view is put forcefully by those questioning the wisdom of total nuclear disarmament.

The disarmament debate has witnessed the emergence of two camps: those arguing that the risks of not doing away with nuclear weapons are too high, and those arguing that the risks of going to zero are too high. This reflects differing world views; one emphasising the need to build trust and cooperation in the international community, the other taking a less sanguine view of future human behaviour. Simply restating these points of view will not enable sound decisions to be made about the optimum numbers of nuclear weapons which should be held by states in current circumstances; the conditions under which total nuclear disarmament could be considered; and the means through which progress can be made to reduce the risks of nuclear war and to contain proliferation.

Progress towards disarmament will inevitably involve moving to lower numbers of weapons, which would change political relations among the major powers. It will also bring to the fore regional conflicts with nuclear dimensions. It is unclear whether this will help or harm efforts to create the conditions of a nuclear-free peace. Many would argue that it is the management of these changes that requires urgent consideration rather than the detailed playing of a theoretical end-game which lies, at best, in a distant future.

Reservations about disarmament will inevitably generate disruption within the NPT review process; not least because the Treaty includes explicit commitments to disarmament. Distrust of and fissures within existing arms control regimes may be the result. There is a clear need to develop genuine dialogue on these issues, notwithstanding the existing divergent views of the regime's states parties. Only through such a debate can the prospect of mutual trust and eventual commitment to collective security arrangements begin to be forged. These are goals which are worth pursuing notwithstanding the many compelling arguments which point towards their, at best, distant achievement.

For progress to be made, the potential threats of other weapons of mass destruction, chemical and biological, will need to be met. For many, nuclear weapons remain a legitimate means to deter the use of CBW and a possible means to respond to their use if this should occur.

Chemical and biological weapons are no longer a 'chilling fiction' but have genuine strategic operational and tactical utilities. There is an urgent need to re-examine the role of nuclear deterrence in dealing with these weapons. The difficulties of dealing with leaderships whose rationales for assessing the costs and benefits of acquisition and use need to be considered. While nuclear weapons continue to exist, they are likely to play a role in deterring CBW; however, the arguments for and against this role need to be explored thoroughly. Even if nuclear weapons are only to be used in the most extreme cases, the implications of such a policy must be explored for arms control, for winning and maintaining a peace and for future decisions on possible CBW use. Relying on nuclear weapons in some circumstances should not undermine efforts to explore alternative options.

Alternative policies may emerge when considering why states decide not to acquire weapons of mass destruction. Such states need to play an increasingly active role if the nuclear arms control agenda is to be further developed, if useful NGOs are to be involved in the process and if a genuinely open debate is to develop about the future of nuclear weapons. They may have a particular role to play in pressing for the integration of 'rogue' states into the international system and multilateral institutions. How will such initiatives be received by existing nuclear weapon states?

Many note an ambivalence or indeed allege hypocrisy in their stance; while agreeing in principle that nuclear disarmament is a 'good thing', they appear to be unconvinced that it is in fact an achievable goal in the foreseeable future. This said, the United States and Russia, for example, have achieved significant reductions in their nuclear arsenals and supported numerous bilateral and multilateral arms control agreements concerning weapons of mass destruction. Difficulties will include negotiating a Fissile Material Cut-Off Treaty and the ratification of, for example, the Comprehensive Test Ban Treaty. Internal divisions within the countries' arms control communities, for example on whether their nuclear stockpiles can remain viable without testing, significantly affect progress. Nevertheless, the governments of both countries appear committed to reducing regional tensions which underpin proliferation and the US, in particular, is seeking to maintain a stable international economic environment not only as a 'given good' but as a means to underpin international security and stability.

The smaller nuclear powers, notably the United Kingdom and France, are similarly supportive of arms control efforts and have moved rapidly towards the establishment of 'minimum deterrents'. They are unlikely to reduce their nuclear arsenals further until substantial reductions have occurred in existing US and Russian inventories. They remain persuaded of the utility of nuclear weapons as a deterrent and also regard existing weapons systems as a 'stepping-stone' to the next generation of nuclear weapons. Their conservative nuclear policies are unlikely to change radically, although the behaviour of the US, Russia and China, the future progress of European integration and developments in the NPT review process may change their policies in future.

China's policy is also unlikely to be adventurous. However, its increasing interest in multilateral arms control regimes and apparent willingness to enforce these more effectively are to be encouraged. Similarly, greater Chinese transparency about its nuclear weapons arsenals and programmes is desirable and should at least match that of the other NPT nuclear weapons states. This would encourage mutual confidence, not least between China, Russia and the United States. Chinese calls for unconditional negative security assurances to all NNWS and for a No-First-Use agreement are unlikely to be matched by the other NWS. Nevertheless, this should not result in a diminution of efforts to involve China fully in multilateral and bilateral efforts to reinforce its commitment to the international non-proliferation agenda; in this context discussions about the impact of theatre missile defence on regional security would be desirable.

If, as many believe, new initiatives and leadership are unlikely to be provided by the NWS in the decade ahead, could the 'threshold' states represent sources of possible innovation? Israeli policies of nuclear self-restraint, sympathy for global non-proliferation and a desire for regional disarmament in the Middle East are likely to persist; nuclear disarmament is considered by Israelis largely in the regional security context. The existence of Arab states' chemical and biological weapons programmes, improving Arab conventional capabilities, and the volatility and hostility of some of the region's leaders are diminishing enthusiasm for arms control in Israel.

A change in Israel's views on the nuclear issue is unlikely. Similarly, opinions in India and Pakistan show little sign of change. Each regards its nuclear capability as representing a deterrent to the other and India also emphasises nuclear deterrence in its dealings with China. Indian insistence that existing multilateral arms control regimes are discriminating and fulfilling exclusively Western interests seems likely to persist; it is unable to offer positive initiatives to advance the non-proliferation agenda as a result. Indian hostility to the United States and existing regimes makes it difficult for either to have a positive impact upon the nuclear *status quo* in the Indian subcontinent. There is similarly little evidence of a desire for change in the Pakistani leadership. Nevertheless, consideration should be given to possible incentives which could be offered to both countries to reconsider their nuclear policies.

It remains an open question how states possessing nuclear weapons, and indeed NNWS, will react to further examples of non-compliance with the NPT regime. There is no agreement in place on the sanctions to be brought to bear if this were to occur.

Urgent consideration needs to be given to the issue of who is to decide if non-compliance has in fact occurred. Some argue that a mechanism needs to be established within the NPT, possibly involving the newly-created Executive Council. Other possible options include using the IAEA, the NPT review process, the UN Security Council, and regional organisations. The US–Russian Compliance Commissions offer a possible model. A thorough evaluation of options is required.

Establishing who is to decide if non-compliance has occurred will not, of itself, ensure consensus regarding a particular incident. Furthermore, even if non-compliance is 'proved', the decision about what to do will remain. Many agree that sanctions and denial of access to relevant technologies and material are insufficient. However, there are differing views about the goal to be achieved when responding to non-compliance: punishment, retribution, a return to compliance, deterring others?

There is an overriding need to develop the political will to act effectively; for this to occur, there must be agreement that non-compliance is a serious problem, that there is a need for real work on the issue, that current responses are unsatisfactory, and most importantly, that states will all act together and not leave the problem to the P5. Strengthening the habit of cooperation on arms control issues across as wide a range of states as possible should be a central goal. States must be persuaded that non-proliferation institutions are 'theirs' rather than a 'Western' or 'American' construct; there must be widespread interest in making these institutions work. For this to occur, the case must be made effectively that non-proliferation is in the security interests of all those subscribing to the regimes.

Can this be achieved without strong leadership? Should and can the United States and China, for example, work together to promote such an arms control agenda? These are questions which both countries, and indeed the broader international community, should rapidly begin to confront. Failure to do so can only lead to a return to the habits of unilateral action or action by groups of the powerful; collective efforts to restrict proliferation cannot be permitted to fail when put to the extreme test.

SECTION

Short Reports

Contents

1

Towards a New Round of Multilateral Trade Negotiations?

Short Report on Conference 500: 2–6 June 1997

Nicholas Hopkinson

1. The December 1996 Singapore Trade Ministers' Conference *inter alia* endorsed the World Trade Organisation's (WTO) 'built-in' agenda, and demonstrated a readiness to continue study on 'new' issues such as competition policy, investment, and trade and the environment. The high expectations attached to Ministerial Meetings can heighten the risk of failure. There is also concern amongst WTO Members that these meetings should not degenerate into routine events although some important decisions should be taken, such as launching a new round.

2. Decisions within the WTO are essentially taken by a small number of active and influential participants. No single developing country Member can effectively block an emerging consensus, while the reverse is true of a major trading power. The growing diversity among developing countries and diversity of issues addressed within the WTO makes it harder for developing countries to agree common positions. Loosening solidarity among developing countries will make them more susceptible to bilateral pressure or 'divide and rule' tactics by major trading powers. Like it or not, developing countries have no other option but to accommodate their policies to the changing WTO landscape.

3. Regionalism and multilateralism are not mutually exclusive. It is often possible to liberalise further and faster in a bilateral or regional context because they can attract more political support than multilateral liberalisation. For example, Asia–Pacific Economic Co-operation can complement the WTO process by moving ahead of the WTO. Regional free trade can also provide an opportunity to develop 'path-finding' agreements which can point the way for solutions to be applied at the multilateral level. Although some regional agreements have some diversionary effects, these are more than offset by the expansion in intra-regional trade.

4. The Multilateral Agreement on Investment (MAI), which will set stricter standards than current multilateral investment rules, could eventually provide a model for WTO rules. However, there is much suspicion amongst third countries as to why Organisation for Economic Co-operation and Development (OECD) countries are negotiating such an agreement since investment flows in the OECD are already relatively free; they wonder if the OECD is trying to set higher standards in order to oblige third countries to accept them later on. MAI proponents counter that already over 30 third countries have voluntarily expressed an interest in acceding to the MAI.

5. Many developing countries allege that industrialised nations' advocacy of international labour standards is a potential first step towards a 'new' protectionism. The argument that labour standards should be equalised through trade measures is flawed for a number of reasons. Cheap imports have little to do with de-industrialisation in developed countries; rather, labour market rigidities, growth of the service economy, and technological change are more salient. Low labour standards are not the primary source of developing countries' comparative advantage; higher labour standards are primarily a consequence rather than a cause of economic growth. The surest way to improve labour standards in developing countries is through economic development, which trade facilitates. Social justice can be promoted more effectively in conditions of trade liberalisation rather than restraint. If the proposed trade and labour standards are applied, one of the first effects will be to increase the frequency of unilateral embargoes and to strengthen protectionist lobbies. International coalitions to counter such vested interests should be formed.

6. Without a new round, results are unlikely in the trade and environment area. If WTO Members continue examining the present full agenda without any tangible results, especially in the trade and environment area, public opinion in industrialised countries will become even more critical of the WTO. As developing countries are interested in speeding up the reintegration of the Multi-Fibre Arrangement into the WTO and securing improved market access for 'sensitive' products, such as agriculture, industrialised countries will have to prepare a package in a future round which is attractive to developing countries. Industrialised countries will have to decide whether environment, investment or social standards should be accorded priority. Given the complementary and mature analytical work under way in the OECD and WTO, trade and the environment might be the obvious candidate for a rule-making negotiation in a possible future round.

7. There is a major debate as to whether and when a new round of multilateral trade negotiations should be launched. By January 2000, the WTO will *inter alia* have to resume negotiations on agriculture and services, and to undertake a major review of Trade Related Investment Measures (TRIMs) and Trade Related Intellectual Property (TRIPs) agreements. A Ministerial Meeting, to be held in the Autumn of 1999, will also have to consider whether many of the 'new' issues are ripe for multilateral negotiations.

8. However, the US believes that in the next four years, major WTO negotiations will have occured in key areas such as agriculture, services and TRIPs. The US regards the WTO as a matured version of the GATT which is not particularly well-suited to another comprehensive round. In particular, the WTO's membership will be both quantitatively and qualitatively different from that of GATT in the late 1980s; the prospective accession of *inter alia* China and Russia would make it more difficult to conclude a next round. Furthermore, loose talk of a new round is likely to undercut efforts in 1997 to reach a successful outcome in financial services negotiations. It would be much better to pursue discrete negotiations already agreed as part of the WTO's 'built-in' agenda. If a particular negotiation fails, as for example maritime services in 1996, then progress in all other issues is not blocked at the same time. Likewise, if an issue is too 'sensitive' to gain a consensus, it would perhaps be better to pursue its negotiation elsewhere, whether bilaterally, in the OECD, or in the context of a regional agreement. The recent successes in the basic telecommunications services negotiations and the Information Technology Agreement should signal confidence in the WTO's ability to make 'real' progress outside the context of a multilateral round.

9. However, most believe package deals are better in mobilising the forces in favour of liberalisation and for getting reluctant governments to open their markets in certain sectors. For instance, it is rather difficult to imagine agricultural negotiations being successful on a self-contained basis. It would also be good to consider visible and invisible trade in parallel, thus preventing services talks becoming too specialised and detached from a broader range of negotiations. Where all negotiations are tied together in a package, countries hesitate to make one part collapse if they know that that will bring down the entire structure. Furthermore, many believe that a new round is needed to provide a counterweight to any residual fears of growing regionalism. By 2000, the matters before the WTO will add up to a critical mass of issues, whether or not one wants to call it a new round.

2

The British German Forum: Same House – Different Dreams?

Short Report on Conference WPS 97/3: 30 June – 4 July 1997

Robin Hart

1. The theme for this year's British German Forum was 'Same House: Different Dreams?' with the underlying question of whether Britons and Germans have a different vision of Europe, our shared home. This theme was explored over a wide-ranging number of issues from the future of EMU to our concern about the environment. Underlying our discussions was the British and German attitude to each subject, and an analysis of the similarities and differences in our approaches. The group concluded that although we may have different dreams on a number of issues they believed that we are increasingly working towards similar dreams, not least because in many ways both countries are becoming more like one another.

2. Our attitudes towards Europe are born from different historical and geographical paths – Britain's geographical location as an island and with a former Empire and Commonwealth, as opposed to Germany's continental situation, its history this century and most recently its reunification. Both countries suffer from historical stereotypes. These are unavoidable, but could be more constructive and cause less ill-feeling. These attitudes and stereotypes undoubtedly affect the approach each country takes towards the common home, Europe. But more and more as the European Union faces up to the agenda of the future, namely ensuring employment and competitiveness in a global economy, monetary union and enlargement, the two countries are likely to develop similar views. Already the two countries seem to be becoming more like one another, for instance German economic reconstruction parallels changes the UK made in the 1980s and early 1990s. For its part, the UK with a new government is embarking upon devolution (closer to the Länder format), is considering proportional representation, and the Bank of England's newly-created independent status has become more similar to that of the Bundesbank.

3. Whatever stereotypes may be in vogue they need to be kept in context, the key element being respect for one another and tolerance of differing viewpoints. There was a feeling that the Forum's generation, the leaders of both countries in the next millennium, had a shared experience and much more in common whether taste in clothes, music, films or concern for the planet, than was true for previous generations.

4. A range of current EU issues were discussed by the group including whether Europe could speak with a common voice in foreign policy; how the different democratic institutions will operate within Europe; the citizen's role within Europe; whether greater co-ordination of justice and home affairs issues is possible; and what the shape of the European Union will be in five years time. Is Europe facing a mid-life crisis at its 40th birthday? Had the Amsterdam IGC focused on the fleas rather than the 'elephant'? Some of these issues were subsequently raised during discussions with the new British Minister of State for Europe, senior policy makers in the FCO, scrutineers of European legislation in the British Parliament and at the German Embassy. A vision was created of an enlarged Europe, of between 7 and 10 extra members, but with little real change in institutional makeup, with a broad EMU operating with some members, leading in effect to a two-class Europe.

5. The implications of enlarging the EU were clearly visible when considering its current institutional arrangements and how to protect European borders. The group were generally in favour of enlargement, but there was more enthusiasm amongst Britons than Germans for a widescale enlargement. The need to reform the CAP was recognised but not discussed in detail. The future focus of the European Union is obviously crucial to all its citizens. One important element the group noted was the need for Europeans to understand the institutions better and what Europe meant for them.

6. There was a call for a pragmatic approach in many areas where different views did emerge. This pragmatic approach was seen most during the discussion on EMU and whether it should go ahead on time. From the group's own poll the majority were in favour of EMU, although the Germans favoured it more than the British who were equally split for and against. The suggestion was made that whilst the overall enterprise of a single currency may be beneficial, there was a danger of Europe becoming locked into a timetable driven by politicians with their own interests. The bicycle theory, whereby if we do not stop pedalling towards EMU the bike will slow, stop and topple is a compelling argument for continuing on the current track. There is fear too that any delay might result in the loss of political commitment towards Europe which could in turn lead to an unravelling of the single market. If EMU is delayed, might EU enlargement be delayed also? Some might argue that a delay might threaten the whole edifice of the EU.

7. But what if we are pedalling towards a precipice? There were good arguments made for an organised delay of up to two years to reconsider some of the issues more carefully, address the fiscal problems, consider the relationship between fiscal and monetary policies and perhaps enable more countries to meet the criteria at the start. The general feeling was that if delay would benefit Europe and bring economic advantages in the long run, it should happen. If EMU does continue on time it might be prudent to expect the worst and hope for the best.

8. Economic development, employment and competitiveness ran through much of the group's discussion. There was concern that Europe is so busy navel-gazing about its institutions and its future that it is taking its eye off the ball of globalisation. Can Europe make its way in the 21st century in what many believe will be a North–South, developed versus developing world? Underlying Europe's competitiveness is business success, and here Britain and Germany had different experiences and cultures which could be shared. Together they could make more impact in a global market. German industry emphasises training, promotion based on expertise, a more egalitarian reward structure, consensus decision-making at Board level, focusing on key successful products and high levels of R and D. The UK is seen as being more innovative, service-driven, focusing on price more than quality, with a differing work culture and more team-driven and ad hoc planning processes. The group provided useful examples of how many companies are now benefiting from the synergy of working together. We also heard about the problems of merging a British and German company, for instance in the financial world. It was felt that the two countries could be more complementary and less competitive in the business context.

9. When discussing the environment it was agreed that all had a role to play. The British have a sensitivity towards fauna and their managed wilderness, and environmental concerns are now within the top three overall concerns (hence the environmental emphasis in the budget). However the green consumer drive has not changed much over the last few years and one of the most serious threats, that of nitrogen dioxide, is not given the priority by consumers – the lovers of cars. Germany has achieved significant reduction in industrial pollution and has taken other measures to protect the local and global environment, at considerable cost. For both countries the question was asked how to alert and maintain awareness of global as well as local issues, and what part individuals can play. Should more measures be imposed?

10. Social welfare was another area which the group examined. Is there a different approach towards how we protect the poorest? Both countries are facing similar problems over funding state benefits to the unemployed, those on low wages and pensioners. In the UK there is a fundamental rethink of the social welfare system; in Germany continuing consideration of how to balance the books and how to pay for old age. Traditionally these have been highly political issues but the Forum participants appreciated that in both countries their generation needs to consider these issues carefully and to care about social welfare.

11. Overall the group concluded that this generation could share the same dreams, recognising that each country in Europe has different interests and priorities. The aim should be to take a realistic and pragmatic approach and compromise where necessary over issues that matter to both our futures. A greater knowledge and understanding of one another would certainly contribute to 'sweeter dreams'.

3

The Media, Democracy and Election Campaigns

Short Report on Conference 502: 7–11 July 1997

Nicholas Hopkinson

1. Sir Winston Churchill stated 'democracy is the worst system of government, except every other!' He might have added that there is a direct correlation between the accuracy, integrity and independence of the media and the health of a free society. Many believe that the prevailing performance of the media in that respect often falls well short of what is needed (and potentially achievable).

2. Has the commercial and highly competitive nature of the industry eroded its value to democracy? Are less-principled journalists generating growing public distrust of politicians and trivialising politics? Are the media being forced to give people what they want rather than report the 'real' story? Or have the media simply become more efficient in investigating and reporting politicians' faults, and as a result created a misleading impression of a deterioration in the quality of democracy? Or are there other reasons for public disenchantment with politics? Have politicians simply contributed to their own low public standing by regularly breaking electoral promises, and behaving in a manner inconsistent with public service? Has the end of the Cold War exposed a long-obscured 'enemy' at home? Or has 'globalisation' reduced the policy options available to elected representatives?

3. In the developing world, hate radio and censorship of the independent press are indicators of potential conflict. The central role of the media in conflicts in the former Yugoslavia and elsewhere has underlined the importance of an independent media as a priority for any conflict prevention and peace-building intervention strategy. Respecting free speech is a prerequisite for ensuring democracy and stability. Assistance for the media should therefore be accorded a higher priority in aid giving. However, the international community cannot simply 'install' an independent media. The other checks and balances of civil society are also esential. Furthermore, media projects should be run by local journalists.

4. Genuine democratic elections require *inter alia* laws and procedures to prevent censorship and to protect the independence and security of journalists. There must be clear media guidelines which lay down criteria for balanced coverage. Direct access time should be commensurate with parties' results in the previous election, how long a party has existed, and the extent of support for the party. Where there is no independent election commission to determine and monitor such guidelines, coverage and access are less likely to be fair.

5. Technology has increased pressures on politicians. They are often now perceived to react either too quickly or too slowly. The media do not initiate change, but they can 'panic' governments and accelerate developments. But only weak politicians are forced to act by the media. Good planning, internal communication, co-ordination, briefing, and making sure all necessary materials are ready well in advance can help ensure public acceptance of government policy. Initiatives, aimed at achieving good headlines for relatively little effort, have to have the required appeal to ensure that the issue is widely discussed. Rebuttals require a good database, speed of response and substance. By effectively attacking the proposals of opponents, there is more chance of ensuring that proposals will be accepted by the public. Another important technique is 'running' a story to take attention away from something that is potentially embarrassing. Knowing what is happening and when is vital. Nothing beats the right headline. Any political party's media operation should be geared to getting there first, and occupying the political ground. However, it is vital that all politicians present an unified front. Otherwise the media will exploit differences.

6. As policies converge, competition for the political centre grows. The resulting ideological 'vacuum' has in some countries been filled by the media and advertising agencies. There is a growing tension between the broadcasters' and political parties' desire to control the political agenda, and their public duty to enhance participation and reflect the range of public debate. Audiences are bored by the erroneous but constant expectation generated by producers that there *is* an explanation for everything, especially when it is too early to make an assessment. The process of managing the message has been taken over from those who generate the content. In effect, politicians may appear to be the source of the message, but they are often cast in the role of mere actors, while journalists are the dramatists. Broadcasters need to show greater detachment from the process, find out what viewers actually want, and broadcast less politics in its present form.

7. Negative advertising is increasingly used by politicians because the message is more dramatic and more easily communicated than opposing parties trying to communicate a similar message. Although there is little evidence to suggest that negative advertising works, politicians increasingly regard it as an 'insurance policy' *should* there be a close political contest. However, citizens are more than mere consumers – they have rights and obligations.

8. Many believe market research is a far more potent influence on politics than advertising. Unfortunately in some countries there appears to be a growing tension between election manifestos and policy based upon inter-active focus group research, and the need to resolve real problems. If democracy is to deliver, it must be widely accepted that politicians must address serious problems, usually through unpopular measures. Opinion pollsters argue they have no incentive to 'guide' the decision-making process, nor do they intend to persuade a person how to act. Opinion polls, like the media, are there to inform and to entertain. As surveys of current opinion, they cannot predict future changes. Although there is some evidence they can influence election outcomes if there is a high turnout, to ban their publication would deprive voters of the one objective and systematic form of information about their views. The electorate would ironically become the only group who would not benefit from polls.

9. It is feared that concentration of media ownership may limit diversity of opinion. However, the motives of the great media proprietors are principally commercial; power takes second place to profit. Accordingly, the media is more likely to follow, rather than lead, opinion because the more the 'mass' the medium attracts, the less it can deviate from its audience or readers. Thus, increasingly, newspapers do not reflect the views of their proprietors. Furthermore, media 'manipulation' is unlikely because there is a complex relationship between knowledge, attitude and behaviour.

10. In spite of differing cultural attitudes over coverage of the private lives of public figures, there is a consensus that if a public figure is involved in crime, conceals information, or endangers public health, the public's right to know ought to take precedence over personal privacy. Over time, media self-regulation, through codes of conduct and press council complaint procedures, may prove to be the most effective way to ensure that the media play a constructive role.

4

Diplomacy: Profession in Peril?

Short Report on Conference 503: 21–25 July 1997

Colin Jennings and Virginia Crowe

1. The role and staffing of diplomatic services are being reassessed in a number of countries. Motivations vary, but include changing demands as a result of the end of the Cold War, an increased emphasis on multilateral diplomacy, the rise of influential new non-state actors, a powerful media with an enhanced ability to highlight issues and to politicise them, and changing political imperatives demanding, for example, more public diplomacy and an ethical dimension to foreign policy. The revolution in information technology and modern communications are also having an enormous impact on traditional practice. Despite the relatively small sums spent on diplomatic activities, resource constraints remain severe for most Ministries of Foreign Affairs (MFAs).

2. The speed of modern travel and communication, and the range and frequency of Ministerial and other multilateral meetings, have raised questions about the role of diplomats. Do they have a distinctive part to play? And if so, what is it?

3. MFAs and their Embassies already undertake a diverse range of activities. In addition to political and economic reporting for their governments, diplomats spend a high proportion of time on trade promotion, multilateral negotiation on such issues as trade and the environment, aid provision, consular and immigration services, and promoting and representing their country. The role of the resident ambassador and his staff has changed as a result of modern telecommunications and with the increasing phenomenon of the non-resident ambassador, special envoys and summits. Personal relationships fostered between Ministers facilitate easy direct contact between them. Agreements can be concluded informally over the telephone without the ambassador being informed. None the less, resident envoys can play a crucial role as 'cross-cultural interpreters'. At summits or on more routine occasions, local knowledge can be the key to identifying ways forward. Diplomats may also be involved in managing and giving information to the press in a way that they did not in the past. A further important role in many governments is that of policy coordination. MFAs are often best placed to draw together the views of a number of government departments into an overall policy or negotiating strategy. Increasingly, NGOs also have the opportunity to make an input.

4. Some argue that most of these roles could be undertaken by non-diplomats equally effectively and at lower cost. For instance, a case can be made on cost grounds for activities such as cultural diplomacy, trade promotion and consular and visa services, being 'privatised' or contracted out. In practice, however, many MFAs already use specialist expertise in such areas from, for example, cultural institutes, government agencies or NGOs. Continuity, objectivity and accountability would undoubtedly be at risk if governments went so far as to establish 'virtual embassies', consisting of a flag and an ambassador buying in necessary services and expertise. Moreover, use of most potential substitutes would risk clear conflicts of interest and aims (e.g. journalists for political reporting, businessmen for trade promotion, or NGOs for aid policy or local lobbying). Non-official sources would also be less likely to command the trust of interlocutors from other governments, particularly on sensitive political or economic issues.

5. Diplomats in some countries already have close links with journalists, NGO representatives and other informed contacts. Such links are mutually beneficial and complementary. But each player has a distinct agenda. None the less, there is often confusion about their respective roles. For instance, businessmen aim to make money for their company. Diplomats seek to facilitate this through political and economic advice, introductions to local contacts, commercial assessments of particular markets, and negotiations with other governments about trade or debt problems, investment terms and international trade agreements. The conference did not identify any convincing arguments that such functions would be better undertaken by non-diplomats.

6. As in other spheres, the IT revolution is having a major impact on the ways in which diplomats conduct their work. But IT benefits are two-edged. There is speed of access to a wider range of information and an enhanced ability to cross-reference it so that better informed decisions can be made. It is easier to prepare, revise and present advice: co-ordination and clearance time can be greatly reduced. Effective public diplomacy, where 'lines' can be co-ordinated and disseminated as soon as Ministers have pronounced, has been facilitated; presentation of documents can be brought up to private sector standards relatively cheaply and easily. Internal administration and co-ordination of MFAs and their outposts world-wide is facilitated. Cash savings may be made as more staff move from tail to teeth.

7. On the other hand, hardware and software are expensive to install and training and documentation costs can be high. Though easy access to tools such as pie charts and graphs can ease assimilation of information, there is a danger of information overload and the problem of how to rate the sources available on the Internet. In some respects, the role of the desk officer at headquarters or local knowledge at post become even more important in assessing such information. Then there is the problem of security: security of the information passed, whether the electronic 'walls' erected are impermeable and whether messages downloaded have been corrupted, accidentally or on purpose.

8. Aside from the practical implications, however, the 'cultural' impact of IT may be profound. The informality of lateral contacts within and between MFAs, and the erosion of the hierarchical attitudes and conventions prevailing in most MFAs, seem likely to increase. In the meantime, many MFAs have the problem of a generation gap between the 'IT literate' and the 'dinosaurs'. While working methods are changing and arguably improving, it can require top level example and even sanctions to convert the latter.

9. EU governments face a further stimulus to change from the continuing evolution of the Union. Logic and the Treaties dictate increasing movement towards an EU Common Foreign and Security Policy. The Commission's External Service, from its origins in technical assistance after Lomé, has developed to become the fifth largest diplomatic service in Europe. Its tasks now include political reporting, as a well as the trade negotiations which are a Commission competence. With recruitment and training the current priorities, there is hope that greater interchange of staff between member state diplomatic services and the Commission's External Services will break down barriers and increase familiarisation with member states' methods. Meanwhile, member states are increasingly co-operating between themselves. Officers are seconded to real jobs in each others' services, there is some sharing of facilities and buildings where new missions have been opened in FSU countries, and there is scope for further co-operation in matters of health, education, transport, communications and joint political reporting. Other tasks may be shared on an agreed basis, though national priorities and sensitivities are constraints. Commission Delegations might eventually represent member states where the latter are not present, closer co-operation between member state and EC missions on common visa and immigration procedures seems likely, while some envisage an EU Consular Service or a privatised consular agency working for the EU as a whole. Meanwhile there is support for a Commission Vice-President for External Affairs to manage Community competences in this area and to work towards a greater coherence with the High Representative for CFSP in the Council Secretariat, as called for at Amsterdam. With business in Brussels acting increasingly as a centre for representatives of national governments, NGOs and other policy actors, the role and status of bilateral ambassadors within the EU, and the tasks they undertake, may well change.

10. Most diplomatic services are confronted with the difficulty of meeting a significant increase in demand with an equally significant decline in resources. This has added extra momentum to the search for more effective management of human and other resources. The British Foreign and Commonwealth Office (FCO) is a prime example of this trend. Management skills are becoming as important as intellectual capability in determining career prospects; private sector techniques are being used to achieve better value for money; and expensive home-based staff are being replaced by local staff in embassies and employed on a greater range of tasks. Out-sourcing is increasing, and business units or other autonomous entities (of which Wilton Park is a prime example as an Executive Agency) are being created out of support and other services and benchmarked by the standards of the private sector. The change from cash to accrual and resource accounting is stimulating a greater awareness of the capital value and costs of buildings abroad, enabling economic rents to be calculated for non-FCO users. Private finance is increasingly employed on joint capital projects such as the new British Embassy in Berlin.

11. The clarion call is for management by performance, although measurement of success is uniquely difficult in a public sector environment where planning can be vitiated by 'events' and changing political imperatives. Resource management is challenging. What are the respective values and costs of analysis, reporting, and influence? How does one charge, for example, for ambassadorial time expended on behalf of commercial enterprises, or on human rights issues? The art is to set policy objectives tightly, but flexibly enough to be workable. Clarity is crucial, and modelling exercises helpful, for example by linking policy aims to the rational distribution of staff in missions.

12. However, private sector practices need to be employed judiciously. The key resource for all foreign services is its people. The vision of a modern diplomatic service which looks beyond a centralised system of personnel to the creation of a network, where Heads of Mission with devolved authority recruit their own staff to meet their strategic goals, may have superficial attractions. But it would put at risk such qualities as loyalty, long term commitment and experience which are central to the continuing effectiveness of foreign services. To a large extent, the composition and career patterns of diplomatic services reflect national culture. In most countries considerable importance is still attached to the public service ethos. In the more fluid employment environment of the US, the average age of new recruits to the State Department is thirty-two, and, a spell in government service is increasingly regarded as part of a working career, rather than a career in itself. The US policy of filling many senior positions with political appointees may stimulate greater movement than would otherwise be the case, but the State Department's career patterns do show that an effective foreign service can be operated with a high level of staff turnover. In some countries, perceptions of the profession as elitist, though not always accurate, have led to urgings that it becomes more representative of the societies it serves. The optimum mix may be a judicious blend of inside and outside experience. Some foreign services may see merit in greater use of five to ten year contracts for government service. This could facilitate easier use of specialists when necessary, greater equal opportunity and a more flexible pool of talent.

13. The danger is that while private sector methods are increasingly employed, the rewards of the public sector in terms of status, pay and promotion possibilities are increasingly uncompetitive. Public service may offer its own rewards, but there is competition for the available talent. Postings abroad are becoming less popular in the light of changing social expectations, notably the widespread reliance on dual incomes, careers and pensions. Flexible attitudes by administrations, imaginative allowance schemes, shorter tours abroad, rewards and appreciation for supporting spouses and partners, and enhanced job satisfaction all have a part to play in mitigating such pressures.

14. Diplomatic services no longer enjoy a monopoly of the practice of diplomacy, as competent and powerful actors multiply. But the profession still demands a range of skills which are not easy to duplicate in any other cadre. Basic core competencies are high personal and intellectual standards, flexibility, an ability to live and work in wildly varying circumstances, and for the public good rather than financial reward. To the traditional qualities such as hard language skills, cross cultural understanding, bilateral and increasingly multilateral negotiating ability, must be added the consular and interpretative skills necessary for public diplomacy, as well as an ability to do the commercial work now so highly rated. Management skills, including those of prioritisation, potential for pro-active preventative diplomacy, co-ordination skills within one's own government, and an ability to do economic work and to link it with political policy considerations, are now key requirements. Diplomats have to be Jacks and Jills of all trades, and masters of some.

15. Most MFAs have long debated the competing merits of employing generalists or specialists. Two areas of policy shed light on this debate: the environment and trade. The former involves problems which cross frontiers, are too big for governments to handle on a national basis and have achieved greatly increased international priority. Effective action requires considerable international dialogue and co-ordination. As in other areas, MFAs are well placed to co-ordinate national approaches to the global agenda. Diplomats tend to be skilled in finding acceptable compromises, factoring in global needs as well as promoting national interests. Population growth, land degradation, water supplies and pollution, changes in the chemistry of the atmosphere, climate change and the destruction of bio-diversity are issues where both specialist knowledge and traditional diplomatic skills must be successfully deployed, whether by MFAs or by 'international policy officers' from home departments. Specialist knowledge on the environment is not too difficult for generalist diplomats to acquire, similar perhaps to the technical knowledge necessary for disarmament and non-proliferation negotiations.

16. Diplomats can also often play a key policy and co-ordinating role, as well as provide expertise and advice in the field, on trade policy and promotion. The chief tasks in this area falling to diplomats are the negotiation of trade policy in bilateral and multilateral contexts, and investment and trade promotion. Diplomats advance their countries' trade and economic interests by ensuring market access, bringing opportunities to the attention of exporters at an early stage, assisting them to penetrate the local market, and attracting foreign direct investment into their own country. Where business is clear in its commercial objectives, diplomatic support can add value with advice, political analysis and representation at senior levels. Where business is unwilling to take the lead in terms of market research and new market entry, the value of governments trying to do the job for them and attempting to 'push water uphill' is doubtful. Government-to-government negotiation is clearly a role for diplomats, creating or protecting areas of competitive advantage for their national companies, which often today includes national 'branches' of multilateral corporations. In all these areas, there is clear advantage in a systematic exchange of views between diplomats and business people on objectives and constraints.

17. Trade promotion is the area with the most overlap between government and business, where governments have an educational and informative role, especially for businesses wanting to enter new markets. Trade promotion activities are frequently considered for privatisation, yet part of trade promotion is marketing a national brand image. This is probably best done by public servants. Clearly, co-ordination between the foreign policy and trade functions is important, hence the close link between trade departments and MFAs. In some cases, it may make sense for MFAs to absorb the trade promotion and trade policy aspects of government, as has already occurred in Canada and some other countries.

18. The root and branch changes in style, culture, substance and organisation that are already occurring in many MFAs suggest that, far from being in peril, the diplomatic profession is showing the necessary flexibility to move with the times. While the needs of smaller countries differ from those of larger ones, and the specific circumstances of each country dictate the priorities for its foreign service, all foreign services need to adapt to new global demands, and to employ highly motivated and skilled individuals with a wide range of experience and aptitude. The distinction from other professionals working in the international arena is in role, not capability. But most MFAs also need to devote more effort to building domestic political understanding of and support for their role. Most governments fail to produce a rational appraisal of the benefits to be derived from an effective and adequately funded diplomatic service, and even those that do often forget that the amount of additional resources required to fund effective diplomacy is minuscule in relation to the economic and other benefits that can be derived and the public expenditure devoted to other areas.

Political and Economic Developments in the Russian Federation: Implications for the West

Short Report on Conference 504: 28 July – 1 August 1997

Chris Langdon

1. The end of the Cold War and the advent of a free market and a nascent democracy in Russia has brought major gains to the West. But the benefits are far from clear to most Russians as they live in a society still in the state of aftershock. The volume of Western aid and investment has been constrained by uncertainty over Russia's political future and by economic and commercial obstacles, as well as by an emphasis in Western countries on tight budgets. Attention has been focused in Western Europe on NATO and EU enlargement and EMU. Relations with the EU are bogged down on issues of dumping.

2. None the less, the West has enlightened self-economic interest in a prosperous and successful Russia. The new government of 'young wolves' is carrying out an energetic programme of reforms. The reforms are not without flaws, but it deserves the support of Western policy makers. Yet inward investment in Russia has been less than in Hungary, a country with a population fifteen times smaller. And the latest area for investment attention is the oil-rich Caspian Basin. Despite all the available evidence that in emerging markets early starters are the winners, most business people have spurned the opportunities, although a number of major international corporations have established strategic positions.

3. While foreign direct investment is only going to play a minor role in Russia's economic transformation, there are clear opportunities for business in infrastructure development, industry, environmental clean-up, agricultural reconstruction, the service sector, training, consultancy and advice. The list of obstacles to investment remains formidable, and will have to be cleared if foreign direct investment is to play its part in economic development, as it has in other regions of the world.

4. The real key to Russia's development will be the mobilisation of its own resources – using its savings, developing a regulated capital market, a law on mutual funds, the creation of pension funds and a savings industry, and the repatriation of the billions of dollars which have been invested abroad. There have already been some signs that capital outflows are being reversed. The key to that will be the prospects for economic growth. Russia needs growth of more than 5–6% to finance massive payments to the IMF and World Bank due in 2001–2, as well as to finance reforms in the social sector and reform of the Russian army. Plans to cut the armed forces to 1.2 million will mean short-term costs as officers are laid off.

5. Growth is also vital to provide clear signals to the population that the economy of misery is shifting. Inflation has been cut to 16–17%, but at a price of a fall in production of 40%. Official forecasts for growth have been scaled back. The latest forecast is for a 2% growth in GDP in 1998, while in the first seven months of 1997 there was a decline of 0.2%. Some government economists estimate that growth of 1.5–2% is possible if the government is able to take a comprehensive series of measures including cutting social benefits, reducing budget spending on public works and dividing the budget responsibilities between federal and regional authorities. Measures to tackle the massive problem of tax evasion are also necessary. Energy prices also have to be kept under control. These measures together with return of some capital from abroad, plus privatisation receipts, and the legalisation of part of the black economy, would make such growth a possibility, but it's a tall order, and requires agreement with the Duma on key policies.

6. Sceptics maintain that the reforms are not tackling the key issue – market failure, or 'transformation decline'. They argue that price liberalisation has not brought in the opportunity for genuine market competition as state control has been replaced by organised monopolies. Privatisation has resulted in huge criminalisation with speculative super-profits extracted by oligarchic elites who have won control of the privatisation process, particularly the energy sector. The rest of the population loses out.

7. The result is a very hostile price structure for Russian manufacturing industry with costs increased through monopoly power of the energy sector. Productive industry is also squeezed by further government policies. Some 70% of all liquid capital is tied up in short-term debt – the method used by the government to cover its finances. It has resulted in high profits for the banks, but also in crippling interest rates of more than 18–20% for productive industry. And the rise in the rouble's real value adds to the uncompetitiveness of Russian industry. It is very difficult for one third of companies to survive in the real economy.

8. Critics of the privatisation process believe that Russia's seven biggest banks are literally running the country. The country's elites are now dominated by four groups: the political leaders and their supporters, the financial and industrial groups, the mass media who serve their interests, and armed groups – the private forces. The interaction between the political and financial and business elites is critical in an economy built on privilege. To obtain privileges a businessman needs a lobbyist within the political system. The dispensing of privileges, the tax inspectorate, the public prosecutors and the police are the levers that can be pulled by the political elites. The political battles within the elite are over privatisation spoils; control of Gazprom, Svyazinvest, or key chemical companies. Businessmen need to invest in politicians to win the spoils, that means that national and regional election campaigns are funded by the financial-industrial groups (FIGs).

9. As well as the FIGs, the role of organised crime and the mafia (350–400 groupings according to one Western estimate) also has to be taken into account in examining political corruption. While the media focus is on the dramatic shootings, the real question is, will the mafia groups eventually be co-opted into the open economy as the black economy is legalised? Why rob the bank if you can own it? And will the state have the political will to suppress those mafia groups who won't be co-opted?

10. In 1997 the Russian media has been the key battleground for the battles between the competing financial and political elites. With the major TV channels and newspapers owned in whole or part by the economic barons, particularly Vladimir Potanin, Boris Berezovsky, and Vladimir Gusinsky, the fight for control of lucrative companies like Svyazinvest has been carried out on prime time television. In 1996 Russian journalists felt justified in not reporting the ill-health of the President as it was not in their own interests or, they felt, good for the future of Russian democracy for the Communists to win. This year their role is relegated to assisting their patrons in their business battles, an experience from which, it must be said, that their colleagues on some Western newspapers have not been immune.

11. In Russia, the result has been to damage the reputation of the new reform team. Boris Nemtsov, seen as uncorrupted when he joined the government in March, has inevitably been tainted by the welter of accusations on television and in the press. The latest polls confirm this. The divisions in the business elite are the next stage of Russia's political development. But it is important not to lose sight of the importance of the political changes made in March with the cabinet of 'young wolves' under the figureheads of Boris Nemtsov, and Anatoly Chubais. It's not just the Cabinet. Reformers also dominate the Presidential Administration under Valentin Yumashev.

12. But will the reforms be supported at the next Presidential elections, providing President Yeltsin's health holds out? Support for Nemtsov, a front-runner, is for his charisma rather than his policies, which will reduce the living standards of many Russians if fully implemented. His lustre has been tarnished in the recent media attacks. Of the other front-runners, the Prime Minister Victor Chernomyrdin, is increasingly in the position of opposition leader, and he cannot be ruled out as a candidate for President. His new roles in chairing the Commission on Military Reform and the State Committee to Protect Investors' Rights have given him new status, and he is the only government figure respected both in the regions and by the opposition in general, so he could play a crucial consolidator role as a centrist.

13. For the opposition, the economy is their best asset, since half the electorate tell pollsters they feel that they did better under the Communists. The current Communist Party leadership under Zyuganov plays the role of constructive opposition allaying Western and public concerns. They have the best machine, but an ageing support base. Their biggest handicap is lack of outlets on national television. They remain the single coherent party, other groupings remain movements around personalities such as Grigory Yavlinsky. Until the election threshold of 5% is removed or reduced, it is hard to see the further development of political parties.

14. Of the alternative centrist Presidential candidates, Alexander Lebed has fallen from front-runner position after his miscalculation on an early Presidential election. Yuri Luzhkov, the reformist Mayor of Moscow, has determination and resources, including a new TV channel, but despite his attempt to build a national standing, he faces the problem that Moscow is loathed by people in the regions.

15. Russia's 89 regions are now major actors in their own rights. Regional governors dominate the political system in their region, and the local media through their local backers. They have greater powers than the Communist Party local bosses had. Their local and international perspectives increasingly diverge from that of the centre. The struggle between Yeltsin and the Governor of Primore is symptomatic of the change in the power relationship as the centre has failed this time to bring a region to heel. The decree in July 1997 giving Presidential Representatives greater financial powers is the latest attempt by Yeltsin to control spending by the regions.

16. Much of the international community's focus on economic changes in Russia centres on the growth poles like Moscow. The reality is that Russia is experiencing a form of enclave capitalism, with a different picture visible just 100 km from Moscow, or in the towns in the Red belt dominated by Soviet era giant enterprises that have no future. All the workers have a vote and are acutely aware of the lack of future for themselves and their children.

17. Concern about the future is articulated by Russian foreign policy specialists. Their fear is that NATO's enlargement and the recent dispute with the EU over dumping show that Russia is being excluded at the national level. While 'soft' integration by companies, regions and sectors is continuing, Western European governments have to awaken to the challenge of globalisation. Russia's educated population, low wage rates and its appetite for Western capital and expertise could provide the opportunity Western Europe needs, they argue. But they also remark on the cautious introspection of many fragile coalition governments in Europe at both a national and an EU level. The question remains how to integrate Russia into the world economy when even developed countries are struggling with the changes brought about by globalisation. The relationship between the EU and Russia will become increasingly critical.

18. In Russia, faith in the new economic system is still conditional and still fragile, highly dependent on individuals. It is not just an economic question but a human one. Western policy has to be sensitive. Russia cannot be expected to switch easily, or without huge problems of transition, to a model of democracy that very few Russians understand and none have experienced.

6

Britain and New Zealand: Refocusing the Link

Short Report on Conference WPS 97/4: 31 August – 1 September 1997

Robin Hart

1. This conference explored the links between Britain and New Zealand, and considered how these could most usefully evolve in the future. The ties between the two countries remain varied and strong, with a shared Head of State, a common language, common values, common heritage, many family links, and shared national interests of a healthy democratic system and economic prosperity. Significant trading links between the two countries, growing out of the 'protein bridge' established at the end of the last century, continue. As leading players in the Commonwealth, Britain and New Zealand benefit from the vibrant global network that membership of this club offers.

2. As the new millennium approaches, political and social changes in both countries provide an opportunity to refocus these traditional links. The constitutional and social changes being introduced by a new Labour government in the UK are matched by the political experiment of coalition government in New Zealand, with a new MMPR (Mixed Member Proportional Representation) electoral system; greater Maori representation in Parliament, not least through the new New Zealand First party, increasing Maori participation and development following land settlements; and the continuation of economic deregulation and social restructuring. Both countries are also seeking to redefine their identity and place in the world: the UK within a changing Europe; New Zealand increasingly within the Asia–Pacific sphere. And both countries will undoubtedly change further. Will New Zealand introduce further constitutional changes? What impact will devolution have on the UK? How will Maori/Pakeha relations develop in New Zealand? How will the UK evolve as a more multicultural society?

3. Against this background of change, the bond between the Britain and New Zealand (NZ) cannot be taken for granted. A continuing programme of action, building on the British government's Link programme, in the economic, political, global and cultural spheres would ensure that both nations gain maximum benefit from their bilateral links.

4. In the economic sphere, the size of the two countries' population and economy varies as does their distance from populated markets, but there are strong mutual interests in trade and investment. Trade levels have nearly doubled in the past 6 years. The UK is New Zealand's fourth largest export market, heavily concentrated on the primary sector but fast diversifying; and some 90 NZ companies have bases in the UK. And NZ remains one of the UK's top 50 markets despite a recent downturn. The UK is the third largest investor in New Zealand, providing dividends for the UK and jobs and technology for NZ. But there are new trade opportunities which should be grasped. New Zealand would benefit from more UK leading edge technological investment, and from producing more 'value-added' products. For those NZ companies investing in the UK, increased use of manufacturing under licence (as successfully demonstrated by Anchor Foods), and employment of their own nationals in UK-based offices would be beneficial. With the diversification of New Zealand's exports, Britain can act as a springboard for entry into the European market. And British companies should be encouraged to share their experience in Europe with New Zealand companies. New Zealand can also act as an intermediary for British (and European) companies operating in the Asia–Pacific region. Genuine partnerships between New Zealand and British industrialists could be forged given compatible business philosophies, New Zealand contacts in the market places and their 'can do' attitude coupled with British expertise in project financing and access to capital markets.

5. Greater political interchange on policy ideas would benefit both countries whether in the field of economic development, social welfare or political reform. The UK could learn much from the successful economic and social restructuring achieved in New Zealand, and from the move to proportional representation; New Zealand might learn from the UK's experience in Europe. If the political relationship is to remain 'special' greater weight needs to be given to it in determining national policy towards specific issues. The UK's handling of the dairy issue and response to French nuclear testing were cited as examples.

6. Both countries retain their outward-looking global nature. The UK is currently greatly focused on Europe, particularly important given the UK Presidency in 1998; New Zealand increasingly focuses on the Asia–Pacific region through its membership of the Asia–Pacific Economic Co-operation, which it hosts and chairs in 1999. But both countries can open windows for the other. Both share the common problems of operating in a global market and can support one another in different fora such as the World Trade Organisation to seek the de-regularisation of trade and investment. And both can also support each other's efforts on the world stage to promote their shared values of human rights, democratic freedom and openness, internal and international justice. Other areas for mutually beneficial co-operation include promoting sustainable development and prudent environmental stewardship; security and defence (where the range of co-operation remains extensive, although here the independent stance of New Zealand on US navy port visits remains an area of difference), and the best approaches to adopt towards Asian countries such as China and Indonesia. Increased dialogue at official and unofficial levels could be highly beneficial.

7. Culturally, ensuring that ethnic minorities play a successful role is a major social and political challenge for both countries. The bi-communal nature of New Zealand lies at the heart of its cultural future. There is a continuing need for a genuinely tolerant and equal relationship between the Pakeha and the Maori. Pakeha dependence on Maori culture to create a New Zealand 'brand' (such as the haka before a rugby game) should not be allowed to inhibit Maori culture from developing in its own way. Bi-culturalism should be encouraged – and the Pakeha may need to lean less on Maori history and more on their own. As a separate point the creation of a New Zealand version of the British Council was suggested as a cost-effective means of promoting modern New Zealand to the rest of the world.

8. Within the United Kingdom the use of anti-discrimination legislation has acted as a lever to enable disparate cultures to co-exist with tolerance and respect. Action to remove racism in sport has had positive effects in other areas of society; employment of multi-ethnic employees by business has provided companies with a competitive edge overseas. Formal education programmes to promote the benefits and values of culturally diverse societies has been crucial in the UK, which is seen as racially more harmonious than its European partners, as is the influential role of the national political leadership through their actions. Such experiences can be shared by both countries to create a just society and a climate of tolerance and fair treatment for all.

9. Bringing people together is crucial for the strong links to be maintained. It happens automatically with 40,000 New Zealanders living in the UK who are free ambassadors for their country. But more could be done to harness this fund of goodwill. Youth exchange is an important aspect of the interchange and larger numbers of young Britons should be allowed into New Zealand for work experience, above the current restriction of 2,000 per annum. Similarly a 2-year stay under the working holiday maker scheme in the UK is not always long enough for New Zealanders. There are growing calls for a deregulation of the movement of people between the two countries. The recent increase in the number of flights between New Zealand and the UK should allow even greater numbers to travel. A visible demonstration by political leaders that the relationship matters would be valued by New Zealand.

10. The concept of refocusing the link is a challenge both to New Zealanders and to Britons. Positive policy measures can be taken by both governments to encourage strong political, economic and social links. It will then be up to the people themselves, and increasingly the next generations, to create and kindle their own special Link and to maximise a partnership based on so much that we have in common.

7

The Europe–Asia Relationship: How Could It Be Improved?

Short Report on Conference 505: 1–5 September 1997

Robin Hart

1. This conference explored the relationship between Asia and Europe in the context of the second Asia–Europe Summit Meeting (ASEM), held in London in April 1998. This follows the inaugural ASEM meeting held in Bangkok in March 1996. ASEM has since acted as a catalyst for a greatly increased Asia–Europe dialogue, at a variety of levels, aimed at stimulating an effective partnership between the two regions.

2. ASEM is an evolving process involving 26 participants, and as such is the largest global inter-regional grouping. Its diverse membership includes developed and developing economies, varying political systems and cultures. Its agenda is set by political leaders, the Heads of Government summits being a meeting of individual politicians, without their officials. Its informal nature and lack of bureaucracy are seen as advantages. ASEM is regarded as part of a Europe/Asia/USA triangle, and a necessary balance to US influence.

3. Over 20 other countries are keen to participate in ASEM, not least given the recently expanded ASEAN and the proposed expansion of the EU. Other applicants include India and Pakistan, Australia and New Zealand and Central and Eastern European countries. There is a generally positive attitude towards enlargement, although many would argue not before the Seoul ASEM III in 2000. The criteria for membership of this new Club still need to be agreed.

4. Europeans are increasingly conscious of the long-term economic opportunities in Asia, the world's most dynamic growth region (despite recent currency problems). Opportunities abound for exports and investment. Asians too recognise Europe as a major market, and for some countries, notably Japan and South Korea (but increasingly other countries such as Malaysia) as an opportunity for long-term direct investment.

5. However, barriers to trade and investment exist for both sides. Europeans face differing tariffs in Asian countries, a closed market in some areas, preferential treatment for domestic products in others, concern over intellectual property, controlled financial markets, bureaucracy in setting up in-country business, and in some cases corruption; for Asians the European anti-dumping measures and differing preferences can inhibit trade. Constructive dialogue on all these issues is needed to ensure market access and a level playing field for all. Varying stages of economic development will make this hard to achieve in the short term. However, businesses from both regions can learn more about each other's business culture and language. European business can also be encouraged to set an example on labour and environmental standards. Asians for their part are benefiting from moving away from mass production to smaller production of diverse goods for the European market. They could also learn from the European experience of developing international norms and setting common standards. Asians trading in Europe will be seeking to benefit from the creation of EMU.

Nevertheless, EU member states remaining outside EMU are unlikely to see a short-term drop in trade with Asia.

6. The ASEM dialogue can be used to discuss economic issues and to emphasise the common desire for economic development. ASEM has already initiated a Trade Facilitation Action Plan working on priority areas for trade facilitation for the business community; and an Investment Promotion Action Plan to promote investments and create a sound and stable regulatory framework. It could also discuss the need for education and training, the common problems of corruption (with this subject raised by Asians first), of labour costs, of unemployment in Europe and cheaper labour in Asia.

7. ASEM can also provide a platform for discussing a range of global trade issues. European members are all part of the EU, Asians members of Asia–Pacific Economic Co-operation (APEC). Discussing issues in preparation for the World Trade Organisation (WTO) negotiations could be mutually beneficial. Regional trading groups have made progress on certain trade liberalisation issues, ahead of multilateral agreements which take much longer to negotiate. But the prospect for co-operation between Europe and Asia is unpromising on specifics. Agriculture is one area where interests differ widely. Chinese membership of the WTO is another. Lessons from APEC might be drawn here. APEC depends heavily on political will to push economic issues forward, but leaves contentious issues for subsequent debate.

8. One of ASEM's strengths is that it includes political dialogue, unlike other regional groupings such as APEC. This is with reluctance on the part of some Asians who are in many cases primarily focused on economic development and see this as the crux of ASEM. Political dialogue is difficult: the Europeans may speak with one voice on many issues but Asians, whose regimes range from autocratic paternalism to communist, clearly cannot speak as one. But this should not mean that dialogue should not happen. Dialogue needs to take place in the right atmosphere, particularly when many Asians consider that the format is more important than the content, and are keen to move slowly. A measured timescale may be needed to allow a 'comfort-level' to be established. Similarly, vocabulary matters – some suggest that political dialogue itself should be called 'the rule of law'. Sensitive handling is needed on such issues as human rights, or universal values as some prefer to call them, as enshrined in the UN Universal Declaration on Human Rights. Europeans recognise that Asians want them to listen more and lecture less. Asians for their part accept that a new relationship with Europe must allow for exchange on difficult and sensitive matters. The suggestion that some of the most sensitive issues could be discussed by a track-two process would overcome the EU's internal divisions and avoid Asian sensitivities in a formal debate. Private diplomacy, building on a track-two approach, might succeed where 'megaphone' diplomacy fails.

9. ASEM can function as a political catalyst, bringing peer pressure to bear on the participants, for instance in informal discussions over Burma. It can also benefit bilateral relationships by providing the forum in which bilateral discussions can take place, for example between Portugal and Indonesia about East Timor, and the UK and Vietnam about refugees. For real improvement in relations between Europe and Asia, frank and honest exchanges of political issues will be needed. In many of the areas of political debate there remains a common agenda but little consensus on the approach or the substance. Confidence-building in this area between the different partners takes time and demands trust and goodwill from all.

10. Security issues have traditionally featured in the Europe–Asia relationship. Europeans have a major stake in Asian stability and most Asian countries welcome their interest. Through various means, Europeans play a significant practical role in the region: peacekeeping in Cambodia; membership of the ASEAN Regional Forum (although here Europe's participation is ineffectual and its method of participation needs to be reassessed), and through European support, now formalised, for the Korean Peninsula Energy Development Organisation (KEDO). Experience in confidence-building measures, in preventive diplomacy and in peacekeeping might be valued further by Asians. The ASEM forum can be used for a meaningful discussion of some of these issues.

11. ASEM can also provide an opportunity to discuss global issues such as development aid, the environment, and the role of the UN. The EU's development aid to Asian countries remains substantial and is only exceeded by Japan. Much aid is devoted to poverty alleviation in rural areas. Other Asian countries with increasing prosperity could participate further in this work. Conversely, in Eastern Europe there are opportunities for greater Asian engagement. Similarly in the environmental field Asians and Europeans can share their know-how, acknowledging the need for environmental protection and recognising that work in this field creates jobs. And discussions on the new shape of the United Nations, or global security such as peacekeeping, the reduction of nuclear weapons and proliferation might be productive, although some are keen that ASEM focuses on short-range issues where Europe and Asia can add value beyond other fora.

12. To ensure that the prejudices, ignorance and misunderstandings which have blighted contacts between Europeans and Asians in the past have no part in the future, greater 'people to people' contact is needed. This is arguably the most important role for ASEM and where the relationship could be most improved. Despite modern communications the peoples of both regions will only come to understand one another better by meeting face to face, and in one another's countries. Cultural awareness could be further enhanced by the indigenous Asian population in Europe.

13. Bringing together the younger generations, students and academics, future leaders, civil society including NGOs, regional and local governments, Chambers of Commerce and national and local media would significantly enhance mutual understanding. At the same time it would involve civil society in the improvement of Euro-Asian relations. Adequate funding is crucial to support civil society-based projects to create mass networks. The establishment of the Asia–Europe Foundation at the Singapore Foreign Ministers' meeting to promote cultural and intellectual exchanges should promote greater contact. Persuading Asians to undertake graduate and post-graduate studies in Europe, rather than the USA, is crucial but needs financial support. The same applies to encouraging Europeans to study in an Asian country. ASEM can stimulate greater student exchange, and should ensure that immigration and red tape do not hinder travel and contact. Similarly the media can have a significant role in raising awareness, and amending outmoded stereotypes.

14. The key to ASEM's current success is its informality and the fact that it is not a negotiating organisation. ASEM's success depends much on the personal chemistry of the political leaders, albeit many of the personalities will change between summits. ASEM has been described as a marriage; a long-term relationship is desired, but as with any relationship this needs to be worked at to prevent a divorce. And a level playing field based on equality is called for. But with summitry and new organisations come traps: a post summit anti-climax, unrealistic goals, too many follow-up activities and 'laundry lists' duplicating other areas of work, too many meetings, and the creation of unwieldy bureaucratic institutions.

15. ASEM needs to avoid these if it is to prosper. It needs to add value to the important relationship between the two regions and its constituent parts. It needs to be seen not just as a talking shop, but a forum with positive results. In the longer term specific plans need to be drawn up, allowing members to budget effectively and taking ASEM as a viable process into the next century. The London and Seoul meetings will therefore be crucial in defining the purpose of the relationship and steering ASEM's future course.

8

Building Stability in Sub-Saharan Africa

Short Report on Conference 506: 8–12 September 1997

Chris Langdon

1. It is clear that the post-independence era in sub-Saharan Africa has come to an end. The fall and death of President Mobutu symbolises the end of the period. It is widely acknowledged in the West as well as in Africa that the experiment in transferring the democratic systems of the colonial masters to their former colonies has frequently failed. Gone also is the era in which African states were pawns in the Cold War. It is now also recognised that imposing a single form of economic structural adjustment since the mid-1980s has not worked. Attempts to impose universal solutions are now widely acknowledged to be inappropriate. And in the 1990s, the international community is seen by many to have failed in recent humanitarian crises. It has insufficient will to intervene. There is now acceptance that imposition from outside cannot produce a system that is stable from within.

2. There is a cautious recognition that the solution to Africa's problems must come from within. The rise of new African leaders is symptomatic of the political changes from within Africa itself. However it remains true that several of the largest countries in Africa (Nigeria, Sudan, Democratic Republic of the Congo (DRC), Angola, and Kenya) are not fully stable.

3. Leaders such as President Museveni in Uganda, President Isiaias in Eritrea, and Prime Minister Meles in Ethiopia, and the new Rwandan government represent the new thinking in Africa. They evolved their approach during long liberation struggles. They point to the failure of African post-colonial leaders and advocate African solutions to provide basic necessities and equality of opportunity and transparent and non-corrupt government. They advocate differing forms of participative democracy rather than Western-style elective democracy which they say is inappropriate. The state has its role but corrupt old style statism is rejected. They believe that it is the government that owns the reform programme. It should set the agenda. It is not for Western donors or non-governmental organisations (NGOs) to impose their solutions. Much aid has been squandered or misdirected in the past they say. National self-reliance, and the development of indigenous business capacity are the key. But they do believe in full participation in the global trading system.

4. Their foreign policy is open to differing interpretation, but it is clear that they believe that it is permissible to intervene to maintain stability, for example in Kivu in former Zaire. This shatters the old OAU consensus on intervention. On the vexed question of Africa's post-colonial borders the approach advocated by President Museveni is that they should be rendered irrelevant rather than redrawn.

5. At the same time, new regional groupings have become more prominent. In Southern Africa, the role of the Southern African Development Community (SADC) is still evolving just three years after democracy came to South Africa. It has had some successes in infrastructure development. It will clearly be some time before it becomes fully effective. It has ambitious plans for a human rights charter and court and a common security regime like the OSCE in Europe. In West Africa, the military arm of the Economic Community of West African States (ECOWAS), the ECOWAS Monitoring Group (ECOMOG), is involved in peace enforcement in Sierra Leone and Liberia. Plans for an African Economic Community (AEC) were ratified by two thirds of the members of the OAU by 1994. However, moves towards economic integration have been disappointing so far.

6. There is a growing consensus in the industrialised world that a country-specific approach that takes into account local conditions and local aspirations is now the only viable approach.

7. That has been shown by the 1997 World Bank's World Development Report which, observers say, represents a watershed in policy. It moves away from the attempt to impose a universal structural adjustment policy to an acceptance that effective government is essential for stability. It rejects 'a single recipe for state reforms'. It also says: 'History has repeatedly shown that good government is not a luxury but a vital necessity. Without an effective state, sustainable development, both economic and social, is impossible'. The report argues that the effectiveness of the state and government reform programmes is directly related to the effectiveness of public institutions. This leads the Bank to focus on institution building. This moves it into areas new to the Bank. The Bank is also advocating 'small steps' which can have a large impact on economic and social welfare. The new strategies are not without risks.

8. There is widespread recognition that even though the success of reform policies cannot be guaranteed, a refusal to undertake reform is likely to be fatal. It is clear that targeted and appropriate assistance has to be given to assist the development of good governance, with appropriate state institutions plus an effective system of laws with an independent judiciary and law enforcement agencies. Other key components of civil society are NGOs of all types and the media. The emphasis is on capacity-building, with aid being targeted at creating the right conditions for the development of civil society.

9. Issues such as corruption have to be tacked at source – the givers abroad as well as at home. Laws such as the US Foreign Corrupt Practices Act prohibiting bribe-giving need wider enactment, or if legislation exists it needs to be used, although the difficulties in achieving a burden of proof in court will be very high.

10. Among the bilateral donors, there has been a general welcome to the principle of Africa-led solutions.

11. France, by far the largest investor and donor, has made what observers say is a historic and irreversible shift in policy with a decision to reduce its political engagement in Francophone Africa. The old network from the Elysee Palace that ran French Africa policy for thirty years, known as the 'reseau Foccart', has gone with the death of its linchpin in 1997. France is cutting its troop presence of 8,500 by between 25% and 40%.

12. Britain has welcomed the rise of a more assertive policy in Africa, and the new Labour government's policy based on concern for human rights and on poverty alleviation has been outlined.

13. In the United States, there is recognition of the significance of the intellectual and generational shift in Africa's renewal. While the US media focuses on the humanitarian crises, US policy-makers acknowledge the economic turnaround shown by the rising growth rates. US investment is rising. Since the 1997 Denver Summit Africa has been given a clear focus. There has been much speculation in the media on the US role in the fall of Mobutu. But US independent observers point out that US government policy was to try to prevent the widening of the conflict and to stop the advance of the Alliance. But its demarches were not credible. It remains true that the result is one that doesn't threaten US interests.

14. It has been strongly argued that the international community failed in Zaire to prevent a humanitarian crisis and that after the failure in Rwanda and the disastrous intervention in Somalia, the international community will be all the more reluctant to intervene in future. NGO observers criticised the relief aid given to defeated militias in the relief camps, allowing them to restore themselves, and thus propagate instability.

15. The international community sent humanitarian aid because it was unwilling to tackle the underlying political issues. Little prospect was seen of a change in that position. For some African observers there is a double standard in that the international community wants to investigate alleged massacres in Eastern Zaire, but turned its back on the genocide of hundreds of thousands of Tutsis in 1994. Attempts to impose a set of conditions on the new government of DRC is grossly unreal they argue, given the condition of the country after so many years of misrule, even if international pressure for elections within two years is relaxed.

16. The crisis in Zaire is symptomatic of the trend toward humanitarian crises in the 1990s. From 1985–9 there were five declared man-made emergencies ongoing each year. By 1990 twenty were ongoing, peaking with twenty-six in 1994. Large scale movements of refugees (5 million a year on average) and internally displaced persons have become the major focus of the international assistance by NGOs, shifting them away from long-term development. This has been encouraged by the media and public perception, and the nature of the aid contract system. Refugee food aid needs constitute a considerable long-term drain on overall food aid resources. The international food safety net has rarely worked for refugees in Africa, and declines in overall availability, coupled with the reorganisation of EU assistance, will increase the vulnerability of refugees, say NGO officials. New approaches to food security need to be developed that allow greater access to income and integration in the host economy.

17. Attempts to cope with the causes of humanitarian crises have led to a debate among the NGOs which has led them into direct conflict with New African leaders. The so-called 'New Humanitarianism' policy argues that neutrality is not an appropriate concept; NGOs should be on the side of the poor and disadvantaged and should speak out when appropriate. As one major international NGO has publicly declared: 'When relief impact is low, the interests of victims are best served by mobilising the international community by bearing witness to violations of basic humanitarian principles and denouncing them.'

18. This approach is still under intense debate within and between the international NGOs. Some argue that it is better for the NGOs to do what they do best – provide humanitarian aid. Going public can have little effect but to endanger local staff and the programme. NGOs can maintain direct pressure off the record on the government concerned. There are also issues of sovereignty, particularly as New African leaders become more assertive.

19. New humanitarianism has inevitably led to strong criticism from certain African governments who argue it is for governments to determine the aid policies in their country. They accuse some NGOs of ill-informed and politically motivated criticism. Much aid to NGOs is wasted on high administration costs as the NGOs have to build their local infrastructure, as high as 83% they say. NGOs do not as a group have a co-ordinated approach, thereby taking a lot of government time in co-ordination. Governments in Eritrea and Rwanda have imposed controls on the work of NGOs. The work of NGOs who operate within government guidelines is acknowledged. The international media, who often work closely with the NGOs in the field, will also have to consider their role as New African leaders such as Paul Kagame have shown strong skills at handling the international media.

20. Avoiding humanitarian crises by preventing conflict remains a goal. However the means to achieve this remain unclear. Ambitious and laudable plans for a system of early warning networks were regarded by many as unworkable. It was unclear whether there would be a willingness to share information, and even if information were collated it was unlikely that the international community, given its recent past experience, would be prepared to intervene. There is no kudos attached to conflict prevention in the way there is for politicians with post-conflict humanitarian relief. And Finance Ministries would see no direct return, however well the case is argued that conflict prevention saves huge sums from being spent later on relief.

21. Initiatives for peacekeeping were also considered, and the possibility of further financial and logistical support for an African peacekeeping force. There are a number of useful training initiatives already. However funding another army would be a complex political and budgetary question for some donor countries.

22. It was clear that the keys to building stability are internal not external. Outside support is necessary but limited. There are some positive signs, such as average annual growth rates of 5%. With the end of attempts to provide simple and universal solutions to Africa's ills from outside, there is a realisation that Africa's economic and political development is going to be a long drawn-out and uncertain process, but one perhaps more likely to produce effective results in the medium term.

9

The Inter-Governmental Conference and Its Consequences: Ensuring Public Acceptance and Building a 'New' Europe

Short Report on Conference 507: 15–19 September 1997

Nicholas Hopkinson

1. In spite of the disappointment expressed by some European Union (EU) Member States after the June 1997 Amsterdam Summit, most participants at this Wilton Park conference believed the Inter-Governmental Conference (IGC) brought about many improvements, although crucial issues remain to be settled. Amsterdam completed the unfinished business of the Maastricht process, improved the democratic quality of the EU, and allowed the future European agenda, in particular the commencement of enlargement negotiations, to stay on track. However, the IGC's major failing was that it did not produce the institutional changes necessary to enlarge the EU. Nor did the IGC discuss other difficult issues, such as reform of the Common Agricultural Policy (CAP) and Structural Funds, which are necessary for the EU to enlarge.

2. Many believe that the positive overall result at the IGC could not have been achieved without a change of government in the United Kingdom (UK). The Amsterdam Summit demonstrated a significant change in the UK's relations with its European partners. The UK can no longer be considered a laggard on most EU issues.

3. There are three alternative interpretations of the Amsterdam Treaty: a new impulse to further integration (fuller use of existing powers under the first pillar, fuller co-operation under the third pillar, and fuller use of existing EU institutions); a symptom of policy and institutional blockage (restricting EU areas of competence, limiting the role for the European Parliament (EP), excluding the European Court of Justice from jurisdiction on free movement, failing to agree institutional changes, introducing the Luxembourg compromise in the second pillar, and general flexibility in the first and third pillars); and an awkward transition mechanism to a different form of union with core obligations of membership and flexibility elsewhere, and uncertainty over the responsibility of the Council and the Commission.

4. Too much flexibility risks undermining the EU. However, flexibility has allowed some Member States to integrate more quickly in certain areas such as the Schengen agreement. If there is too much uniformity, some fear nationalism could grow, ultimately tearing the EU apart. New Member States will probably be offered lengthy transitional periods but this does not initially increase the flexible nature of the EU. However, once inside the EU, new Member States are likely to press for arrangements that will probably increase the scope of flexibility.

5. Little progress was made in communitising the Common Foreign and Security Policy (CFSP). However, the inclusion of the Petersberg tasks and of the principle of respect for human rights and fundamental freedoms are important developments, although it remains to be seen how these tasks will implemented. There remains a divergence of views within the EU on security policy. One view is that the EU should not duplicate NATO as a military structure, IGCs are not a proper forum to discuss European security, and many of the resolutions on the CFSP are questionable. The other is that the goal of a European defence identity is best pursued in an EU context.

6.   Much was achieved at Amsterdam to communitise third pillar issues such as visa policy, asylum, immigration, refugee and external frontier arrangements. Decision making in these areas will be considerably simplified, conflicting competences will be eliminated, and time-consuming ratification procedures will be avoided. However, much again depends on how these measures are implemented.

7.   Institutional change, the major unfinished business of the IGC, will not be made before the necessity arises, probably after the enlargement negotiations are completed. Some fear that an IGC specifically devoted to institutional reform could be used to delay enlargement, largely because there are differing national perceptions of the urgency and commitment to enlargement. A weak deal from such an IGC, perhaps along the lines of the Ioannina Agreement, threatens enlargement. The EP has indicated that it may not give its assent to enlargement unless institutional reform is substantive. Nevertheless, it is widely believed that another IGC is not required to resolve institutional issues. If the EU is fit for 15 Member States, it is just as fit for 20. All that is needed is the political will to tighten-up procedures and to implement new institutional rules.

8.   In order for the EU to be effective, the Commission should have no more than the present 20 members, a ceiling that may be sustainable if, as the Amsterdam Treaty suggests, large countries give up their second Commissioner. An EU of more than 20 members would require either a Commission with standing and rotating members or a general rotating system. A smaller number of Commissioners is opposed. An enlarged EU will also require a redistribution of seats in the EP – the only politically feasible way to do this is to scale down the existing distribution; it could not be done according to a proportional representation of the population.

9.   The next enlargement will shift the balance fundamentally towards smaller countries. For example, new eastern members could block any decision in the Council. The issue of re-weighting of voting rights itself is probably the only case where there is a clear clash between large and small Member States. What divides Member States is not their size, but their interests. Small states believe it would be dangerous to disturb the present voting balance which is founded on the equality of states. To prevent deadlock in the IGC, a decision on possible solutions, such as a dual majority voting system, was postponed until 2000 or later.

10.   There is time before the next enlargement is likely, perhaps around 2003, to overhaul the CAP and Structural Funds. Structural and Cohesion Funds need to become simpler, more affordable and better targeted. This process is likely to be painful, especially for Cohesion countries. The amount of regional funding is likely to be scaled down, especially when it is not used. For example, the Italian Mezzogiorno uses only 20 per cent of the funds available to it. Structural Funds could also be used more efficiently, and the private sector could become more involved in infrastructure projects. Economic growth in the EU may provide the least painful solution. For example, annual growth of 3 per cent of GDP suggests that an additional 1.2 billion ECU could be available for Structural Funds spending even though relative contributions would be scaled down.

11. European publics are reacting to IGCs with increasing incomprehension as each IGC is portrayed as vital, but then the decisions reached appear to be relatively unimportant and decisions on controversial issues are postponed to the next IGC. It is anomalous that the EP has no right to amend the Amsterdam Treaty, even though it may be the institution that is best placed to scrutinise its provisions. Nevertheless, it is believed that there will not be a repeat of the Maastricht referendum crisis, in part because there is some optimism that the more modest nature of the Amsterdam Treaty will contribute to its ratification in the UK during the UK Presidency, and to a possible positive vote in the May 1998 Danish referendum.

10

India and Pakistan at Fifty

Short Report on Conference 508: 29 September – 3 October 1997

Virginia Crowe

1. Changing economic realities are overtaking the urgent strategic and political considerations which dominated India and Pakistan's first fifty years. They are having to adapt to a new climate induced by global change and the end of the Cold War. The deeply rooted mutual hostility which shaped their respective national ethos and the exploitation of religion for political purposes have to make way for a more constructive dialogue if opportunities for peaceful coexistence are to be grasped.

2. The Kashmir dispute remains a major barrier to the normalisation of relations between India and Pakistan. Employing the parallel strategies of working *round* the issue, as well as *at* the issue, is a pragmatic approach to an impasse. A role for third parties as mediators is resisted by India, which regards any internationalisation of the dispute as unacceptable.

3. Armed forces confront each other across a long and volatile border, reflecting fundamental insecurity and mutual mistrust. The nuclear option has arguably kept the peace, but military spending is costing both India and Pakistan dear in terms of economic and social development.

4. The Pakistani economy is considered to be in a state of crisis, and though India's bold deregulatory reforms are applauded, they are neither complete, nor assured. Reform of the public sector is perceived as a pressing necessity. Progressive privatisation of trade and production, fiscal reforms to reduce deficits, the raising of savings levels, a commitment to export-led growth supported by efficient exchange rate management and selective infrastructure investment, and tough measures to attack endemic and corrosive corruption are required in both countries.

5. Closer bilateral trade links between India and Pakistan are a route to both greater mutual understanding and economic development. Unofficial trade figures suggest trade complementarity and a huge potential which could be developed if the restricted list of imports and non-tariff barriers could be eased (and preferably abolished), and tariffs cut. Problems of adjustment would be inevitable, especially for the smaller partner. Infrastructure would need improvement, with co-ordination of rail, road and port links, the removal of third country port restrictions and the opening of the Wagha border to facilitate trade.

6. The prospects of India and Pakistan emulating the Asian tigers in the near term are questionable. Foreign Direct Investment and Foreign Institutional Investment are actively sought, but some potential investors detect a lack of commitment in practice, whatever the rhetoric, and a lingering perception of foreign investment as exploitation. Investment is not made easy, with difficulties in finding local partners, unreliable procedures and bureaucratic delay, and critical shortfalls in adequate infrastructure and power supplies.

7. South Asia has the highest incidence of poverty, the most illiteracy and malnourishment of any region in the world, arguably because its culture embraces appalling neglect of its women. This has contributed hugely to deprivation being passed on between the generations. The degree of gender inequity is a major factor distinguishing the South Asian economies from the East Asian tiger economies. There should be more investment to counter the problems of illiteracy, health care and population growth. Education could help reduce ethnic and class tensions.

8. Issues of governance are central to every aspect of development. Democracy in India seems firmly rooted, though in a weakened Parliament and hindered by a cumbersome bureaucracy, but reinforced by a strong independent judiciary. Pakistan, inheritor of lopsided institutions and feudal traditions, is witnessing a breakdown in the mechanisms of governance, where pressure for reform and popular activism is leading to the development of structures of civil society which are paralleling and overtaking government institutions. There is recognition in both countries of the need for administrative reforms to promote efficiency, transparency and accountability but they are difficult to institute for both political and social reasons.

9. Governance, development and poverty are closely linked to environmental issues. A clean environment has been declared a human right in both India and Pakistan, constituting a common challenge. State and community action to improve the environment; co-operation on issues such as trade in gas and power through a regional grid; and co-operation on vital water issues, infrastructure for the urban poor and on solar power for the rural poor could benefit both countries. However, the state of relations between the countries makes it difficult to achieve progress.

10. The facilitation of contacts and frank exchanges at every level is necessary if such fruitful co-operation is to flourish. Though a number of structured non-governmental dialogues are usefully conducted, contacts between peoples and organisations in the two countries remain minimal. An easing of the visa regime would be a highly desirable and simple practical measure to facilitate such exchanges.

11. Regional co-operation based on the South Asian Association for Regional Co-operation (SAARC), is developing somewhat slowly. Suggestions are made that SAARC might usefully be strengthened, and include a security dimension in tandem with its trade and economic functions. SAARC and the South Asian Free Trade Association (SAFTA) have a useful continuing role to play in normalising Indo-Pakistan trade relations, which could help defuse the wider tensions. A variable geometry of triangles and quadrilaterals of nations associated in a multi-layered, multi-dimensional format is being constructed in the region and beyond, which could ultimately form the basis of a Commonwealth or United States of South Asia, and which links SAARC countries to ASEAN.

12. The ASEAN model of regional co-operation is cited as a relevant example for South Asia, since it comprises developing nations. Nine countries with different traditions, political systems, religions, language and levels of development work together in the interests of peace, security, stability and prosperity, forging a certain emerging identity, with 'unity in diversity'. Traditional disputes and ideological differences have not been allowed to impede the drive for regional economic growth. Whether economic considerations can be such a driving force in the culture of South Asia may be problematic.

13. The experience of the European Union, another potential role model, is that to be effective, a long term vision, a political dimension, and a supra-national element are essential additions to the economic dimension which, it is suggested, SAARC might usefully consider. Ideas for an overall Treaty or Charter, and a Council of South Asia with echoes of the Council of Europe and its cultural exchanges, Charter of Human Rights and Court, and particularly, the idea of functional sectoral associations such as a South Asian Water Community, command interest.

14. For India and Pakistan much in the new millennium will depend on how successfully economic opportunities are seized and whether they can move from confrontation to co-operation. The success of their respective relationships with ASEAN, for example, is said to depend on economic factors such as the continuation of Indian economic reform, but also on the jettisoning of habits of confrontation. There is reluctance within ASEAN to import conflict, and a perception that India and Pakistan are obsessed by bilateral issues.

15. The two, however, share cultural affinities and compelling interests even beyond those being generated by the dynamics of regional trade. They share perceptions of P5 discrimination on nuclear issues, of a trade and economic regime developing to their disadvantage in WTO and ILO, and a concern to develop and secure access to the resources and trade potential of Central Asia. Such commonalities and the experience of working together on them may influence a rapprochement.

16. The painful legacy of fifty years ago may simply be overtaken by the modalities of the new high-techology consumerist society where private sector interests are increasingly the arbiters, and existing tensions may eventually be mitigated by generational change, recognition of common interests and mutual accommodation. In the meantime, however, there is a risk that India and Pakistan may be marginalised by the effects of their confrontation and less able to play an appropriate role in world affairs. Courageous initiatives, leadership and magnanimity are called for, supported by patient painstaking confidence-building measures at every level. The task is huge, but so are the potential rewards for a whole subcontinent.

11

Multilateral Control Regimes in the 21st Century: The Impact on Chemical and Biological Weapons

Short Report on Conference WPS 97/5: 3–5 October 1997

Richard Latter

1. There is a need to reaffirm the importance of arms control in maintaining international stability and security, to demonstrate to governments and their leaders that efforts to prevent the proliferation of weapons of mass destruction remain important, notwithstanding the disillusionment of some with the achievements of arms control and, to many, its perceived inordinate cost and irrelevance in the face of new threats and risks.

2. The success of arms control should be measured against the following tasks: maintaining stability between major powers; integrating aspiring powers; insulating the world community from local conflicts; punishment of transgressors; the effective management of technology diffusion; and engaging the United States in the international system at its 'uni-polar moment'.

3. Multilateral arms control regimes are not a panacea for the achievement of these goals; nor can they totally prevent proliferation. However, their use of a combination of verification and confidence-building measures supports the maintenance of an international norm against weapons of mass destruction. Nevertheless, most observers agree that there is a need to increase the direct role of states in implementing the regimes and that the regimes need to be supplemented by regional and bilateral agreements and cooperation.

4. The 'difficult' proliferation cases, for example North Korea and in the Middle East, need to be dealt with individually as they are not readily dealt with within the framework of a multilateral regime.

5. The expectation that verification procedures within regimes will be 100 per cent effective is unrealistic. As a consequence, there has to be a balance between costs incurred and the effectiveness of the provisions purchased; the sensible application of the premise of 'diminishing returns' is essential. However, publics and governments must be made aware of the significant potential and actual costs which would be incurred if arms control regimes were allowed to lapse.

6. The Chemical Weapons Convention offers the prospect of a chemical weapons (CW)-free world in the 21st century. Its intrusive verification regime, based upon mandatory declarations and the inspection of sites where chemical weapons could be produced, diminishes considerably the possibility of covert CW production. The access to technology-sharing which will be made available to signatories and the threat of trade restrictions for non-compliance further underpin the regime's potential. However, the fact that a number of states remain outside the regime and possess chemical weapons remains problematical. There is a need to press these countries to join the regime; the ratification of the CWC by the Russian Duma is an early priority.

7. Existing security and trade regimes governing the use of and trade in infectious diseases need to be strengthened. The Biological Weapons Convention (BWC) needs to be reinforced in the near future by the introduction of a verification protocol to complicate further and deter efforts to acquire BW and to underpin confidence among states that such weapons are not being acquired by their neighbours or potential adversaries. To this end it is essential that some form of 'non-challenge visits' be permitted to enable checks to be made by international inspectors of the accuracy of mandatory declarations. These would be backed by field or facility investigations to be carried out if and when BW programmes are suspected to exist.

8. Nuclear weapons remain an international problem and the regional conflicts which have motivated the three 'threshold states' and a small number of suspected proliferators to acquire or seek to acquire such weapons need urgently to be addressed. Furthermore for the Nuclear Non-Proliferation Treaty to retain widespread support, it will be necessary to reconcile differing views of the regime's fundamental purpose: whether it is intended to manage an international system in which a few states retain nuclear weapons and further proliferation is to be stemmed, or whether the regime represents but a temporary stage on the road to global nuclear disarmament. A failure to reconcile these differing views will inevitably lead to frictions as the regime is reviewed on a five-yearly basis. In this context, the role to be played by nuclear weapons in deterring the use of biological weapons needs to be clarified (see below). Additional priorities should include: a greater emphasis on warhead destruction rather than the dismantling of delivery systems; supporting UNSCOM activities in Iraq; and maximising the effectiveness of International Atomic Energy Agency (IAEA) inspection procedures.

9. Ensuring the continued relevance and effectiveness of these regimes will require leadership and the evolution of more cooperative inter-state relations on arms control issues. Those leading the non-proliferation effort must be willing and able to set a good example; take due account of other states' potential reactions; use diplomatic means to avert crises; offer a mixture of inducements and pressures; seek what is realistic rather than 'perfect'; anticipate that irrational behaviour will be encountered; and appeal to states' shared interests and values.

10. Where should this leadership be sought? During the Cold War period western states looked to the United States to give a lead and, indeed, the United States has continued to lead on a variety of issues including the Middle East Peace Process and its associated arms control elements, and resolving the North Korean nuclear programme crisis through the initiation of the KEDO arrangement. Nevertheless, some take the view that the US is increasingly disinclined to set the arms control agenda. The priorities of the US Administration are essentially domestic and elements of the Congress are at best dubious about arms control arrangements. Concerns about the rising costs of arms control agreements, their apparent inability to prevent proliferation completely and doubts about the efficacy of verification combine to mute US leaders' enthusiasm. These elements are all the more apparent in the Russian Federation where arms control is increasingly driven by domestic economic and social concerns. The combination of severe domestic problems and the confrontational politics of the Duma, which effectively precludes the rapid ratification of arms control treaties, offers little evidence that Russian leadership will be forthcoming in this area. Domestic concerns, principally economic development, similarly command the attention of the Chinese leadership; while specific arms control issues do feature regularly on China's foreign policy agenda, for example, the introduction of theatre missile defence in East Asia, the country's relative lack of experience in the arms control field points to at best a modest contribution. While China takes a close interest in the deliberations of the Non-Aligned Movement (NAM) group of countries, aspirations to lead the group appear to be muted and it is unclear whether such aspirations would be well received in the NAM itself.

11. With 'great power' leadership uncertain, other countries should be encouraged to play leading roles on particular arms control issues. The positive example set by Australia in recent years demonstrates the possibilities which exist. Promoting arms control agendas in specific regions could be facilitated by major regional players. For example, South Africa could play a role to consolidate arms control regimes in Africa. At another level, arms control initiatives may increasingly be launched by sub-national or non-governmental groups; the recent case of the Landmines Convention is illustrative.

12. If leadership on arms control issues appears likely to be diffused among a number of international actors, the development of a more cooperative approach by all parties will be required. Progress will be governed less by dramatic initiatives of 'the few' than by a collective sense of commitment by 'the many'. It is far from clear that such a collective commitment will materialise in the near future or that it will prove to be an effective means through which arms control policy can be developed. This is a source of concern if predictions that weapons of mass destruction, notably biological weapons, are likely to be used in the decade ahead.

13. Establishing how to react to such use is an urgent priority. Many argue that it must be made clear to potential users that they will not gain advantage and that retribution will be decisive and overwhelming. Whether a 'decisive' response should include the use of nuclear weapons and/or the destruction of the offending regime remains a controversial issue. Furthermore, there is a need to consider whether deterrence will be enhanced by explicitly setting out the means through which a 'reaction to use' will be made, or whether continued ambiguity would be preferable. These and related issues need urgently to be taken up by the international community, perhaps by the United Nations Permanent Five, by the US and its immediate allies, or by an *ad hoc* group of interested nations. There is a need to think through how to respond in cases of BW use by an unidentified state, by a non-governmental actor, by elements within a collapsing state, or in situations of limited use and low casualties. While many would take the view that the response should be 'appropriate' and 'proportional', it remains essential that interested states agree on a limited range of appropriate responses from which a choice may be made if and when a crisis arises.

14. Such consultations need not be exclusive and should incorporate as wide a range of states as possible. A failure to develop an agreed position among states subscribing to the norms and practices of international arms control regimes would inevitably lead some countries to fall back upon national policies and capabilities; a fragmentation of commitment to the maintenance of stability and security through collaborative efforts could result. It is essential, therefore, that the practice and habits of collaboration and cooperation which have begun to develop through the maintenance of existing arms control regimes should be enhanced.

12

How Can Europeans Best Maintain European Security?

Short Report on Conference 509: 6–10 October 1997

Richard Latter

1. There are no immediate security risks of sufficient magnitude to threaten the existing European security system. Current problems, including for example Bosnia and instability in the Mediterranean, are important but containable. However, a more fundamental need remains to avert the re-emergence of hegemonic powers in the region and there is a requirement to forge a genuine capacity for joint action by European states.

2. Such cooperative action is difficult to develop because of states' existing divergent national interests and policies, an increasingly nationalistic reaction to European integration and economic globalisation, and a renewed emphasis on democratic decision-making within existing nation states.

3. The European Union and its enlargement offer potential means to overcome these problems. However, the envisaged enlargement will make the evolution of a genuine Common Foreign and Security Policy (CFSP) more problematical not least because of the involvement of more states in decision-making. For this reason, reinforcing CFSP will require the exercise of considerable political will and determination by those who favour its strengthening, and the need to adapt EU institutions to undertake enlargement may offer them an opportunity to establish the EU as a political entity between the US and Russia with a genuine global voice and role.

4. Envisaged changes under the Amsterdam Treaty are but first steps in this process: the introduction of a new Planning and Early Warning Unit and the appointment of a 'high representative of the EU Council'. Such changes offer the prospect of improvement in the coherence, continuity and capacity of the EU's external activities. However, the European Union will have to do things differently if it is to persuade its population that even more cooperative decision-making is desirable; the issues of national identity and democracy will have to be dealt with if CFSP is to be developed further.

5. This will be true not least in the newly-independent countries aspiring to membership, for example in the Baltic region, which view membership of the EU and other western institutions as a means to guarantee their national integrity and domestic economic and social stability and to underpin their good relations with Russia and other eastern neighbours.

6. Facilitating similar goals in North Africa and the Middle East will require EU attention and action, perhaps sooner than many anticipate given the economic and social regression which is occurring to the south of Europe. Failures of economic development are being compounded by the lack of legitimacy of many Mediterranean governments which may yet generate extremes of violent political conflict similar to that already occurring in Algeria. The EU will need to strengthen the

Barcelona Process and act in a more coordinated and proactive way if it is successfully to contribute to the prevention of further instability. Furthermore, for success to be achieved differences of emphasis in EU and US policies in the region will need to be addressed.

7. Difficulties may be anticipated between the EU and the US across a range of issues as CFSP evolves, notwithstanding the generally positive attitude of United States governments towards the EU. US declaratory policy remains committed to the evolution of a 'genuine' European partner. There is support (albeit low-key) for EMU, and the US–EU Transatlantic Agenda has met with some successes. However, US frustrations regarding trade issues and the slowness of EU policy evolution and US ambiguity about working with the EU on major international problems point towards continued frictions in the transatlantic relationship.

8. In contrast, the EU's relations with its large eastern neighbour, the Russian Federation, seem likely to be relatively untroubled. Russia is little concerned with EU enlargement and CFSP, not least because of its domestic concerns, but also because of a belief that Russia's security problems will be to its south and east in the future. Russian fears of marginalisation in Europe and its overwhelming interest in its trading relationship with western Europe suggest the evolution of a positive cooperative relationship for the foreseeable future.

9. In these circumstances Europeans appear to have the luxury of taking time to consider how best to organise to meet their future defence needs. Support exists for a genuine European Security and Defence Identity with an independent capacity to conduct military operations globally, notably but not exclusively in France. Others foresee a far more modest European defence capability which is to evolve in collaboration with the United States under a NATO umbrella; the constraints of declining defence expenditures in Europe may preclude the evolution of a 'European' capability and many feel comfortable with continued US leadership and engagement in the region. Nevertheless, *genuine* partnership between Europeans and Americans will require a greater European 'input', the generation of improved European military capabilities and, as a consequence, a greater European voice in cooperative US–European defence decision-making. This would inevitably affect the relative weight of American and European views both when taking decisions and when controlling operations, and military commands when decisions are implemented. While talk of US unilateralism and hegemony may be exaggerated, US–European relations *are* changing. For Europe to play a more equal and perhaps more independent role, more thought must be given to what is *desirable* in the longer term as well as to what is *practical* in the near term.

10. Much will depend upon future US policy. There is a tension between a US desire to act unilaterally to secure US interests and its wish to work cooperatively with others to the same end. The United States is in Europe because of its interests in the region, but these are but a part of a wider network of interests of a global power. The latter may not always sit well with Europeans' regional concerns. To some, this means Europe has to be able to defend these alone, while others emphasise the need to work with the US to seek agreed and mutually-beneficial policies. However, these goals need not be mutually exclusive and can be pursued simultaneously; but to do *either* Europeans will have increasingly to be prepared to act collectively and to pay for the military capabilities which will be required.

11. Moving in this direction is not a current European or EU priority. Many are content with existing cooperative arrangements in NATO. Goals appear to be modest, focusing, not least, on the lessons of former Yugoslavia and the conduct of future Peace Support Operations (PSOs).

12. The Amsterdam Treaty envisages that the 'Petersberg Tasks' including PSOs will be an EU responsibility and activity. The Western European Union and NATO are already working on how best to approach such operations and a complementary linkage is emerging between the EU/WEU/NATO; WEU-led operations can call on NATO/US military assets at need. Peace Support Operations will inevitably involve members of the EU/WEU/NATO but will also require the presence of non-members. Priorities for future planning include: establishing clearly the role of non-members in the conduct and planning of operations; improving the quality of coordination between national contingents; dividing tasks to maximise efficiency; allocating financial responsibility; and developing a clear PSO doctrine. There is an overriding need to ensure that the involvement of many states and organisations, as occurred for example in Bosnia, does not make the conduct of such operations unmanageable.

13. Conducting military operations requires that correct equipment be available and that there is assured access to sources of supply and re-supply. An independent CFSP and related defence elements will require access to a European defence industry which many would argue does not yet exist. European states continue to have their own national procurement processes and maintain separate defence industries. The recent US rationalisation of its defence industry into three large defence corporations requires a rapid European response, namely, the cross-border merging of existing European defence companies (new companies should be concerned exclusively with defence), the establishment of a single market for defence within the European Union, the creation of a single procurement process across Europe, and discussions between military staffs regarding common requirements. While there is a widespread recognition that 'something must be done', progress to date remains slow.

14. The gradualism of European efforts to establish CFSP, more cooperative defence arrangements and an integrated defence industry are perhaps acceptable if there is no immediate foreseeable threat to the region. Does any such threat loom which could and should generate greater urgency? Proliferation of weapons of mass destruction (WMD) represents one possibility. While the threat of nuclear weapons is not new to the sub-continent, the widening availability of chemical and biological weapons and related long-range delivery systems to an increasing number of countries is worrying. These may be deployed against European troops or homelands within a decade. A European response has been to reinforce support for ongoing non-proliferation efforts, not least relevant international non-proliferation regimes, and to consider supplementing these with counter-proliferation policies, including pre-emption and the destruction of WMD at source; improving the protection available to individuals, particularly military forces; and maintaining deterrence by establishing credible counter-threats. However, these deliberations have not resulted in European states or the EU establishing a common position on these issues; for example, on whether or not to develop a theatre missile defence system, whether to work with the US on such a project, or whether to buy a US system 'off the shelf' if such becomes available.

15. While these options are under consideration in a number of national capitals the prospects for a collective decision on the issue within the EU do not appear to be high. This is partly because such issues command little attention in national governments which are increasingly concerned with domestic and other issues. There is an urgent need for the security and defence communities within Europe to reassert the importance of security and defence issues within national and EU agendas. An increased sense of urgency is required to generate the political will to deal with these issues at the European level.

13

Justice and Home Affairs in the European Union

Short Report on Conference 510: 13–17 October 1997

Robin Hart

1. The Treaty of Amsterdam has created an extremely complex framework for co-operation in the field of Justice and Home Affairs (JHA). The resulting flexibility is the price to be paid for making progress by consensus decision-making. Officials and practitioners will struggle to implement the measures required by the Treaty over the next 5 years or so. The incorporation of the Schengen acquis into the European Union (EU), allowing border-free travel within the Schengen area, is likely to be problematic, and will result in tiers of 'ins' and 'outs' of EU members and non-members, implications of which will only slowly become obvious. In matters of immigration and asylum (also to be communitarised, without three EU members) the absence of a common political objective will mean crafting policies in practice could prove difficult.

2. European co-operation works best in police and judicial work, in particular against the growing problem of drugs and organised crime. The creation and development of the European Drugs Unit (EDU) is the most tangible example of JHA co-operation so far and builds on the growing cross-border police links developed by the practitioners.

3. The implications of the changes made in the field of JHA by the Amsterdam Treaty on every EU citizen, third country nationals and Europe's neighbours, including EU applicant countries, will only slowly become apparent. Flexibility, patience and greater political direction will be needed if progress towards greater co-operation in any of these fields is to be achieved.

4. The Treaty of Amsterdam, signed by Foreign Ministers on 2 October 1997, seeks to maintain and develop the European Union as an area of freedom, justice and security for its citizens. The framework for JHA co-operation established under the Third Pillar of the Maastricht Treaty of 1992, was significantly altered, and developed, at Amsterdam. But Amsterdam satisfied few and is regarded as a compromise having been agreed by official-less Ministers late at night. It may also have demonstrated the limit of consensus on what the 15 can aspire to. The lowest common denominator of what is acceptable to national self-interest features throughout. Not legally binding until the Treaty is ratified by all member states, expected in 1999, there is much to be done in preparation for implementation. Interpretation will undoubtedly be contentious in some areas given the apparent ambiguities in some of the Treaty text. And there are worries about whether implementation can take place in some areas without either lengthy legal wrangling or subsequent challenges at the European Court of Justice (ECJ). If nothing more, Amsterdam has set a heavy and complex agenda for the next 5 years on JHA issues.

5. To date there are many areas where Europe has worked collectively under the Third Pillar; the swift reaction to the paedophile problem in Belgium and the joint action against sex tourism being recent examples.

Where there is a will at a practical level, for example police and judicial cross-border contact, co-operation can be very effective. However many of the policies recommended and instruments adopted post-Maastricht have had little effect; agreed conventions and some joint actions still need ratification by all members. It was hoped by some that Amsterdam would make more significant changes than it did.

6. In their desire to achieve greater freedom of movement, essentially driven by economic aims, the negotiators at Amsterdam have created a complex situation. The new Title IIIa, on free movement, immigration and asylum, is to be added to the First Pillar of the EU. Incorporating the Schengen acquis into the relevant part of the Treaties is also part of the move to create a more solid legal framework for an area of free movement. The three attached protocols to Title IIIa (Article 7a Protocol, UK Protocol on Free Movement and the Danish Protocol) allow for flexibility and 'opt-ins'.

7. Amsterdam has not provided a common interpretation of 'freedom of movement', but it has created additional flanking compensatory measures, thus tilting the balance towards security as against free movement (and ensuring the need for identification of EU citizens in order to identify those who are not). The difficulties in creating a common and agreed immigration and asylum policy, which so far does not exist, to replace the range of existing current objectives coping with individual national problems, will continue to stretch what is possible for EU member states acting by consensus. Serious and sensitive immigration issues such as readmission (where agreements with third countries may be causing more problems than they solve) and the question of temporary protection and burden sharing (with associated social costs) still need tackling.

8. Incorporating the Schengen acquis into the legal framework of the Union, as part of the drive towards freedom of movement, is likely to prove extremely problematic, and a lot of questions need to be answered in the process. Will the existing Schengen texts need to be changed to coincide with EU legislation with all this entails, and despite the desire of Schengen countries not to reopen the texts? What can be transferred into the First Pillar, what to the Third? Schengen has created tiers of 'ins' (including Schengen states Norway and Iceland which are outside the EU) and 'outs' (UK and Ireland). Serious questions remain to be answered about the extent to which those outside could actually 'opt-in' in practice, given the need for unanimity from those already involved.

9. European immigration and asylum issues need to be considered in a wider context, being inextricably linked to the issues of frontiers. The link increasingly made between immigration and crime however is not always accurate or healthy, and often based on preconceptions and media hype. Concern about the rise in drug trafficking and organised crime across EU borders, increasingly arising from outside the EU, has given added impetus to European co-operation both by practitioners on the ground and at the political level. Co-operation in police and criminal judicial matters remains a Third Pillar issue post Amsterdam, thus retaining its intergovernmental nature and the need for unanimity, although making provision for small groups of member states to develop closer co-operation.

10. The fight against organised trans-border crime needs to be flexible, proactive and adaptable, involving close co-operation between all involved. The management of information is a crucial aspect but there remain differences between those keen to centralise information and those recommending it be kept where it is needed, and data protection issues still need to be resolved. A project-based approach encouraging regional police co-operation is supported. Europol (European Police Office) and EDU are tangible signs of growing European law enforcement co-operation to tackle an expanding list of crimes. But it only goes so far, providing a limited operational support role, which is the maximum politically achievable so far. Europol is likely to develop into what member states want it to be based on their needs. Important questions about the accountability of Europol, and more generally of police offices operating extra-territorially, will need to be solved.

11. Customs co-operation, the administrative aspects of which are already achieved under the First Pillar in connection with the Single Market, will be enhanced in the Third Pillar by the Naples II convention on customs co-operation once it is signed and enters into force. This will also provide greater powers to national customs agencies to co-operate with one another.

12. Judicial co-operation in criminal matters lags behind police co-operation. Given that is impossible to harmonise legal processes, greater mutual recognition and co-ordination of other member states' judicial processes is crucial. Ways of speedy co-operation will be ever more important, as will understanding the legal systems, and legal changes of member states. The judiciary have a leading part to play in assisting the co-ordination, given that the obstacles to judicial co-operation are often at a very basic level. Points of national contact could be set up between states to hasten the exchange of judicial information and requests for assistance. The recommendations of the High Level Working Group, reporting after the Dublin Council, are welcomed by many. It called specifically for an assessment of the practical effects on the fight against organised crime of a 'closer union or harmonisation' of member states' legislation in this area.

13. The need to crack down on serious crime is not exclusive to EU members, and questions about the appropriate forum are raised. Is the EU not in danger of duplicating the Council of Europe's Conventions, for instance in mutual assistance?

14. Judicial co-operation in civil matters lags behind that in criminal matters, with one convention so far being agreed. This area too will transfer to the First Pillar after entry into force of the Amsterdam Treaty.

15. The implementation of the provisions of Amsterdam significantly alters the way the institutions will be involved in JHA co-operation, including the Council; the European Commission, with the unusual non-exclusive right of initiation on many issues over the next five years; the European Parliament, with an initial consultative role in many areas; and the European Court of Justice which has increased opportunities for involvement. The transition period set by many of the Treaty Articles could be an uncomfortable period, depending heavily on good co-ordination. Also, national Interior and Justice departments, more used to focusing on domestic issues, are being increasingly involved with their own Foreign Ministries and their European counterparts involving a change of culture and practice.

16. There are serious implications of Europe's developing JHA policies for both its neighbours and applicant countries. They need help in facing their different problems, not least their long land borders, the growing numbers of potential EU immigrants waiting in transit in neighbouring countries, and the increase in trafficking in illegal immigrants. Assistance from the EU is necessary if Europe's eastern neighbours are not to be seen as acting as a buffer zone to what some describe as 'Fortress Europe', not least given that a buffer has implications of being expendable. Applicant countries will be expected to reach the standards of existing EU members in many areas of JHA. But they should be allowed to contribute to the discussions, particularly in areas where the EU itself is still creating the ground rules rather than being treated to a 'structured monologue'. The period of transition for new members will be an important stepping stone for applicants.

17. Changes to the framework for co-operation in the EU's JHA will undoubtedly affect the EU's relations with third countries such as the USA or Canada. Without a legal personality in this area the EU cannot itself conclude treaties with third countries on issues such as readmission. There is concern that the more there is refinement of policies, the less able Europe is to speak to other countries.

18. For EU citizens there continues to be a need to ensure openness and accountability. It would be ironic if Amsterdam, which was supposed to create a Treaty for its people, is less easy for the European citizen to comprehend. Amsterdam may have made some JHA areas more open, particularly those to be moved to the First Pillar, but much could still be done. There is a need to monitor and evaluate the effectiveness of the policies. JHA also has poor image throughout Europe and the media can play a part here.

19. Changes made in the field of JHA at Amsterdam may have demonstrated the end of political consensus within Europe on these issues. Increased flexibility will result in different levels of participation and a multi-tiered approach. There is much on the agenda to be worked out and implemented and the sheer complexity of some of the issues is daunting. Clear political will is needed to drive the agenda through, similar to that for creating the Single Market or EMU, if an area of freedom, justice and security is really to be achieved for its citizens. The next 5 years will be crucial in determining just how far Europe is prepared to co-operate in areas which have traditionally been regarded as coming within the sovereign jurisdiction of national governments.

14

George C. Marshall and Dwight D. Eisenhower: Their Legacies and Visions and the Future of the Atlantic Community

Short Report on Conference WPS 97/8: 24–25 October 1997

Nicholas Hopkinson

1. This conference commemorated the fiftieth anniversary of George C. Marshall's famous speech of 5 June 1947 at Harvard University. With Europe in ruins after the Second World War, leaders on both sides of the Atlantic saw economic assistance and European integration as ways to promote European economic recovery.

2. George C. Marshall and General Dwight D. Eisenhower were two extraordinary men with great ability, courage, dedication, and foresight. Both men organised and believed in international alliances as the way to preserve global peace and build prosperity. Although the idea of commitment of more funds to Europe was a departure for the American public and politicians after the war, Marshall secured the massive funding needed to help rebuild war-torn Europe. Although many in Europe and the US believed Germany was still an enemy, Marshall and Eisenhower successfully argued that the West must solve the German 'problem' or the Soviets would resolve it in their favour. In entering into membership in the North Atlantic Treaty Organisation (NATO), the US in effect abandoned its past policy of belonging to 'entangling' alliances.

3. The Marshall Plan was much more than a 'generous' transfer of funds from the US to Europe. Not only did it help contain the spread of Communism in Europe, it encouraged Europeans to help themselves by requiring governments to submit domestic policies to international scrutiny, and promoted outward-looking economic policies which helped create competitive economies. The Marshall Plan is the cornerstone of the prosperity that both Europe and North America enjoy today.

4. Marshall and Eisenhower believed that European unity would be a source of economic strength and a contribution to future peace. While Jean Monnet is called the 'father' of the European Community, George Marshall can be regarded as its 'godfather'. The Marshall Plan underpinned the dramatic post-war shift in French policy towards Germany and created an economic and political environment which enabled the future European Union (EU) to flourish.

5. For almost fifty years, the relationship between Europe and North America was dominated by the political and military threats faced by the West. It has become a truism that the end of the Cold War has softened some of the cement in the transatlantic relationship. The main threats to Atlantic security are no longer from an ideologically-opposed bloc, but are more diverse in nature such as the resurgence of nationalism in the Balkans and elsewhere, terrorism, drug-trafficking and international crime.

6. While transatlantic security structures have been effective, transatlantic economic structures remained relatively weak, largely because the Marshall Plan organisation, the OEEC (the predecessor of the OECD), remained an inter-governmental association. As a result, at times the EU and the US have appeared to have rival rather than complementary interests. Without a strengthened inter-regional framework, the risk is that differences, mostly over trade issues, rather than common interests, will define the transatlantic relationship. Nevertheless, there is great potential for the EU and US to co-operate in foreign policy and economic areas because they share the same democratic and cultural values, have an enormous diversity of trading and other links, are members of the same key international organisations, and have similar industrial and regulatory structures.

7. Without a serious enemy, the purpose of NATO is often questioned. While some argue that NATO should die along with disappearance of the Soviet threat, the predominant view is that NATO should be retained because it keeps the US actively involved in Europe. If US military forces left Europe, the region would be less stable. The tragedy in the former Yugoslavia demonstrates that the EU is still not a credible security actor, and that NATO remains indispensable to the provision of military security in Europe. Furthermore, NATO remains an 'insurance policy' against a possible resurgence of nationalism in Russia.

8. In the post-Cold War world, publics in the EU and US have increasingly focused on domestic problems. The EU is concerned with its enlargement to Central and Eastern Europe, instability in the Russian Federation and North Africa, high unemployment, and the advent of Economic and Monetary Union (EMU). Some argue that the single European currency so preoccupies the EU that it makes it more difficult for it to focus on long-overdue economic reforms such as reform of labour markets, overly generous state pension schemes and the Common Agricultural Policy. It is countered that such reforms are currently politically difficult; once the single currency is in place, EMU will force the pace of economic reform. Meanwhile, the US and its citizens are preoccupied with crime, job security, other domestic economic issues and meeting economic challenges from Asia.

9. Some fear that the US is losing the art of alliance management, a talent that both Eisenhower and Marshall possessed and knew that was essential to the US national interest. If the US and EU do not co-operate, especially in the economic sphere, then there will be a greater temptation to act unilaterally. Recognising that old bonds need to be continuously renewed, in recent years many in the US and the EU have been looking for new ways to strengthen the transatlantic relationship.

10. US–EU economic co-operation is likely to be more successful than co-operation between other economies because industrial, commercial and regulatory structures are similar; there is extensive foreign investment in each others' economies; and because there is considerable exchange of staff. Given the enormous scale and depth of these ties, the US and EU have a mutual interest in eliminating barriers to trade. Investment, standards, government procurement, and competition policy are areas where the most concrete progress in liberalisation can be achieved in the short term. Such 'path-finding' agreements could more firmly anchor the US and EU to the multilateral trading system.

11. However others, especially Asians, are concerned that a closer US–EU link could harm the multilateral trading system. Excluding East Asia from any future bilateral arrangements would be a mistake, especially as US trade with the Pacific is greater than US trade with the EU, and because US trade with Asia is growing more rapidly.

12. Marshall established a lasting positive American attitude towards European unity. In spite of some serious disputes between Europe and the US, successive American governments remained convinced that European unity is in the best interest of the US as well as Europeans themselves. As an important 'door' through which the US 'approaches' Europe, the US would like to see the United Kingdom (UK) play a strong role in a cohesive Europe – this would be good for the UK, the EU and for the US. Given the UK's close ties in the past to the Commonwealth and continuing close ties with the US, it is hard for the UK to come to terms with Europe. While 'Eurosceptics' in Britain fear the loss of sovereignty to European institutions and believe the UK should build upon the transatlantic relationship and old Commonwealth ties, the new British government elected in May 1997 wants to play more of a leading role in Europe. As a result, some would argue that the UK's relations with the EU and the US have already been enhanced.

15

Political Stability in the Balkans and South-East Europe

Short Report on Conference 511: 27–31 October 1997

Chris Langdon

1. The crisis in the Balkans has moved south. While the principal focus of Western involvement remains Bosnia and the Bosnian Serb Republic, developments in Serbia, the Former Republic of Yugoslavia (FRY) and in Kosovo also require close attention from policy-makers and analysts.

2. Political events in Serbia have to be viewed with concern. In the elections for the Presidency of Serbia in December 1997 there is a real prospect of a victory by the extreme nationalist candidate who narrowly won the previous invalid round. The political strength of FRY President Slobodan Milosevic seems to be weakening. One sign of this is the victory of the reformist candidate in Montenegro's Presidential elections which will have an impact on Milosevic's power-base as the President of the FRY. A weakened Milosevic with Serbian voters apparently seeking a strong man and thus voting for an extreme nationalist is a dangerous prospect.

3. The most obvious flashpoint is the FRY province of Kosovo with its majority Albanian population. Preparations there for an infrastructure of organised violence are said to be under way. There have already been a series of attacks on police stations. This has to be taken in context with the frustration felt by young Kosovans at the failure to resolve running issues such as Albanian language education.

4. Ethnic Albanian communities in the Former Yugoslav Republic of Macedonia (FYROM), where tensions are also quite high, mean that the risk of spill-over has to be considered. While Albania has been the beneficiary of a successful donors conference in October, its stability cannot be taken for granted, as events showed earlier in 1997. And two other countries in the region, Bulgaria and Romania, are only one year into ambitious economic and political reform programmes.

5. In the Bosnian Serb Republic, the Assembly elections on 23 November 1997 will begin to resolve the key question of whether there is a domestic political alternative to Radovan Karadzic's Serb Democratic Party (SDS). If a credible coalition can be formed including President Biljana Plavsic's newly formed Serb National Alliance (SNS) party, then the next question for the international community will be the economic restructuring of Republika Srpksa. A long-term political settlement will take much longer, well after the full range of elections due in September 1998. But the lack of democracy in Serbia provides a fertile environment for the clique in Pale.

6. In Bosnia-Herzegovina, the question is: can the need for international support over the medium term be reconciled with the US domestic political agenda? Intervention may not have been wholly successful, but many argue that there is a moral imperative to stay and assist the process of reconstruction and democratisation. Society cannot be reconstructed in two years. That means agreeing the successor force to SFOR after June 1998 and the US role in it, and also looking at long-term development issues going beyond the September 1998 elections. It also means examining the international structures put in place after the 1995 Dayton Agreement.

7. As part of that re-examination of the Dayton structures, the international community would do well to look again at the lessons learnt in Bosnia-Herzegovina and in Albania. They pose questions for future peace-keeping operations, and on how the EU runs a common foreign and security policy effectively.

8. Serbia remains the key to stability in the region in many ways. The domestic situation in Serbia is bleak. The deepening economic crisis, the impact of economic isolation, and the largest number of refugees in the region, help to explain why the Milosevic regime is weakening. But it would be foolish to write Milosevic off. And a weakened Milosevic is potentially dangerous.

9. Both the Parliamentary and Presidential elections have been seen as a rebuff to Milosevic. The elections were boycotted by the Albanian community and part of Serbia's divided democratic opposition movement (a decision of questionable wisdom). In the September 1997 Parliamentary elections the governing parties' JUL-New Democracy won 110 of the 250 seats, a surprisingly low number given the electoral system. The opposition Serbian Renewal Movement won 45 seats. But the far right nationalist Serbian Radical Party (SRS) won 82 seats. The SRS, which is led by Vojislav Seselj whose war crimes are well documented, blends nationalism imperceptibly into fascism. Seselj has taken over the nationalist stance once espoused by Milosevic himself. Seselj and his party attract support from the poorly paid factory worker, the dispossessed, members of the armed forces, and also from many, including students, seeking a strong-man – the eternal problem of Serbian politics. Some Serb observers say it is wrong to assume that the Serbian electorate has necessarily become more nationalist. Seselj has tried hard to paint himself as a moderate in local terms. It is, they say, also rooted in Serbia's communist past, and it is a reaction to economic sanctions against Serbia and the perceived lack of assistance for Serbia's refugee problem. And 50% of the electorate did not vote, some through passivity, some as a result of the boycott by part of the opposition. The disunity in the democratic opposition plays into Seselj's hands as he appears an effective figure compared with the bickering democrats. Whatever the causes, parallels with the Weimar Republic are made with increasing frequency by Serbian observers. They also say that the international community's carrot and stick approach (with relatively little of the former) may have assisted the negative developments within the Serbian domestic political scene.

10. In the October 1997 Serbian Presidential elections Seselj beat Milosevic's nominee in the second round, but since less than 50% of the electorate voted, the election was invalid. On 7 December 1997 and possibly a later second round, Seselj will stand against Milan Milutinovic, the FRY Foreign Minister and close friend of Milosevic. It is uncertain if Milosevic will give more public support to Milutinovic.

11. Milosevic's own position as FRY President has been affected by the victory of the reformist Montenegrin Premier Milo Djukanovic in the Presidential elections in October. The next political battle in Montenegro, Parliamentary elections in 1998, is already looming with Milosevic's ally, the outgoing President Momir Bulatovic, determined to win a majority.

12. A Seselj victory in Serbia would pose severe difficulties for Western governments. The next twists and turns in Serbian and FRY politics are impossible to predict; but what is going on in Serbia is seen as a tragedy for the Serb people and for the region as a whole. It is too strategically important to be allowed to 'stew in its own juice' given its proven capacity to destabilise most of its neighbours simultaneously.

13. It is clear that Western policy-makers will have to focus on Kosovo in particular. It has long been seen as a potential tinder-box. Since Kosovo effectively lost its autonomy, the non-violent civil disobedience campaign has been led by Dr Ibrahim Rugova, leader of the Democratic League of Kosovo (LDK). There have been divisions within the leading politicians of Kosovo in recent years on strategy. But what is new is that the consensus on moderation is being broken by two new forces. First, students pushing for education in the Albanian language to be reintroduced in schools and universities are prepared to go to the streets. The demonstration on 29 October 1997 passed off relatively peacefully. International observers reported heavy police brutality during an earlier protest and they report that the police continue generally to abuse and mistreat Albanians. The protests are likely to continue as the balance of fear has been breached, say local observers. The issue behind the protests is that the memorandum of understanding on Albanian language education has not been implemented over a year after it was agreed.

14. Second, there is the rise of violence by Kosovar groups. International observers say that the pattern of violence has changed to a more frequent and sophisticated pattern. The Serb authorities say the Kosovo Liberation Army (KLA) is responsible for attacks on eleven Serbian police stations and for killing over 30 people. Twenty alleged members of the KLA are on trial in Pristina.

15. The Serbian police cannot go out at night, there is a vicious cycle of violence that Kosovar observers say has potentially no end. There are signs of further preparations being made – increases in the price of pack-animals is apparently one indicator. Firearms can be obtained locally, though tens of thousands of weapons are available in Albania. The next phase, observers predict, is the development of a political infrastructure for violent groups. As it is very clear that none of the present Kosovar political organisations advocate or support political violence, the political ideology behind a campaign of violence has yet to be outlined. An increase in violent activity in the spring of 1998 is predicted by some.

16. The potential consequence of rising violence in Kosovo coupled with the political dynamics developing in Belgrade is clear to all. It is true that doomsday scenarios have been outlined before by commentators. But one of the lessons of Bosnia is that more preventive activity upstream is essential to prevent such a conflict breaking out. This is particularly important in Kosovo as the possibility of spill-over cannot be ruled out. Pressure on the Serb authorities by the international community is ongoing.

17. In the neighbouring FYROM, which has its own Albanian minority (of about 20%), tensions are high in the Western part: in Gostivar 3 Albanians were killed and 100 injured on 9 July 1997 in demonstrations over the use of Albanian flags, and the Albanian language university in Tetovo is a long-running issue.

18. Albania is the other key factor as it is recovering from its own political crisis. There have been recent moves to normalise relations between Tirana and Belgrade. But with President Milosevic continuing to insist that Kosovo is a domestic FRY issue, Albanian Prime Minister Fatos Nano has been heavily criticised by the leadership in Pristina for his compliant stance.

19. While Albania itself appears more stable, and there is no doubt that Operation Alba achieved its objectives, Albania has been described as the first armed camp in Europe. In all, 625,000 guns were released. Some weapons were returned under an amnesty, but that still leaves one gun per male inhabitant. There has been a large amount of damage to the economy and to the infrastructure such as schools. The $600 million pledged at the October donors' conference has been set aside for a balance of payments programme up to March 1998. Longer and medium term financial agreements are under negotiation. For many Albanians remittances will continue to be a vital source of income. The harvest was sufficient, but there is a problem of cereal deficiencies. And there will be major problems in the supply of water and power.

20. There is a clear difference between the North of Albania – the area of Berisha's support where in some places there is no effective police force and no rule of law – and the South. Relative stability has returned in the South where the rebellion was at its most intense, and where the ruling coalition has much of its support. Issues for the international community include assistance for democratisation and the restructuring of civil society, the media and the police forces, and the redrawing of the constitution. And over the longer term, support for democratic normalisation. In Albania as in other parts of the region, stability needs democratisation. That will require a change of generation.

21. The elections for a new Bosnian Serb Parliamentary Assembly on 23 November 1997 are the first real test of whether political forces who advocate the rule of law and the implementation of the Dayton process can achieve a majority. The issue is whether President Biljana Plavsic's newly created SNS can win enough seats together with the other opposition parties to create a governing coalition that can run Republika Srpska (RS) until the multiple elections in September 1998. President Plavsic is seen by Western observers as a transitional figure. But it would be foolish to assume that Radovan Karadzic and his SDS will give up the levers of power easily. And as the Bosnian Serb Member of the collective Presidency, Karadzic's ally, Momcilo Krajisnik is able to block progress on key parts of the Dayton process. The political scene in Serbia itself gives the Pale leadership a background in which to operate.

22. If the SDS and their allies in the Serbian Radical Party are defeated in the November elections, the issue for the West is the provision of assistance for the RS. Figures in 1996 showed that only 2% of international assistance came to RS with 98% going to the Federation. The lack of investment on education and health care and pensions is clear. On pensions the rate in Sarajevo is 45 DM a month, in RS it is 25 DM a month. Spending on health in the RS is 25% of the rate in the Federation. The disparity in assistance is partly because the international community did not want to reward the regime in Pale, and also because the Bosnian Serbs did not send a delegation to the donors conference in April 1996 on legal grounds. The gap has reached dangerous proportions. If there is political progress in the November elections, then it is important that voters feel that it is worth voting for pro Dayton parties by the time of the September 1998 elections.

23. (a) The first phase of reconstruction is over in the Federation. The second and harder phase over the next two years is about to begin. The issues are building a business climate: privatisation, developing banking and tax revenue collection systems. A sustainable economy has to be developed that is integrated into the European economy and has access to international financial markets, and can attempt to regain markets lost during the war. It is estimated that the war damage amounts to $20 billion and another $20 billion is needed for investment and to upgrade production facilities to put the Federation and RS back on their feet.

After a slow start the international community has created the infrastructure to provide the necessary assistance for economic development, and a donor conference in the spring is proposed to tackle the issue of refugee return by providing further accommodation facilities, 'swing-space' to assist the return process.

However a very large range of problems remain to be tacked. Corruption has got much press coverage. Specialists say it is not true that the economy is totally corrupt. International assistance projects are carefully monitored. There are important issues that have to be tackled including smuggling and customs revenue evasion as well as corruption. The lack of a functioning state with the failure to agree on Ministry buildings and staffing means there is not a proper administration. Meetings of Ministers and legislators are too infrequent to ensure that laws are passed in due time. The privatisation law was passed in October 1997 after a delay of a year. There has also been no agreement on a number of laws including those on a temporary currency design, on unified licence plates and on national symbols, despite the deadlines set by the Peace Implementation Council (PIC) at Sintra in May 1997.

(b)   There are longer term issues on the military side, including the Presidency's Standing Committee on Military Matters (SCMM), which is designed to be the constitutional mechanism in which military matters are co-ordinated. The rules of procedures have been agreed, and it had its first full meeting in September 1997. It is due to met again in November.

In terms of NATO, observers contrast early concerns over 'mission creep' with SFOR's robust action in taking control of transmitters to prevent Pale television broadcasting propaganda. It is now an active partner in the elections and in the reconstruction process.

(c)   The issue now after the September 1997 Municipal Elections is to get local government and local coalitions going. Since people were allowed to vote in the municipality in which they registered for the 1991 census, thousands of people displaced during the war voted for municipalities in what are now parts of the other entity. The OSCE and the Office of the High Representative have drawn up an Implementation Plan for Elected Officials. The OSCE has said it will not issue a final certification until every municipal council has convened with all members. Enforcing the election results on the ground will be difficult.

24. One issue is whether the powers of the High Representative should be increased. This brings up the question of whether there should be a Dayton Two. While there is a consensus that the Dayton Agreement is deeply flawed there are many reasons for arguing it is the least worst option. It is clear that the civilian structure was not given enough emphasis during the negotiations or in the initial implementation. The determination of the United States to by-pass the United Nations, and create a new civilian structure has left a legacy of problems which have to be considered for future operations.

25. Many recoil at the idea of Dayton Two on the grounds that as it would be impossible to negotiate. The most contentious issue is partition. One model cited is that of cantons. Advocates say that multi-national societies are an American vision that doesn't necessarily work in Europe. Instead they cite European models such as Switzerland or Belgium. Such a model is attractive for the Bosnian Croats of Herzegovina. Others describe full partition for Bosnia as morally wrong and strategically reckless. SFOR, they say, would have to herd refugees to ethnic ghettos – a Bosniak mini-state is not viable unless there are international forces stationed there in perpetuity.

26. The timetable for US military involvement is also getting in the way of the process. However it is clear that the debate is still ongoing within the Clinton Administration on the retention of American presence on the ground after June 1998. There are press suggestions that a decision could be made by the time of the meeting of NATO Defence Ministers in early December. There is a consensus in Europe that there has to be a replacement force for SFOR after June 1998, and that it is vital that the US maintains a significant presence on the ground.

27. The role of the OSCE needs to be decided. For example the Provisional Election Commission, which has supervised the elections since September 1996, has no mandate after the 23 November 1997 elections in the RS.

28. The arrest of war criminals is still unresolved – human rights observers argue that they are an infection of society. There has been some progress with the agreement that 10 alleged war criminals from the Bosnian Croat side go to trial in the Hague. But the Hague Tribunal is seen by Croats and others in the region as an instrument of political power rather than an impartial court.

29. Policing is a long-term issue as there will be other conflict prevention missions where a strong policing element is also required. The UN International Police Task Force (IPTF) is described as a Cinderella organisation. It has no standing reserves. Unlike national armed forces who are easily deployed there is no simple way of recruiting civilian police for international duties. Not all countries have standing police forces. There has been insufficient funding, and the standards of the contributed forces is variable. The IPTF's mandate is due to expire at the end of 1997. This is a problem that those involved in peace-keeping need actively to consider. NATO Secretary-General Javier Solana has recently proposed a permanent international police force, which he argued, could improve the international community's ability to manage crises, if well-funded and well-equipped and available quickly.

30. The European Union has to consider the lessons from Operation Alba which operated under the previous Maastricht Treaty rules. The revision of the Treaty text on Common Foreign and Security Policy (CFSP) by the Inter-Governmental Conference (IGC) at the Amsterdam Summit left open questions such as when the Union considers a future force and whether only the contributing members, or all EU members, participate in the decision-making process.

31. One of the practical successes of Alba was the establishment of an ad hoc co-ordinating body: the Political Steering Committee consisting of the Political Directors of the eleven troop contributing countries and a range of international organisations including the OSCE, WEU, NATO and ICRC. It set the political framework, and acted as interlocutor with the UN Security Council and the Albanian authorities.

32. The crisis in Albania also shows the importance of crisis prevention. The failure to react to the rigging of the 1996 elections, highlighted by the OSCE at the time, allowed the pyramid scandals to blow up into a full scale crisis by March 1997.

33. Conflict prevention remains the key. It may be unglamorous and Treasuries will begrudge the costs. The aim is not to solve the situation, but to bring it under control. This has often been said before, but is often forgotten as crises blow up apparently unexpectedly, as Albania did in 1997. It is therefore vital that the international community watches events in Kosovo and Serbia and the FRY with great attention, particularly as so much attention will be on EMU and EU enlargement.

34. For the long term, it is clear that the international involvement will need to be prepared for a long and painful haul until there is the emergence of local political stability, with domestic institutions beginning to function without artificial respiration from outside. Even then success is not guaranteed.

16

The Relationship Between Greece and Turkey: Can It Be Improved?

Short Report on Conference WPS 97/10: 31 October – 2 November 1997

Colin Jennings

1. The end of the Cold War has produced a far less static world, but the relationship between Greece and Turkey appears to be stuck in a time warp. The Greeks feel militarily threatened, while the Turks feel strategically besieged. This is directly contrary to the security and the economic interests of both countries, and carries the risks of a future crisis erupting which could be hard to control (as the dispute last year over Imia/Kardak vividly demonstrated). The international community, and especially the European Union (EU), has a major interest in a far better relationship between the two countries.

2. The mistrust between the two countries is not, of course, of recent origin. But as the second millennium draws to a close, enlightened opinion in both countries is calling for a rapprochement based on mutual benefit. Both countries have fallen into the trap of holding up a mirror image of each other: politicians appeal too readily to nationalistic sentiment, the media and educational systems highlight hostility rather than shared needs, and governments allow themselves to be led by public opinion rather than seek to shape it.

3. Yet a reduction in tension would have obvious benefits. Cuts in Greek defence expenditure would greatly facilitate major national objectives of modernising the economy and joining a single European currency. A more positive relationship with Greece coupled with the improvements in human rights and a Cyprus settlement, called for in the European Commission's Agenda 2000 document, would greatly assist Turkey's aspirations to join the EU. This would in turn strengthen democracy and stability in Turkey.

4. In addition to political and public distrust, there are three areas in particular which cause tension: Turkey's links to Europe; air and sea rights in the Aegean; and Cyprus. The conference identified ways in which progress could potentially be made on all three of these:

(a)   the Greeks argued that it was in Greece's interests that Turkey should join the EU as soon as the Copenhagen criteria had been met. Some felt that Greek governments had made the mistake of leading criticism of Turkey within the EU and blocking such measures as the provision of financial assistance under the Customs Union. It was welcome that Foreign Minister Pangalos publicly supported Turkey's European vocation in 1997, implying eventual Turkish membership of the EU. Greek governments should work to promote this. This would have a very positive impact in Turkey given that EU membership had become a top national priority;

(b)   on the Aegean, it was argued that both sides devoted more economic resources to protecting their possible future rights than could possibly be gleaned economically from the exploitation of those rights. There was a need for each side to understand and not to distort the position of the other. Some Greek participants suggested that, while a global negotiation on the Aegean was ruled out, movement on specific issues would inevitably lead to movement on others. It was suggested that there could be merit in considering ways in which experts could be brought in for a fresh review of ways of achieving progress, possibly with outside chairmanship;

(c)   on Cyprus, both countries should seek to work together as in the 1950s to encourage a settlement on the island in line with UN resolutions, and meeting the security concerns of both communities. The involvement of NATO might help to provide reassurance over security. The EU dimension could, if managed with due regard to the interests of all concerned, help to promote a resolution of this dispute.

5. But progress on these issues lay largely in the hands of governments. Far-sighted leadership was undoubtedly needed on core political and security issues. There was a case for taking some steps unilaterally out of self-interest and to demonstrate goodwill. The core aspirations of the two countries involved common visions of the need for stability, democracy and prosperity. These pointed to finding ways of developing a relationship of interdependence including joint pursuit of common goals. In this context, non-governmental efforts to improve bilateral links could also benefit from an enlightened vision of the future by the two governments. Non-governmental links could make a real impact provided they were supported by politicians. Contact between the two countries was at a woefully low level, and the authorities on both sides often created difficulties for those wishing to meet. The deliberate and sustained effort made by the French and German governments after the Second World War to promote a wide range of contacts between their citizens showed what could be achieved if governments made a determined effort to remove long-standing hostility.

6. The conference unanimously called on the two governments to create a fund (if possible backed by the EU) to pay for a wide range of non-governmental meetings between Greeks and Turks designed to increase knowledge and understanding between the two countries. It was pointed out that stopping the purchase of one tank each would fund the cost of an enormous number of meetings. Contact in a number of areas could be particularly fruitful:

(a)   Members of Parliament from the two countries should establish regular meetings away from the confrontational environments on the Council of Europe or the European Parliament;

(b)   historians and educationalists should meet to recommend less confrontational language in school books;

(c)   the study of each other's language, culture, etc. should be encouraged in universities;

(d)   the steps already recommended by businessmen from the two countries to reduce regulations, promote trade and tourism, increase cooperation in the insurance, financial and shipping sectors, and work on joint infrastructure projects should be actively supported by the two governments and further bilateral business meetings encouraged;

(e)   media cooperation should be promoted, e.g. to facilitate regular meetings between the heads of the television news departments, programmes about each other's countries and dispassionate discussion of the bilateral relationship in the media;

(f)   meetings of Greeks and Turks in the areas bordering each other in the Aegean should be strongly backed;

(g)   cultural exchange programmes should be initiated, including town-twinning, youth visits, arts exhibitions, etc.;

(h)   other normal contacts between neighbours, such as sports matches and meetings of environmentalists should be encouraged;

(i)   contact should be established between academic institutions, especially those working on strategic issues.

7. As a Greek participant commented, Greece has a bigger stake than any other EU member in a democratic, stable and prosperous Turkey. EU membership for Turkey and pending that, the clear prospect of it, would promote these aims. The Greek government should therefore do all it can to help achieve it. And as a Turkish participant observed, the conference demonstrated that the Greeks have gained national self-confidence through their membership of the EU and are therefore prepared to be more far-sighted. There was an urgent need for both sides to translate this into action to avert another self-defeating downward spiral. Some proposals were made to pursue that goal and discussions to refine them set in hand.

17

Economic and Monetary Union:
Economic and Political Implications

Short Report on Conference 512: 3–7 November 1997

Nicholas Hopkinson

1. The majority view in this conference was that Economic and Monetary Union (EMU) will start on time on 4 January 1999 with 11 European Union (EU) Member States, including Italy, participating. By 2003, every EU Member State will participate in EMU. Although EMU will be sustainable, the first major tensions may occur when the European economic cycle next turns down, perhaps around 2005.

2. EMU will provide clear benefits to companies, especially Small and Medium Enterprises, in the form of exchange rate stability, lower inflation and lower interest rates. Of the many benefits, the lower cost of capital will by far be EMU's major benefit. The real obstacle to growth in the EU has not been labour market inflexibility, but inefficient capital markets. The anticipated integration of European capital markets and a major rationalisation of the European banking sector will be a major boost to EU competitiveness.

3. Those against EMU, whether in principle and/or in practice, argue that European leaders will commit a major mistake when they decide in May 1998 to proceed with EMU because companies and governments are not well prepared. The advantages of EMU do not obviously outweigh the risks – the gain is simply not worth the pain. Although it is conceded that there will be benefits from exchange rate stability, the benefits of EMU for investment and employment are less certain. EMU cannot be sustained because the European Central Bank (ECB) will not have the instruments to do its tasks. Should EMU run into difficulty, the fallout would go beyond economics. For example, asymmetric economic shocks would lead to demands for fiscal transfers. As the EU budget is small, only 1.27 per cent of EU GDP, Member States would probably have to bail-out other Member States. This would provoke outcries from taxpayers in some Member States. In order to avoid upheaval, EMU should be delayed for five years. However, most believe that postponement of EMU is no longer likely; furthermore, postponement would lead to the abandonment of the entire project. According to one analogy, if one postponed the marriage date, then couples wouldn't get married and they wouldn't have children.

4. It is widely believed that heads of government in May 1998 will pre-announce the rate at which their currencies will be converted into the Euro, a decision that it is hoped will enable currencies to 'glide' smoothly into EMU and avoid instability and massive currency speculation. The majority view was that speculation in the run up to EMU is unlikely to succeed. Already George Soros has stated that EMU will be a 'non-event'. Nevertheless, disagreements, whether real or perceived, between central bankers and the politicians, could still cause turbulence in international currency markets.

5. Although there will be a few teething problems, EMU is unlikely to collapse. The main risk attached to EMU is a systemic collapse of the banking system. While some believed that EMU may have to change in light of events, the majority view was that European economic and social systems, particularly in Germany and in Mediterranean countries, will have to reform because of EMU. EMU is likely to accelerate reform of many social systems, especially generous state pension provision in Mediterranean Member States.

6. It is hard to predict whether the Euro will be a hard or soft currency. Nevertheless there is a good possibility that the Euro will become a strong currency because central bankers will not suddenly implement a loose monetary policy once the ECB is established. Furthermore, the ECB will be more immune to political pressures because it will operate outside national political frameworks. There needs to be an effective check on the ECB to ensure that it is accountable. Some believe that this is best done at the European level, perhaps by the European Parliament. Federalists and Eurosceptics agree that political scrutiny at the European level may be the outcome, but they do not agree that this should be the goal.

7. The British Chancellor of the Exchequer's late October 1997 statement favouring entry into EMU in principle was revolutionary in the British political context. While some believe his statement did not go far enough, others believe it went too far. The lack of synchronisation of the British economic cycle with the rest of the European economy is regarded as the most important short-term barrier to British entry. Perhaps a more important barrier is that the British government does not want to run too far ahead of public opinion which is still largely opposed to the abolition of the pound sterling. Nevertheless, the recently launched Euro preparation programme and the future referendum campaign are likely to build public support that will facilitate the United Kingdom's entry into EMU.

8. The success of EMU is also important for countries seeking to join the EU. Should EMU fail, enlargement would be postponed indefinitely. By voluntarily seeking to meet the EMU convergence criteria, candidate states will reinforce their economic reforms and promote growth, and as a result enhance their chances of qualifying for EU membership. In particular, Central and East European Countries (CEECs) must continue to lower their deficits through privatisation programmes and structural reform, especially reform of social security systems. If these policies are sustained and if CEECs join the EU around 2002, a few CEECs may join EMU in 2004 with most joining around 2009.

9. Markets will determine whether the Euro becomes an international reserve currency. However, the initial use of the Euro as a reserve currency is likely to be low. The US will lose seignorage income as use of the Euro increases. If the Euro and dollar become the two major global reserve currencies, and with efficient futures and derivatives markets, the use of gold as a reserve currency could decline. Although the Euro may supplant the US dollar in US–EU transactions, it is unlikely to supplant the dollar in US–Asian transactions.

10. The impact of the new currency will be deflationary, in part because there will be greater price transparency across Europe. This in turn is likely to increase pressure for harmonisation of fiscal policies and taxation rates.

11. Although there has been considerable progress within the last year in preparing for the introduction of the Euro, many companies need to accelerate planning. The cost to companies of converting to the new currency will not be materially significant. By not having adequate corporate strategies, accounting systems and the right machinery in place, there is a possibility that some companies could go bankrupt. However, the scale of bankruptcy is not expected to be significant. In the absence of banknotes and coins circulating during the three-year transition period between 1999 and 2002, the Euro will become widely used through cards and electronic means. As the Euro is introduced, communication with the public about EMU and its implications will be important.

12. The physical introduction of the Euro, on a no compulsion and no prohibition basis during the transition period, is a dynamic process that is moving faster than originally expected. Although this three-year period serves as a 'comfort' zone for some Member States, others are beginning to question why it must be so long. The focus of discussion about EMU has therefore moved beyond debating its pros and cons towards ensuring that the concrete preparations for EMU are properly in place.

18

The Transatlantic Relationship: Strengthening Dialogue and Cooperation

Short Report on Conference WPS 97/6: 10–14 November 1997

Richard Latter

1. The close relationship between European and North American states is likely to remain strong for the foreseeable future. The United States remains proactive and engaged in Europe and its presence is supported by West European governments because of historical security ties, mutually compatible national interests, and shared values.

2. However, problems are emerging, notably over trade and commercial issues, which may make future cooperation more difficult.

3. Nevertheless, friction between the 'West' and the rest of the world deriving from the rise of new economic powers, notably in Asia, and increasing differences over standards of trade may serve to draw North Americans and Europeans together. For this to occur, transatlantic partners will have to deal with problems associated with perceived differences between Anglo-Saxon and Continental models of capitalism; the rise of regionalism within the global economy (notably driven by EU integration and the creation of NAFTA); and the need to maintain the impetus of global trade liberalisation and to promote further reductions of barriers to trade.

4. It will be mutually beneficial for North Americans and Europeans to further strengthen security links; to help to maintain one another's prosperity and economic interdependence; and to ensure mutual respect is maintained as solutions to economic problems are sought.

5. A clarification of mutual perceptions is required, particularly between leadership elites in the United States and the European Union. European concerns about perceived US uncertainty regarding EU integration need to be allayed; the idea that Americans are less than enthusiastic about European integration because they will have to deal with an 'equal partner', and be less able to command unquestioned leadership, needs to be put aside. Europeans must reassure Americans that a stronger Europe will remain committed to the pursuit of economic prosperity and political stability in collaboration with North American partners.

6. More specifically, there is an urgent need to resolve differences arising from the Helms–Burton legislation, from recent WTO rulings on bananas, concerning acceptable levels of carbon dioxide and other pollution emissions, and regarding the utility of the United Nations and its future reform. These differences must not be allowed to reinforce a trend towards the re-nationalisation of Western countries' foreign policies.

7. While a partnership across the Atlantic is generally perceived to be to a 'common good', some fear increasing US global domination, noting the negative economic trends in Europe which point towards its relative economic decline; this would prompt a reduction of US interest in the region and its willingness to cooperate with European partners. Measures must be taken to reverse European loss of competitiveness, low growth, high long-term unemployment and the general lack of economic flexibility in European economies. Europeans must be encouraged to invest venture capital in higher risk enterprises and in the high technology sector. A buoyant European economy is essential for the maintenance of a genuine partnership.

8. Proposals to this end include the creation of a North Atlantic Economic Community to provide a framework for commercial cooperation akin to that existing in APEC. This framework would facilitate both continued US engagement in Europe and more outward-looking European economic policies. It could be a reaffirmation of a 'Western vision'; but it remains to be seen whether this idea will attract significant political support on either side of the Atlantic.

9. The integration of Central Europe into Western institutions is essential even as a redefinition of 'the West' and Western policies occurs. Integration efforts must be strengthened further and prospects for this are encouraging given the enlargement agendas established in 1997 by the European Union and NATO and the fact that both organisations have retained 'open doors' for possible additional members. Any 'redefinition of the West' must extend beyond the purely economic realm. Significant security risks remain and the states on either side of the Atlantic can best deal with them on a collaborative basis. For example, problems exist to the south and south-east of Europe which are already generating instability and giving rise to terrorist incidents which affect citizens of the transatlantic countries.

10. Terrorism and associated criminality, not least the possible challenge of terrorist use of weapons of mass destruction, must be faced in a cooperative way. Actions should include increased and more effective sharing of intelligence; standardisation of legal provisions where possible and at least a better understanding of one another's legal systems; increased personal contacts; and improved police cooperation. A common 'zero tolerance' of terrorism is essential.

11. Despite a general commonality of view regarding terrorism, how best to react to states' sponsorship of terror groups has generated US–European friction. Divisive issues include the circumstances in which economic sanctions should be introduced, whether the laws governing such sanctions should apply extraterritorially, and the impact of anti-terrorism efforts on the commercial position of a nation's companies.

12. Such potentially explosive cocktails of security and economic issues are a long-standing feature of transatlantic relations; it has often been feared that they would adversely affect cooperation on security issues and NATO solidarity. However, the security situation in Europe has altered radically. No major threats to Western European states' territories exist following the end of the Soviet threat. As a consequence, NATO is restructuring to be able to deploy military forces outside Europe to undertake the tasks of threat prevention, instability management, and peace support. This change is occurring at different speeds in different countries.

13. Partially as a consequence, some perceive a difference of emphasis in US and European policies; Americans placing greater emphasis on military responses to security risks and Europeans stressing the need for diplomatic and negotiated solutions. A 'disconnect' between US global concerns and the essentially regional European focus is felt to be apparent. There is a growing US view that NATO must be used to defend common US and European interests outside Europe and there is US concern that some European governments are at best ambivalent about the prospect. The growing technology gap between the United States and Europe needs to be diminished if Americans and Europeans are to contribute equally to future Alliance operations. Europeans will need to develop a significant force projection capability and a related commitment to cooperate with the United States as an equal partner in undertaking military operations outside the European theatre.

14. Such a future European role has by no means universal appeal, not least because of the envisaged costs involved. While some advocate the evolution of a genuinely independent European Security and Defence Identity, of a *Europe puissant,* others are less enthusiastic, not least because they fear an erosion of national sovereignty should such a project be realised. Others take the view that a European security partnership with the US remains essential, that sufficient European resources must be dedicated to building up required defence capabilities, and that political decision-making backed by sufficient political will must be put into place to enable Europeans to act effectively in the defence and foreign policy fields. A near-term goal would be the adoption of a central role by Europeans in the conduct of post-SFOR operations in Bosnia.

15. Progress on these issues will require an effective NATO Alliance. Support for this defence organisation must be maintained during a period in which there is no immediate direct threat to its members. The degree to which NATO is to function as a collective defence or a collective security organisation, or a combination of the two, has to be clarified.

16. It is important that the traditions of consensus within the Alliance and the commitment to coherent policies be retained. As the role of the Alliance changes and expands, it is necessary to ensure that resources are available to carry out commitments effectively and that the Alliance does not become over-stretched.

17. Strengthened cooperation between the Alliance and non-NATO states is necessary, for example to conduct peace support operations effectively. There is a particular need to clarify relationships and increase cooperation with Ukraine and Russia.

18. Changing NATO and maintaining cordial transatlantic economic relations will require consistent public support over a number of years and media attitudes will affect levels of support. While the media legitimately seeks to report upon differences and inconsistencies between North American and European governments, it is important that such reporting should be responsible. This will be particularly important when crises occur which increase the normally low levels of public interest in foreign policy issues.

19. Despite frictions, the habit of collaboration and tradition of mutual support existing across the Atlantic remain strong. With responsible leadership and mutual respect, the prospects for a close and mutually-beneficial transatlantic relationship are good as the twentieth century draws to a close.

19

The United Nations in the Twenty-First Century

Short Report on Conference WPS 97/9: 14–16 November 1997

Sam Daws

1. The conference examined where the UN's comparative advantages lie as it seeks to combine universality with subsidiarity, and to adapt to changes in the geopolitical landscape. It considered whether the *Track 2* reform proposals of Secretary-General Kofi Annan herald radical change or mere institutional reshuffling.

2. There has been limited recent progress on *Track 2*, the regular budget assessment scale and Security Council reform. Caucuses such as the Non-Aligned Movement (NAM) and the G77 may be viewed as restricting progress through their emphasis on group consensus, but may be needed in response to a 'politics of exclusion' whereby major developing country powers are left out of fora such as the G7/G8. The unique influence of the United States, for good or ill, is also significant in the creation of the present impasse.

3. Most conflicts are now intra-State. The centre–periphery model can be applied to the structural imbalances inherent in such conflicts. Successful conflict prevention entails power-sharing within a country; the sense of common belonging combined with the value of diversity; the building of democratic practices and values; a strong (but not oppressive) State; non-divisive leadership; the political will to act on early warning data; and a spectrum of mechanisms and actors. It is long term, highly unglamorous, very difficult, but entirely necessary.

4. Successful UN peace-keeping requires political will; from this flow workable mandates and commensurate resources. The tragedy of Bosnia was that UN peace-keepers were sent in when there was no peace to keep and were replaced by NATO war-fighters when there was no war to fight. Peace-keepers in Bosnia were criticised for not taking sides against one of the factions, exactly what *was* criticised in Somalia. Delegating peace-keeping to regional organisations is hampered by a lack of financial and logistical resources, a potential lack of impartiality, and the absence of regional mechanisms in some parts of the world.

5. The UN can mount both traditional Cyprus-type operations and more 'robust' or 'credible' operations, under Chapter VII. It cannot mount protracted combat operations. Agreed definitions of command and control, and improvements in logistical support are essential. The military can only supply a security umbrella; if the underlying peace process is not a success, then the military operation will have only achieved an expensive cease-fire. Over-reliance in the Department of Peace-keeping Operations on Gratis Military Officers (GMOs) from developed countries is undesirable, but phasing out GMOs without budgeting for their replacement should be avoided.

6. *Globalisation* presents the UN system with the transnational phenomena of crime, terrorism, and drugs. Addressing such problems is intrinsic to, not additional to, UN work for peace, development, and human rights. Co-operation and integration on a pragmatic basis is preferred over institutional merger as a means of dealing with them. Effectiveness may be diminished because of the reluctance of States to share intelligence and security information. Emphasis on drugs could be shifted from a supply-side to a demand reduction approach.

7.   Humanitarian action is more than humanitarian assistance. The basic aim of UN humanitarian action should be human *security*, with the key to security being physical rather than legal *protection*. In Bosnia the Security Council failed to provide an adequate mandate or number of troops to protect civilians in UN 'safe areas'. In Rwanda, the international community rejected UN Secretariat requests for additional troops that might have contained the genocide. The awakened interest in humanitarian issues in the Council may be less indicative of a new spirit of resolve to act on humanitarian issues than a sign that agreement on political, let alone military, action cannot be reached. Many questions remain. At what point does maintaining silence in order to gain access to victims of human rights become complicity in those abuses? What measures can be taken to ensure that, in the absence of political and military action to resolve a conflict, aid provided does not contribute to its perpetuation? If humanitarian norms are being flouted, at what point do humanitarian agencies withdraw?

8.   The UN has a key role in humanitarian norm setting, and in ensuring integration of humanitarian action with the political/conflict resolution and development/rehabilitation processes. An integrated UN field and headquarters approach is preferable to the bureaucracy of a 'super agency'. The fulfilment of State responsibilities depends upon the realisation that humanitarian norms and behaviour are compatible with national interests, especially national and sub-regional security concerns.

9.   UN human rights work, whilst facing chronic under-funding, must move from standard-setting to implementation. Economic, cultural and social rights are as important as civil and political rights. Problems with the justiciability of the former arise more from how to agree on a timeframe within which to measure progress, than in the elaboration of evidential standards. Equality and justice for women, and the rights of children and minorities, should be central concerns. Human rights education, sensitive to indigenous value systems, can help entrench universal cultural rights. National protection systems can be strengthened through the ratification and implementation of international treaties. Confidence-building measures are needed to move beyond the frame of 'accusers and the accused'. Attacks on the impartiality and even physical security of rapporteurs have increased. Perceptions of inconsistency stem from variable political will to act in similar cases, and from selective use of UN and regional mechanisms.

10.   To entitle the UN Secretary-General to request advisory opinions from the International Court of Justice (ICJ) could be problematic. If the legal matter concerns an inter-State dispute the parties might as well go directly to the Court. Recourse to advisory opinions may undermine the use of the Court's binding contentious procedure. There may be drawbacks to allowing non-State actors, be they international organisations or NGOs, to become *litigant*s through an amendment to Article 34 of the ICJ Statute.

11. The meaning and practical implementation of judicial review of Security Council decisions by the Court remains elusive; what is the distinction between interpretation and review? Can the Court challenge a Security Council finding that a threat to international peace exists? Even if it cannot, can the Court examine the measures taken by the Security Council to ensure their proportionality to the wrong done, or their compatibility with other existing legal obligations?

12. A proliferation of standards and institutional approaches exist in inter-State relations, international organisations, and in international regimes reflecting national enforcement systems. Legitimacy problems have arisen where international law has been applied to individuals, both in the legal basis of *ad hoc* tribunals, and in the uneven nature of normative processes (e.g. the death penalty being used in national Rwandan courts, but not in cases before the International Tribunal for Rwanda).

13. On the development front, infant mortality rates and life expectancy have improved sharply since the 1960s, some developing countries have made striking economic progress, and the world conferences have set clear goals and targets for the 21st century. On the down side, ODA has declined by 14% since UNCED, and shows little sign of reversal. The Least Developed Countries are unlikely to benefit from the Multilateral Agreement on Investment (MAI), nor do they receive much Foreign Direct Investment. Debt reduction/elimination has still been elusive. 'New and additional resources' to fund the South after Rio have not materialised.

14. Some governments have doubts about the channelling of ODA though UN agencies. Country level coordination between UN agencies and the Bretton Woods institutions is vital. Reconciling the economic, social and ecological objectives of sustainable development is difficult without a mechanism to implement Agenda 21; an Inter-Governmental Panel on Financing Sustainable Development could be established. When the money spent on dog and cat food in the US is greater than the budget of a dozen developing countries, progress in development may ultimately depend upon changes to the spiritual underpinnings of society.

15. The UN is in essence a global communications agency; its comparative advantage lies in its ability to both frame and lead the debate on an issue. As an advocate for the poor, the UN must also have the capability to act as a global persuader. Many people respect the UN but do not see its relevance to them. The *Track 2* proposals are a modest beginning for the real reorientation needed in both image and substance.

The Secretariat should have freedom in implementing the priorities set by Member States; micro-management by States, and by some UN officials, has been harmful to its effectiveness.

16. Controversy surrounds whether the Secretary-General should be merely the servant of Member States, or be given a higher profile to exercise moral authority promoting the values of the UN directly to the peoples of the world. These two approaches are potentially reconcilable if the Secretary-General is regarded as spokesman, advocate and implementer of a consensus arrived at by Member States.

17. The credibility of the UN has been harmed in the past when the Secretariat has been required to defend the UN as an institution when criticism, e.g. over Srebrenica and Somalia, should have been targeted at the failure of political will by Member States. UN staff must carry out the mandates entrusted to them, but could be permitted to report publicly when they have been given insufficient resources to execute a given mandate.

20

Japan's Role in the World

Short Report on Conference 513: 17–21 November 1997

Robin Hart

1. Japan is undergoing significant economic and political reform. Japan's global role is also evolving. With extensive overseas investment, significant trading links and sizeable overseas development aid (ODA) Japan is increasingly acting as a global player, taking a more active part in building and sustaining the new post-Cold War order. Japan's foreign policy agenda will continue to be dominated by managing and balancing the key relationship with the USA, by the desire and need to strengthen and improve diplomatic ties regionally, and by building bilateral relationships with China, Russia, Korea, and the Asian region. Although not seeking a leadership role, Japan is concerned when others do not welcome its involvement in global issues, as is demonstrated by the current debate over Japan's permanent membership of the United Nations Security Council. As Japan acknowledges, the legacy of the past still needs to be dealt with correctly when managing future diplomatic relations. As Japan becomes a more normal state its traditional diplomatic 'constructive ambiguity' will be challenged and Japan will face hard choices.

2. Japan's role in the world has become more of a domestic political issue since the Gulf War, when Japan was criticised for not joining the coalition or supplying men and materials, despite significant contributions to its costs. If Japan is to play a larger international role however, the key question of the constitution is raised. There is now a majority in Japan expressing revisionist views, particularly since the Gulf War. But there is still a large majority against the use of collective self-defence and the existence of armed forces. The constitution is likely to become a serious political issue over the next 5 to 10 years which, in turn, will determine Japan's foreign policy. A recommended revision of Article 9, proposed by the Yomiuri Shinbun in 1994, included a number of new provisions: existing self-defence forces would be given legal basis; it opposed weapons of mass destruction; and it provided for Japanese contributions to international peacekeeping.

3. Since 1993 Japan has experienced significant political change with coalition and multi-party government, shifting party realignment under the new electoral system and party de-alignment among voters. Many predict future changes to the political scene. Others are confident that the changes and reforms taking place will create a stable democratic system within the next 2–3 elections. But internal reforms (including reform of the administration, economic structure, financial system and fiscal policy) will only be successful if there is clear political vision and effective policy implementation. Constantly changing Prime Ministers does not help stable foreign policy decision-making.

4. Opinions on Japan's economy range from optimistic to pessimistic with many believing that the current situation is quite dire. Japan is regarded as a sick man of the OECD, despite being the world's second largest economy; a recent report showed signs of recovery in all OECD countries apart from Japan. The recent Stock Market crises and bank closures have exacerbated the situation. The most pessimistic future scenario suggests that there will be no return to productivity growth, which will have disastrous effects, including a pension funding problem and potential unemployment. This scenario fears a policy vacuum with the economy becoming 'rudderless' and more volatile. There is concern as well about too enthusiastic an embrace of an Anglo-Saxon form of corporate governance, relying on take-overs and bankruptcy rather than stable financial relations. The optimistic scenario suggests productivity recovering to some extent, an independent Bank of Japan taking a broader view of its remit, increased stabilisation, and a range of new corporate governance models being gradually introduced.

5. Key factors determining Japan's economic future are the decline in birth-rate and an ageing society resulting in the reduction of the productive labour force, exacerbating the current downturn in production. In order for Japan to meet current global economic requirements there is a strong need to undergo significant economic reform. This has begun but, as witnessed by recent events, there is still much to be done. Significant additional reforms are needed to improve Japan's economic fortunes and encourage growth: first in the macro-economic structure, developing an open market, and deregulation in logistics, energy, telecommunications, finance (the Big Bang), and distribution reforms; second, in the redistribution of income, for example, the Social Security system. Education is also in crucial need of reform. To produce the skilled workforce Japan needs there must be higher standards, more vocational courses, fewer graduate lawyers and economists, and university entrance must be related to ability.

6. Experts worry that fiscal policy is being driven by concern about fiscal deficit and extreme productivity pessimism. The question of who is supervising the bankers is also raised. The monolithic Japan Inc structure has to be unharnessed. Many call for a continuing process of self-scrutiny and self-renewal.

7. Japan's influence on the world stage will be determined by how Japan's economy develops, its openness to foreign goods and services and its international competitiveness. A significant factor determining foreign policy will continue to be Japan's heavy dependence (81%) on imported energy, notably the 80% of oil imports which come from the Middle East. Japan is also highly dependent upon imported food, self-sufficiency being only 49%. Many argue that in an era of globalisation Japan will need to assert its economic influence by becoming more involved in the global debates about regulations and standards, proposing alternative thinking and undertaking lobbying activities, and becoming a standard setter rather than a standard taker. This can only happen if Japan's underlying economic performance improves. The currency crises in Asia provide Japan with an opportunity to become more involved locally, and also for the Yen to become a key local currency. The creation of an Asia Monetary Fund (AMF), a proposal promoted by Japan, would internationalise the Yen and propel Japan into playing more of a leadership role in South East Asia. However, to become reality it would need South East Asian acceptance (and it may never come into existence, being incompatible with the International Monetary Fund).

8. In the Asia–Pacific region, Japan's role is evolving but remains defensive. There is no appetite, amongst either the Japanese public or elite, for an expanded role, although there is an increasing desire to be regarded as a 'normal' country. Japan does not seek regional leadership, preferring to be in partnership with the US and to operate on a multi-lateral level. However Japan's self-defence force is now sizeable (a larger navy than the UK, significant air defences, anti-submarine warfare and mine-sweeping capabilities). The kinds of forces Japan should have must be key issues for Japanese defence and budget planners, not least given the expected budget cuts. The current systems and capabilities already give Japan the capability to do more than it does at present. Japan's crisis-management is regarded by some as a weakness, particularly with regard to the Gulf War, with a need to improve inter-agency co-ordination.

9. Undoubtedly co-operative relations with the US continue to be at the core of Japan's foreign policy, covering security, economic and global issues. The US–Japan alliance plays a crucial role for Japan's security, and in the view of its signatories is an insurance policy promoting peace and stability in the wider region. The recently revised guidelines established a clearer and more effective definition of the defence co-operation and logistical support which Japan would provide to the US at times of contingencies affecting Japanese security. But Japan remains a junior partner. Some would argue that the revision maintained the status quo and lost the opportunity for a fundamental rethink of US–Japan defence roles, not least because of Japan's insistence, and US acceptance, that Japan cannot exercise collective self-defence. For US defence planners there is still uncertainty about whether Japanese forces would be 'in' or 'out' in a real regional crisis. US public opinion would be unlikely to tolerate a crisis situation in Korea where Japan was unwilling to use its air and naval forces to help prevent North Korean attacks on Americans and South Koreans. The Treaty, although revised, has an uncertain long-term future. Some worry that if Japan decides it cannot exercise collective self-defence, the Treaty may not survive a further 45 years. Others believe that significant progress has been made and that the review launched a process of intensive dialogue between Japan and her neighbours that is in the long-term interest of the region. Continuing dialogue about the guidelines with Japan's Asian neighbours will be crucial. Japan–US relations involve much more than security: economic links are crucial but there is still a lack of constructive dialogue on some key trade issues.

10. Relations with China continue to develop, with a flurry of senior visits between Beijing and Tokyo. The two countries are leading trade partners (with Japan having a trade deficit), and Japan is a major aid donor to China. However despite a deepening economic relationship, there is much on the bilateral agenda to create an uneasy political relationship: the revision of the US–Japan Guidelines; the territorial dispute (Diaoyu Island); and the Taiwan issue. To become good neighbours will take time and effort from both sides, maximising trust and co-operation and minimising difficulties, a fact both countries recognise since public distrust of one another has grown over recent years. Specific proposals to improve Sino-Japanese relations include a further tightening of economic links, confidence building measures, increased student exchanges, a strengthening of dialogue including annual leaders' summits, and increased involvement in multilateral fora.

11. A sound trilateral relationship embracing Japan, China and the US is of the utmost importance for stability in the Asia–Pacific region. Each country has to work at its relationships, and Japan would welcome further progress in US–China relations. China, for its part, is less sanguine about Japanese reform. China remains concerned at the enlargement of Japan's diplomatic efforts, and over the implicit concept of a Chinese threat in the revised US–Japan guidelines.

12. Japan is anxious to build her relations with Russia: Heads of State meetings are cementing the trust between the two countries; economic relations are developing with various agreed programmes; Japan is promoting Russia's participation in APEC; and there are exchanges on defence and security issues. Japan believes that the Northern Territories issue, the one thorn in relations, should be resolved by the end of the century and there is hope that a peace treaty can be concluded by 2000. Japan is keen to work with the KEDO partners and has provided significant food aid to Pyongyang. Building creative links between Seoul and Tokyo is important both in its own right and in the context of possible future reunification.

13. There is a paradox that Japan has an increasing sense of confidence in South East Asia at a time of economic regional crisis. With a cut in Japan's ODA to the region, however, a different policy may evolve. Most countries in South East Asia are keen that Japan plays a greater regional role, but they want this to be independent from the US. Some, remembering history, are more uneasy about Japan's involvement. The AMF, should it happen, is one option where Japan may become more constructively involved, although concern is voiced about Japan being the dominant player (although Japan is already active in the Asia Development Bank). The ASEAN Regional Forum (ARF) is another, where Japan's quiet and constructive support, particularly to funding non-governmental work, is recognised. Other examples include peacekeeping in Cambodia, and the recent Japanese support to Thailand during the currency crisis. However Japan does not always regard itself as Asian: being part of the Asian side of ASEM can be uncomfortable. South East Asia is keen to ensure good Japanese–Chinese relations so that they do not have to choose between the two, for instance over the Taiwan Straits issue.

14. Japan views Europe as an important partner. And Japan is important to Europe. The Japan–Europe relationship should be seen in a wider tripolar context including the US. There is an opportunity for a new and more balanced relationship. Greater partnership can be achieved in a number of areas from research and development to security, industrial policy and parliamentary dialogue. Business opportunities for Europeans in Japan should be exploited. Inward Japanese investment to Europe continues to be extremely important. There are also possibilities for partnership in ODA, in the development of KEDO (EU support for KEDO might act to demonstrate Europe's commitment to the area in the way that Japan has supported development in Europe), on Myanmar, and Bosnia. The Japanese could lobby the European Union to a greater extent and therefore engage in the discussions which affect EU–Japanese relations. People to people contact also remains important. It is in Europe's and Japan's mutual interest to deepen and widen the dialogue.

15. A key tool in Japanese foreign policy has been the significant provision of ODA. In 1995, Japan was the largest global donor providing aid to over 150 countries (half going to Asian neighbours), and it was the biggest donor to about 50 recipient countries. However, the ODA to GNP ratio is only 0.2%, ranking 19th out of 21 OECD countries. Japan supports self-help efforts, balancing humanitarian aid, poverty alleviation, supporting social development and strengthening economic infrastructure, through a range of loans (now untied), grants, technical co-operation and aid through international organisations. Although Japan's ODA has played a unique role in Japan's foreign policy, this role is now in danger given severe budgetary pressures. A 10% cut will force Japan to focus on efficiency and effectiveness. Japan has been a world leader not just in volume but in contributing to the long-term vision of development work. However Japan could learn from others in making its aid more co-ordinated and improving its quality. Other donors wish to see Japan supporting the proposal to relieve the debt of the poorest nations. Concern is also voiced at what is seen as ambiguous conditionality, for example, mixing food aid to North Korea with other policies towards North Korea. The question is raised whether Japan's foreign policy will be weakened if her ODA is reduced.

16. Japan has successfully employed soft diplomatic skills in its foreign policy, whether through ODA, cultural diplomacy or its involvement in global issues such as the environment (as the host of the Kyoto conference). As such it is demonstrating a new diplomatic way in the New World order which is recognised and admired by many. The challenge for Japan will be to balance its relations with its neighbours and the wider world. The development of Japan's domestic agenda will be crucial in determining this.

21

Cultural Diplomacy at the Crossroads

Short Report on Conference 514: 24–28 November 1997

Virginia Crowe

1. Overall pressures to reduce government spending, a relative reduction of resources available for the promotion of cultural exchange, the global communications revolution, and changing political imperatives favouring anti-elitist, inclusive and accessible public diplomacy are compelling cultural diplomacy to change direction.

2. Cultural exchange may be personally enriching, but governments' expenditure on it has to be seen to be justified, so that it is not regarded as 'an optional extra'. Promoting a certain identity and image of a society brings political and commercial benefits. Culture is inherently political, in that it embodies the values of its society, reinforced by the way in which it is promoted. Cultural exchanges generate trust and long term understanding transcending transient political crises. National images promoted by national cultures have commercial implications: where once the trade followed the flag, today commercial benefit is said to follow the dance troupe (or the football team). Increasingly cultural diplomacy must be seen to earn its keep, a difficult task when its benefits are hard to measure.

3. The medium is still the message, and there are implications in how cultural diplomacy is conducted and by whom, whether as an arm of foreign policy through Ministries of Foreign Affairs (MFAs), or through National Cultural Institutes by a cadre of expert and specialist 'cultural diplomats'. There is logic in putting external cultural relations directly under the wing of MFAs, as the US State Department, for one, has recently done, when they are used as a tool of government and part of public diplomacy. But 'embassies tend to keep people out, whereas national cultural institutes bring them in', and though there may be cost and tax advantages in siting cultural activity in diplomatic missions, there is also advantage seen in distancing culture from day to day political business. There is anyway a striking disparity between the numbers of military and cultural attaches employed in Embassies.

4. There are contradictory demands on cultural diplomats, to offer new services, as in countries of the former Soviet bloc, and to run high quality events which have general appeal, while facing competition from other channels of cultural exchange when under pressure to reduce costs. The danger is that cuts generate a spiral of declining effectiveness, second class events, and rising cost per client. The challenge is to be flexible and innovative, suiting methods to circumstances, focusing on joint ventures and new partnerships. Activities at regional and local levels are taking on a new significance, since states, the traditional 'containers' of culture, and primary actors in cultural diplomacy, are eroding, and their boundaries not necessarily synonymous with the cultures within them.

5. Language teaching is increasingly important to those National Institutes in larger states as a means of generating resources to defray costs, though questions are also raised about publicly subsidised competition for potential private sector initiatives. Language is important to cultural diplomacy and a sensitive issue for small states, because it is so closely linked to national identity, and because for minorities it can act as a barrier. Language can be simply a medium, rather than a Trojan horse for a national culture with all its accompanying political and commercial baggage. Language teaching materials increasingly reflect the receiving nations' national, social and cultural aspirations and need not be vehicles of cultural and linguistic imperialism. However, given the level of investment, the supplier will often be keen to maximise the returns, both quantifiable and non-quantifiable. Language teaching is very often what the customer wants; it is a tool which grants access, and it facilitates exchanges at the practical as well as the cultural level.

6. Cultural diplomats are having to learn new skills, to be good managers, to maximise efficiency, to develop new accounting and monitoring tools, to leverage resources and maximise sponsorship for national culture. Business, whether local, national or multinational is increasingly important in supporting cultural activities which benefit their image. The natural tendency is for business sponsorship to go to popularly acclaimed excellence; less glamorous, controversial and innovative activities are less likely to win support. If the private sector is to benefit from established success, should it not also contribute to the nurture of developing talent? Questions about accountability, transparency and public access to co-sponsored events are also relevant. It is important for government and business to work in partnership to share in the development and projection of national and corporate images, with governments having a key role in setting priorities and private sector finance supplementing, not substituting for, government.

7. The possibilities and limitations of sharing scarce resources are debated. Where there are shared values and regional commonalities there can be advantages. The countries of the European Union for example, while embracing a rich cultural diversity, share core values which could be the basis of a Common European Cultural Policy, difficult as that is to frame. Educational and cultural programmes such as PHARE, TACIS, Erasmus, Socrates and Leonardo reinforce and propagate such values inside the Union and externally, and may provide a useful model for other regions. Multicultural exchanges however, should have identifiable actors. There is a strong case for bilateral exchanges, which facilitate not only government to government, but also people to people contacts and those between cultural institutes and interest groups. A globalised world may even have greater need of them to counter intercultural prejudices and stereotypes of the East/West, North/South variety, which foster generalisations about, for example, 'Asian values' which may not appropriately reflect regional diversity. Bilateral and multilateral exchanges should be complementary.

8. Any trends towards cultural blocs however, risk the 'clash of civilisations' threatened by Huntingdon. Relations between Islam and 'the West' are a present and future challenge for cultural diplomacy, bedevilled as they are by mutual ignorance, misunderstanding and negative stereotypes exploited by the media and politicians for their own ends. Islam is as far from a monolith as is 'the West'. Cultural differences do not of themselves imply conflict, except where there is conflict present for other reasons. Some cultural differences have for so long been exploited to justify conflict, that hostility and antipathy have become part of the cultural dialogue. Informed by powerful social, political and economic factors, and notably the lack of a democratic culture, the recent Balkans war where Christians were pitted against Muslims, arguably embodied aspects of this. Opportunities to further mutual understanding through cultural exchanges need to be actively developed, with monitoring of the media and incipient Western Islamophobia nipped in the bud, and a certain subtlety and wisdom required in the presentation of Western values in Islamic contexts.

9. While it is innately anti-authoritarian and democratic, the effects of the Internet cannot yet be assessed, but it has a huge potential as a tool of cultural diplomacy. Its dynamic growth may breed some unease at the lack of signposts or control; it is currently heavily American and European; and there are questions about the nature, authenticity and political bias of the information it purveys, and how it may be assessed and managed. Together with the emergence of multicultural societies through immigration and the increased opportunities for contact and communication afforded by travel, the Internet may be contributing to the creation of an underlying world culture, where a common structure of political and cultural values is allied to diverse and special identities. The erosion of 'Eurocentrism' seems inevitable and implications for cultural diplomats remain to be recognised.

10. At the same time there is also a fear that an imbalance of exchanges and a flow of information facilitated by the Internet and global communications, will lead to the values of the technologically advanced transmitting societies swamping those of the receiving societies as they 'modernise' and change. There is a perception that the overwhelming influence and benefit is to 'the North' and 'the West'. Needs and preferences are currently seen to dictate an instrumental approach to cultural exchange, and priority for language teaching as a vehicle for joint development and technological advance, over access to the personal enrichment brought by the Arts, seen as benefiting a limited elite. The challenges in North/South and East/West cultural relations centre on finding ways to promote true exchange, to achieve mutual cultural enrichment and understanding, and appreciation of cultural diversity.

11. Fears of leaving cultural exchange to the mercy of free market economics are exemplified in the film industry, a powerful cultural influence. Concerns centre around Hollywood's pre-eminence which is leading to American cultural dominance, the erosion of local culture and the destruction of the film industry in smaller countries. The strength of national cultural resilience, the vigour and creativity of smaller nations and the power of a quality 'product' developed for a home or niche market to earn its keep at home, and win markets abroad, may however be underestimated in the debate.

12. Cultural exchange will accelerate as modern communications develop with or without state guidance. The role of the state is under close scrutiny: it seems increasingly to be that of an involved supportive facilitator, empowering people and enterprises to do what they do best in an increasingly free market. None the less, the state's part in promoting an appropriate national image in the context of popular diplomacy seems irreplaceable. The national images and values projected have to have credibility and popular relevance, maintain highest artistic standards and be delivered cost effectively. The maintenance and promotion of cultural diversity in the face of the allegedly homogenising effects of market forces and the Internet, must remain a shared goal for all those working in the field, to the spiritual benefit of all humankind.

22

Central and Eastern Europe and NATO and EU Enlargement

Short Report on Conference 516: 15–19 December 1997

Chris Langdon

1. Enlargement will change the map of Europe and transform the composition of both NATO and the European Union (EU). For the first time in the European Union's history entry has been virtually guaranteed before the negotiations begin to ten Central and Eastern European countries, plus Cyprus. Negotiations begin this Spring with the five countries agreed at the Luxembourg Summit. The other five candidate countries in the region are said by the European Commission to be in a 'training ground' for eventual entry rather than a waiting room. The year 2002 is regarded by the Commission as a perfectly possible entry date for a well prepared candidate. However, others argue that a date nearer 2005 is more likely for the front-runners, given the range of issues to be resolved, the ambivalence of some existing EU members, and the need for institutional reform. As a result, countries at the end of the process, such as Bulgaria and Romania, are unlikely to enter before 2010–15.

2. The preparations for entry will require very painful adjustments from all the applicant countries. It is accepted within the Commission that the resources implied in their Agenda 2000 document are not calculated on the applicant countries' needs, which are many times greater. There are different approaches to the resource issue within the existing EU members, with the major EU net contributors rejecting any increase in contributions and the net recipients resisting any loss of resources.

3. On joining the EU, new members will become eligible for funds from the Common Agricultural Policy (CAP) and the structural funds regional aid budget, which account together for 80% of the Community budget. Extending CAP and regional funds to new members as they are now is politically unacceptable. The pre-accession debate over structural funds is likely be intense. And fireworks are predicted in the round of EU budget discussions after 2006, when some of the new entrants will be able to argue their case from within. Structural funds are predicted by some to be even harder to resolve than the CAP, which is itself a political and economic problem of major proportions.

4. The key problem will be to keep the EU budget within its current ceiling of 1.27% EU GNP, whilst also reassuring current beneficiaries that they won't be major losers, and ensuring that the new applicants are not second-class members of the Union. Agenda 2000 provides a carefully calculated formula that maintains the expenditure limit of 1.27% of EU GDP, and it assumes that some additional funds will be available through economic growth in the period 2000–2006. The Commission projects a small increase in CAP funds, a small reduction in regional aid for the existing members, and 75 billion ECU of funds being available for the applicant countries. Some analysts calculate that this is just one thousandth of the EU's GDP in the period between 2000 and 2006. That translates as 130 ECU per head for the top five applicant countries, and 60 ECU per head for the second five, compared with the 400 ECU per head that, for example, Portugal gets from structural funds.

These figures also highlight the problem of the applicant countries with the greatest needs getting the lowest level of financial support, at least until the front-runners join.

5.   The Commission's stated aim is to achieve a cohesive and dynamic Union avoiding tiers of members. For that, extensive reform of EU institutions is needed. However the overall vision of a Europe of 26 remains cloudy at best, some critics say. They argue that there is no clear timeframe or target date for first and last accession, leading them to fear that the whole process could be undermined by the failure to enunciate a strategy. It was President Mitterrand who said it would be a tragedy if the final applicant joined the EU just as it ceases to function through institutional paralysis. The new Amsterdam Treaty has taken few of the basic steps necessary to streamline EU institutions for enlargement. Another inter-governmental conference is due before the EU expands beyond 20 members.

6.   Longer-term issues include the shape of an EU of 26: will there necessarily be tiers, given that EMU is not a condition of membership and given the different states of the economies of the new members? The relationship between 'Little Europe' and Big Europe' remains a matter of speculation. And will a Europe of 26 be more effective in running a coherent CFSP than a Europe of 16? Relations between a Europe of 26 members and South-East Europe will also have to be considered.

7.   The relationship between the European Union and Ukraine and Russia will also be critical. Russian frustration at the level of duties levied by the EU on Russian exports was openly expressed by Prime Minister Viktor Chernomyrdin when he met the President of the European Commission in 1996: 'the question of granting Russia the status of a country with a market economy – that is the central question'. Russia's place in Europe is a pressing issue for policy-makers, EU as well as NATO.

8.   On the economic agenda, the uncertainties highlighted by the crisis in Asia lead some to argue that the EU should focus on improving competitiveness. They suggest that the EU cannot restructure without enlargement. It has to consider economic restructuring and stop pretending that the problem does not exist. If Poland, for example, is the most competitive centre for Japanese car manufacturers because of its low labour costs, this will siphon off jobs from Western Europe and this has to be taken into account in a planned way. However, Western economists say this Polish competitive advantage will be relatively short-lived, and the political consequences given the high levels of unemployment among some of the existing member states mean that such a planned restructuring would be political dynamite.

9.   One of the central issues for policy-makers dealing with Central and Eastern Europe is the plethora of institutions which do not co-ordinate their policies as effectively as they should. Dialogue between NATO and the EU and the responsible desks in national capitals has to be expanded. The problem needs solving at a very high level. The WEU has a clear role as a bridging institution over the next decade as the EU evolves its security policy. There are several other bodies – including the Council of Europe, OECD and, for separate reasons, the OSCE – which have expanded their membership to take account of the post-Cold War changes in Europe, as well as new bodies such as the Euro-Atlantic Partnership Council. Problems include the difficulty for small countries of staffing all the relevant desks in their ministries and missions with capable officials to deal effectively with these institutions, the risks of turf fights between institutions and inconsistencies of approach, and the potential problems of co-ordination and advance planning.

10. It is also abundantly clear that sub-regional co-operation has to be fostered as the EU enlarges. It encourages states to improve bilateral relations, it fosters cross-border co-operation and the strengthening of economic ties, and it develops experience of multilateral organisations. Sub-regional groups have especially useful roles to play bringing together countries in the first tier of enlargement with neighbouring countries who are in the second five, and with some of their neighbours, thus bridging some of the new emerging divides in Europe.

11. Since 1989 six sub-regional co-operation groups have been created, including the Central Europe Free Trade Area (CEFTA) which is now perceived as having a useful and lasting rule, even after four members start EU entry talks. Its current membership of six (Czech Republic, Hungary, Poland, Romania, Slovakia and Slovenia) is likely to expand to include Bulgaria this summer. A number of countries have also said they would also like to join eventually, including Croatia, Latvia, Lithuania and Ukraine. CEFTA countries have to determine how to develop the organisation structurally and how they can deepen and widen, as several CEFTA member states have advocated.

12. Another leading regional group is the Council of Baltic Sea States (CBSS), which has eleven members. The CBSS Prime Ministerial Summit in Riga in January 1998 dealt with long-term regional co-operation issues involving the states in the Baltic Sea basin. As far as relations between the three former Soviet Baltic nations are concerned, the inclusion of just one in the first tier of EU membership requires a great deal of maturity in the relations between the three countries and with Russia.

13. Security is an important issue as the EU expands, particularly as third pillar justice and home affairs topics move to the first pillar agenda. Borders are one such issue; the tightening of one border will have an impact on other borders bottling up or diverting damaging phenomena into neighbouring countries especially the Newly Independent States (NIS) and the Balkans. Means to control terrorism, asylum, material smuggling, and economic migration have to be considered.

14. The signing of the NATO accession protocols with Poland, Hungary and the Czech Republic paves the way for the three to enter in April 1999, assuming early ratification by NATO member Parliaments, including the US Congress. In the meantime the three states will have active observer rights to over thirty committees in Brussels, though they will not take part in the decision-making processes.

15. As well as the issues of the cost of burden-sharing, the education and training of the military are pivotal over the medium and long term. This involves not just issues of training procedures, but also policy and doctrine. Soldiers need to be trained in the 'communality of thinking' and also in taking responsibility. In Bosnia, NATO troops are pro-active while troops from one applicant country have worked on the principle of 'no orders, no action'. Command and control procedures also need to be changed, and new members have to adapt to NATO's strategy of mobile projection of forces.

16. A great deal of logistical preparation remains to be done. Before that can be achieved, the education process needs to be successful. There are still problems of resistance within the military and foreign ministry – old Moscow era thinking can prevail, leading on one occasion to the NATO Mission of a new member being by-passed by its military who didn't want to deal with the diplomats at their own Mission. Civilian control of the military will also require further work on a technical level. But some progress has been made on education. In the Czech Republic, 72% of the military polled recently were in favour of NATO membership, compared with 45–52% of the population as a whole. Acceptance by public opinion of the costs of both NATO and EU enlargement is critical.

17. There has been much speculation on how public opinion will change as citizens become more informed of the costs of membership. In Hungary the lessons from the NATO referendum in November 1997 raise questions for policy-makers involved in EU as well as NATO enlargement. The number of Hungarians in favour of NATO membership went up from 74% in opinion polls in October to 85% in November's referendum vote (albeit with a turnout of 49.24%). The polling evidence suggests that ambivalent voters reacted to the pro-NATO campaign and the favourable press coverage by switching to a 'yes' vote, according to polling analysts. On EU entry, the number of Hungarians polled who believe there will be more advantages than disadvantages has fallen from 69% in 1996 to 57% in 1997. The question therefore is whether to run information campaigns which make people aware of the costs and problems of membership if the increased realism will make them less likely to vote in favour of entry. Hungary's NATO referendum experience suggests that a well-run campaign on the merits of entry can be effective in winning over the ambivalent. An important issue for political elites in the first wave countries is who should run public information campaigns: officials in government ministries, or is it better to leave it to public information professionals?

18. Pro-reform political elites in a country such as Romania, who have seen their bids for entry of both the EU and NATO delayed, have to decide how to maintain the domestic reform process when their political authority has been damaged. The authority of the Romanian coalition has been diminished because of its campaign theme in the November 1996 elections that Romania would be invited to join both the EU and NATO if a pro-Western reformist government was elected. The result of the decisions by NATO and the EU is to decrease Romanian public support for reform politics and Euro-Atlantic integration and to diminish popularity of democratic leaders. It is predicted by Romanian specialists that the position of leftist and xenophobic forces will be consolidated. Since December 1997, the coalition's position has been significantly weakened by in-fighting caused by internal pressures.

19. It will become clear over the coming months whether the steps agreed at the Luxembourg Summit, aimed at making the 'outs' feel included in the process, achieve the desired results. A great deal will depend on the effort put into relations with the second tier countries. Some observers say that EU entry as late as 2010–15 will put severe strains on Bulgaria and Romania's ability to reform. They warn that given the fragility of the reform process and the potential for instability in the region, there are risks of a new 'fault-line' developing in South-East Europe. The risk of new divisions arises not just in the south;

> it is hard to ignore the co-incidence of several indicators – 'integratability', state cohesion, civilizational factors – which would point to a fundamental rift along fault-lines somewhere to the north of Serbia and west of Belarus. Yet even those who find themselves on the right side can hardly be at ease with the prospect of a 'permanent frontier' between 'cosmos and chaos' lying so close to home. (Ian Bremner and Alyson K. Bailes, 'Sub-regionalism in the Newly Independent States', *International Affairs* (1998), pp. 131–148)

20. It is clearly vital that Western European policy makers, while focusing on their top foreign policy priorities of EMU and the negotiations with the six top tier countries, also give due attention to the external and internal problems faced by the second tier countries. The problems that Latvia and Lithuania face given their geographic position cannot be underestimated. And Slovakia must not be ignored, although it will only be clear after the Parliamentary elections in September 1998 whether the opposition is able to win power and to satisfy Western critics of the country's political development sufficiently to bring it back into the running for entry.

21. In Slovakia as in the rest of Central and Eastern Europe, internal factors remain central given that the biggest barrier to EU entry is the problem of economic management and restructuring. Central to the success of economic reform will be the ability of the governments to persuade their populations that the gains of enlargement are worth the pain of the restructuring process it entails. The experience of the Maastricht Treaty has shown the dangers of decisions being taken within narrow elites. This is important enough in Western European democracies, but even more critical in Central and Eastern Europe less than a decade after the ending of fifty years of totalitarianism.

SECTION

Lists of Speakers

Conference 489: International Co-operation Against Drugs and Crime: Are Societies Losing the War?

Monday 27 – Friday 31 January 1997

BARBOSA, Rubens	BRAZIL Brazilian Embassy, London
CAMERON-WALLER, Stuart	INTERPOL ICPO-Interpol, Lyon
CLUTTERBUCK, Richard	UNITED KINGDOM Exeter
DORN, Nicholas	UNITED KINGDOM Institute for the Study of Drug Dependence, London
GREGORY, Frank	UNITED KINGDOM University of Southampton, Southampton
GUIDO, John	UNITED STATES OF AMERICA Embassy of United States of America, London
LEVI, Michael	UNITED KINGDOM University of Wales, Cardiff
NORMAN, Paul	UNITED KINGDOM University of Portsmouth, Portsmouth
ÖLANDER, Jan	SWEDEN Swedish National Police Board, Stockholm
PLUMBLY, Derek	UNITED KINGDOM Foreign and Commonwealth Office, London
TUPMAN, Bill	UNITED KINGDOM Exeter University, Exeter
ULRICH, Christopher	UNITED STATES OF AMERICA Fife
WILLIAMS, Phil	UNITED STATES OF AMERICA University of Pittsburgh, Pittsburgh

Conference 490: Europe's Development Aid

Monday 3 – Friday 7 February 1997

AARONSON, Mike	UNITED KINGDOM Save the Children Fund, London
BLACKHURST, Richard	UNITED KINGDOM World Trade Organisation, Geneva
BOSSUYT, Jean	BELGIUM European Centre for Development Policy Management, Maastricht
CLAY, Edward	UNITED KINGDOM Overseas Development Institute, London
COX, Aidan	UNITED KINGDOM Overseas Development Institute, London
DOYLE, Sean	EUROPEAN COMMISSION European Commission, Brussels
FEENEY, Patricia	UNITED KINGDOM OXFAM, Oxford
HAMBURGER, Friedrich	EUROPEAN COMMISSION European Commission, Brussels
HILSUM, Lindsay	UNITED KINGDOM Channel 4 News, London
JONCKERS, Jos	EUROPEAN COMMISSION European Commission, Brussels
KINNOCK, Glenys	EUROPEAN PARLIAMENT European Parliament, Brussels
LAGO, Ricardo	EBRD European Bank for Reconstruction and Development, London
LAING, Stuart	UNITED KINGDOM Foreign and Commonwealth Office, London

MAJANEN, Pertti	FINLAND Ministry of Foreign Affairs, Helsinki
MANNING, Richard	UNITED KINGDOM Overseas Development Administration, London
MAXWELL, Simon	UNITED KINGDOM Institute of Development Studies, Brighton
OMURA, Masahiro	OECD Development Cooperation Directorate, Paris
POOLEY, Peter	EUROPEAN COMMISSION European Commission, Brussels
ROBERTS, John	EUROPEAN COMMISSION European Commission, Brussels
ROBINS, Nick	UNITED KINGDOM International Institute for Environment and Development, London
RYRIE, Sir William	UNITED KINGDOM London

Conference 491: NATO's Role in the Twenty-First Century

Monday 10 – Friday 14 February 1997

BILYNSKI, Markian	UKRAINE Pylyp Orlyk Institute of Democracy, Kiev
BLOCH-LAINÉ, Amaya	FRANCE CREST – Ecole Polytechnique, Paris
BROCK, George	UNITED KINGDOM *The Times*, London
DANIELSEN, Dagfinn	NORWAY Norwegian Military Mission to NATO, Brussels
GOULDEN, Sir John	UNITED KINGDOM UK Permanent Representative to the North Atlantic Council, United Kingdom Delegation to NATO, Brussels
HUNTER, Robert	UNITED STATES OF AMERICA US Permanent Representative to North Atlantic Council, Brussels
JAKOBSON, Max	FINLAND Former Finnish Ambassador to United Nations, Helsinki
KEHOE, Nicolas	NATO NATO Military Committee, Brussels
KOZHOKIN, Yevgeny	RUSSIA Russia's Institute for Strategic Studies, Moscow
KRUZICH, Joseph	UNITED STATES OF AMERICA American Embassy, Stockholm
LENZI, Guido	WEU Western European Union Institute for Security Studies, Paris
LESSER, Ian	UNITED STATES OF AMERICA Rand Corporation, Santa Monica

MORGAN, Patrick

UNITED KINGDOM
Department of War Studies,
King's College, London

ONYSZKIEWICZ, Janusz

POLAND
Member of Polish Parliament,
Warsaw

VOIGT, Karsten

GERMANY
Bundestag, Bonn

Conference 493: Western Military Intervention in the Developing World: Why, When, How and Where?

Monday 3 – Friday 7 March 1997

BATTILEGA, John	UNITED STATES OF AMERICA Science Applications International Corporation, Greenwood Village
CARLE, Christophe	UNIDR United Nations Institute for Disarmament Research, Geneva
COBBOLD, Richard	UNITED KINGDOM Royal United Services Institute, London
ENGEBERG, Katarina	SWEDEN Swedish Armed Forces, Stockholm
FREEDMAN, Lawrence	UNITED KINGDOM Department of War Studies, King's College, London
GARDEN, Timothy	UNITED KINGDOM Royal Institute of International Affairs, London
GOWING, Nik	UNITED KINGDOM BBC World Television, London
HOFFMAN, Bruce	UNITED KINGDOM University of St Andrews, Fife
JOSEPH, Robert	UNITED STATES OF AMERICA National Defense University, Washington DC
MAKAROV, Sergei	RUSSIA Ministry for Civil Defence, Moscow
OROSZ, Stephen	NATO NATO, Brussels
SINGH, Jasjit	INDIA Institute for Defence Studies and Analyses, New Delhi

VALLANCE, Andrew

UNITED KINGDOM
SHAPE, Mons

von HIPPEL, Karin

UNITED STATES OF AMERICA
King's College, London

WILLIAMS, Michael

UNITED KINGDOM
International Institute for Strategic
Studies, London

Conference 495: Oil and the Middle East Economies

Monday 17 – Friday 21 March 1997

AL DUKHEIL, Abdulaziz

SAUDI ARABIA
Consulting Centre for Finance and
Investment, Riyadh

AZZAM, Henry

SAUDI ARABIA
National Commercial Bank, Jeddah

GAUSE III, Gregory

UNITED STATES OF AMERICA
The University of Vermont,
Burlington

GHORBAN, Narsi

IRAN
Asian Pacific Inc, Tehran

HORSNELL, Paul

UNITED KINGDOM
Oxford Institute for Energy Studies,
Oxford

JONES, Peter

CANADA
Stockholm International Peace
Research Institute, Solna

KARAWAN, M

UNITED KINGDOM
International Institute for Strategic
Studies, London

KARMI, Ghada

UNITED KINGDOM
School of Oriental and African
Studies, London

POLLOCK, David

UNITED STATES OF AMERICA
US Department of State,
Washington DC

RIVLIN, Paul

ISRAEL
Moshe Dayan Centre for Middle
East and African Studies, Tel Aviv

ROBERTS, John

UNITED KINGDOM
Methinks Limited, Edinburgh

SAKR, Naomi

UNITED KINGDOM
Economist Intelligence Unit,
London

SICK, Gary

UNITED STATES OF AMERICA
Gulf 2000, New York

TAECKER, Kevin

UNITED STATES OF AMERICA
Saudi American Bank, Riyadh

YAMANI, Mai

SAUDI ARABIA
School of Oriental and African
Studies, London

Conference 500: Towards a New Round of Multilateral Trade Negotiations?

Monday 2 – Friday 6 June 1997

ABEL, Gerhard

OECD
Director, Trade Directorate,
Organisation for Economic
Co-operation and Development,
Paris

AKRAM, Munir

PAKISTAN
Ambassador, Permanent
Representative of Pakistan to the
United Nations Office, Geneva

BAYNE, Sir Nicholas

UNITED KINGDOM
Chairman, Liberalisation of Trade in
Services (LOTIS) Committee, British
Invisibles, London

CURTIS, John

CANADA
Senior Policy Adviser and
Co-ordinator, Trade and Economic
Policy Branch, Department of
Foreign Affairs and International
Trade, Ottawa

FLETCHER, Ian

EUROPEAN COMMISSION
WTO and OECD Unit, Directorate G,
DGI, European Commission,
Brussels

HODA, Anwarul

WORLD TRADE ORGANISATION
Deputy Director-General, World
Trade Organisation, Geneva

MacLAREN, Roy

CANADA
High Commissioner, Canadian High
Commission, London

METZGER, Jean-Marie

FRANCE
Permanent Representative of France
to the World Trade Organisation,
Geneva

REITERER, Michael

AUSTRIA
Minister-Counsellor, Permanent
Mission of Austria to the European
Union, Brussels

ROBERTS, Christopher

UNITED KINGDOM
Deputy Secretary and Director-
General of Trade Policy, Department
of Trade and Industry, London

ROLLO, Jim

UNITED KINGDOM
Chief Economic Adviser, Foreign
and Commonwealth Office, London

SEE, Chak Mun

REPUBLIC OF SINGAPORE
Ambassador, Permanent
Representative of Singapore to
the United Nations Office, Geneva

SIKKEL, Rien

NETHERLANDS
Head, Investment Department,
Ministry of Economic Affairs,
The Hague

STERN, Paula

UNITED STATES OF AMERICA
President, The Stern Group Inc,
Washington

STOLER, Andrew

UNITED STATES OF AMERICA
Deputy Chief, Permanent Mission of
the United States to the World Trade
Organisation, Geneva

SUN, Joun Yung

KOREA
Ambassador, Permanent
Representative of the Republic of
Korea to the United Nations Office,
Geneva

SUZUKI, Yoichi

JAPAN
Director, First International
Organisations Division, Economics
Bureau, Ministry of Foreign Affairs,
Tokyo

WOOLCOCK, Stephen

UNITED KINGDOM
Senior Research Fellow, The
European Institute, London School
of Economics and Political Science,
London

Conference 501: Prospects for Peace and Stability in East Asia

Tuesday 17 – Friday 20 June 1997

BOISSEAU DU ROCHER, Sophie	FRANCE National Foundation of Political Sciences, Paris
CHIA, Siow Yue	SINGAPORE Insititute of Southeast Asian Studies, Singapore
COSSA, Ralph	UNITED STATES OF AMERICA Center for Strategic and International Studies, Honolulu
DING, Kuisong	CHINA China Institute of Contemporary International Relations, Beijing
GRANT, Richard	UNITED STATES OF AMERICA Royal Institute of International Affairs, London
HENN, Charles	THAILAND International Affairs and Law Forum, Bangkok
HOARE, James	UNITED KINGDOM Foreign and Commonwealth Office, London
HOSHINO, Toshiya	JAPAN Japan Institute of International Affairs, Tokyo
JAWHAR bin Hassan, Mohamed	MALAYSIA Institute of Strategic and International Studies, Kuala Lumpur
LEIFER, Michael	UNITED KINGDOM London School of Economics and Political Science, London
SALMON Jr, Charles B.	UNITED STATES OF AMERICA Asia–Pacific Center for Security Studies, Honolulu

SEGAL, Gerald

CANADA
International Institute for Strategic
Studies, London

SHIN, Dong-Ik

KOREA
International Institute for Strategic
Studies (IISS), London

WANANDI, Jusuf

INDONESIA
Centre for Strategic and
International Studies, Jakarta

Conference WPS 97/3: The British German Forum: Same House – Different Dreams?

Monday 30 June – Friday 4 July 1997

ARROWSMITH, John

UNITED KINGDOM
Senior Research Fellow, National
Institute of Social and Economic
Research, London

BROOMFIELD, Nigel

UNITED KINGDOM
Former British Ambassador to
Bonn, Blackheath

BUDDE, Katrin

GERMANY
Member of Sachsen-Anhalt Landtag;
Deputy Chairwoman of the SPD
Parliamentary Group, Magdeburg

FISK, David

UNITED KINGDOM
Chief Scientist, Department of the
Environment, London

GLEES, Anthony

UNITED KINGDOM
Department of Government, Brunel
University, Uxbridge

HEUERDING, Henning

GERMANY
Supervisor of Capital Markets
Division, Coopers & Lybrand,
London

KIELINGER, Thomas

GERMANY
Journalist and Author, Bonn

KREILE, Michael

GERMANY
Institute of Political Science,
Humboldt University, Berlin

LAYDEN, Anthony

UNITED KINGDOM
Head, Western European Union
Department, Foreign and
Commonwealth Office, London

MONAR, Jörg

GERMANY
Director, Centre for European
Politics and Institutions, University
of Leicester, Leicester

PATEL, Bharti	UNITED KINGDOM Acting Director, Low Pay Unit, London
PATERSON, William	UNITED KINGDOM Director, Institute for German Studies, University of Birmingham
SCHUHMACHER, Jürgen	GERMANY Director, Bremer Landesbank Capital Markets plc, London
SCHUSTER, Barbara	GERMANY Deputy Director-General, Fundamental and Economic Aspects of Environmental Policy, Federal Ministry of the Environment, Bonn
SOSKICE, David	GERMANY Director, Labour Market and Employment Science Centre, Berlin

Conference 502: The Media, Democracy and Election Campaigns

Monday 7 – Friday 11 July 1997

BICKHAM, Edward

UNITED KINGDOM
Managing Director, Public Affairs
and Corporate Policy, Hill and
Knowlton (UK) Limited, London

BORDEN, Anthony

UNITED KINGDOM
Executive Director and Editor,
Institute for War and Peace
Reporting, London

BUTLER, David

UNITED KINGDOM
Fellow, Nuffield College, Oxford
University, Oxford

CARVER, Richard

UNITED KINGDOM
Head of Africa Programme, Article
19, International Centre Against
Censorship, London

FLETCHER, Winston

UNITED KINGDOM
Chairman, Bozell UK Holdings,
London

HILL, David

UNITED KINGDOM
Chief Media Spokesman, The
Labour Party, London

HOWARD, Anthony

UNITED KINGDOM
Broadcaster and Obituaries Editor,
The Times, London

HUDSON, Lucian

UNITED KINGDOM
Strand Editor and 1997 UK Election
Editor, BBC World Television,
London

INGHAM, Sir Bernard

UNITED KINGDOM
Chairman, Bernard Ingham
Communications; Chief Press
Secretary to Prime Minister
Thatcher (1979–90), London

MERLOE, Patrick	UNITED STATES OF AMERICA Senior Associate for Election Processes, National Democratic Institute for International Affairs (NDI), Washington
NICHOLSON, Emma	UNITED KINGDOM Former Liberal Democrat Member for Devon West & Torridge, House of Commons, London
OÑATE, Santiago	MEXICO Ambassador, Mexican Embassy, London
RAZZALL, Tim	UNITED KINGDOM Party Treasurer, Liberal Democrats, London
ROBINSON, W.G. (Gerry)	OSCE Deputy Chairman, Provisional Elections Commission and Senior Counsel, Organisation for Security and Co-operation in Europe (OSCE), Mission to Bosnia and Herzegovina, Sarajevo
SÄVE-SÖDERBERGH, Bengt	SWEDEN Secretary-General, International Institute for Democracy and Electoral Assistance (IDEA), Stockholm
SEYMOUR-URE, Colin	UNITED KINGDOM Department of Politics & International Relations, University of Kent, Canterbury
WAKEHAM, Lord	UNITED KINGDOM Chairman, Press Complaints Commission, London
WORCESTER, Robert	UNITED KINGDOM Chairman, Market & Opinion Research International (MORI), London

Conference 503: Diplomacy: Profession in Peril?

Monday 21 – Friday 25 July 1997

ARTHUR, Michael

UNITED KINGDOM
Director, Resources, Foreign and
Commonwealth Office, London

BIANCHERI CHIAPPORI, Boris

ITALY
Secretary-General, Ministry of
Foreign Affairs, Rome

CAMERON, Fraser

EUROPEAN COMMISSION
Foreign Policy Adviser, DG1A,
European Commission, Brussels

CHASE, Howard

UNITED KINGDOM
Senior Policy Adviser, The British
Petroleum Company plc, London

HANRAHAN, Brian

UNITED KINGDOM
Diplomatic Correspondent, BBC
News, London

HENRIKSON, Alan

UNITED STATES OF AMERICA
Director, Fletcher Roundtable,
Fletcher School of Law and
Diplomacy, Massachusetts

HOCKING, Brian

UNITED KINGDOM
Reader in International Relations,
Centre for International and
European Studies, Coventry
University, Coventry

KURBALIJA, Jovan

MALTA
Head of Unit for IT and Diplomacy,
Mediterranean Academy of
Diplomatic Studies, Msida

LEWIS, Patricia

UNITED KINGDOM
Director, UN Institute for
Disarmament Research, Geneva,
London

LINK, Joan

UNITED KINGDOM
Head, Personnel, Finance and
Planning for FCO Support Services,
Foreign and Commonwealth Office,
London

LUY, Julius Georg

GERMANY
Head, Task Force on Future
Development, Federal Ministry of
Foreign Affairs, Bonn

MATHESON, Alexander

NEW ZEALAND
Adviser, Management and Training
Services Division, Commonwealth
Secretariat, London

MATSUURA, Koichiro

JAPAN
Ambassador of Japan to France,
Paris

MORRIS, David

AUSTRALIA
First Secretary and Deputy Head of
Mission, Australian Embassy,
Dublin

NEWTON, Alastair

UNITED KINGDOM
Deputy Head, Policy Planning Staff,
Foreign and Commonwealth Office,
London

QUAINTON, Anthony

UNITED STATES OF AMERICA
Director of Personnel,
Department of State,
Washington DC

ROY, Jean-Michel

CANADA
Counsellor (Commercial/Economic),
Canadian High Commission,
London

TICKELL, Crispin

UNITED KINGDOM
Warden, Green College, The
Radcliffe Observatory, Oxford

TORRY, Peter

UNITED KINGDOM
Director, Personnel, Foreign and
Commonwealth Office, London

Conference 504: Political and Economic Developments in the Russian Federation: Implications for the West

Monday 28 July – Friday 1 August 1997

FALL, Sir Brian

UNITED KINGDOM
Principal, Lady Margaret Hall,
Oxford; Former British Ambassador
to the Russian Federation

GALEOTTI, Mark

UNITED KINGDOM
Director, Organised Crime &
Eurasian Research Unit (ORECRU),
Keele University, Staffordshire

GLAZIEV, Sergei

RUSSIA
Director, Information and Analysis
Department, Council of Federation,
Moscow

KORTUNOV, Andrei

RUSSIA
President, Moscow Public Science
Foundation, Moscow

KRYSHTANOVSKAYA, Olga

RUSSIA
Head, Department of Elite Studies,
Institute of Sociology, Russian
Academy of Sciences, Moscow

LAND, Ralph

UNITED KINGDOM
Chairman, Russia–British Chamber
of Commerce, London

LEBEDEV, Vladimir

RUSSIA
Consultant, Department of Strategic
Assessments and International
Affairs, Defence Council of the
Russian Federation, Moscow

LLOYD, John

UNITED KINGDOM
Associate Editor, *New Statesman*,
London

MELVIN, Neil

UNITED KINGDOM
Lecturer, Russian and Central Asian
Politics, Leeds University, Leeds

NIKONOV, Vyacheslav

RUSSIA
President, Polity Foundation,
Moscow

PAVLENKO, Sergei

RUSSIA
Deputy Head, Main Department of
Control Administration of the
President of the Russian Federation,
Moscow

PETROV, Nikolai

RUSSIA
Senior Consultant, Carnegie
Endowment for International Peace,
Moscow

SAKWA, Richard

UNITED KINGDOM
Professor of Russian and European
Politics, University of Kent,
Canterbury

SOSNOVSKY, Anatoly

RUSSIA
Deputy Director for Foreign Affairs,
ORT – Russian Public TV, Moscow

Conference WPS 97/4: Britain and New Zealand: Refocusing the Link

Sunday 31 August – Monday 1 September 1997

BELICH, James	NEW ZEALAND Department of History, University of Auckland
DELAMERE, Tuariki	NEW ZEALAND Associate Treasurer, Parliament Buildings, Wellington
FALLOON, John	NEW ZEALAND Former New Zealand Cabinet Minister (Inland Revenue and Statistics); Associate Finance Minister, Agriculture and Forestry, Masterton
FRASER, Andrew	UNITED KINGDOM Chief Executive, Invest in Britain Bureau, London
HOWELL, David	UNITED KINGDOM Former Chairman, House of Commons, Foreign Affairs Select Committee, London
O'BRIEN, Terence	NEW ZEALAND Director, Centre for Strategic Studies, Wellington
OUSELEY, Herman	UNITED KINGDOM Chairman, Commission for Racial Equality, London
QUINLAN, Michael	UNITED KINGDOM Former Permanent Under-Secretary of State, British Ministry of Defence; Director, Ditchley Foundation, Ditchley Park, Enstone
REEVES, Paul	NEW ZEALAND Former Governor-General; Chairman, Fiji Constitution Review Commission; Visiting Professor, New Zealand–Asia Institute, Auckland

SPANJAARD, Jeremy

NEW ZEALAND
Overseas Regional Manager for
Europe, New Zealand Trade
Development Board (TRADENZ),
Hamburg

Conference 505: The Europe–Asia Relationship: How Could It Be Improved?

Monday 1 – Friday 5 September 1997

BAGINDA, Abdul Razak	MALAYSIA Executive Director, Malaysian Strategic Research Centre, Kuala Lumpur
CHIRATHIVAT, Suthiphand	THAILAND Director, European Studies Programme, Chulalongkorn University, Bangkok
FATCHETT, Derek	UNITED KINGDOM Minister of State, Foreign and Commonwealth Office, London
FERDINAND, Peter	UNITED KINGDOM Director, Centre for Studies in Democratisation, Department of Politics and International Studies, University of Warwick, Coventry
GODWIN, Peter	UNITED KINGDOM Head, Export Finance; Chair, Asia– Pacific Advisory Committee, Commerzbank AG, London
HERNADI, Andras	HUNGARY Director, Japan East and South East Asia Research Centre Institute for World Economics, Budapest
HINDLEY, Michael	UNITED KINGDOM Member of European Parliament, Brussels
IWAKUNI, Tetsundo	JAPAN Member of House of Representatives, Tokyo
JIRAPAET, Krirk-Krai	THAILAND Ambassador, Permanent Mission of Thailand to the World Trade Organisation, Geneva

KIM, Jong Bum

KOREA
Research Fellow, Korean Institute
for International Economic Policy,
Seoul

NUTTER, Julie

UNITED STATES OF AMERICA
First Secretary, Economic,
American Embassy, London

PARK, Jin-Ho

KOREA
Counsellor, Embassy of the
Republic of Korea, London

RÜLAND, Jüergen

GERMANY
Professor of Political Science,
Rostock University

SEET-CHENG, Mary

REPUBLIC OF SINGAPORE
Director, Directorate II (Europe/
North America), Ministry of Foreign
Affairs, Singapore

SEGAL, Gerald

UNITED KINGDOM
Senior Fellow, Asian Security
Studies, International Institute for
Stategic Studies, London

STOKHOF, Wim

NETHERLANDS
Director, International Institute for
Asian Studies, Leiden

WESTERLUND, Percy

EUROPEAN COMMISSION
Director, Directorate F, DG1,
European Commission, Brussels

ZHAO, Gancheng

CHINA
Deputy Director, Shanghai Institute
for International Studies, Shanghai

Conference 506: Building Stability in Sub-Saharan Africa

Monday 8 – Friday 12 September 1997

AJELLO, Aldo	EUROPEAN UNION General Secretariat of the Council of the European Union, Brussels
AKINYEMI, A. Bolaji	NIGERIA Consultant on International Affairs, Cambridge
AKUFFO-ADDO, Nana	GHANA Member of Parliament, Accra
BOWDEN, Mark	UNITED KINGDOM Save The Children Fund, London
CHARLE, Josias	SOUTH AFRICA *The Sowetan*, Johannesburg
CHIKOTI, George	ANGOLA Vice Foreign Minister, Luanda
CHILUMPHA, Cassim	MALAWI Minister of Justice and Attorney General, Lilongwe
CHINAMASA, Patrick	ZIMBABWE Attorney General, Harare
CLAPHAM, Christopher	UNITED KINGDOM Lancaster University
DALES, Richard	UNITED KINGDOM Foreign and Commonwealth Office, London
de ALMEIDA SAMPAIO, Luis	EUROPEAN UNION Council of the European Union, Brussels
GORDON, David	UNITED STATES OF AMERICA Overseas Development Council, Washington DC
IBER, Davies	UNITED KINGDOM International Society for Human Rights, Serekunda

ISAIAS AFEWERKI, President	ERITREA President of Eritrea, Asmara
KABEMBA, Claude	SOUTH AFRICA Centre for Policy Studies, Johannesburg
KADAGA, Rebecca	UGANDA Minister of State for Foreign Affairs, Kampala
KUKAH, Matthew	NIGERIA Catholic Bishops Conference of Nigeria, Lagos
NEWTON, Alastair	UNITED KINGDOM Foreign and Commonwealth Office, London
POOLEY, Peter	UNITED KINGDOM British African Business Association, London
RAZAFIMAHALEO, Herizo	MADAGASCAR Vice Prime Minister, Antananarivo
SMITH, Stephen	FRANCE *Liberation*, Paris
TCHEYAN, Nils	WORLD BANK The World Bank, Washington
TOURÉ, Amadou Toumani	MALI Bamako

Conference 507: The Inter-Governmental Conference and Its Consequences: Ensuring Public Acceptance and Building a 'New' Europe

Monday 15 – Friday 19 September 1997

ARNOLD, Elisabeth

DENMARK
Deputy Speaker; Vice-Chairman, European Affairs Committee, Copenhagen

BUDD, Colin

UNITED KINGDOM
Director, EU and Economic Affairs, Foreign and Commonwealth Office, London

CORBETT, Richard

EUROPEAN PARLIAMENT
Labour Member for Merseyside West, European Parliament, Brussels/Strasbourg

DOHMES, Johannes

GERMANY
Director; Deputy Head, European Affairs Department, Federal Ministry of Foreign Affairs, Bonn

ESPADA, João Carlos

PORTUGAL
Senior Research Fellow, Institute for Social Sciences, University of Lisbon

JACOBS, Francis

EUROPEAN PARLIAMENT
Principal Administrator, Committee on Institutional Affairs, European Parliament, Brussels/Strasbourg

JESIEN, Leszek

POLAND
Research Fellow, College of Europe-Natolin, Warsaw

MAGANZA, Giorgio

EUROPEAN UNION
Legal Adviser, Secretariat of the Council of the European Union, Brussels

NEYTS-UTTEBROECK, Annemie

EUROPEAN PARLIAMENT
Second Vice-President, Liberal, Democrat and Reformist Group, European Parliament, Brussels/Strasbourg

PERRAKIS, Stelios	GREECE Secretary-General for European Affairs, Ministry of Foreign Affairs, Athens
RODRIGO, Fernando	SPAIN Deputy Director, Spanish Centre for International Relations (CERI), Madrid
SCHELTER, Kurt	GERMANY Permanent Secretary, Federal Ministry of the Interior, Bonn
SEIXAS DA COSTA, Francisco	PORTUGAL Secretary of State for European Affairs, Lisbon
SMART, Victor	UNITED KINGDOM Assistant Editor, *The European*, London
STATHATOS, Stephane G.	GREECE Ambassador (retired); Vice President, Hellenic Foundation for European and Foreign Policy (ELIAMEP), Athens
VIBERT, Frank	UNITED KINGDOM Director, European Policy Forum, London
WHITTY OF CAMBERWELL, Lord	UNITED KINGDOM Government Whip, House of Lords, London
WILLIAMSON, David	EUROPEAN COMMISSION Former Secretary-General, European Commission, Brussels
WORCESTER, Robert	UNITED KINGDOM Chairman, Market & Opinion Research International (MORI), London

Conference 508: India and Pakistan at Fifty

Monday 29 September – Friday 3 October 1997

AHLUWALIA, Sanjeev S.
INDIA
Senior Fellow, Tata Energy Research
Institute (TERI), New Delhi

AHLUWALIA, Isher Judge
INDIA
Professor, Centre for Policy
Research, New Delhi

AHMADI, A. M.
INDIA
Former Minister of Justice, New
Delhi

BAKHT, Zubair
PAKISTAN
Secretary-General, UK–Pakistan
Business Forum, London

BRAY, John
UNITED KINGDOM
Principal Research Consultant,
Control Risks Information Services,
London

EVANS, Paul
CANADA
Visiting Scholar, The Asia Centre,
Harvard University, Cambridge

FENN, Nicholas
UNITED KINGDOM
Former British High Commissioner,
New Delhi

FOSSATI, Emiliano
EUROPEAN COMMISSION
Director, South and South East Asia,
Directorate-General 1B, European
Commission, Brussels

GIDOOMAL, Ram
INDIA
Chairman, South Asian
Development Partnership, Sutton

HAIDAR, Salman
INDIA
Foreign Secretary, Ministry of
External Affairs, New Delhi

HAYWARD, Anthony	UNITED KINGDOM Chairman, The Baring Peacock Fund, Baring Asset Management Ltd, London
HOSSAIN, Kamal	BANGLADESH Senior Advocate, Supreme Court of Bangladesh, Dhaka
JABBAR, Javed	PAKISTAN Former Federal Minister for Petroleum and Natural Resources, MNJ Communications (Private) Ltd, Karachi
JAYAWARDENA, Lal	SRI LANKA Economic Adviser to the President of Sri Lanka and Deputy Chairman, National Development Council, Colombo
KABRAJI, Aban Marker	PAKISTAN Regional Director, South and South East Asia IUCN, The World Conservation Union, Karachi
LODHI, Maleeha	PAKISTAN Editor, *The News*, Rawalpindi
MACRAE, Christopher	UNITED KINGDOM Head of Mission Section, Foreign and Commonwealth Office, London
MITRA, Amit	INDIA Secretary-General, Federation of Indian Chambers of Commerce and Industry, New Delhi
NOMAN, Omar	UNDP Senior Programme Manager, United Nations Development Programme, New York
OSMANI, Siddiq	BANGLADESH Professor of Development Economics, University of Ulster at Jordanstown, Newtownabbey

QURESHI, Shah Mahmood   PAKISTAN
Former Minister of State for
Parliamentary Affairs, Islamabad

RAZA, Rafi   PAKISTAN
Former Federal Minister and
Author, Karachi

SEGAL, Gerald   CANADA
Senior Fellow, Asian Security
Studies; Director, ESRC Pacific
Asian Programme, International
Institute for Strategic Studies (IISS),
London

SEN GUPTA, Bhabani   INDIA
Director, Centre for Studies in
Global Change, New Delhi

Conference WPS 97/5: Multilateral Control Regimes in the 21st Century: The Impact on Chemical and Biological Weapons

Friday 3 – Sunday 5 October 1997

ADAM, Rudolf

GERMANY
Director of Nuclear Disarmament,
Federal Ministry of Foreign Affairs,
Bonn

DELPECH, Thérèse

FRANCE
Adviser to the High Commissioner,
National Atomic Energy Agency,
Paris

DUNN, Lewis

UNITED STATES OF AMERICA
Corporate Vice-President and
Operation Manager, Science
Applications International
Corporation, McLean

GEE, John

AUSTRALIA
Deputy Director-General, Technical
Secretariat Organisation for the
Prohibition of Chemical Weapons,
The Hague

KISSELEV, Sergei

RUSSIA
Counsellor, Embassy of the
Federation of Russia in the
Netherlands, The Hague

MOODIE, Michael

UNITED STATES OF AMERICA
President, Chemical and Biological
Arms Control Institute, Alexandria

OUYANG, Liping

CHINA
Research Fellow, China Institute of
Contemporary International
Relations, Beijing

PEARSON, Graham

UNITED KINGDOM
Honorary Visiting Professor in
International Security, Department
of Peace Studies, University of
Bradford

REID, Gordon

UNITED KINGDOM
Deputy Head of Non-Proliferation
Department, Foreign and
Commonwealth Office, London

ROBERTS, Brad

UNITED STATES OF AMERICA
Member, Research Staff, Strategy,
Forces and Resources Division,
Institute for Defense Analyses,
Alexandria

STEYN, Benjamin

SOUTH AFRICA
Special Adviser, South African
Mission to the Conference on
Disarmament, Geneva

TAYLOR, Terry

UNITED KINGDOM
Assistant Director, International
Institute for Strategic Studies,
London

Conference 509: How Can Europeans Best Maintain European Security?

Monday 6 – Friday 10 October 1997

BOYER, Yves

FRANCE
Deputy Director, Centre for
Research and Study on Strategies
and Technologies, Paris

ENGBERG, Katarina

SWEDEN
Adviser, Defence Committee,
Ministry of Defence, Stockholm

GREENWALD, Jonathan

UNITED STATES OF AMERICA
Former Minister/Counsellor for
Political Affairs, US Mission to the
EU

JANKAUSKAS, Kestutis

LITHUANIA
Head of Security, Policy Division,
Ministry of Foreign Affairs, Vilnius

JOFFÉ, George

UNITED KINGDOM
Director of Studies, Royal Institute
of International Affairs, London

McELHANEY, Doug

NATO
Deputy United States Permanent
Representative, North Atlantic
Treaty Organisation, Brussels

MORTIMER, Edward

UNITED KINGDOM
Assistant Editor, *Financial Times*,
London

RICKETTS, Peter

UNITED KINGDOM
Deputy Political Director, Foreign
and Commonwealth Office, London

SANBERK, Özdem

TURKEY
Ambassador, Turkish Embassy,
London

SIMPSON, John

UNITED KINGDOM
Mountbatten Centre for
International Studies, Southampton
University

TITLEY, Gary

EUROPEAN PARLIAMENT
Labour Member for Greater
Manchester West; Foreign Affairs,
Defence and Security Co-ordinator,
Party of European Socialists,
European Parliament, Brussels

TRENIN, Dmitri

RUSSIA
Deputy Director, Carnegie Moscow
Centre, Moscow

ZIELONKA, Jan

NETHERLANDS
Joint Chair in Political Science
(European Studies), Department of
Social and Political Studies,
European University Institute, San
Domenico Di Fiesole

Conference 510: Justice and Home Affairs in the European Union

Monday 13 – Friday 17 October 1997

AUDENAERT, Glenn

BELGIUM
Commissioner, Judiciary Police;
Manager, Europol Home Desk,
General Police Support Service,
Brussels

BARANY, Eduard

SLOVAK REPUBLIC
Director, Institute of State and Law,
Slovak Academy of Sciences,
Bratislava

COLVIN, Madeleine

UNITED KINGDOM
Senior Legal Officer, Justice,
London

DE JONG, Dennis

NETHERLANDS
Counsellor (Justice), Permanent
Mission of the Netherlands to the
European Union, Brussels

DE KERCHOVE
D'OUSSELGHEM, Gilles

EUROPEAN UNION
Director, Directorate-General H,
General Secretariat of the Council of
the European Union, Brussels

DEN BOER, Monica

NETHERLANDS
Senior Lecturer, European Institute
of Public Administration,
Maastricht

DORR, Noel

IRELAND
Tanaiste's Personal Representative
on the IGC, 1996–97; Former
Permanent Secretary, Department of
Foreign Affairs, Dublin

DZIALUK, Igor

POLAND
Deputy Director, Department of
International Affairs and European
Law, Ministry of Justice, Warsaw

FLYNN, Don

UNITED KINGDOM
European Projects Worker, Joint
Council for the Welfare of
Immigrants, London

GREGORY, Frank

UNITED KINGDOM
Senior Lecturer, Department of
Politics, University of Southampton

MAROTTA, Emanuele

ITALY
Management Team, Europol Drugs
Unit, Europol, The Hague

MONAR, Jörg

GERMANY
Director, Centre for European
Politics and Institutions, University
of Leicester, Leicester

PELSEZ, Elisabeth

FRANCE
Liaison Magistrate for the French
Government, Ministry of Justice,
The Hague

SPENCER, Sarah

UNITED KINGDOM
Director, Human Rights Programme,
Institute for Public Policy Research,
London

TORDOFF, Geoffrey

UNITED KINGDOM
Liberal Democrat Peer, House of
Lords; Chairman, Select Committee,
European Communities Committee,
London

TURNBULL, Penelope

UNITED KINGDOM
Institute for German Studies,
University of Birmingham

WALKER, Timothy

UNITED KINGDOM
Director-General, Immigration and
Nationality Department, Home
Office, London

Conference WPS 97/8: George C. Marshall and Dwight D. Eisenhower: Their Legacies and Visions and the Future of the Atlantic Community

Friday 24 – Saturday 25 October 1997

AMBROSE, Stephen

UNITED STATES OF AMERICA
Boyd Professor of History and
Director, Eisenhower Center,
University of New Orleans

BAYNE, Sir Nicholas

UNITED KINGDOM
Chairman, Liberalisation of Trade in
Services (LOTIS) Committee, British
Invisibles, London; Former High
Commissioner of the United
Kingdom to Canada

BEVERIDGE, Albert

UNITED STATES OF AMERICA
President and Chief Executive
Officer, George C. Marshall
Foundation, Lexington

BONSOR, Sir Nicholas

UNITED KINGDOM
Former Minister of State (1995–7),
Foreign and Commonwealth Office,
London

GOODPASTER, Andrew

UNITED STATES OF AMERICA
Chairman, The Atlantic Council of
the United States, Washington DC

INGRASSIA, Lawrence

UNITED STATES OF AMERICA
London Bureau Chief, *The Wall
Street Journal*, London

JOHNSTON, Donald

OECD
Secretary-General, Organisation for
Economic Co-operation and
Development, Paris

KORB, Lawrence

UNITED STATES OF AMERICA
Director, Center for Public Policy
Education and Senior Fellow,
Foreign Policy Studies Programme,
The Brookings Institution,
Washington DC

LADER, Philip

UNITED STATES OF AMERICA
Ambassador, Embassy of the United
States of America, London

PENNINGTON, Janet

UNITED KINGDOM
Historian, Steyning

REYNOLDS, David

UNITED KINGDOM
Fellow, Christ's College, Cambridge
University

ROBERTS, Sir Frank

UNITED KINGDOM
Vice-President, European Atlantic
Group, London

SCOWCROFT, Brent

UNITED STATES OF AMERICA
Founder and President, The Forum
for International Policy,
Washington DC

von MOLTKE, Gebhardt

GERMANY
Ambassador, German Embassy,
London

WALTERS, Vernon

UNITED STATES OF AMERICA
Former US Ambassador to the
Federal Republic of Germany
(1989–91)

ZOELLICK, Robert

UNITED STATES OF AMERICA
John M. Olin Professor of National
Security Affairs, US Naval
Academy, Washington DC

Conference 511: Political Stability in the Balkans and South-East Europe

Monday 27 – Friday 31 October 1997

CVIIC, Christopher	UNITED KINGDOM Journalist, London
de FRANCHIS, Amadeo	ITALY Director-General for Political Affairs, Ministry of Foreign Affairs, Rome
GOW, James	UNITED KINGDOM Department of War Studies, King's College, London
HAJRIC, Mirza	BOSNIA-HERZEGOVINA Adviser for Foreign Policy and Implementation of Dayton Agreement, Bosnia and Herzegovina Presidency, Sarajevo
NEVILLE JONES, Dame Pauline	UNITED KINGDOM Managing Director and Head, Global Business Strategy, NatWest Markets, London
O'SULLIVAN, Rory	THE WORLD BANK Director, World Bank Resident Mission to Bosnia-Herzegovina, Sarajevo
PARTOS, Gabriel	UNITED KINGDOM Albanian Section, BBC World Service, London
PETTIFER, James	UNITED KINGDOM Visiting Professor, Institute of Balkan Studies, Bath
PRICA, Milos	BOSNIAN SERB REPUBLIC Banski Dvor, Banja Luka
REHN, Elizabeth	FINLAND UN Special Rapporteur for Human Rights, Ministry for Foreign Affairs, Helsinki

ROBERTS, Ivor	UNITED KINGDOM HM Ambassador, British Embassy, Belgrade
ROBINSON, Gerry	OSCE Deputy Chairman, Provisional Elections Commission and Senior Counsel, Organisation for Security and Co-operation in Europe (OSCE), Mission to Bosnia and Herzegovina, Sarajevo
SCHULTE, Gregory	NATO Director, Bosnia Task Force, NATO Headquarters, Brussels
SURROI, Veton	FRY (KOSOVO) Editor-in-Chief, *Koha*, Pristina
TUDJMAN, Miroslav	CROATIA Deputy Director, National Security Office, Zagreb

Conference WPS 97/10: The Relationship Between Greece and Turkey: Can It Be Improved?

Friday 31 October – Sunday 2 November 1997

AKARCALI, Bülent	TURKEY Member of Parliament for Istanbul; President of the Turkish Democracy Foundation, Ankara
COBBOLD, Richard	UNITED KINGDOM Director, Royal United Services Institute, London
DUNA, Cem	TURKEY AB Consultancy and Investment Services, Istanbul
MANOS, Stefanos	GREECE Member of Parliament; Former Minister of the National Economy, Athens
MORTIMER, Edward	UNITED KINGDOM Assistant Editor, *Financial Times*, London
PRATT, Martin	UNITED KINGDOM Research Officer, International Boundaries Research Unit, Mountjoy Research Centre, Durham
RICKETTS, Peter	UNITED KINGDOM Deputy Political Director, Foreign and Commonwealth Office, London
ROBINS, Philip	UNITED KINGDOM St Anthony's College, Oxford
ROZAKIS, Christos	GREECE Professor of Public International Law; Member of the European Commission of Human Rights, University of Athens

Conference 512: Economic and Monetary Union: Economic and Political Implications

Monday 3 – Friday 7 November 1997

BISHOP, Graham

UNITED KINGDOM
Salomon Brothers International
Limited, London

DAVIS, Philip

EUROPEAN MONETARY INSTITUTE
Deputy Head, Stage Two Division,
European Monetary Institute,
Frankfurt-Am-Main

DESMOND, Richard

UNITED STATES OF AMERICA
Group Treasurer, BAT Industries,
London

FLIGHT, Howard

UNITED KINGDOM
Conservative Member of Parliament
for Arundel & South Downs, House
of Commons, London

KAISER, Rolf

EUROPEAN COMMISSION
Adviser to the Director-General,
Directorate-General II, European
Commission, Brussels

MÜNCHAU, Wolfgang

GERMANY
Economics Correspondent,
Financial Times, London

NÖLLING, Wilhelm

GERMANY
Professor, Department of
Economics, University of Hamburg

ONOFRI, Paolo

ITALY
Secretary-General, Prometeia
Associazione, Bologna

PORTES, Richard

UNITED KINGDOM
Director, Centre for Economic
Policy Research (CEPR); Professor of
Economics, London Business
School, London

RADICE, Giles

UNITED KINGDOM
Labour Member of Parliament for
Durham North, London

SAMECKI, Pawel

POLAND
Under-Secretary of State, Ministry
of Finance, Warsaw

STEVENS, John

EUROPEAN PARLIAMENT
Conservative Member of the
European Parliament for Thames
Valley, European Parliament

TUOMIOJA, Erkki

FINLAND
Chairman, Social Democratic
Group, Parliament of Finland,
Helsinki

Conference WPS 97/6: The Transatlantic Relationship: Strengthening Dialogue and Cooperation

Monday 10 – Friday 14 November 1997

CARRUTH, Reba Anne	UNITED STATES OF AMERICA Assistant Professor, Strategic Management and Public Policy, School of Business and Public Management, Washington DC
FRASER, Simon	UNITED KINGDOM Office of Sir Leon Brittan, European Commission, Brussels
FREEMAN, Harry	UNITED STATES OF AMERICA Executive Director, The MTN Coalition; President, The Freeman Company, Chevy Chase
FROST, Ellen	UNITED STATES OF AMERICA Senior Fellow, Institute for International Economics, Washington DC
GROEN, Harry	NETHERLANDS Amsterdam
HEISBOURG, François	FRANCE Senior Vice-President (Strategic Development), MATRA Defense-Espace, Paris
HOEKEMA, Jan	NETHERLANDS Spokesman on Foreign and Security Issues, D66 Democraten, Netherlands Parliament, The Hague
KUGLER, Richard	UNITED STATES OF AMERICA Distinguished Research Professor, National Defense University, Washington DC
LEWIS, Flora	UNITED STATES OF AMERICA Journalist, Paris

ÖLANDER, Jan	SWEDEN Former President, Europe 2000; Foreign Policy Adviser, National Swedish Police Board, Stockholm
ROLLO, Jim	UNITED KINGDOM Chief Economic Adviser, Foreign and Commonwealth Office, London
SCHEFFER, Paul	NETHERLANDS Journalist, Amsterdam
SYMONS of Vernham Dean, Baroness	UNITED KINGDOM Parliamentary Under-Secretary of State for Foreign and Commonwealth Affairs, Foreign and Commonwealth Office, London
von MOLTKE, Gebhardt	GERMANY Ambassador, Federal Republic of Germany, London
WALLACE, William	UNITED KINGDOM Liberal Democrat Spokesman on Defence, House of Lords; Reader in International Relations, The London School of Economics and International Relations, London
WILCOX, Philip	UNITED STATES OF AMERICA Bethesda
WOLF, Martin	UNITED KINGDOM Associate Editor and Economics Commentator, *Financial Times*, London

Conference WPS 97/9: The United Nations in the Twenty-First Century

Friday 14 – Sunday 16 November 1997

CRAWFORD, James

UNITED KINGDOM
Lauterpacht Research Centre for
International Law, Cambridge

GIACOMELLI, Giorgio

ITALY
Former Executive Director, UNDCP,
Vienna

HIGGINS, Rosalyn

INTERNATIONAL COURT OF JUSTICE
International Court of Justice, The
Hague

KAMAL, Ahmed

PAKISTAN
Permanent Representative of
Pakistan to the United Nations,
New York

LEWIS, Stephen

UNICEF
Deputy Executive Director, UNICEF,
New York

MALLOCH-BROWN, Mark

WORLD BANK
Vice-President, External Affairs,
The World Bank, Washington DC

NDIAYE, Waly Bacre

SENEGAL
Special Rapporteur on Extra-
judicial, Summary or Arbitrary
Executions, Centre for Human
Rights, Geneva

OTUNNU, Olara A.

UGANDA
President, International Peace
Academy, New York

RAMCHARAN, Bertie

UNITED NATIONS
Director, Africa Division 1,
Department of Political Affairs,
United Nations, New York

SPETH, Gus

UNDP
Head, United Nations Development
Programme, New York

THAROOR, Shashi

UNITED NATIONS
Executive Assistant to the
Secretary-General, United Nations,
New York

van KAPPEN, Franklin

UNITED NATIONS
Military Adviser, Department of
Peacekeeping Operations, New York

VIEIRA de MELLO, Sergio

UNHCR
Assistant High Commissioner for
Refugees, Geneva

WESTON, Sir John

UNITED KINGDOM
United Kingdom Permanent
Representative to the United
Nations, New York

Conference 513: Japan's Role in the World

Monday 17 – Friday 21 November 1997

AUER, Jim

UNITED STATES OF AMERICA
Director, Centre for US–Japan
Studies and Co-operation,
Vanderbilt Institute for Public
Policy Studies, Vanderbilt
University, Nashville

BAGINDA, Abdul Razak

MALAYSIA
Executive Director, Malaysian
Strategic Research Centre,
Kuala Lumpur

COBBOLD, Richard

UNITED KINGDOM
Director, Royal United Services
Institute for Defence Studies,
London

CONNORS, Lesley

UNITED KINGDOM
Lecturer, Department of Political
Science, School of Oriental and
African Studies, London

CORBETT, Jenny

CANADA
Nissan Institute of Japanese Studies,
Oxford

FORD, Glyn

EUROPEAN PARLIAMENT
Labour Member of European
Parliament for Greater Manchester
East

GRANT, Richard

UNITED KINGDOM
Head, Asia–Pacific Programme,
Royal Institute of International
Affairs, London

HAMA, Noriko

JAPAN
Director, Mitsubishi Research
Institute, London

HAYASHI, Sadayuki

JAPAN
Ambassador, Embassy of Japan,
London

HEWITT, Adrian

UNITED KINGDOM
Deputy Director, Overseas
Development Institute, London

KAKIZAWA, Koji

JAPAN
Member of House of
Representatives; Former Minister
for Foreign Affairs, Tokyo

KOMACHI, Kyoji

JAPAN
Deputy Chief of Mission, Embassy
of Japan, Moscow

KOMATSU, Keiichiro

JAPAN
Exports to Japan Unit, Department
of Trade and Industry, London

MATTHEWS, Juan

UNITED KINGDOM
Regional Director, Asia Pacific, AEA
Technology

NOGAMI, Yoshiji

JAPAN
Ambassador, Japanese Permanent
Delegation to the OECD, Paris

NUMATA, Sadaaki

JAPAN
Minister Plenipotentiary, Embassy
of Japan, London

SONE, Yasunori

JAPAN
Professor of Political Science, Keio
University

STOCKWIN, Arthur

UNITED KINGDOM
Director, Nissan Institute of
Japanese Studies, St Antony's
College, Oxford

TAKAHASHI, Kunio

JAPAN
Director of Research Co-ordination,
The Japan Institute of International
Affairs, Tokyo

TAKAHASHI, Fumiaki

JAPAN
Deputy Director-General, Economic
Co-operation Bureau, Ministry of
Foreign Affairs, Tokyo

TANIGUCHI, Tomohiko

JAPAN
European Bureau Chief, *Nikkei Business*, London

UDA, Shinichiro

JAPAN
Chairman, Shinsei Kenkyukai (Institute of Promotion of Policy Reform); President, LSE Forum in Japan, Tokyo

WOOD, Bernard

OECD
Director, Development Co-operation Directorate, Organisation for Economic Co-operation and Development, Paris

YANG, Bojiang

CHINA
Deputy Director, Division of Northeast Asian Studies, China Institute of Contemporary International Relations, Beijing

Conference 514: Cultural Diplomacy at the Crossroads

Monday 24 – Friday 28 November 1997

AUBLIN, Laurent

FRANCE
Director, Cultural Affairs, Ministry
of Foreign Affairs, Paris

BRIX, Emil

AUSTRIA
Director, Austrian Cultural Institute,
London

CLARK, Peter

UNITED KINGDOM
Special Adviser, Middle East and
North Africa, British Council,
London

CRYSTAL, Professor David

UNITED KINGDOM
Editor, The Cambridge
Encyclopaedia, Gwynedd

FULTON, Barry

UNITED STATES OF AMERICA
Project Director, Diplomacy in the
Information Age, Centre for
Strategic and International Studies,
Washington DC

GURNAH, Abdulrazak

TANZANIA
Senior Lecturer in English,
Rutherford College, University of
Kent, Canterbury

HANSON, Sir John

UNITED KINGDOM
Director-General, The British
Council, London

HASSAN, Fuad

INDONESIA
Governor, Asia–Europe Foundation,
Jakarta

LOIELLO, John

UNITED STATES OF AMERICA
Associate Director for Educational
and Cultural Affairs, US
Information Agency,
Washington DC

NIZAMI, Farhan

INDIA
Director, Oxford Centre for Islamic
Studies, Oxford

PAPANDREOU, George

GREECE
Alternate Minister for Foreign
Affairs, Ministry of Foreign Affairs,
Athens

POWELL, Nik

UNITED KINGDOM
Chairman, European Film Academy,
Berlin, London

TONINI, Frank

UNITED STATES OF AMERICA
Deputy Managing Director, The
Motion Picture Association,
Brussels

TWEEDY, Colin

UNITED KINGDOM
Director-General, Association for
Business Sponsorship of the Arts,
London

Conference 515: Building an Effective International Consensus Against Nuclear Proliferation: What More Can Be Done?

Monday 1 – Friday 5 December 1997

AHMED, Samina	UNITED STATES OF AMERICA Sandia National Laboratory, Albuquerque, New Mexico
BAILEY, Kathleen	UNITED STATES OF AMERICA Lawrence Livermore National Laboratory, Livermore, CA
BELOBROV, Iouri	RUSSIA Embassy of the Russian Federation, London
CLARKE, Michael	UNITED KINGDOM Centre for Defence Studies, King's College, London
DAS, Suranjan	INDIA Peace Research Centre, University of Calcutta
DAVYDOV, Valery	RUSSIA Russian Academy of Sciences, Moscow
DELPECH, Thérèse	FRANCE National Atomic Energy Agency, Paris
DHANAPALA, Jayantha	UNITED NATIONS UN Department for Disarmament Affairs, New York
HOOPER, Richard	IAEA International Atomic Energy Agency, Vienna
KIBAROGLU, Mustafa	TURKEY Bilkent University, Ankara
LEVITE, Ariel	ISRAEL Ministry of Defence, Tel Aviv

MOODIE, Michael

UNITED STATES OF AMERICA
Chemical and Biological Arms
Control Institute, Alexandria, VA

MÜLLER, Harald

GERMANY
Peace Research Institute, Frankfurt/
Main

ROBERTS, Brad

UNITED STATES OF AMERICA
Institute for Defense Analyses,
Alexandria, VA

SCHEINMAN, Lawrence

UNITED STATES OF AMERICA
Monterey Institute of International
Studies, Washington DC

TOUKAN, Abdullah

JORDAN
Adviser to HM King Hussein,
Amman

WULF, Norman

UNITED STATES OF AMERICA
US Arms Control and Disarmament
Agency, Washington DC

ZHANG, Tousheng

CHINA
The China Foundation for
International and Strategic Studies,
Beijing

Conference 516: Central and Eastern Europe and NATO and EU Enlargement

Monday 15 – Friday 19 December 1997

ANDRZEJEWSKI, Piotr	POLAND Counsellor, The Presidential Chancellery, Warsaw
AVERY, Graham	EUROPEAN COMMISSION Chief Adviser, Enlargement, Directorate-General for External Political Relations, European Commission, Brussels
BAILES, Alyson	UNITED KINGDOM Director, Political Affairs, Western European Union, Brussels
HÜBNER, Danuta	POLAND Head, Committee for European Integration, Warsaw
HUGHES, Kirsty	UNITED KINGDOM Head, European Programme, Royal Institute of International Affairs, London
HUSZ, Dora	HUNGARY Researcher, Szonda IPSOS (Media, Opinion and Market Research Institute), Budapest
KALDOR, Mary	UNITED KINGDOM University of Sussex, Brighton
PEARCE, Howard	UNITED KINGDOM Head, Central European Department, Foreign and Commonwealth Office, London
SANDOR, Dorel	ROMANIA Director, Centre for Political Studies and Comparative Analysis, Bucharest
SAUDARGAS, Algirdas	LITHUANIA Foreign Minister, Vilnius

SEDIVY, Jiri

CZECH REPUBLIC
Institute of International Relations,
Prague

SZENTIVANYI, Gábor

HUNGARY
Ambassador, Hungarian Embassy,
London

WASZCZYKOWSKI, Witold

POLAND
Deputy Head, Polish Mission to
NATO, Brussels

Index

Index compiled by Susanne Atkin